The Chinese Liberal Spirit

SUNY series, Translating China

Rogert T. Ames and Paul J. D'Ambrosio, editors

The Chinese Liberal Spirit

Selected Writings of Xu Fuguan

Translated and edited by

DAVID ELSTEIN

Cover image of Xu Fuguan and the handwriting sample used by permission of his son, Hsu Woochun.

Published by State University of New York Press, Albany

For information, contact State University of New York Press, Albany, NY
www.sunypress.edu

Library of Congress Cataloging-in-Publication Data

Name: Elstein, David, translator and editor.
Title: The Chinese liberal spirit: selected writings of Xu Fuguan / David Elstein,
    editor and translator.
Description: Albany : State University of New York Press, [2021] | Series:
    SUNY series, Translating China. | Includes bibliographical references and
    index.
Identifiers: ISBN 9781438487175 (hardcover : alk. paper) | ISBN 9781438487182
    (ebook) | ISBN 9781438487168 (pbk. : alk. paper)
Further information is available at the Library of Congress.

10 9 8 7 6 5 4 3 2 1

For my parents, who instilled in me a love of learning

Contents

Acknowledgments

My greatest debt is to Xu Fuguan's son Hsu Woo-chun (Xu Wujun). He not only agreed to give permission to translate some of his father's work, but took time to meet with me personally to share stories about his father and give me scans of nearly all of his published work. I only hope that he is pleased with the result.

Dr. Donald Sturgeon's Chinese Text Project (Ctext.org) has been an invaluable resource. I do not know of a better collection of digital texts in Chinese studies, and it would have been virtually impossible to track down the sources of nearly all Xu's quotations without it. The wealth of materials available there without a subscription fee is nothing short of astounding.

Huang Chun-chieh generously met with me to answer questions about some uncertainties in the texts and saved me from a number of errors.

The library staffs at SUNY New Paltz, Academia Sinica, and the National Central Library of Taiwan were of great assistance in locating materials. Lee Ming-huei of Academia Sinica and Pong Wen-berng of National Taiwan University helped with the arrangements for research trips to Taiwan. Much of the translation and editing work was done in Taiwan while I was on a research fellowship at the Center for Chinese Studies of the National Central Library, courtesy of the Taiwan Ministry of Foreign Affairs. I would like to express my thanks for their support.

Finally, I thank my wife Chen Shuyuan for reading assistance, unflagging encouragement, and always taking on a little extra at home to give me a chance to work.

A Note on Language

This volume uses the pinyin Romanization for all Chinese terms and personal names, except for people who prefer an alternative spelling. In these instances, I use their preferred spelling and provide the pinyin for the first use. In place of "Confucian" and "Confucianism" I use "Ruist" and "Ruism" for greater fidelity to the Chinese terms, which are not derived from Kongzi (Confucius).

Preface

My Father

HSU WOO-CHUN

My father, Professor Xu Fuguan, was one of the leading members of the New Ruist movement of the twentieth century. His life, faith, and learning were strongly related to the modern history of China.

My father was born on January 31st, 1903, in a poor hill village in Xishui county about 120km south of Wuhan, China. He received rigorous Chinese classical training until twenty-three, then attended a military academy in Japan, where he was highly attracted to socialism.

He was commissioned Major in 1932, fought the Japanese in the field, and was promoted to Major General. In 1943, he was stationed in Yan'an for five months as the KMT's CCP liaison officer, where he got to know Mao Zedong and Zhou Enlai in person. After he returned to Chongqing, President Jiang Jieshi was impressed by his report and assigned him to his staff. He was then associated closely with Jiang through the 1940s.

More than 90 percent of Chinese were farmers at that time, and my father suggested repeatedly to Jiang that the KMT needed to understand the farmers and fulfill the farmers' needs. He proposed a "Land for Farmers" plan, which regulated the amount of land each landlord could own, with the requirement to sell extra land to tenants at an affordable price. The "Land for Farmers" Plan was implemented in Taiwan in 1953, thus changing the social structure, setting the foundation for later industrialization, and strengthening KMT rule in Taiwan.

Chinese people suffered the most from civil wars, and therefore my father believed that China must adopt the democratic system so that power could be transferred peacefully. However, Jiang Jieshi considered consolidating power as the top priority in Taiwan. Jiang also designated his son Jiang Jingguo to be his successor and asked my father to pledge loyalty to his son, which was completely against my father's will. My father cut himself off from Jiang, found a teaching job in college in 1952, relocated to Tunghai University in 1955, and started his academic career at the age of fifty-two.

My father wrote and published commentaries, offering his observations, comments, and suggestions on political, social, and cultural issues from 1949 on. He was the most respected and popular commentator of the time. However, his insistence on democracy irritated the KMT. The KMT kicked him out of the party in 1957; then, with the cooperation with Tunghai University, forced my father to retire at the age of sixty-six in 1969, and cut my father off from any academic position in Taiwan, effectively exiling him to Hong Kong in 1970. Because my father did not have regular academic positions in Hong Kong, his main income source was writing. He left more than one thousand commentaries, more than half of which were written in Hong Kong.

I was asked to resign from a Taiwan chemical research institute in 1979 without being told why, and then took a marketing position with a petroleum company in Hong Kong in 1980. That was the first time I got to see my father often since I left home for college in 1954, for almost two years. We carried on conversation in Xishui dialect, exchanging views and ideas freely, mostly about China. His position was firm and clear that the fate and well-being of the Chinese people is the most important issue, and personal feelings should be left aside. He believed Deng Xiaoping was the right man to reconstruct China, and suggested that China needed to resume the private property system. However, whenever I asked him why he did not take up Beijing's invitation to visit, he just changed the subject without answering. That was nothing unusual to me at that time, because he never talked about his own life, and we respected his privacy.

When my father was last hospitalized in Taibei in February 1982, the KMT offered full care. My father wished to leave as a free man, so we did not accept the KMT's offer and held a family service instead. A four-star general in full uniform offered his condolences. My father retired from the army in 1946. How, where, and when did they cross paths with each other?

After my retirement in 2001, by reading my father's commentary articles and from memories and documents, I came to have a better picture of my father's life. He was a man who stood by the people and tried his best for them. And I believe that the major difference between his academic works and the other scholars' is his believing that a true Ruist should take the well-being of the people as the first priority, not the perfection of academic research.

Among other things, I found that I lost my Taiwan research job in 1979 because I am Xu Fuguan's son. And my father did not visit Beijing to protect me from the KMT. I wish I could say to him: "Please just do as you wish, Daddy."

I want to sincerely acknowledge Professor Elstein's great effort in introducing my father's works to the Western world.

Introduction

David Elstein

Some explanation ought to be offered for an entire book dedicated to Xu Fuguan's thought, who is not the most prominent New Ruist thinker. He is by no means a household name in Chinese communities, and I would speculate that his writings are not frequently read in philosophy classes. He never had the ambition to develop the kind of philosophical system that his contemporaries Tang Junyi and Mou Zongsan did. While like other scholars of the period (including the two just mentioned), he wrote voluminously, he never published anything in English, other than the jointly authored "Declaration on Behalf of Chinese Culture Respectfully Announced to the People of the World," and how much of this document his contributions represent is not clear. The present volume represents the first appearance of any of his individually authored works in English.

The question, then, is why we should be interested in the thought of this particular twentieth-century Chinese scholar. I will answer that in several ways. First, due to his background he had greater connections with the significant historical and political figures of the time than most scholars. I would surmise not many had personal relationships with both Mao Zedong and Jiang Jieshi (Chiang Kai-shek). As a general in the Nationalist (GMD) army, he had a closer look at the military and political situation than most. Xu's writings thus provide an intriguing perspective on the fall of mainland China and the early years of GMD rule of Taiwan.

Second, Xu is both more accessible and more congenial philosophically for most modern English speakers than Mou or Tang, his contemporaries who are more widely studied in the Sinophone academic world. Both were fond of neologisms based on classical Chinese works, frequently reference nearly the entire history of Chinese thought, and constructed their philosophical systems in response to dense German philosophers (Kant in Mou's case, Hegel in Tang's). Without significant acquaintance with these philosophers, as well most of the history of Chinese philosophy, it is very difficult to understand their systems, which tend toward elaborate metaphysics. Xu was very critical of this metaphysical turn, arguing that it misconstrues Chinese thought. While his works are not always easy—the frequency of classical Chinese quotations from a wide variety of sources being the most troublesome for the translator—he generally is more approachable for the reader. This is surely in part because most of what is translated here was published in semipopular journals that aimed to reach an audience outside of academia.

Philosophically, his rejection of metaphysics means he turns out to have more in common with the more ontologically reserved positions common in Anglo-American philosophy. Xu is not committed to naturalism at all; it is difficult to pin down his position precisely, but certainly he believes that there are truths that are neither logical nor scientific. Yet he is closer to that than many other representatives of New Ruism, and it is not hard to see how his thought could be modified to fit within a naturalistic worldview. In his rejection of anything like divine revelation as a source for morality, he shares a great deal with many modern Western ethical philosophers.

Finally, Xu is an excellent representative of the dominant New Ruist view of democracy, a view which only recently has found any representation in Anglophone works on Ruist political thought. The interpretations of Ruist political thought that get the most attention are mainly antidemocratic to some degree, strongly critical of a focus on individual freedom, and favor a significant meritocratic component to government to avoid the problems of voter ignorance and bias. Xu rejects all of these positions. He was an unfailing supporter of *more* democracy in Taiwan (and China, eventually), he strongly believed in the importance of individual freedom (while having grave reservations about liberalism in the British tradition in particular), and having lived in such an environment, he was highly suspicious of any claims to meritocratic rule. Instead, his interpretation of Ruism is that it *requires* democracy. It would not be too strong to say modern liberal democratic institutions at long last provide the environment where it would be *possible* to realize Ruist political goals.

I have found his arguments here fascinating and incisive, and while he may be overly optimistic about the reality of democracy, his claims are worth serious consideration. At the very least, as someone well acquainted with life in a dictatorship that claimed to be governing in the people's best interests, his criticisms of it deserve attention by anyone who thinks meritocratic government is a realistic possibility. Scholars who hope for that should perhaps be careful what they wish for: Xu's own life illustrates that those in power often don't look kindly on criticism from intellectuals.

Xu Fuguan's Life

Xu Fuguan 徐復觀 was originally named Bingchang 秉常 and born to a peasant family in Xishui county, Hubei province, on January 31, 1903.[1] His early education was at home under the tutelage of his father. When he was fifteen he began to attend Wuchang First Normal School. During this period of schooling, he chose the style name Foguan 佛觀 for himself. Showing a talent for scholarship, he was admitted to Wuchang Academy of Chinese Studies at twenty-one. After graduating he had difficulty making a living and so in 1926 he joined the Nationalist (GMD) Army. Around this time, Xu had his first contact with modern political work: first the writings of Sun Zhongshan (Sun Yat-sen), then Marxism and other economics and philosophy. By the time he went to Japan to study in 1928, he had lost interest in reading anything else, particularly the Chinese literature he had grown up with. After studying economics for a year at Meiji University, he was unable to continue paying tuition and left. In 1930 he returned to Japan, this time attending army officers' school.

After the Japanese invasion of Manchuria in September 1931, Xu returned to China and continued advancing through the ranks during the War of Resistance against Japan, working his way up to the rank of general while seeing combat action. He married Wang Shigao in 1935, and they remained together for forty-seven years. In 1942 the Nationalist command sent Xu to Yan'an as GMD liaison with the Chinese Communist Party (CCP) army there as part of the United Front to resist Japan and he stayed there for several months. During this period he had several personal meetings with Mao Zedong, forming a favorable impression of him and Zhou Enlai. Xu thereafter became something of the GMD expert on the CCP. After leaving Yan'an, Xu went to Chongqing, the temporary capital during the war, in late 1942.

There he had two meetings that impacted the rest of his life. He met Xiong Shili in person for the first time, and reported that Xiong's severe scolding of his shallow method of reading completely changed his attitude toward scholarly pursuits and reversed more than fifteen years of disdain for "thread-bound [i.e., traditional] books."[2] He had already expressed a wish to retire from the military, and his meetings with Xiong strengthened his desire to leave the army and return to serious scholarship. It was Xiong who suggested changing his name from Foguan 佛觀 to Fuguan 復觀. Xu was also invited to meet with Jiang Jieshi (Chiang Kai-shek) to give his opinions on the CCP, beginning a significant personal acquaintanceship with Jiang. Xu did retire from the army in 1946, shortly after the conclusion of World War II, but remained a member of the GMD and was a personal secretary to Jiang Jieshi for a period.

Jiang was impressed with Xu and when the Chinese government moved back to Nanjing, Xu accompanied Jiang and advised him on how to rebuild the country and win more popular support. One of Xu's recommendations to restore land to the farmers became the basis for the later GMD land reform plan in Taiwan. When Jiang resigned from the presidency for a time and retired to his hometown of Xikou, Xu stayed with him for forty days in early 1949. However, it was becoming clear to Xu that the GMD situation was hopeless and the Communists would win the civil war. He left China with his family for good in May 1949. Later that year he started the journal *Democratic Review* in Hong Kong, which became one of the main New Ruist journals and the source of many of the articles translated here. Though Xu was very critical of the GMD government, *Democratic Review* was initially funded by members of the party, with Jiang himself providing some of the early funds.[3]

After moving back and forth between Hong Kong and Taiwan, Xu settled in Taizhong, Taiwan, in 1952 and began to make good on his ambition to become a scholar. That year he took his first teaching position, teaching a course on international organizations and the international situation at Taizhong Agricultural School. The following year he became a full-time instructor, teaching first-year Chinese. In 1955 Donghai (Tunghai) University was founded as a private Christian university in Taizhong. Xu was invited to teach in the newly established Chinese department. He would remain there for the next fourteen years. Even while teaching, Xu was an outspoken critic of many policies of the government and strongly favored more democracy in print, though this resulted in his expulsion from the GMD in March 1957. Then he had to cease publication of *Democratic Review* in 1966 due to lack of funds. As a result of his criticisms, he was eventually forced to retire from Dong-hai University in 1969. Unable to get another job in Taiwan, he spent most of his remaining years in Hong Kong. During a visit to Taiwan in 1980, he was diagnosed with cancer. Xu passed away in 1982 in Taiwan.

Xu's Scholarship

Xu's research always had a particular ambition: defending and promoting Chinese tradition as he saw it. His writings show great preoccupation with "the question of Chinese culture." While never defined precisely, his concern was to articulate the value of Chinese tradition in the face of three threats. The first two were overt attacks on Chinese tradition, going back to the May Fourth era. One of these threats was the Communist government on mainland China. Although Xu had some early interest in Marxism, he could not tolerate the antitraditional aspect of Chinese Communism, which became even more severe during the Cultural Revolution. His strong views against Communism were based on the materialist view of human nature (which he felt denied morality by reducing it to class interest) and the revolutionary aspect, which wanted to discard tradition.

His split with the liberal camp in Taiwan was due to the same rejection of tradition and their overly narrow view of knowledge. The liberal camp in Taiwan, including Hu Shi 胡適, Zhang Foquan 張佛泉, and Yin Haiguang 殷海光, also advocated discarding the outdated culture (which they usually identified as Ruist) in favor of complete Westernization. Much like the Communists, they held Ruism responsible for China's lack of modernization which made it vulnerable to imperialism. Xu shared the concern with modernization, but felt that China had to modernize within its tradition rather than by trying to discard it.

The third threat was from an incorrect interpretation of Chinese culture, Ruism in particular. This came from the GMD. Perhaps as a response to the explicit antitraditionalism of the CCP, perhaps because they felt that it would be politically useful, the GMD government promoted their interpretation of Ruism in Taiwan,[4] which focused on elitism, deference to political authority, and maintenance of hierarchy. While claiming to preserve Chinese tradition, in Xu's view they had no understanding of it, and he dedicated much of his work to arguing that Ruism was in fact politically liberal and democratic, with space for individual freedom. Yet unlike the liberals, he upheld universal morality based on the Mengzian conception of human nature, which he felt was the correct characterization of what being human is. His scholarship is thus fundamentally directed toward supporting his understanding of Chinese tradition.

A central element of this is "concern consciousness" (*youhuan yishi* 憂患意識), which is the term he developed to describe the central focus of the Chinese intellectual tradition. Rather than disinterested search for knowledge of the world, which he identifies as the goal of Western intellectual traditions, Chinese intellectuals were concerned about fixing social and political problems. Concern consciousness is an awareness of the possible consequences of one's actions and sense of responsibility to have a positive impact on the world, understanding that one's choices have significant effects. For intellectuals in particular, it meant a duty to work to improve society, even at the expense of one's own interests. Xu is frequently critical of the intellectuals of his time for looking out for themselves, rather than standing up to speak truth to power. The value of an intellectual is about much more than only scholarly accomplishment.

The true measure of scholarship is, in fact, how it develops a person's character, not their contribution to knowledge. He had no objection to scientific investigation, indeed considering it important and necessary. It could be another way of making a contribution to morality. What he was concerned about was a kind of scholarship that denied morality entirely in favor of mere pursuit of knowledge. "A person's value as a scholar should not merely be determined by his research achievements. It should also be determined by his sincerity in learning and by his character."[5] As the essays in this book make clear, Xu had no respect for the philological and historical approach to humanistic study. He believed Chinese scholarship went on the wrong track with Qing dynasty evidential research, and the introduction of Western methods of scholarship only exacerbated this trend. By focusing only on the meanings of terms, scholars of this type miss the spirit and true meaning of classical texts. Speaking of Qing dynasty scholars, he said, "In reality, while they read a lot of books, they didn't understand a single sentence of what the ancients said that was important."[6] He would probably say the same about Hu Shi and scholars like him.

Xu's Thought: Human Nature and Ethics

As previously stated, Xu rarely presented his thought systematically, instead writing articles of various lengths in response to other articles or political events going on at the time. Therefore, in order to provide a guide to the reader for the following translations, I outline some of his major themes here.

HUMANISM

A central theme running through one of his best-known monographs, *A History of Chinese Theories of Human Nature: The Pre-Qin Period*, is the development of Chinese thought from religion to a humanistic mindset. While not denying the importance of religious practice in Chinese society, the mainstream of Chinese thought was not religious from a very early period, in contrast to premodern European thought. This is one of Kongzi's major advances, in Xu's mind. The story he tells of the early development of Chinese thought (in the Zhou dynasty) is a story of progression from reliance on external, supernatural forces to recognition of the locus of control within human beings.

The early mindset that Xu identifies, typified in Shang dynasty oracle bone divination and hints in early texts about propitiating spirits, involves seeking approval from supernatural forces. It transfers responsibility from human beings to spirits, making their approval and disapproval the standard for human action. In essence, Xu thinks of the category of "religion" as akin to divine command theories of morality. While Kongzi, for example, never denies the existence of spirits, their will does not define good or bad action. Xu observes how Kongzi consistently refused to say much about spirits, instead always drawing attention back to human beings and individual choice and action. For example, when Ji Lu asked about serving the spirits, Kongzi responded, "When you are not able to serve people, how can you serve spirits?"[7] This is in stark contrast to the Mohists, who argued strongly for the importance of conforming to heaven's will and treating ghosts with care.

Ruism is foremost a kind of humanism for Xu, meaning it locates value within the human and is fundamentally concerned with improving the life of human beings, not pleasing supernatural beings. This gives Ruism its characteristic focus on "life," which is the highest value. This means first of all caring for people as biological beings, thus not doing them harm and providing what they need to survive. It also means respecting people as moral agents and helping them to realize the moral side of their nature as well. And this is all justified without reference to supernatural agents. Ruism recognizes the reality of choice in people, rather than displacing it to a supernatural being. This is another aspect of concern consciousness: awareness that one is ultimately responsible for one's own choices and actions.

Since the will of heaven or spirits does not provide the warrant for ethics, Xu believes Ruists had to look elsewhere, and they found it in internal experience. He therefore gives less attention to Xunzi, since Xunzi thought that, at least initially, people have no internal inclination to morality and have to learn it from an external source. This conflicts with Xu's idea of humanism, and so he focuses much more on Kongzi and Mengzi and later Ruists who also emphasize a kind of internal experience, such as Wang Yangming. In fact, internal experience (*neizai jingyan* 內在 經驗) could be called a technical term for him. It refers to introspective sorts of experiences that may be elicited by contact with some object or situation in the world, but are ultimately located within the person. Ethical value is not objective in the sense of existing outside the human heart-mind, though it is still universal, because people's heart-minds are identical in the relevant capacities. This is why scientific confirmation of morality will always be impossible: morality cannot be proved by any sort of knowledge of the external world. Only internal experience can confirm it. That possibility of internal experience and moral response is what makes human beings human and worthy of respect.

HUMAN NATURE

Like the other twentieth-century New Ruists,[8] Xu is committed to Mengzi's doctrine that human nature is good. For him, that means human beings have the capacity to go beyond self-interest and, at the highest level, to eradicate the distinction between self and other. Even for those who do not reach that point, there is a capacity for moral responsiveness that is sincerely motivated by care for others. Xu frequently talks about benevolence (*ren* 仁), which he sees as the fundamental moral quality. It can be understood as sincere concern for another's well-being.

Defining human nature as including this potential to extend beyond self-interest is a way of expressing the universality of moral agency and is a crucial underpinning of democracy for Xu. As discussed above, Xu's disagreement with liberals such as Yin Haiguang were not over the goal: there wasn't much disagreement about the form of democratic government. Differences over the importance of tradition were one factor, but there was an additional philosophical point. Xu believed that the liberal belief that democracy could be established on a view of human beings as motivated fundamentally by self-interest was fatally flawed. He was critical of the excessive individualism he found in Anglo-American liberalism in particular, and thought this could not be the basis of a stable democratic society. His understanding of human nature in no way denies that people have their own interests that they will and should pursue, but it allows for other-regarding motivations as well. It is necessary to develop this aspect of human nature if democratic practice is going to work. Hence, he argues that democracy needs something like the Ruist conception of human nature to last.

We need to look at his approach to knowing human nature to appreciate Xu's distinctive contribution to New Ruist thought. The belief that human nature is good and that democracy needs Ruism is common to other New Ruists of the period, not unique to Xu. About the same time as Xu was writing his essays on democracy, Mou Zongsan was putting together the ideas that he would publish as *The Way of Authority and Governance* in 1959. What is particular to Xu is his rejection of metaphysical understandings of Ruist thought. Unlike Mou and Tang Junyi, he believed Chinese thought could not be profitably understood as a kind of metaphysics or idealism. He was certainly not a materialist, but he never put human nature on a higher ontological level outside the ordinary material world. There is a certain similarity between Xu and Jean-Paul Sartre, though as far as I can tell he did not know of Sartre's work. That is, Xu's claim that Ruism is not religious can be extended to attempts to elevate something other than God to a transcendent place and source of ultimate value, whether Hegel's spirit or Kant's noumenal self. There is one world, the one in which physical phenomena are described by science.

Xu frequently cautions against using Western philosophical models to understand Ruist thought. Chinese thought's starting point was fundamentally different than Greek philosophy, which began with trying to understand the natural world. Chinese thought began with moral practice, and always had a more practical concern to realize moral action. Chinese and Western thought have fundamentally different characters for him. As a consequence, Chinese philosophy did not excel in understanding the physical world, and this should be left to science.[9] Rather than metaphysics (*xing er shang xue* 形而上學), Chinese philosophy is properly understood as embodied learning (*xing er zhong xue* 形而中學). While there are questions about exactly what this means, at minimum it has two implications for Xu: following the Chinese philosophical tradition means not erecting metaphysical systems, and the source of morality has to be found within human nature.

KNOWLEDGE

In much of his work, Xu says there are two knowing faculties in the heart-mind, which grasp different sorts of content. "Heart-mind" is the way I have most often translated *xin* 心, because the word does also refer to the physical organ in the chest and because Chinese thought traditionally did not strictly separate affective and cognitive mental states. The heart-mind has a cognitive nature (*zhixing* 知性) and a moral nature (*dexing* 德性). The former is the source of knowledge of objects, external phenomena. The latter is the source of self-knowledge and values, which are rooted in human nature.

Western culture excelled in developing the cognitive nature, which led to natural science and the great technological advances of the industrial period. Xu believes these discoveries have had great value, and it is very important to have the better understanding of the natural world that science provides. This is something that was not developed sufficiently in Chinese culture, and Xu believes it is critical to remedy this.

However, as human nature is not a part of the external world, it is not something that can be discovered scientifically. Scientific knowledge is very important, but not all knowledge is scientific. The way to understand human nature is through the moral nature, not the cognitive nature. This means that research in psychology, for example, cannot demonstrate the truth of moral values. Rather than concluding that moral values are not real, Xu regards this as a flaw in psychology, and by extension a limit to the scientific approach generally. Moral values have to be discovered by internal experience, not investigation of phenomena.

EMBODIED RECOGNITION

One key form of internal experience that Xu discusses extensively is what he calls "embodied recognition" (*tiren* 體認), a major epistemological concept for him. He adopted this term from Xiong Shili, who in turn drew it from the work of the Ming Ruist Wang Yangming. Characteristic of Xu, he does not provide a clear definition of the term. In "The Culture of the Heart-Mind," chapter 9 here, he identifies it as awareness of the four moral feelings Mengzi presented. He also calls it an inward cognition of oneself. It therefore appears to be a direct, immediate awareness of the moral feelings that he identifies as human nature, a sort of self-verifying experience that cannot be denied, psychologically if not logically.

An example, perhaps, is Mengzi's description of a person seeing a child about to fall into a well. In such a situation, anyone, according to Mengzi, would have a feeling of alarm and compassion, not based on any self-interest (which Mengzi is careful to exclude), but simply concern for the innocent child about to suffer great harm.[10] Liu Honghe described it as a spontaneous, prereflective response to the suffering of an innocent.[11] Xu says that we do not necessarily understand why we have this reaction, but we don't need to: the feeling cannot be denied.[12] The phenomenological reality of the moral response is itself sufficient justification.

Analyzing this sort of example further, it is clear that there are two dimensions. There is obviously an empirical dimension: the subject in this instance has to see the child in danger in order to have the moral reaction. While Xu does not make this point, we may further add that as a matter of human psychology, people tend to respond much more strongly to that kind of direct, immediate perception of possible suffering than to more distant, secondhand information (such as testimony about children in danger in another country). And so the moral reaction is causally dependent on some empirical knowledge, which belongs to the cognitive nature. Yet this information alone is not sufficient. In a manner analogous to Hume, Xu argues that mere facts do not generate a moral response or motivate any kind of action. Even if one is taught what is good, without caring about the good it will not lead to action. For action to be possible at all, there have to be some inherently existing motives.[13] Embodied recognition is awareness of those motives, the moral responses that belong to human nature. Without awareness of those, the witness might indifferently observe the child fall to her death, a reaction Xu thinks is psychologically impossible for most people.

So this is a kind of experience, in that it is awareness with particular content that happens at a particular time. But though it is causally dependent on some information about the world (such as seeing the child in this example), what the agent then becomes aware of is something in herself, not the world. This is why Xu tends not to call it empirical knowledge exactly, which for him means knowledge of something separate from the agent, but internal experience. Yet as he also makes clear, it is not knowledge of some higher reality: the heart-mind known through embodied recognition is not separate from the physiological body. The "embodied" part of embodied recognition is crucial.

THE IMPORTANCE OF PRACTICE—*GONGFU*

Related to Xu's emphasis on embodied recognition is his focus on practice, specifically practice in the real world (*xianshi shijie* 現實世界). Instead of elaborating metaphysical theories, what Ruist philosophers focused on was moral practice in the real world and how to improve it. The method for this is *gongfu* 工夫—mostly familiar from martial arts contexts but meaning any focused effort generally. In Xu's case, *gongfu* usually means the process of moral cultivation. He says of *gongfu* that it "takes the self, especially the inner spirit, as its object for achieving a particular kind of goal. In the theory of human nature, the work of the inner spirit to realize the hidden potential of the origin of life and make manifest the source of morality—only that can be called *gongfu*."[14] This is an endless process in the pursuit of moral perfection that can never be fully or permanently achieved.

Ruism to him is not about constructing moral theory but improving moral practice. Xu's concern with practice is also visible in the earlier Ruist scholars that he chooses as exemplars. Although he is critical of Wang Yangming for neglecting the significance of greater knowledge of the world, his frequent commendation of Wang's attitude toward *doing* in the real world comes across in these essays. Embodied recognition is not an intellectual sort of knowing, and that critical internal experience suggests that conventional philosophical study is not very helpful. Studying moral theories alone won't produce embodied recognition: that has to be realized through action in life.[15]

This is again where Chinese and Western cultures diverged. Western culture, Xu was quick to admit, was superior in its realization of the cognitive nature and knowledge of the external world. However, it was not as advanced as China in development of the moral nature. This was where Chinese thought excelled, and where it can make a contribution to world culture. One manifestation of this is the early appearance of a free society in China, by which he means a society where advancement depends on individual effort and not status determined at birth. Xu credits Kongzi with realizing this in China, centuries before the Enlightenment ushered such freedom into Europe. The goal of modernization should be to remedy the deficiency in the cognitive side while retaining the advances of the moral side.

Xu's Thought: Politics

The most obvious point in Xu's political thought is his unwavering commitment to democracy. In a world where the value of democracy is under serious question, and where many people in East Asia in particular doubt whether democracy is suitable for their societies, this is itself noteworthy. Xu gives few details about what he means by democracy, but from what he does say it includes many typical features of liberal electoral democracy: multiple political parties, near-universal voting rights, rule of law and mechanisms for orderly transfer of power, a constitution, and protections for freedom of speech, publication, and assembly. He was no revolutionary when it came to political institutions. Most of these were already found in the Republic of China constitution at the time; he simply wanted the government to live up to them.

As already stated, Xu's primary concern, outside of advocating for democracy, is showing that there is no conflict between democratic government and Ruist political ideals. Far from a conflict, democracy will actually make possible the realization of these ideals. For Xu, democracy is what Ruists *should* have been advocating all along, but the historical realities in which they lived made that impossible and all they could do was try to mitigate the excesses of autocratic and hereditary rule. Thus, pursuing democracy does not require giving up Chinese culture, as both liberals and conservative elements of the GMD argued. There is no contradiction in having a democratic Ruist society.

RUIST POLITICAL IDEALS

Xu's approach to justifying democracy is to examine Ruist political ideals, describe how they could not be realized in the historical political conditions, and argue that democracy will allow for better, even full, realization of these ideals. The way he does this is based on the view of human nature described above, both the moral aspect that represents true human nature for him, and his refusal to separate the moral person and the physiological or material person.

Politics has a moral goal for Xu: the ultimate goal of Ruist politics is to allow people to realize their moral natures as much as possible. This provides a test for good government: a government that represses the moral responses or simply doesn't allow for their full development is not a good government. Government must provide room for the free development of the moral nature, while also encouraging its growth through suitable education. So Xu is not a liberal, if that means endorsing value neutrality. He does not believe government needs to or should be neutral concerning the good human life, but neither can it force a certain view on people. Government can encourage the Ruist view of the person through education, but not use coercive measures to force people to adopt it.

Xu's objection to using coercion to support any moral view, including Ruist values, has two sources. The first is due to what he calls the primary value in Ruist thought: life. He means a biological notion of life primarily, so that caring for the physical self takes priority over caring for the moral self. In other words, coercion and punishment—the power of the law—must not be used to harm the physical body in the name of improving the moral self. The first duties of the government are to refrain from causing harm and provide the conditions for people to satisfy their material needs. Since the moral self cannot be separated from the physiological self, one cannot improve the former by harming the latter. This includes requiring people to deny their basic preferences. This is what he believes Communists do. It is wrong for the government to try to ignore people's preferences, the foremost of which is life. Yet at the same time, he insists that preferences cannot be the basis of morality (as in utilitarianism).

The other reason is that he believes morality has to be freely chosen, not coerced. He frequently quotes *Analects* 2.3: "If you guide the people with decrees and reform them with punishments, they will evade them and have no sense of shame. If you guide them with virtue and reform them with ritual, they will have a sense of shame and correct themselves." The way Xu understands this is government coercion can indeed regulate people's behavior, since they will try to avoid punishment, but it cannot bring them to realize true morality. As discussed above, this has to be an internal experience, in which the moral person recognizes her moral nature. This means it is something that each individual has to realize themselves. Coercion simply cannot do this. True morality must be realized under conditions of political freedom.[16]

How Democracy Works

The goals of Ruist politics—care for the people's material welfare and support for their moral development—are captured in the traditional idea of *minben* 民本, the people as foundation. Xu describes how Ruist thinkers urged rulers to put the people's preferences ahead of their own and do what was best for them. However, they did not have a political structure available to make that happen consistently. Rulers might either fail to understand correctly what the people's preferences are, or they might know but find it too difficult to ignore their own preferences, which Xu recognizes is a very challenging thing to do. That is what democratic institutions should aim to instantiate: a system that allows the people to make sure their preferences are followed. Traditional Ruism never had this.

The most basic component of democracy for Xu is thus elections, since that is the mechanism by which the people enforce their col-lective will on the government. The other components of democracy mainly follow from consideration for what is necessary for elections to be effective. Taiwan at the time was formally a democracy, since there were periodic elections, but there was only one party and vote buying was commonplace. Furthermore, the legislature was stacked to support President Jiang, and there was no effective separation of powers. Media were quite restricted as well, as the GMD owned the mass media. Hence, he believes it is necessary to have more political parties, rule of law and separation of powers, and free expression and publication so people can become informed and express their views. Xu's ideal is for the rulers to have no preferences at all, or at least to act as if they don't.

In response to criticisms that democracy was inferior to decision making by an educated elite (as the GMD represented themselves)—very close to the position of contemporary Ruist meritocrats—Xu's response is that scholarship and government are entirely different endeavors. Scholarship or academia, the pursuit of knowledge, is indeed qualitative:

as he says, the opinion of one scientist is worth more than ten thousand ordinary people. But carrying this idea over to politics leads to totalitarianism. In scholarship, the goal is to converge on truth and eliminate falsehood, but through a process of presenting evidence and convincing other scholars of one's view. In politics, however, what will happen is that the government will use its power to enforce its view of the truth and eradicate opponents. This is what was happening in China, and, to a large extent, in Taiwan.

Politics is quantitative: the standard of what is right is what the majority supports. The minority can always try to change majority opinion, and this is one important reason for free expression. But if the majority rejects a certain government policy, then it should not be implemented even if the experts in government disagree. Freedom of thought has to be protected, which means the people must be able to exercise their abilities to make political evaluations and judgments. Respect for the equality represented by universal moral nature requires this. While this may result in suboptimal government policies at some points, there is always the possibility for change. However, this has to come from the people.

Another way Xu makes this point is by distinguishing the form and content of government. Content is the particular proposals, laws, and policies that address specific political issues; form determines how content is decided and implemented; typically, the procedures inscribed in the constitution. In a democratic system, the democratic form sets limits on what content is possible; that is, a law that would dissolve the legislature and give a lifetime executive supreme power would not be possible. Ideally, form determines how content can be advocated, opposed, and realized; the content of government changes but the form does not. He makes this distinction largely in response to claims that Taiwan is a government of the Three Principles of the People, the political ideology of Sun Zhongshan (Yat-sen), father of the Republic of China. As such, realizing the three principles is a higher value than democracy (even though democracy is one of them). Xu's response is that there is no conflict: democracy is the form, and the three principles are one possible content. Democracy is not committed to any particular content (other than that which is necessary to preserve that form). The adoption of any doctrine or policy must go through the democratic process, so the people can choose the three principles if they want, but that has to be a choice made democratically. It cannot be above the democratic process.

THE SIGNIFICANCE OF RUIST DEMOCRACY

Xu makes two overarching points in his political thought. The first is that democracy represents the best opportunity for realizing Ruist political ideas. It is not a guarantee, both because the practice of democracy may not live up to its promise and because his views on putting the form of democracy above any specific content means that it is possible that the electorate will support other content, not Ruist values. He appears to recognize and accept this possibility, though he would surely try to change their views if that happened. For people committed to continuing Chinese culture and Ruism, Xu argues that supporting democracy is part of that.

His second point is that democracy needs to be built on a moral foundation: the Ruist conception of human nature or something very close to it. There is necessarily a question of morality in politics; the two cannot be entirely separated. He finds modern liberalism deeply dissatisfying for attempting to set aside the moral dimension. This treats people like animals, merely pursuing satisfaction of their desires. It is not only an insult to human dignity, it cannot work. Such a conception of human beings cannot provide a stable foundation for democratic theory. He appears to think that this way of thinking about human beings as essentially self-interested at best results in democracy as a *modus vivendi*: people want to be able to pursue their interests with no restraints, but recognize that they have to accept some restrictions to avoid conflict.[17] If they think they can get away with avoiding these restraints and accumulating more power, they have no reason not to.

In Xu's Ruist understanding, people are not only self-interested. We want to care for others and get along with them. Commitment to democracy is necessary to realize important goods in human life. It furthers people's interests, rather than only getting in the way of the pursuit of their desires. Belief in the Ruist conception of human nature thus gives people more reason to support democracy, and hence Xu thinks it will finally have a stable foundation. It makes government into an important source of good, not something to tolerate grudgingly. Whether there are alternatives to the Ruist view of humanity that would achieve the same thing is not something he considers, and it would be an interesting question for further study. Various critics of liberalism have been making similar arguments for years, but Xu stands out for making this point sixty years ago.

Influence

Xu had virtually no impact on the political situation of his time. He was essentially forced into a second exile in 1969 due to his criticisms of the government and had very little success in encouraging any democratic reforms. Jiang Jieshi died in 1975 and his son Jiang Jingguo became the next president. Jiang Jingguo began to relax political persecutions and tolerate more dissent, though Xu did not live to see this. It is not surprising that Xu proposed this for his epitaph: "Here lies the son of a peasant village who once tried his hand at politics while deeply loathing it—Xu Foguan."[18] Personal conflicts with members of the liberal group, notably Hu Shi and Yin Haiguang (though Xu reconciled with him at the end of Yin's life—see chapter 3), meant that there was little cooperation between the liberals and New Ruists even when they shared the goal of democratic reform. This surely weakened both sides.

In academia, philosophy in particular, his influence has also not been that significant. This is not so surprising when he disclaimed being a philosopher and indeed much of his work was on literature, history, and aesthetics. His historical conclusions about early Chinese texts are mostly dated at this point, surpassed by the major recent discoveries of excavated material which has shed tremendous new light on many ancient texts as well as by advances in text criticism. While he had some dedicated students, some of whom edited later publications of his works, he did not inspire later generations of scholars the way Mou Zongsan did.

Where I believe he *could* have influence is helping to reorient what Ruism is about. The growth of academic philosophy in the Sinophone world as well as (some) greater interest in Chinese thought among Western-trained philosophers means that debates have proceeded at a high level of abstraction, delving into metaethical concerns such as what form of ethical theory Ruism is and which characteristics or virtues in Ruism are fundamental and which are derivative. A lesson to draw from Xu's work is that Ruism is not any kind of ethical theory. It is a philosophy about improved ethical practice: making people better, not refining theoretical arguments. Xu emphasizes that Ruism must be about practice, and practice in the real world. It is something to realize in one's life. Several contemporary Ruists have expressed concerns about Ruism turning into an academic field. Xu reminds us that it is foremost a way of living.

Part One

Autographical Essays

Chapter 1

My Life of Study

Translator's introduction: Xu's writings include a number of autobiographical pieces such as this, in which he describes his educational background. It was relatively unconventional even for his day. After initially studying to be a teacher, he decided to join the army for a better chance at making a living. Then he went to Japan, first to study economics and then to officers' training school. His early education was very traditional, focusing on classical Chinese works. He had little contact with the new subjects imported from the West until he joined the army. Not many people in his time had the chance to get graduate education, but Xu didn't even finish college. He was largely self-taught.

The influence of Xiong Shili on Xu's scholarship is clear. He first met Xiong during the war, after Xiong had earned quite a bit of fame for *New Treatise on the Uniqueness of Consciousness*. Xu credits Xiong with restoring his interest in traditional Chinese culture and scholarship, which he maintained for the rest of his life. His description of Xiong's severe criticism of his reading method is particularly vivid, and it obviously made a strong impact on his approach to research for the rest of his academic career. As Xu describes elsewhere, he believes the purpose of learning is building character more than accumulating knowledge. He is briefly but intensely critical of Hu Shi, who strongly favored a more empirical approach to humanistic study—Xu refers to him as a fake. Yet

The Finest Selected Writings of Xu Fuguan, 311–319, first published in *Literary Star* 4, no. 6, December 1959.

he did not reject Western knowledge, feeling that it might contribute to understanding Chinese literature, history, and thought. Although his own research was always focused on China, he read Western works extensively as well.

Ever since I learned to read at age eight I could not go two or three days without opening a book, even in the midst of serving in the army during wartime.[1] However, one could still say that I never read or understood a single book until I was forty-seven or forty-eight. Because my life of study is so contradictory, perhaps writing it down can serve to provide lessons from my mistakes for many youth with aspirations to study.

The reason I always read was because of an interest in reading. But now I understand that interest in reading without adding a purpose will not bring any results. Reading for forty-odd years, naturally I browsed very broadly. However, now I understand that merely reading quickly and extensively without reading thoroughly and becoming familiar with several sizable volumes of classical works will not provide any basis for scholarship. This is the lesson I draw when looking back on my experience.

My father's life was a life of taking examinations, but he never attained any rank. The reason my father wanted me to read was to attain some rank by examination. This never failed to arouse my distaste, and influenced my education when I was young tremendously. As soon as I learned to read, it was new and old together. By "new" I mean textbooks, starting with volume one and reading through to volume eight. Then it was *A Model for Argument and Speech*. Then *The Gate of Ink*.[2] This book is a collection of essays by successful examinees and *jinshi* holders.[3] On top of that, I also read essays by Tan Yankai.[4]

As for the "old," starting with the *Analects* I read through the Four Books and Five Classics.[5] Additionally, I read *Broad Debates of Donglai*, *Ancient Writing Styles in One Hundred Chapters*, *Zenith of Ancient Writings*, *Annals Easy to Understand*, and later switched to *Imperial Comments on the Comprehensive Mirror [of the Past], Edited for Perusing*.[6] Other than the last two, I had to recite these from memory. After reciting, I would have to explain a chapter.

This study of new and old materials went on for a while, until I was about thirteen. During this period, I loved reading poetry, but my father wouldn't allow it. At that point, the civil service exam had already been abolished,[7] but my father apparently thought it would be brought back. The final civil service exam had only tested essay writing, not poems and rhapsodies. I found a color printing of *Strange Tales from a Chinese Studio*.[8] While I was devouring it eagerly, my father found out and tore the book up and burned the pieces. When I started high elementary school[9] and got out from under my father's thumb, I spent those three precious years entirely in reading old works of fiction. One could say it was an emotional reaction.

When I was fifteen, I entered Wuchang First Normal School, still mixed up. At that time, our level in Chinese was probably much higher than that of Chinese department university students today. Our Chinese teacher was a man from Anlu[10] named Mr. Chen Zhongfu. His skill in Tongcheng school writing was especially deep,[11] and he taught extremely well. The man who corrected our homework was Mr. Li Xizhe from Wuchang.[12] His scholarship was based on the masters of the Zhou and Qin periods, and his achievements were also very high. The homework he assigned always inspired one to do real study. We did an essay every two weeks: he would give the assignment on Saturday afternoon and we would hand in our roll of paper on Monday of the week after, giving students enough time to plan out their compositions. He always returned our essays in order from good to bad. At that time, I didn't care about my other work; I only took writing seriously, and I was quite full of myself about my ability. But every time, he handed back my paper second or third from last. I would think that Mr. Li probably didn't understand my essay. But when I would get a look at the essays of my classmates next to me, they really were better. How could this be? Often I would cry secretly, unable to understand it.

I spotted a copy of *Xunzi* on a classmate's desk once and opened it up. The line I had read in my textbook, "Blue dye comes from the indigo plant and yet it is bluer than the indigo," came from here![13] My curiosity aroused, I borrowed it and read it straight through without pausing, finding it tremendously interesting. From this I learned of the pre-Qin masters, which opened up a new world of reading for me and I read them from morning until night. Because my interest in Zhuangzi was very high, and moreover he is not easy to understand, I would get five or six annotated editions from the library and compare them. Once I'd read the various masters, my choices in books were naturally not the same as before. What I had thought was good before now I found wasn't worth a cent. Books I'd felt no interest in previously I now found myself wanting to read. From that point on, I didn't pay much attention to writing and only focused on reading. That same frame of mind I'd had for fiction I now applied to reading Liang Qichao, Liang Shuming, and Wang Xinggong (apparently he was talking about the scientific method), as well as works by Hu Shi and others on scholarship.[14]

Once, in my third year, Mr. Li suddenly handed back my essay first, and from that point on I was usually first or second. Furthermore, I found out that the principal Liu Fengzhang and some of the teachers had begun to praise me behind my back. Slowly I came to understand that the quality of an essay is not only a matter of open and shut, free-flowing technique, but requires content. For a typical essay, there is only content when there is thought. Thought has to be inspired and nurtured from classical works with value, and moreover come to fruition in the atmosphere of the period. By the time I was twelve or thirteen I already had a grasp of the rhythm of old writings, but thinking back on it, this probably did me more harm than good.

My common sense about thread-bound books was obtained from five years as a normal school student.[15] After that, although I was a student for three years at the [Wuchang] Academy for Chinese Studies, I had already lost the feeling of novelty for reading and so I did not improve much. There were two peculiar things about that entire long period of study. The first is that until November 1926, one could say that I read nothing on the contemporary political situation. I didn't have the slightest impression of this ism or that party. The way I began to have some connection with political thought was in December 1926 when I was stationed in Huangpi[16] and Mr. Tao Ziqin was my brigade commander.[17] I was a secretary at a battalion headquarters and he asked if I had read Sun Zhongshan's doctrine, the Three Principles of the People.[18] I said that I hadn't, and he felt that this was very odd. Then he gave me a copy of *The Three Principles of the People*, wanting me to read it. This is how I began to have some connection with political thought.

The other peculiar thing is that although I had read a lot of thread-bound books by this time, when I think back I had not obtained the key to studying. This is because although many teachers had been very good to me, not one of them really guided me when it came to how to study. Add in my own personality of leaving things up to fate and going along, and it meant that I had no goal I was trying to achieve by study, nor did I have a particular direction or foundation. I was like a wanderer who spends money as soon as it comes into his hand. Even if the amount of money that passes through his hands is not small, at the end of things his hands are still empty.

Starting in 1927, through Sun Zhongshan's writings I started coming to know about Marx, Engels, materialism, and so on. Later, when I went to Japan,[19] if it weren't that sort of book I had no interest in reading it. While at the army officers' school in Japan I organized a Society for the Group That Doesn't Read especially to read this kind of book. This lasted until about the time Deborin was subject to criticism.[20] It included philosophy, economics, political science, and so on. Even the Japanese translation of the Soviet periodical *Under the Banner of Marxism*—we didn't miss a single issue. After I returned to China and served in the army, I neither spoke nor wrote of these matters, but in truth they filled my spiritual space between youth and maturity, until about 1940. Probably from 1942 to 1948, I filled the spiritual space formerly occupied by Marx-Engels thought with the simpleminded idea of "saving China through saving the GMD." After I returned from Japan, for more than ten years of precious time I read a lot of books related to military work out of a competitive mindset. Now when I think back to that period, I still feel distracted.

It was in 1942 that the military command sent me to Yan'an as a liaison officer [to the CCP].[21] There I read Clausewitz's work on war theory while living in a cave for six months, but I also gave up on it then.[22] Unless one understands the Seven Years' War as well as the French wars from the Revolution to the Napoleonic wars, and in addition has a background in German philosophy from Kant to Hegel, it is impossible to understand this book completely. It was my third time reading it in Yan'an. That time I happened to understand the course of thought that shaped the structure of his book and grasped his conclusion. Then I truly understood that he wasn't telling us some formulas for fighting a war, but teaching us a method for understanding and grasping war. Almost all great books give their readers a method for reaching a conclusion, and so give their readers some training in thought. After reading this book, when I went back to look at what Yang Jie had said, it really was "the words of a small child pretending to explain things."[23] I had already taken copious notes at that time and had planned to write a book when I returned to Chongqing,[24] however, due to procrastination and indolence, my interests shifted and more than ten years of effort on military theory all came to naught. It is really a matter for regret. However, one can learn from this that unless one grasps the most essential things in a certain field of study, one will be a layman for his whole life.

The courage to resolve to knock[25] on the door of study was inspired by Xiong Shili.[26] My shift from twenty years of a mindset of rejecting Chinese culture to having a greater understanding of it was also due to Mr. Xiong's inspiration. I wore my army uniform on my first visit to see him at Mianren Academy in Jingangbei town, Beibei, in Chongqing. I asked for instruction about what books to read. He told me to read Wang Fuzhi's *Assessment after Reading the* Comprehensive Mirror.[27] I said that I had read it years ago. Displeased, he answered, "You didn't understand it. You should read it again." After a while, I went to see him again and said I had finished reading it again. He asked, "What did you get out of it?"

Then I told him about all the places where I didn't agree with it. Not letting me finish, he angrily scolded me. "How can you read anything, you idiot! The content of any book has some good parts and some bad parts. Why don't you find the good in what he wrote first, instead of picking out the bad? Reading your way, you can read a hundred, even a thousand books, and what benefit will you get from them? First you should understand the good in a book and then criticize the bad. It's like eating: through the process of digestion you absorb the nutritious part. For example, in the *Assessment*, such and such part has such significance, and in this other part, his understanding is quite profound. Do you remember? Do you understand? Your way of reading has no promise!"

He scolded and scolded until this army general was dumbfounded. My mind was spinning. This gentleman could scold so fiercely! He read so thoroughly! So in reading, one first had to understand the meaning of each book! This was a cursing that brought me back from the jaws of death. I fear it would be a cursing that would bring back from the jaws of death any youth, grownup, or elder who were full of themselves but had not entered the gate of real study! In recent years, whenever I meet someone who believes there are no books worth reading, I know that they are someone who puts off life with small cleverness.

Afterward, every time I would meet with Mr. Xiong and discuss a particular cultural question, he would listen to my opinion and then in a scolding but exhorting manner say, "You idiot! Have I not already thought through this kind of shallow viewpoint? But [because of these reasons] . . . how could this be persuasive? Taking it up a level, one could think in this way . . . but this is also not persuasive. I arrived at my conclusion only after several layers of analysis." Through this constant forging from the old gentleman, I gradually struggled to free myself from my shallowness and also to not let myself be covered up by the shallowness of the general mood of the time. I slowly realized that I should pursue something spiritual. Opening books in order to pursue something and reading books for no particular goal are two completely different sorts of activities in terms of their effect.

Since 1949, when I had no real connection with actual politics, my one way forward was reading. My initial plan was to use all my time reading books on Western philosophy while my mind was still sharp, and also to take a little time to read about politics. I would only go back to thread-bound books when I was about sixty. However, this plan had to change in the middle because of teaching. But within the constraints of what was possible, I still read Western books related to my work. For example, to teach The Literary Heart-mind Carves Dragons[28] I read more than three thousand pages of Western literary theory. To teach Records of the Historian[29] I put together a sequence and copied down passages from the historiography of Ranke, Croce, and Meinecke, as well as Cassirer's narrative of synthesis.[30] This is because one must put Chinese literature and history to the test before one can talk about where it is valid and where it has problems. If I hadn't taken extracts from more than three hundred thousand words of Western ethical theory, I could not have understood Zhu Xi and Lu Xiangshan, nor could I have written "Explaining [Lu] Xiangshan Studies."[31] This is why I often urged students in the Chinese department at Donghai University to learn English well.

Some friends laughed at me when I read philosophy books, saying, "Are *you* going to be a philosopher?" That's right; I couldn't, nor did I want to. But I had my reasons. First, I wanted to understand the basic questions in Western culture and the routes that they took in order to find answers. In some intangible way, these would often become a clear contrast with the questions of Chinese culture. Second, I often felt that Western philosophical works were often impoverished in their conclusions, but when critiquing other philosophies and analyzing phenomena and facts, then they had the highest sharp and orderly ability. A person's mind is like a knife. Reading this kind of book is like sharpening a knife on the finest and smoothest grindstone.

I did not get a direct benefit from this work; that is, I didn't become a philosopher. But I did get a side benefit. First, whenever I met someone who took himself to be an academic authority and pressured others with Westernization, I knew in what field he was a fake expert as soon as I heard him. I could go back and look through some related books and prove he was a fake expert (such as Mr. Hu Shi).[32] Although I offended no small number of people this way and isolated myself further, this was still very important. Many people get frightened by this sort of fake expert and go down the wrong path for their whole life, or even don't dare to go down a path but delay applying their time and energy for their whole life. Second, my reading for those years seemed to be a little more meticulous and deeper than the average person. I could find some issues in frequently read materials that had been ignored by past readers, but were nonetheless important. Perhaps it was because that dull knife of my brain had been cleaned and sharpened against the grindstone.

After wasting an immeasurable amount of energy, I slowly groped toward my own way of reading. First, for the past ten years I have refused to read second-rate or lower books.[33] Nor do I read books unrelated to my research unless absolutely necessary. There would always be some first-rate scholars or books from every area that people would recommend. These books were typically voluminous, with more profound content. Naturally, sometimes there were exceptions. When one has read things like textbooks and pamphlets and then wants to go up to a higher level of reading, one will actually feel it's particularly difficult because the gap spans so many mediocre and shallow views. Moreover, it's often like a country woman whose arms are covered with gilded copper bracelets. She feels she's very fancy, but it's all not worth a cent. Better to wear one ring of real gold which would have some value. This is the reasoning behind reading less, but only reading first-rate works. I used to read every word of the writings of Lu Xun and Kawakami Hajime.[34] I also read several thick books on economics as well as a number of works on military affairs. Up until 1952 I was still copying passages from four Japanese translations of Laski's writings.[35] This was all a waste because it has nothing to do with my current research. I wasted far too much of my energy on this kind of work. Now that I'm approaching old age, I hope I won't waste energy this way again.

Second, when I'm going to read a classical work or research some question in classical writings, I first read thoroughly whatever related research I can get my hands on, especially from contemporary writers. Then I carefully read the original text. I feel that research by later scholars can provide a guide to the original text and, further, one gets a sense of the level of research and the results in that area. However, if one uses this kind of work to take the place of reading the original, then one is forever sitting at someone else's knee and wasting one's whole life. It is easier to understand and evaluate both the original and later research by reading later scholars' research and then reading the original. Additionally, one will often discover that there is still a lot of work for us to do. I have read a number of essays by scholars of reputation these past few years, writing that is polished and elegant. But once I checked their work against the original text or material, it was often quite disappointing. As for things written entirely for the fee, best not to touch them at all. So when I teach, I encourage students to aim high and read more original texts.

Third, copy important passages when reading. Usually I will mark up an important book while I read. When it's marked up, then I write down particular passages. I don't have the practice of making notecards. Notecards might be suitable for gathering ordinary materials, but they have no point with ancient books that need to be read carefully. I would feel I understood many spots in a book while reading, but then once I started to note down passages, I would find that I didn't understand clearly what came before. The work of copying passages is actually the work of sharpening one's reading. Additionally, as I get old my memory is getting worse. I can't grasp the content of a whole book at once. Copying passages can jog my memory and guide me along the contents of the entire book, joining together to form several important ideas. This is most mindless work, but in a life of reading I have only gotten some benefit from the past few years of this mindless work.

Actually, one doesn't get any nutrition from the food while one is eating. One gets the nutrition while resting after eating, or during some idle period. The digestion of books, too, often happens in a period of temporary idleness after reading. Sometimes it's through thinking of a new question, and sometimes it's in the manner of an animal that chews its cud, chewing over what one has read, intentionally or unintentionally turning it over in one's mind, that one begins to digest what one has read. Furthermore, many doubts, difficulties, and questions find the light of resolution in an instant. When I was reading Mr. Lai's work on the *Changes* at twelve or thirteen, I could never understand the various relations of the hexagrams.[36] My father couldn't understand them either. One day during lunch I suddenly put down my bowl and chopsticks and said, "Father, I get it!" My father said, "What did you get?" Then I explained how to understand the relations between the hexagrams, but my father still didn't believe me and took out the book to look at each hexagram, and sure enough I was not mistaken. I've had many of this kind of experience in my life. I think that everyone has.

If a person reads a book and has no questions in his mind, then he hasn't absorbed the book. Then one just has to put one's mind to reading it again carefully. If one has questions after reading a book, then he has opened the gate of this book and will naturally hasten to continue the effort to understand. I'm not sure if I've entered the gate of scholarship or not, but there are always many questions pressing at me and urging me on. The strength that supports my life comes from two sources: one is my wife and the four children she bore, and the other is the books on my shelf. Now my wife and I are getting old, and our children have become independent one by one. Soon this phase of sentiment will come to an end. I only hope that I can maintain the mood of a kindergarten student to let me study for another twenty years and continue to write down the questions in my mind. That might be enough to say that I have squared my accounts with my ancestors.

Chapter 2

The End of *Democratic Review*

Translator's introduction: This brief essay commemorating the end of *Democratic Review* is a revealing look at Xu's relationship with President Jiang Jieshi, his life after leaving China, and his personal mission. In it, he describes how he came to start *Democratic Review* in hopes of contributing in some way to perpetuating and restoring Free China, which he believed had to be achieved through support of the GMD. Although he had left the army by this point, he was still a member of the party and close with Jiang, to the point where Jiang personally provided some of the startup funds.

It may be that Jiang thought that Xu's journal would be more supportive than it turned out to be, though the very title *Democratic Review* was a clue that Xu did not approve of Jiang's authoritarian policies. Still, even when Xu and other writers were critical of the government, the GMD continued providing financial support, aside from the interruption that Xu mentions. It was only fully withdrawn in 1966, at which point Xu had to cease publication. This was part of a larger move to suppress dissent by the government starting around 1960. Still, Xu escaped any personal consequences for a while longer, until 1969 when he was forced to leave Taiwan.

The article also makes clear the connection Xu saw between maintaining Chinese culture and the hope for Free China in the future.

The Finest Selected Writings of Xu Fuguan, 194–98, first published in *Democratic Review*, August 15, 1966.

Without appreciating this, it would perhaps be odd to see articles on literature and history in a journal that was purportedly about politics. The culture question *was* political for Xu. He did not have a great deal of respect for most members of the GMD, who he felt were motivated by selfish interests. To him, their moral failings and the corruption in the government were due to losing touch with Chinese culture and its emphasis on morality. The future of Free China for him depended on greater appreciation for true Chinese culture, which would restore a sense of value.

There is always something to say of a publication when it begins, but what is there to say when it ends? Moreover, once one thinks of the adage with profound implications, "Past or present there is no feast that does not end," then when *Democratic Review* says its final goodbye to its readers and writers, it is understandable that I, the founder, give not the slightest sigh of regret. The following are simply a few words reluctantly thrown together in order to do *something* on the occasion of this conclusion.

In the spring of 1949, President Jiang [Jieshi] of Fenghua[1] resigned the presidency and went to live in Xikou,[2] and I received a telegram and left Guangzhou to go attend him. At the time the collapse of the country was already a fact and President Jiang of Fenghua was giving serious thought about how to turn around the fortunes of the nation. I suggested starting a journal in Hong Kong for the following three reasons:

First, given President Jiang's great hopes for me at the time, I had no reason not to take part in his major task to restore China. However, I understood very early that my foolish disposition was entirely unsuited to actual politics. By starting a journal in Hong Kong, which was soon to become the front line in the battle [over China], and undertaking some responsibility for the intellectual battle, I could maintain considerable distance from actual politics and it might be something I could continue all the way through. In those darkest times, only thought could provide a ray of light and hope. So at that time that kind of battle line was absolutely necessary.

Second, carrying out the major task of restoring China could not in any case be done apart from the Nationalist Party (GMD) and the upper-class liberals in society. However, I also understood very early that Nationalist Party members and Chinese liberals only differed in what kind of unfortunate situation they were in;[3] in their views on personal interests they differed not at all. Unless we did serious reflection on the great disaster [of losing China to the CCP], it would be impossible to place any hope in these people who only understood selfishness and personal advantage. Reflection makes an appeal to each individual's conscience, but the awareness of conscience relies on criticism and stimulation of thought. This requires a journal dedicated to thought.

Third, when I was in Nanjing[4] I often discussed the problem of China with Mr. Mou Zongsan and Mr. Tang Junyi,[5] which at its root is a problem of culture. Because of the collapse and disorder of [traditional] culture, and because China's intellectuals had completely lost their original nature and become more corrupt and base day by day, there was no way to start discussing the work of building the country. Therefore, one fundamental part of the work of building the country was starting with some effort toward culture. By setting the main cultural direction, those corrupt and base people could take hold of the standard constituted by this direction and begin to stand up. This opinion of ours should at least be offered to society as a topic for common exploration and discussion. This too means that we cannot be without a journal.

This idea to start a journal received President Jiang's support. In front of President Jiang, a budget of ninety thousand Hong Kong dollars[6] was provided, half by Mr. Zheng Yanfen and half by Mr. Tao Xisheng.[7] Mr. Tao had not yet got hold of his half, so President Jiang made up the shortfall. After that, with two months of planning Mr. Zhang Pijie[8] assumed the position of editor-in-chief and on June 16, 1949, obtained a publication code for a bimonthly journal. At that point we were anxious; it was truly a precarious and desperate situation. Those who had fled from the mainland to Hong Kong were too occupied hiding out. A number of old friends were sweating anxiously for me, urging me that it was unnecessary to waste this kind of useless effort. My own state of mind was also not just "I don't know where I'll be next year," but "I don't know where I'll be next month or tomorrow."

In his remarks inaugurating the journal, Zhang Pijie wrote, "Especially in a moment when we face quick extinction, we cannot avoid facing the realities squarely . . ." That phrase "moment of quick extinction" that he used truly reflected our mood at the time. Yet exactly because we felt it was a moment of facing extinction, we thought our responsibility was even greater. Before that moment of extinction, we wanted to sow a few seeds of the culture to allow the nation to take its stand. We started our work with a confidence approaching obstinacy. After each issue was printed, besides distributing them through the mail Mr. Wang Ganyi 王干一 and Mr. Zhang Zhenwen 張振文 each took a small basket and personally went to look for vendors to promote sales.

Once *Democratic Review* began to publish it developed in accord with the above-mentioned motivations. Mr. Tang Junyi began his unearthing of the Chinese humanistic spirit with his deep and pure pen. Mr. Mou Zongsan developed moral idealism in his unaffected but robust manner. They both wanted first to let everyone stand up as people to combat the Communist Party's treating people as things. Both of them philosophically critiqued Mao's Party for its extreme materialism, practicality, and contradictions.[9] Qian Mu's[10] essays took a clearer and cleverer approach, his great reputation attracting many readers. Mr. Hu Qiuyuan[11] published the weighty "China's Tragedy" under the pen name You Zhiping 尤治平. These were all playing the most important roles in cultural reflection. Of course, there were other significant great works from other authors that were compiled together.

In political reflection, since I understood politics more, I published a few critical essays, thinking to establish the major task of restoration on a foundation of democratic government. Additionally, I thought to use the power of democracy to wash away old stains and lay down a new road for life. As for criticism of the actual situation of the Communist Party, I, along with Zhang Pijie and Wang Ganyi (later joined by Zheng Zhuyuan[12] and Jin Dakai 金達凱), made a consistent effort to concentrate on the objective and close aspects. It is not that we didn't recognize the importance of encouraging natural science, but because the CCP also encouraged science and so was no different than we in that respect, we put it behind the battle front for the time being.

The real problem came from ourselves. Some people began to say, "Mr. Xu takes money from the GMD and uses it to insult them." If one does not recognize the necessity of renewal through reflection, then this criticism is not wrong. But apart from the desire for renewal through reflection, why would we work on this journal? If one were to follow this criticism to its logical conclusion, *Democratic Review* would have closed long ago. That it could continue until now is in part because in our gravest financial straits the Committee for Free Asia[13] subsidized part of our printing costs. When the Committee subsidies ended, the GMD resumed some symbolic support until now. Hence, we cannot but be grateful for President Jiang's tolerance, as well as for the enthusiasm of some friends who gave unconditional assistance from the flanks. As someone who helped to the very end, I should especially mention Mr. Tu Songqiao's 涂頌喬 name.

After publishing for probably five or six years, the aspects of *Democratic Review* directed to actual politics became thinner day by day and, almost imperceptibly, it turned toward specialized discussion of the cultural problem. The point of our discussion of the cultural problem was originally for cross-cultural communication between China and the West. However, we continuously discovered that Chinese culture, this historical tradition of five thousand years and common possession of seven hundred million people, was threatened by totalitarians and colonialists and their running dogs. They carried out large-scale, planned attacks to distort, slander, and humiliate it beyond all bounds of common sense, with the common goal of achieving complete eradication. If no one resolutely stood up and said some words of justice to respond to this circumstance, not only would this show that the Chinese nation was already spiritually dead, it would be a disgrace for all of humanity itself. The ancient Greek and Roman nations have long since disappeared from history, but the culture they left behind is still respected and passed on in academia and in people's consciences. How is that the Chinese culture, possessed by seven hundred million living souls, can be such a source of inferiority and self-abasement that they want to get rid of it themselves? Or get rid of it through relying on the power of colonialists?

As I pointed out in an essay about fifteen years ago, if the people of mainland China are to be able to stand up against totalitarians, they will have to rely on the ethical teachings of Chinese culture, which are founded on the view that human nature is good. In view of this, cleansing the stains of historical association with despotic government from Chinese culture and letting its position that human nature is pure be shouted to mainland China and all of humanity: this is the great mission of this age. At the time I wrote those words, I had not estimated how quickly things would happen, that now there would be a life and death struggle between Chinese culture and Maoist totalitarian thought in the inner apparatus of the CCP.[14] To conclude, regardless of where one begins, among all journals out there, *Democratic Review* straightened up and arose to speak on behalf of besieged Chinese culture, and this was not a conflict with the mission with which it had been founded.

We also knew that a journal should be run as a business enterprise. However, due to the nature of this journal, its environment, and the abilities of the circle of friends who managed it, we could not develop in this direction. At the same time, because we took the standpoint of Chinese people and Chinese culture to speak the truth, we did not need to, nor could we, find sufficient support from any quarter.

"When the oil is used up the lamp goes out": this is indeed the fate of this journal today. As an individual, I am ashamed that I merely have the attitude of thinking seriously about problems but lack the ability to adapt to reality. Where I feel no shame in my heart is that ever since I left China I received the assistance of *Overseas Chinese Daily*[15] and so I never took a penny from *Democratic Review*, even subsidizing it to some extent. And all the friends who participated in the work of *Democratic Review* received the smallest salary or even volunteered their time. For example, Mou Zongsan, Liu Baimin 劉百閔, Xie Youwei,[16] and Lang Weihan 郎維瀚 received no compensation. In the last few years, it became a one-man show of Jin Dakai, whose hard work needs no further mention. As for the registration fees taken out after ceasing publication, they will still be reserved for publishing works related to Chinese culture.

From the point of view of *Democratic Review* ending, we might consider our struggle on behalf of Chinese culture a failure. Naturally, a small minority has no power to defeat the united pressure of great numbers of totalitarians and colonialists. But over the past eighteen years every one of the friends involved in starting *Democratic Review* has made great advances in scholarship and research centered on Chinese culture, which strengthened further our confidence that "China will not die, Chinese culture will not end." With a common attitude of "render to Caeser the things that are Caesar's, and to God the things that are God's," we firmly believed that the flame of this stick of incense would continue on in our hands. Chinese culture is a culture that was born from and grew out of concern consciousness.[17] It must grow and flourish anew in the native soil of the fatherland where the concerns are the deepest and concern consciousness is the strongest. I dare to make this prediction here.

Finally, I naturally want to thank everyone who supported us, and our many authors and readers.

Xu Fuguan
August 9, 1966, Donghai University dormitory

Chapter 3

Mourning My Enemy, Mourning My Friend

Translator's Introduction: Yin Haiguang 殷海光 (1919–1969) was, like Xu, a refugee who fled to Taiwan in 1949. (Haiguang was his pen name; his personal name was Fusheng.) There, as Xu hints in his essay remembering his friend, their paths gradually began to diverge. Yin became one of the main editors and contributors of *Free China*, the primary liberal publication in Taiwan. Hu Shi and Fu Sinian were also involved with this journal, and as such it was closely associated with the pro-Western, anti-tradition viewpoint as well as the empirical approach to history, which Xu rejected. Yin Haiguang gradually became very critical of the GMD and Jiang Jieshi personally. These were among the likely factors that led to the change in their relationship. Xu was of course a committed defender of traditional Chinese culture, Ruism in particular, and while also critical of the government's policies, did not attack Jiang personally.

Yin later also became a professor of philosophy at National Taiwan University and developed a reputation as one of the foremost representatives of liberalism in Taiwan. He published widely and in general advocated an empirical, scientific approach to knowledge and freedom from tradition. Many of his publications angered the government and he was eventually forced out of his job at National Taiwan University, while *Free China* was also banned and its editor in chief Lei Zhen arrested for sedition. In this essay, according to Xu's account, he came to reconsider

Ruist Political Thought and Democracy, Freedom and Human Rights, 327–34, first published in *Personages and Thought*, 1969.

the value of Chinese culture at the end of his life. In addition to Xu's personal reflections on Yin and their relationship, the essay is also noteworthy for Xu's discussion of the distinct roles for scientific knowledge and values, and for his brief defense of Kant as the best bridge between Eastern and Western thought, when in most of his writings Xu opposes founding Chinese thought on metaphysics.

Mr. Yin Haiguang left this world on September 16, 1969. I wrote this essay on the 18th to record my sorrow and it was published on the 22nd in Taibei's Independent Evening News *with the headline completely changed. Now I have submitted it with the original headline restored to republish in* Personages and Thought.—*Fuguan*

The year before last (1967), around the end of spring or early summer, I received a letter in Hong Kong from Mr. Jin Guangji, telling me Mr. Yin had been admitted to National Taiwan University hospital and had surgery for stomach cancer. However, his cancer had already spread and he had only three to six months to live. Although over the last decade and more, in culture and thought Mr. Yin had gone from my friend to my enemy, nevertheless, after I received Mr. Jin's letter my heart was heavy for days. Soon after I wrote him a letter entreating him to figure out some way to send three thousand dollars[1] on my behalf for Mr. Yin's medical expenses, whether he wanted to accept it or not. I returned to Taiwan from Hong Kong at the end of June and went to his house to see him and he looked vigorous beyond all my expectations. But just like when we suddenly ran into each other at [Charles] Fu Weixun's wedding,[2] as soon as he saw me his manner hardened a little. After some time, we were talking and joking again.

At that time, the Cultural Revolution in China was a dark cloud over everything. I told him no matter what Mao Zedong does, our nation can get through the hard times and will stand up again. He listened to what I had to say, half analysis and half trying to console him, and was obviously quite excited. Half-jokingly I said, "On the basis of semantics, you used to oppose using terms like 'country and 'nationality.' But in truth, if we did not have sincere love for our country and nationality, we would not write so much and arouse so much trouble. In my opinion, a true liberal is naturally also a patriot. You are no exception!" Very seriously, he admitted the truth of what I said. As our conversation went on, he continued to reveal his fervent hopes for the country and nation with a youthful passion. What he opposed was using the country and nation as a tool to satisfy the desire for personal power.

II

In July of that year I received a letter from Mr. Yin, who wanted to come to Donghai University [in Taizhong] to see me. I wrote back saying he would be welcome. He came and stayed for four days, often discussing cultural problems with me. I discovered that his attitude had already shifted; he maintained his cautious respect for Chinese culture and believed that he had made many mistakes in a book he wrote on Chinese culture (I never read it so I don't clearly remember the title).[3] He believed that logical positivism could not touch the question of value, and that this question is critical. I merely listened placidly, refraining from actively expressing my own opinions for fear that if my words were not cautious it might harm him in his weakened condition. A lot of it was things he would have been unwilling to say or admit earlier. In surprise, I asked him, "How has this change happened?" He answered, "I have been influenced by cultural anthropology in recent years." A little earlier, from his sickbed, he had expanded on three reasons for his shift to Chen Guying.[4] First, memories from his hometown. Second, his student Chang [Zhang] Hao.[5] Third, half of Xu Fuguan['s ideas]. In my understanding, apart from the memories of his hometown, which was the strongest, the other reasons he mentioned were all external. The real reason is that Chinese culture took shape in concern and can only be truly felt in concern. In those years, he had felt deep concern.

In those four days he also brought up that a department at Harvard had invited him to do research but he had still not obtained an exit permit. He asked whether there was anything I could do. I said, "The reason they [the GMD] are doing this is because they're afraid you'll say bad things about them in America. What is your view on this?" He replied, "Abroad, I would never speak ill of them. They don't understand me at all." I believed him entirely and so I suggested, "You should write a letter directly to Mr. So-and-so, who should know what to do." He accepted my suggestion and said that Mr. So-and-so and I were old friends. I told him, "In political circles, it's not a question of being old friends or not. But if you want me to write a letter I will do so with the utmost sense of responsibility." The matter was resolved as I suggested, but he still did not leave. But when he wanted to send back the letter from National Taiwan University offering [continued] employment on the condition that he could not teach,[6] I strongly discouraged him.

III

Ever since then, I often thought of him with concern, but in order to avoid unnecessary trouble I never went to see him. At the end of June this year I took part in the oral exams for the graduates of National Taiwan University graduate school of philosophy and learned that his illness had recurred and he had been readmitted to the hospital. When I hurried to see him I found he had already returned home to rest. I visited him in the middle of August and to offer some comfort I said to him, "No matter what, the spirit of resistance that you showed is something to be treasured given the long history of despotism in China. For that alone, you will be immortal." He answered, "I do not resist; I transcend. I hope Mr. Xu will also take the route of transcending." I understood what he meant by transcending and, laughing, I said, "I transcended a long time ago, but can't transcend the label of traitor to the Chinese people."

He and I heatedly discussed the question of culture. He said to me, "We can't say that Karl Jaspers[7] doesn't understand science. But he said something which shocked me. He said, 'Even if we knew all scientific knowledge, about people themselves we would still know nothing and it would be no help at all.'" He went on and on talking about how science could not represent culture. We could not determine that people living in a prescientific time were not happy. Whether scientific achievement is a blessing or a curse for humanity is still difficult to determine. The most important thing is to resolve the question of human values. Yin said, "Many people who talk about Chinese culture strenuously try to graft science onto Chinese culture; this is really to overestimate the importance of science, thinking that if Chinese culture lacks science it has no value. The fact is, even if Chinese culture has no science it would do no harm to its lofty value. However, for China's present situation, it of course is important for defining and determining knowledge according to strict standards."

He said many other similar things displaying his elevated wisdom. I urged him to put these thoughts down, not in an essay form but rather as recorded sayings.[8] He said, "It's too hot now, but I've resolved to start writing on October first." He further said, "I hope to live five more years to complete my aspirations concerning Chinese culture." When I heard this I was very distressed: with his condition, how could he put it off until October? How could he live five more years? Fortunately, at my suggestion he finally allowed his student Chen Guying to record some fragmentary thoughts.[9] I once said to some friends, "Haiguang explores scholarship sincerely and so now, his thought and experience are reaching a stage of maturity. If he could live twenty more years, he would surely have great accomplishments. It is a misfortune for academia that he contracted this illness." Later on, some students reported my remarks to him and he broke down in tears in his bed.

IV

On August 25, Chen Guying sent over some materials dictated by Mr. Yin that he had taken notes on, along with a letter signed by Mr. Yin. It might have been the last letter he wrote to a friend, so I copy it here:

Mr. Foguan:[10]

What you brought up on the morning of August 15th about the difficulty of propagating and developing purely rational thought under a despotic regime stimulated a lot of thought on the matter in me, for which I am very grateful. On August 20th you visited my home along with Mr. Tang Junyi to inquire about my illness, and that visit also elicited some thought about some fundamental problems with intellectuals today. Mr. Tang set an example of the manner of being a Ruist and made achievements in moral idealism, but not knowledge. His academic capabilities, his training in thought, and his personal talent and ability are evidently not up to the task of achieving his goal. From the past to the present, morally charismatic people are often like this.

We have known each other twenty years and you are a person I often bring up as someone I dislike but you are still one of the people I greatly admire in my heart. This contradiction is certainly due to the sparks and upheavals of different lives. The source of the creative power of an age is perhaps dialectically[11] fostered in this kind of difference. Now the calls for the restoration of Chinese culture seem very loud. However, they are devoid of substance, nothing more than empty bubbles. In my opinion, understanding of Chinese history, society, and culture are still largely undeveloped virgin territory. They await the effort of scholars of real talent and substance. "The mountains and streams go on without end and there seems no way through, but among the dark willows and the bright flowers, there is another village."[12] As far as the actual circumstances, then the condition of some intellectuals seems to be that there is nowhere to go, but when it comes to opening up new worlds of concepts and knowledge, there are no limits at all.

The most important matter for conscientious people today is establish a self which surpasses the realities. It is not necessary at all to care about success or failure and praise or blame in the outside world. In an age when it is difficult to discern right and wrong we must study the wisdom of separation, of shaking off all dregs and purifying our souls, and then mounting the back of the great Peng bird, setting our sights a thousand miles away,[13] and galloping in spirit between past and present. Yet at the same time, we can achieve a true understanding of the ins and outs of Chinese history, society, and culture, like a modern prospector. If you, sir, could slightly adjust your cognitive schema, perhaps you could make a higher level of effort in this respect.

At this time, I am wrestling with the demon of cancer and if I am able to recover, I hope in the near future to discuss all these matters of past and present with you, and you can treat me to a meal of turtle and eel. I joke! I sincerely wish you health and happiness.

Yin Haiguang
August 24, 1969

When I finished reading his letter, it made me even sadder about his earnest desire to live.

V

It was probably on September 7 or 8 (I don't have the habit of keeping a diary and my memory is poor, so I don't remember dates clearly) that I learned his condition had worsened considerably and I rushed to see him again. When she answered the door, Mrs. Yin told me, "He can't talk at all. Talking makes the pain worse." After entering his room, she and I both urged him not to speak. But he insisted. "Mr. Xu has come, so how can I not talk?"

Pausing frequently, he said, "Newton once said that he owed his achievements to standing on the shoulders of giants. You, Mr. Tang [Junyi], and Mr. Mou [Zongsan] made certain contributions to Chinese culture, but I fear you didn't stand on the shoulders of giants enough. (He mentioned a couple of works of American sociologists.) Chinese culture cannot be grasped through the ideas of four particular people. First, it cannot be grasped through Darwin's ideas on evolution. This idea has led many people astray. (Note:[14] For Chinese culture the main achievement is in human values, which manifest in morality, literature, and the arts. These all should not be assessed by a theory of evolution.) Second, Kant's a priori theory should not be used. (Note: Kant is precisely the giant to build a bridge from the West to the East. If Mr. Yin had lived three to five more years, he would have corrected this opinion.) Third, it cannot be understood through Hegel's systematic philosophy. (Note: This is partly correct.)[15] Fourth, it cannot be understood through Marxist thought. Chinese culture does not evolve [jinhua 進化] but adapts [yanhua 演化], through adversity accumulating to such depth. I have only now discovered my passion for Chinese culture. I hope to live fifteen more years to give my all for Chinese culture." I simply listened quietly for fear of stimulating him to talk more, and used gestures to indicate he should not speak.

I left to let him rest when he reached a certain break in his discourse. He probably went back to National Taiwan University hospital on September 12 and when I visited him on the thirteenth his eyes were already closed more often than not. Yet when I told him, "For the rest of my life, I will not forget the hopes you expressed for me in your letter," the corners of his mouth lifted in a little smile. When I saw him on the fourteenth, he looked like a skeleton in his bed. On the evening of the fifteenth he had much more vigor, and I wondered whether this was what is called "a rally at the end." I didn't go on the sixteenth and that night he died.

Chinese intellectuals have lived under the whip of what Legalists called the two handles—reward and punishment—and the vast majority of them turned into mollusks.[16] Their special trait is that they believe only the pleasures of food and sex are real and all knowledge and values are fake. Not only is it not easy to find one who can love his own character and have real integrity, it is also not easy to find one who respects and pursues knowledge in their scholarship. Mr. Yin never reached maturity in his scholarship. Furthermore, his attitude toward culture and politics often tended to an extreme. However, the refined light of his strong backbone and true passion shined on many of the mollusks, taking away their voice and revealing their true colors. Academically, he started from a position of scientism but changed to appreciate the limits of scientific values, which illustrates his passion for and sincerity toward scholarship.

He always had some misunderstandings of Mr. Tang and Mr. Mou. He did not realize the new direction he took was exactly what they had been advocating for years; knowledge must be pursued through empirical methods but human values cannot be built relying on knowledge alone, much less can knowledge replace human values. However, he had even greater contempt for the superstition that the "cultural gentry" believed in.[17] He once emphasized individualism but hated selfish and self-interested people. He donated his body to the hospital, an illustration of his respect for science and proof of the connection between compassion and science. I am already old[18] and it is not likely that I can make much further effort in study. But I hope some future intellectuals of ambition can take inspiration from Mr. Yin's character and develop their own foundation for duty to the country and nation. I hope they can grasp the zeal for and [proper] orientation toward academic inquiry from his scholarly transition. In this respect, I hope he attains immortality.

Part Two

Ethical and Political Thought

Chapter 4

Two Layers of the Chinese Political Problem

Translator's introduction: This article is where Xu articulates and defends his important distinction between the form and content of government, insisting that democracy belongs to the form, and can embrace virtually any content. As he argues, form has to take precedence over content, so that any concrete political proposal has to go through the democratic process to be legitimate. This is what distinguishes democracy from communism and other totalitarian ideologies for him: respect for the process is valued over specific outcomes.

At the time, the government in Taiwan was still planning for a counterattack to retake mainland China, and the need to oppose communism was used as an excuse to delay implementing democratic reforms. One of the messages of Xu's article is that this is a false dichotomy: enacting democratic forms would strengthen the country and make it better able to oppose communism. Hence, he brings up the examples of the United States and UK successfully defending against Nazism and fascism in World War II. Democracy unites a country better and so has instrumental benefits as well as being morally justified as a superior form of government that respects the individual.

Democracy is the form of government that recognizes the universality of human nature and gives space for the free development of the individual and reason. "Personality" functions as a technical term for

Between Academia and Politics, 31–45, first published in *Democratic Review* 2 no. 18, March 16, 1951.

Xu; it is roughly synonymous with human nature—that which defines a person as something more than a thing or an animal. It does not mean the particular traits an individual happens to have, but what is universal in humanity. This is what he means when he talks about realizing one's personality. Reason as well has a somewhat different meaning. The Chinese term (lixing 理性) might be rendered as "patterned nature" and again refers to what is essential in people, which is not necessarily to be identified with the exercise of rationality in the strict sense. Xu does believe people's free exercise of "reason" in this broader sense will converge, due to shared human nature.

This is why he sees democracy as a universally valid form of government. As he clearly explains, democracy means free elections and protections of certain fundamental rights. As he does elsewhere, he argues that this is the natural progression of Ruist thought. Even today, some other scholars argue for a very different "Chinese" or "Ruist" understanding of democracy (usually much more limited and less democratic), while Xu strongly advocated modern liberal democratic institutions. These are not accidents of Western history for him, but the government that best accords with universal human nature.

I

I refer to the various positions regarding political problems as "political content." The methods of selecting political positions to put into effect I refer to as "political form." Totalitarian states only permit one type of political content and therefore do not distinguish between content and form. Democratic states, however, have already established political forms, and thus now need only debate political positions and do not need to debate methods of putting positions into effect. Free China [Taiwan] is in the midst of a transitional period. As far as the entire government goes, subjectively speaking it has not publicly stated it is a dictatorship, but objectively speaking it is not seriously pursuing democracy. Hence, the political problem of our country requires another level of effort. First, there must be effort to establish a democratic political form (only a democracy can constitute a political form, which will be explained below). Then, with this political form we can realize the political positions that people hold. The first layer is the political structure, the latter is the political function.[1]

We must seek agreement at the first level, but at the second level there is no harm in diversity. Those who agree on a certain political position, [no matter] the degree to which they agree, cannot go past this form in order to reach the goal on which they agree. Those who oppose a certain political position, [no matter] the degree of their opposition, cannot go past this form in order to reach the goal of their opposition. That way it is possible for diverse political content to be accommodated with a common political form. Political content is a variable, and has to be a variable. Political form is a constant and could also be called the constant way. When variables are applied within a constant, when the constant controls the variable and the variable adapts to the constant, this makes the working of government like the alternation of day and night or the way the sun and moon alternately shine without ever falling out of sequence. Only this can be called setting up the model for a state.

Now, we can unite our strength to fight communism. In the future we can preserve the unity of the state, plan for its continued order and security, and overcome the historical tragedy of the cycle of order and chaos. Recently, I have been looking for a way forward for our government and once wrote an article on "the center" in politics (in vol. 1 no. 2 of this journal: "On the Mainstream of Politics: A Look at the Development of History from the 'Center' Line of Politics") to plan out a general direction. Although I haven't changed my concept of the political center, I realize this is just political content, merely a subjective idea and insufficient to reveal the great system or define the differentiations. Political content that is determined within a strict democratic system: the result of that is probably the political center. This is why I have especially spelled out the two layers of politics to allow people who discuss government to grasp more easily the great distinctions and great tendencies.

Confronting this dangerous and difficult transition, some people simply talk vacuously of democracy, not realizing that democracy is only a political form. Within this form, there still needs to be concrete content, otherwise it is impossible to resolve the present real problems. Then there are others who are simply smugly self-satisfied with their own proposals, only making an effort on the second level of political content and writing off the effort for the first level, which is establishing the political form, even to the point of denying that there are these two levels. This results in failing to distinguish structure and function, the constant and the changing, and hence that which necessarily changes is held up as the constant way. Then the real constant way of government cannot be established. Both types of people have their prejudices and their blind spots. The reason these prejudices and blind spots cannot be resolved is either because they have suffered some great trauma and have not yet been able to arouse a sense of compassion, or because they have met with serious difficulties and have not stimulated their seeds of wisdom.[2]

What I wrote above is common sense about politics. Not only will it not incite debate, it does not even need to be said. But since China has been caught in many historical and practical problems, the result is that even the commonsensical is not common sense, to the point where people don't wish or don't dare to bring it up for discussion. Nowadays, after suffering great pain we feel that we can only stop the source of chaos by first establishing the constant way of government and creating the circumstances for everlasting great peace. Therefore, we cannot but disentangle these knots and offer them for concerned people to consult.

II

The first difficulty is an inchoate Communist Party influence. Based on the simplistic proposition "there is no content-free form nor any unformed content," it concludes that form and content cannot be separated. After I published the opinion piece "In Democracy We Trust" in *Democratic Review* (vol. 2, no. 6), a few young people raised doubts about this point. Here I have to give a commonsensical explanation. In regard to a certain thing in itself, then content is a condition of it constituting a form.[3] At this point, form and content indeed cannot be separated. However, if we are speaking regarding the relationships and mutual interconnections of several things, then it is possible to abstract the unique parts out and abstract the common aspects together into a common form. Furthermore, in regard to concrete things, then we may say that a certain thing is the form for something else. And one thing may be the content of something else. The meaning of "content" is more particular, while the meaning of "form" is more what is held in common. One form can encompass many different contents but one content cannot simultaneously be part of multiple forms. Content and form are relative terms and their connotation is relative as well.

Take a bowl, for example. A condition for it to be a bowl is for it to have the form and content that constitute a bowl. At this stage, form and content cannot be separated. However, if we look at the bowl and what it holds, then one bowl can hold many different things. Then the bowl can be said to be the form of what it holds, and what it holds can be said to be the contents of the bowl. In regard to democratic government itself, then freedom of thought, speech, publishing, assembly, and voting; the minority following the majority and the majority respecting the minority; and other such principles constitute the content of democratic government. Apart from this content, there is no democratic government.

At this stage, form and content indeed must be identical. But when it comes to applying them to concrete political problems, then all kinds of thought and speech can be subsumed within the principles of freedom of thought and speech. All kinds of majority and minority positions can be subsumed within the principles of the minority following the majority and the majority respecting the minority. Then those subsumed positions are political content and that which they are subsumed within is political form. Only a democratic government makes subsuming all kinds of differences its fundamental content. So only democratic government possesses political universality and can constitute the form of government. The reason the Communist Party does not admit this distinction between form and content is because it does not admit that more than one political content can exist within a political form. This is why it is a totalitarian government. How can we fall into their conceptual trap?

However, democratic government becoming political form also went through an evolutionary process of humanity developing political self-awareness. The nineteenth century is typically called a flourishing period of democracy, but since at that time capitalism was the political content, capitalism and democracy were mixed together and there was not a full consciousness of the distinction between form and content. In the mid-century, J. S. Mill often drew a symmetry between democracy and socialism in his major works *Principles of Political Economy* and *Autobiography*, believing politics had the possibility of advancing from democracy to socialism, proof that he considered democracy to be concrete content. In the latter part of the nineteenth century, the term *democratic socialism* was created, then the Second International was constituted, unifying the two opposing terms in Mill's thought. This indicated a belief that democracy and socialism could be united under certain circumstances, but this was a blending of political content and not in fact an awareness that democracy could be abstracted into the form of government.

This blend did, however, gradually lead people to understand that because first there was capitalist democracy and then there was socialist democracy, it is possible to look at democracy as not wedded to some particular content. We can look at this as the transition of democracy toward realizing its "formal" meaning. In the twentieth century in Great Britain, the Liberal Party, the Conservative Party, and the Labour Party took turns holding power under the same political form with different economic views as their content. There was no incompatibility and still less any bloody revolution. At that point, the fact that democracy could be abstracted into a political form and subsume diverse content within this universal form to become the constant way of human politics became evident. At their annual meeting last year, the Labour Party declared themselves democratic socialists "realizing socialism under democracy," thus formally subsuming content within form. The universal and particulars of politics each assumed their proper place. Compared with the earlier "socialist democracy," which mixed together the concepts of form and content, there is a difference of significance from beginning to end. It constituted a major advance in political life.

Politics is a kind of application of power. Any individual or group that obtains political power will always hope that their positions and influence become the constant way of the state, passed on from one age to the next without end. However, any political position or political body, no matter how excellent, has not only a relative but a subjective existence. As relative, they cannot exclude other political positions. As subjective, they lack universality and cannot become an unchanging constant way. The reason democracy can be abstracted into political form and develop its universality is precisely because it does not have to be wedded to a certain position or body and can have objective existence. When certain political positions or a body is chosen to occupy the dominant position, we can say that at that point that it has gone from subjective and personal to objective and public. Then the party that was defeated cannot take any measures to exact revenge on the victors, other than working for the electorate and trying to obtain greater objective approval. Hence, within this form there is competition among the content but not hatred. This is because the power to determine political positions does not belong to the advocates of the position themselves, but rather to an objective power outside them: the power of the electorate.

Any good political position, if it does not go through this way of obtaining objective approval from this political form but obtains a dominating position through some plot or violent means, then even if it is indeed good, it can only be the subjective good of its advocates. They have no right to demand its embrace by other political bodies or by the people. This will invariably result in a situation of mutual conquest and overthrow. If we have democracy, there is no need to talk about revolution. Democracy and revolution are antipodal terms, and this is the reason why. Dictatorship and totalitarian government by nature inevitably end tragically. This is the reason why.

III

The second difficulty is that opposing Russia and communism at present requires concentrated power. If democracy is overemphasized, then since democracy and liberty cannot be separated, will this make matters and discussion more complicated, causing division of authority and weakness? This is definitely not a problem when considering the entire world. When the world fights for democracy and freedom or to preserve the liberal democratic way of life, can we say that this is just lies to put a pretty face on things? Furthermore, we do not perceive any problem of concentrating strength when liberal democratic countries such as Britain and America mobilize and prepare. However, when restricted to Free China, then this is indeed a problem, which we should have clarified already but have not dared to, or do not even wish to clarify. Some people say the reason we lost the mainland is because we weren't democratic enough. Others believe that everyone contending over liberal democracy destroyed it. In reality, this is a question that history will answer clearly, not something that propaganda of the people involved can resolve.

The issue now is not to reevaluate democracy, but for each person to reevaluate his understanding of democracy and the sincerity of his past commitment to it. There is a fork right now: one side leads to democracy, the other to dictatorship. No one publicly wants to say they want dictatorship or that they don't want democracy. Other than these two, is there some other alternative that is neither dictatorship nor democracy? The objective demand is that we straightforwardly take one path: this is where the political crux lies. If we hesitate to confront this crux, then the wellspring of political power will be in danger of drying up. In regard to this, I would like briefly to make the following several points:

What I should point out first is that the establishment of democracy was based on the awakening of human reason. The preservation of democracy is constructed upon a foundation of common human reason and concomitant equality of personality. Trusting in reason and respecting the person, one cannot but trust in and respect freedom. Freedom is a necessary condition for developing reason and nurturing personality. Because reason is necessarily endowed in each person, the result of its free development in a certain time and place will always form into a relative mainstream. Hence, democracy can trust in the majority and let them make decisions. Since reason displays its content in many aspects and perfects its development in a process of sifting the good and bad, it cannot be fixed into one mold, still less rely on violence. So democracy must safeguard the minority and not suppress it.

At the same time, formation of the individual personality is based on free self-awareness of reason. Individual self-awareness of reason means having a responsibility to reason, and therefore freedom under democracy necessarily produces the concepts of rule of law and personal responsibility. Furthermore, individuals with self-awareness of reason will, responding to the demands of reason, naturally join together to accomplish the great mission of the time. Just as people now who do not want to be slaves will naturally join together to oppose Russia and fight communism. So freedom and organization are seemingly contrary but actually complementary.

Individuals who do not have self-awareness of reason can only pile up like rubble, with no true vitality imbued in them. Such organization cannot be called powerful; still less can it last. Those who discuss liberalism now are still mostly stuck at the stage of practical individualism. This is negative, utilitarian freedom, entirely insufficient to undertake the mission of the time. Yet we have to understand that, without political freedom then on the one hand, since people cannot have any sense of responsibility to the government and on the other hand have an instinct to protect themselves, of course their idea of freedom will tend toward negative, utilitarian, practical individualism. From a social point of view, this kind of freedom has to reach the point of breaking up practicality and reconstructing it. Only then can it advance in the direction of idealist, personalist freedom. This is what the people responsible for the government should be alarmed about.

The Communist Party doesn't believe that reason can solve common problems or that equal persons can undertake common tasks, because they don't believe people have common reason or equal personality. And so there is only totalitarianism—only tyranny. Only totalitarianism and tyranny can hold together their fixed political content and form. When regarding the situation of the Communist Party, we should trust that they are heading toward extinction. We must then build a political environment in which countless people can freely reason in order to encourage the enthusiasm of countless people and liberate their power. When only a minority can reason and the majority is not permitted to; when only those in power can reason and the governed cannot, then this is not reasoning. At its worst, it is not something for which the majority would want to be responsible. The reasoning of the governors is shown in their policies. The reasoning of the governed is shown in their criticism. So in democracies one hears only criticism of the government, while in dictatorships one can only hear laudatory songs. In countries that are neither democracies nor dictatorships, one can hear only silence.

In actuality, human reason cannot vanish. This is why in the despotic period there was the tradition of "direct words and serious remonstration"[4] and even in dictatorships there is self-criticism within the ruling group. These give some level of regulation after reason has disappeared and assuage the subconscious demands of the reason they too possess. Criticism is the basic measure of democracy. Yet today there is still a minority who occupies positions of authority over the masses but still feels that criticism from the masses is taboo, that it is tantamount to rebellion. This is truly a baffling riddle.

Secondly, the plots and tricks of the Party penetrate everywhere. If there is liberal democracy, will that make it difficult to guard against traitors and protect national security? Of course, childish techniques of guarding against traitors and protecting national security will become difficult. This fact simply demonstrates that we have not established a foundation for intelligence work, and that under democracy the character, knowledge, and skills demanded by this kind of work must be developed to a higher level. Those responsible should work hard to adapt to the demands of the general political direction and its principles; they cannot instead distort the general political direction and its principles to adapt them to the demands of their work. Government is a very practical matter. I do not wish to smear this whole kind of work as many others do.[5] And among those who occupy these posts, there are indeed many good men who are mainstays[6] of the job who sacrifice and struggle. But in any matter, there are appropriate limits. When one goes beyond these limits, then a positive turns into a negative. Further, in the great realization of liberal democracy, the power of positive social morale vastly outweighs the power of mere passive guarding. When have the security bureaus of Britain or America ever felt the burden of liberal democracy?

Also, would the people who boost the Communist Party perhaps also want to give it the security of liberal democracy? This should not even be a question. The Communist Party is the greatest enemy of democracy and freedom today. Anyone who really loves freedom and democracy must be absolutely anticommunist. There is absolutely no room to maneuver here. In this day of red flames billowing to the sky, when life and death, survival or extinction, are decided in a moment, then those who are not themselves communists but are speculators willing to promote them should also not be tolerated. But the title of "booster of brigands" should not be tossed around lightly. In order to fight communism more effectively, everyone who opposes communism should have the responsibility and the right to criticize or spur on those in power, and they cannot be casually framed as being "boosters of brigands." Simply put, within Free China there should be no freedom for communists or their supporters, but freedom to oppose communism. Otherwise, who can by themselves bear the great responsibility of fighting communism?

IV

The third difficulty is that the present founding principles of the state are the three principles of the people.[7] If we were to take democratic political form as the constant, categorizing it as the goal of the first level, then does that mean that realizing the three principles of the people has to be put on the second level, where it is considered to be changeable political content? This is indeed my belief. However, this is not to diminish the value of the three principles, but rather to put them in their appropriate place. Furthermore, this is exactly in accord with Mr. Sun's wishes. Mr. Sun personally created the Republic [of China] and put republicanism into practice, and from this we know that he intended to realize his three principles in a democratic republic, not that he thought that the three principles have an independent political form apart from democracy. Mr. Sun continually exhorted his comrades to put the three principles into practice. When he moved to uphold constitutionalism twice, he exhorted the people to preserve the democratic republic.[8] The distinction between the two levels of inner and outer is readily apparent.

The principle of people's rights in his doctrine is obviously democracy. It is just that in its realization he laid down some rules concerning particular steps and methods, which were permeated by some impure factors. When he resigned the presidency in the first year of the Republic after the National Assembly was established, his intention can be favorably compared to George Washington's refusal of a third term, although it did not lead to lasting stability. As for democracy, it was first destroyed by Yuan Shikai's stealing power and calling himself emperor.[9] It was destroyed again by the warlords' seizing territory and separating from the central government.[10] And it was destroyed a third time by the shameless corruption of the politicians of the time. Mr. Sun fixed his resolve from the beginning to carry out revolution, dividing it into three phases of military government, provisional government, and constitutional government. This appears to be at odds with his intent in the first year of the Republic.

However, the period of military government did not mean military activity across the entire country, but military activity in one province, and so this period was in fact very brief. The provisional government meant putting local self-government into practice, something quite different than the later baojia[11] or government administration systems. Its direction was still constitutional government, global democratic government. Then it is not hard to infer that from beginning to end the three principles of the people were encompassed within the form of democratic government. This general direction in government began to become obscured after being influenced by communism and German and Italian fascism. Today, the government has long since declared itself democratic, so democracy is the form and the three principles are the content. Form can encompass content, but content cannot encompass form: this is universal. Only this way of thinking conforms to the essence of the three principles. Therefore, although I am a believer in Mr. Sun, I never felt that there should be the right for there to be "one [who] stands with head above the multitudes,"[12] making the three principles stand over and above democratic form.

Moreover, any doctrine or "ism" has a fundamental spirit. This fundamental spirit can overcome the limits of place and time to become a lasting treasure for humanity. At the same time, this spirit must be applied to practical problems to produce particular conclusions. These conclusions are for the purpose of resolving the problems of a certain time and place and so necessarily are limited in time and place. As circumstances of time and place change, the earlier solutions gradually begin to conflict with the fundamental spirit. Those who bear responsibility for history and culture have to go through their already ossified, expired conclusions to bring the original, fundamental spirit to the fore, and create new conclusions for humanity. The cultural spirit of benevolent nature that Kongzi and Mengzi established can last forever, but the human relations they practiced have to change along with the times. The spirit of the natural philosophers of Greece of trying to understand nature paved the way for modern Western science, but the specific conclusions of their time became straw dogs long ago.[13] Thus, we can grasp the eternal in history and culture and also observe what changes.

Unending creativity while knowing what should change and what should remain constant: this is the path to evolving. Mr. Sun's three principles of the people brought together and expressed as one the three major political issues that emerged one by one out of human history. He made them regulate and supplement each other to constitute a proper political direction for humanity. This is where his greatness is. So we can say the fundamental spirit of the three principles is the unvarying principle of human political life, suspended between heaven and earth to last forever. However, the aspect that takes shape in policy is naturally limited by time and place, and can and should change. In recent years many people have not deeply investigated the fundamental spirit of the three principles; they have merely grasped at one segment or branch as a political shield, causing their political significance to wither, and consequently the spirit of the three principles becomes ossified. It is not that Mr. Sun's wisdom was inadequate, but rather that everyone does not try to improve [their understanding].

V

The fourth difficulty is the conviction [some have] that China has traditional Chinese democracy and need not imitate the West. To make a strained effort to imitate Western democracy will only increase confusion. For example, parties and elections, the backbone of Western democracy, in China have gone nowhere. This proves their point [they think].

As for traditional Chinese democracy, my friend Mou Zongsan pointed out that in Chinese history "there was democracy of administrative power but not democracy of political power," in his major work "Analyzing the Development of the Spirit of Our National History."[14] The reason is as Hegel said: in China there was substantial[15] freedom but not subjective freedom (freedom of individual self-awareness).[16] Mou also pointed out that because there was no democracy of political power, democracy of administrative power was not secured. Because there was no subjective freedom, substantial freedom was often destroyed.[17] Hence, he believes that China has to move toward subjective freedom and democracy of political power.[18] Mr. Mou's argument surely can be the final conclusion and resolve most disputes concerning this issue.

We might say that traditional Chinese Ruist culture long ago established the foundation for the democratization of Chinese politics, and that Chinese traditional politics long ago did a lot of preparation for the democratization of Chinese politics. The reason it could not take the step onto the road of modern democracy earlier is, in Mr. Mou's view, because Chinese culture lacked "the analytic spirit of the fulfillment of reason";[19] which is to say that it had developed benevolence but was deficient in developing knowledge.[20] But once we realize this, then we must force the development of analytic knowledge to achieve science and democracy. Mr. Mou presented his ideas in detail and his argument is accurate. So we only need consciously to take the great step in the common direction of all humanity and go forth to complete the journey that Chinese history and culture could not. Going from the particular to the universal is a necessity of the development of human reason. Thus, history must be the unification of the individual and the global. I do not believe China has any particular democracy.

It is a fact that the elections and political parties of recent years have been unacceptable. A friend in Taiwan sighed and said to me, "Getting elected as a city or county council member takes twenty or thirty thousand Taiwan dollars.[21] A mayor or county administrator, two or three hundred thousand dollars. These people work for the public welfare, yet when you ask them to contribute a hundred or two hundred dollars, they won't do it. Now it takes so much money for one council member or mayor to get elected, and their way of thinking is hard to understand." Elections in Taiwan are still more advanced than in mainland China, since there is voting after all. In China for the most part they do away with the voting step. Granting that what my friend said is certainly worth reflecting on deeply, if we look a little at the causes, it is because Chinese intellectuals are still bound by the traditional spirit of relying on connections to become a *xiucai*.[22] When they take part in elections or political parties, it is not from awareness of subjective freedom or to strive for the realization of the democratic spirit and democratic system. It is just a disguised extension of the spirit of relying on connections to pass the *xiucai* exam.

Moreover, since people who adopted the ideas and words of the Communist Party during the Political Consultative Assembly[23] in China enjoyed some advantages and had their success go to their heads, to this day they still think discussing democracy means engaging in party machinations, and that by doing so, they can immediately share in the spoils. They endlessly spout bizarre views that their party carries out the Way on behalf of Heaven, not having a sliver of shame. Little do they know that under democracy, the status of political parties is not determined by the parties themselves, but is decided by the voters. From the point of view of democracy, any political power[24] that does not derive from the decision of the electorate is a kind of theft. A democracy needs parties to make decisions easier for the voters, not so parties can take the place of voting.

Henceforth, parties in a democracy are parties that [should] demand conditions for free elections, demand putting free elections into effect, preserve democratic principles, and compromise on minor points but not give in on major issues. Creating conditions for free elections is especially important. Some people mistakenly believe that merely having elections is practicing democracy. Little do they know that the CCP also has elections; German and Italian fascists as well had elections. Elections have to go through a filtering process with freedom of thought, speech, publication, and assembly. They need an atmosphere with these freedoms to be considered democratic elections. Only then are elections on the right track. To sum up, the elections and parties of the early Republic were, looking on the bright side, a transitional phenomenon of a transformative historical period. Or more negatively, they were just a cheap trick. A transitional phenomenon has to transition toward an end. A fake, cheap trick can't really be held responsible for the loss of face it causes. Can China stop at this point? Can it go back to the old road of democracy of administrative power without democracy of political power? Therefore I say that only by honestly and forthrightly pursuing democracy can we establish the foundation of our country and the foundation for great peace and unity. The key is "honestly and forthrightly": no one can use it for their advantage or come up with some new variety.

VI

Recently, a number of people have said that we lost at the hands of the CCP because we did not put into practice the principle of the people's welfare.[25] As a description of the baseness and corruption of the warlord regimes, which exploited and killed the people, and when confronting the main content of the government, this is an indisputable fact. But the political crux is how to make it so that base and corrupt warlord regimes are not tolerated by the government, put social and political activity on the right track so as to attain peace and stability, and allow people to follow their nature and care for their own lives.[26] This will make it possible to walk the path of the principle of the people's welfare. To achieve this, firmly establishing the form of democratic government and setting up the dimensions for founding the state is in fact a more pressing matter than the people's welfare. The "Gospel of John" chapter 10 says, "Most assuredly, I say to you, he who does not enter the sheepfold by the door, but climbs up some other way, the same is a thief and a robber. But he who enters by the door is the shepherd of the sheep."[27] Democratic political form is the entrance to democracy. Those who truly intend to have democracy must go in by this door to avoid suspicion of being a thief or robber and sending the country into an unending catastrophe. The CCP flaunts their slogan of "bread for the people" and because of this do not enter by the door of democracy. This is why today it has indeed become the number one bandit. We can definitely take this as a warning from history.

At this critical juncture of resisting the Soviet Union and opposing communism, I bring up this view, which some people might misunderstand. But if we only could calmly assess past and present disasters and even more calmly consider future problems, [then we would understand that] even if we could quickly counterattack and even if this counterattack went well, then with the political situation the way it is now how could we possibly unite the power of the whole country? How could we guarantee political unity to quickly pick up the pieces in the aftermath and minimize disorder? After a counterattack it is impossible for there to be only one political power. I would ask: Who has confidence in conquest, using one political power to subjugate the others? Even if one is confident that it is possible, how would the country endure it? We have to establish an objective standard so that each power has objective restraints in hopes that they can compete and there can again be peace: contention that does not sink into chaos. This is the powerful application of democratic political form.

All subjective things—individual or group—without going through the objectification of the political form cannot obtain objective recognition without any debate, and still less can they constitute a constant for the country's government. Hence, they cannot serve as a standard for ensuring the country's political unity. This is not just a matter of theory but circumstances as well. Without a thorough understanding of this point, all efforts will be in vain: the greatest loss for individuals, for groups, and for the nation. Two historical examples are worthy of admiration: one is George Washington and the other is the British royal family. Washington declined a third term as president when the United States had need of him at the time. However, Washington didn't just look at the interests of that time and certainly not just his personal interests. He wanted to set an example and establish a firm foundation for American democracy, and because of this the United States has had uncountable benefits.

The British royal family saw the way trends were going and put itself above political disputes, becoming a symbol for unifying the kingdom. It adapted itself to democracy and so became an unmoving constant for British government. Political parties in Britain win and lose in elections, but these have no impact on the royal family. How could it be that in the royal family, no one exceeded most people in talent and wisdom? But they maintained a stance of being useful by being useless, and this is of great use to the country.[28] This is truly an outstanding feat of turning decline into something miraculous in human history. Because of what the military reported to the throne, the Japanese emperor only learned half and therefore was still enmeshed in disputes [over government policy] and was nearly overthrown this time.[29] From now on, he will have to emulate the British royal family further if he is to maintain the unbroken line of the ages.

As for those with real governmental responsibilities, Churchill is a good model. He rescued Britain from a crisis where its survival was at stake, but did not use his wartime powers to restrict speech. Once he lost the election, then although that Parliament was not yet over, his renowned political authority had already ended. But he had no resentment over the fact that the electorate had forgotten his outstanding achievements. This is the sort of great scene that is revealed in the common practice of democracy. If not for the restrictions of the democratic political form, then considering Churchill's individual personality, it is difficult to say whether he could have been that great. So the restrictions democracy puts on individuals and groups actually help them achieve.

Our tragedy is that up until now, when we draw back the curtain on what happened behind the scenes of our political figures of all sorts, these great heroic figures of all time were all self-made. And so there was no way for objective, universal political constants to get off the ground. Should heaven favor China and transforms these heroes of outstanding spirit into politicians of talent and loyalty, endowed with great common sense, then the country will truly have a turning point and our suffering will not have been in vain.

Chapter 5

The Construction and Advancement
of Ruist Political Thought

Translator's introduction: This article is an exemplary illustration of Xu's
main political and social concerns as well his intellectual method. The
opening section defends the idea of a constant Way that humanity can
understand and instantiate in life (including in government), while also
noting that each historical situation is unique and so the Way has to
be adapted to the particular historical conditions. Based on this idea,
he criticizes cultural conservatives who opposed any change in political institutions as well as those who were radically antitraditional and
wanted to discard all traditional culture. Democracy, he argues, is a
natural development of Ruist political thought and should be welcomed.

In the next section, Xu provides his analysis of traditional Ruist
political thought. As he often does, he provides extensive quotations from
a number of traditional sources to illustrate what rule by virtue means.
He emphasizes two points: rulers had to put the people first, caring for
the people's interests over their own, and rule by virtue operated through
rituals rather than the coercive means of law and punishment. Then in
the third section, he argues that democracy will provide the best structure
to realize Ruist political ideals, while also considering why historically
democracy failed to develop in China. His answer to this question is

Between Academia and Politics, 47–60, first published in *Democratic Review* 3, no. 1,
December 16, 1951.

that Ruism always considered government from the rulers' perspective, and never developed a sense of political consciousness and agency in the people. The current governments, and he probably means both in China and Taiwan, are the worst of both Chinese and Western models. They have the unlimited power of Chinese politics without the sense of moral responsibility, and the struggle for political power characteristic of Western politics without the rights that guarantee protection for individuals. Dedication to real democracy while preserving the Ruist ideal of rule by virtue and the use of ritual is the only way forward. Additionally, democracy needs Ruism to give it a moral foundation; otherwise it is merely a balancing of different interests.

Our Attitude toward Chinese History and Culture

The formation of any kind of thought will always be influenced by the historical conditions of its time. The uniqueness of history thus turns into the uniqueness of a kind of thought. Perhaps there would be no motivating cause to bring out this kind of thought without this uniqueness, and thought would lose its significance for undertaking the mission of that time. Whether a historical form of thought has vitality in the present or not depends entirely on the degree to which it can reveal universality from its unique conditions. Put differently, it depends on truth of the universality that the formation of its uniqueness relied on, and the degree to which people of later times can realize this. Uniqueness changes, but the truth of the universality behind uniqueness, which it relies on, is constant and unchanging. The reason why historical study is possible and why it is valuable is because it reveals the nondual relationship between the changing and the constant.

Constancy is embodied in change while keeping a rein on it, so that humanity can ceaselessly advance in the practice of the unchanging Way that makes humanity human in their own specific, unique historical conditions. Some people do not admit that there is an unchanging constant Way behind the current of historical change. They denigrate history and despise tradition, believing they themselves stand fully outside the category of history and create themselves relying entirely on their own power. They don't understand that this sectional way of thinking is to associate themselves with ordinary animals who lack historical awareness and pave the way for the materialists of today, the Communist Party.[1]

On the other hand, some people hold fast to the relics of a historical period that is already vanished, sticking to the specific, unique things that have to change. They want to force these relics into the new specific, unique conditions, which is to confuse a historical phenomenon with a natural phenomenon. It's not just that they cannot understand the present by sticking to ancient ways, but that they are often imprisoned by particular historical phenomena and so they obliterate the constant Way of universality that constitutes unique phenomena. In name, they respect history, but their attitude is actually an affront to it. The worst part is that this misplaced effort can be easily used by schemers. Some such schemers like to use the word *revolution*, while others like to use the mentality of holding onto the past. Still others like to combine the two to get an advantage from both sides.

Therefore, our stance toward Chinese culture should not be the reckless overturning of the May Fourth period, nor should it be ignorant defense. Rather, what we should do is discern the universal, eternal, unchanging Way behind particular historical conditions that runs through the current of history, and further see how it was limited by the specific historical conditions of the past. Because of these restrictions, sometimes circumstances don't reveal enough of it, or the way they reveal it has some deviations. At this point, we should consider what kind of new practices are required by new historical conditions to allow the unchanging Way to be revealed more completely and correctly and converge with the major current of human culture. This will also make schemers unable to make use of Chinese culture to aid their evil designs. This is our mission.

Ruist thought forms the mainstream of the Chinese national spirit. Its starting point is using humanity's own power to resolve their problems.[2] So the issues raised by Ruism are always concerning "cultivating oneself" and "governing people"; moreover, these are two sides of the same issue, what is called the beginning and end or the root and branch of one matter. This is why governing people in Ruism has to start with cultivating the self, and cultivating the self must end up with governing people. The inner sage and the outer king are the inside and outside of one thing. And so, looking at it from one angle, Ruist thought is mainly ethical thought, but from a different angle it is also political thought. The distinguishing characteristic of Ruist thought is exactly not separating ethics and politics. Naturally, this also shows that it is a form of thought in its early stage that did not later develop completely separate fields of inquiry. For now, I will only look at Ruism's achievements, its limitations, and how it needs to advance in the aspect of political thought. Then we can begin to once again reveal the constant Way it embodies through a renewed practice to continue benefiting humanity.

The Structure of Ruist Political Thought

From the point of view of its highest ideals, we may well call Ruist political thought "rule by virtue."[3] From the point of view of the object of most of its effort, we may well call it "making the people the foundation." For realization of the ideas in an object, ritual is the warp and weft throughout.

Respect for people is the starting point of rule by virtue; it expresses faith in human nature. Foremost, Ruists firmly believe that "people possess this constant way, and love this perfect virtue."[4] Hence, rulers must first perfect the virtue in themselves and thereby allow everyone to perfect the virtue of their common nature. The relationship between rulers and ruled is a relationship of shared virtue, not a relationship of power and coercion. Virtue is the common basis of what makes people human. When people can perfect their virtue, they interact with and forget each other in the common basis of humanity, each nurturing their life and following their nature.[5] This is the goal and highest attainment of government.

The critical part is that the rulers can first perfect their virtue. As the *Analects* says, "To govern means to be correct. If you lead with correctness, who would dare be incorrect?"[6] and "One who rules by virtue may be compared to the Pole Star. It remains in its place while the other stars revolve around it."[7] The *Mean* says, "The gentleman sets his mind on reverence and the world is thereby pacified."[8] All express this idea. The three guiding principles and eight steps of the *Great Learning* are a systematic account of this kind of rule by virtue.[9] In fact, the source of this idea is very early. The "Canon of Yao" chapter of the *Documents* says, "[Yao] was able to make the outstanding and virtuous illustrious in order to show affection to the nine peoples. With the nine peoples harmonious, he regulated all the people, making them shine brightly, and united the myriad states in harmony. The black-haired people were transformed and lived in concord."[10] This differs with the "cultivate, order, govern, pacify" steps of the *Great Learning* only in the level of detail of the theory; the fundamental ideas are not different.

The earliest credible text related to political thought in China is surely the *Documents*. The case for rule by virtue in its first chapter was already stated above. The second chapter "Counsels of Gao Yao" first says, "[He must] take care for his character and cultivate his thoughts for a long time," and, "There are nine virtues of conduct." "Display three of these virtues daily" and "Strictly and solemnly respect six of these virtues daily."[11] This known as the invariant thought of the two sovereigns and three kings,[12] and was brought together to its pinnacle in "The Great Plan." The focal point of "The Great Plan" is "the constant principle was then given order,"[13] which means rule by virtue wherein everyone follows their nature to perfect order. This is a kind of political thought that is internally enacted.

The rulers' internally enacted moral cultivation is usually more important than external restrictions and constructions. Rulers don't take a stand on power and utilize power to restrict some kinds of action, but mainly take a stand on their natural allotment, doing the moral cultivation to be an inner sage. From inner sage to outer king is simply a kind of function of "extending the self to others,"[14] a function of expanding and filling out. The reason one can extend, expand, and fill out this way is the belief that human nature is good and "everyone can be a Yao or Shun."[15] As long as the rulers can build the center to establish the periphery, then "when the wind blows the grass will bend,"[16] and then everyone will live a reasonable life within their own natural allotment.

Government is primarily the most centralized form for resolving [problems in] interpersonal relations. The basic intention behind rule by virtue is for everyone to blend their relationships harmoniously through their internal virtue and not to use power, or even human-created laws and regulations to oppress and tie or bind people together. Of course, oppression and tying by power is intolerable and legal binding is only an external force, even if it is effective. External forces need to be based on a foundation of internal relationships, otherwise in the end the bonds will not be secure and people's nature will not be able to develop freely. Rule by virtue aims at using the virtue people already have to establish internal relations between them. The way Ruists see it, only internal relations are natural and reasonable. In China, whenever one mentions "techniques of governing" one then has to bring up "correcting people's heart-minds." If their heart-minds are disordered then they lack virtue, which means the loss of internal, reasonable relationships.

The human heart-mind is fundamentally correct. The reason it becomes incorrect is usually due to someone with power and influence misusing these, causing the people to lose their virtue and [correct] heart-mind. Then not only does society lack a standard for building the center to establish the periphery, but he [the ruler] will certainly abuse his position, his conduct will be unreasonable, rewards and punishments will be mixed up, and as a result people's normal and reasonable life will be destroyed. Then evil and cunning elements in society will have free rein to do evil to guarantee their survival, and then how could the world not be in great disorder? On the eve of the fall of China, all legitimate workers and businesspeople, dedicated and law-abiding soldiers, and determined and self-motivated intellectuals could not go on living. In other words, the only way to live was to compete in society immorally. As a result, the immorality that existed from time immemorial evolved into the unprecedented pain of mutual ruin.

Looked at this way, Chinese Ruists' position of rule by virtue seems to be the most practical position to address the root of the problem. It is not unrealistic or illusory. Perhaps some people will ask why it is that although many people, past and present, talk about benevolence, rightness, and morality, their actions are exactly the opposite of what they say. This principle is very simple: virtue or its lack is a matter of practice, not a matter of talking. When someone in the position of a ruler talks about virtue, the first thing to look at is whether he is public-spirited and the way in which he uses his power. Of course, the unjust will often pretend to do what is right, but then they have to deceive and walk a fraudulent path: the longer they do the more difficult it is to get on the correct track. It is [as Mengzi] said, "When it arises in their heart-minds, it harms their governing":[17] in the end it cannot be concealed.

Whenever there have happened to be rulers of such hypocritical character, their lack of virtue has first been laid bare to the world. They will even dismiss their own officials out of lack of virtue, their closest and most trusted followers. This kind of action and response between the unvirtuous, and the chaos it brings, can be a kind of negative confirmation of how rule by virtue can produce order. Using morality as a tool to abuse power actually reveals the most egregious immorality. If we were to not advocate virtue because of this and not try to use virtue to shed light on everything, we would only increase social chaos and fall deeply into their trap. Then normal relations between people could not be recovered and we would lose the means to bring order out of chaos.

The concept of "the people are the foundation of the state" in the *Documents* relates to rule by virtue as exterior and interior.[18] Chinese political thought rarely emphasizes establishing the concept of the state, but especially emphasizes confirming that the people are the only [proper] object of government. It is not just the belief that "Heaven gives birth to the people and established rulers to oversee them [for their benefit]."[19] The primitive religious concept of heaven was concretely implemented in the people, elevating the people to the position of gods.[20] "Counsels of Gao Yao" said, "Heaven's sharp hearing and sight comes from our people's sharp hearing and sight. Heaven's display of awesome power comes from our people's display of power," and "Great Declaration" said, "Heaven sees as my people see."[21] In the *Zuo Tradition*, Ziyu, supervisor of the military in Song and Ji Liang of Sui both said, "The people are the masters of the gods."[22] The "Zhou Speeches" of the *Speeches of the States* says, "When the people are harmonious, then the spirits send down blessings" and "Heaven inevitably follows what the people want."[23] Therefore, the people do not merely have the standing to be "governed by others" in a position below the rulers; they also have the standing to represent Heaven and the spirits in a position above the rulers. We can see from this that Mengzi's "the people are the most valuable"[24] is simply an unvarying idea in Chinese political thought.

The spirits over the ruler, the state the ruler relies on, and the ruler himself all exist for the benefit of the people, according to the orthodoxy of Chinese thought which is Ruism. All of them manifest their own value in their value for the people. One might say that spirits, states, and rulers are all empty positions and only the people have substance. So it is not only that Ruist thought does not recognize the political positions of tyrannical rulers and corrupt officials who harm the people for their evil schemes. Orthodox Chinese thought also does not recognize the political positions of rulers who rule for the sake of power, who cannot "use themselves to nurture the world" but "use the world to nurture themselves."[25] This thoroughgoing emphasis on the people constitutes one of the unique characteristics of Ruist thought.

Rejecting the idea of politics as power from the point of view of rule by virtue also means rejecting the warning that the state is just a tool of suppression. Rejecting the idea that rulers themselves have some special rights from the point of view of the people as foundation also means rejecting the warning that rulers and ruled are strictly opposed classes. Since rule by virtue is government enacted internally, in personal interactions the emphasis is not on adding restrictions to the external relationships, but on positively influencing and eliciting what people already have in their own nature, making them become conscious of it themselves so as to fulfill their duties as people.

Law emphasizes external control while ritual emphasizes internal motivation, so naturally rule by virtue favors ritual over law as the tool it relies on for governing. Zhu Xi said, "Ritual is the ordered design of Heavenly Pattern, the formal principle of human affairs."[26] Mr. Xiong [Shili] of Huanggang in his *Essential Instructions for Reading the Classics* explained it this way: "This formal principle is not purely founded on the external. The Heavenly Pattern of my heart-mind naturally responds to what it encounters in an appropriate fashion. This appropriate fashion means that it follows the relevant distinctions in all things, putting them in the sequence they should have. In the heart-mind, it is called 'the ordered design of Heavenly Pattern'; when it is enacted externally it is called 'the formal principle of human affairs.'"[27] More simply, it is ritual.

Virtue and ritual are fundamentally one, not two different things. Hence, the *Analects* said, "If you guide the people with decrees and reform them with punishments, they will evade them and have no sense of shame. If you guide them with virtue and reform them with ritual, they will have a sense of shame and correct themselves."[28] Institutions are external arrangements and punishments are forms of external coercion. Virtue is inherent in human nature and ritual is its general form of action. Institutions and punishments go together, and so do virtue and rituals. Since the motivating power of government is based on the virtue of human nature which people all share, then "where human footsteps trod, where boats and carts penetrated"[29] is where the virtue of the rulers reaches. Then there is not only no opposition between rulers and ruled, there is no opposition of self and other. "If anyone in the world drowned, it was if he had drowned them himself. If anyone starved, it was as if he had starved them himself." "King Wen looked on his people as he would someone injured."[30] "[Act] as if caring for an infant."[31] A ruler who governs by virtue merges himself within the ruled, becoming one body with them, and there is nothing artificial in this. And of course, what they use to join inner and outer and give expression to higher and lower is primarily ritual.

The fundamental spirit of ritual as far as the self is concerned is emphasizing respect. Respect is overcoming the petty self. And so "The Minor Rituals" says, "Never be disrespectful."[32] As far as others are concerned, it is emphasizing deference. Deference is extending the greater self. And so the *Analects* says, "If one can govern the state with ritual and deference, what difficulties would there be? If one [can]not govern the state with ritual and deference, what use is ritual?"[33] In Ruist thought, rule by virtue, making the people the foundation, and rule by ritual are all connected. The political sphere of Ruism is the highest sphere of human life. Hence, the opening of the *Great Learning* says, "The way of the great learning consists in illuminating clear virtue, in renewing the people, and in stopping at the highest good."[34] The highest good is the end of human life in Ruism, and the end of government as well.

Ruist Political Thought and Democratic Government

Modern Western democratic government springs from self-consciousness. As far as government goes, self-consciousness means one upholds and struggles for one's own right to life, independence, and self-mastery in regard to others, especially rulers. The first phase of the basis for democratic government is the natural law of "freedom and equality of human life." The second is the [social] contract theory of mutual agreement. Natural law and contract theory are both premises and means for contending for individual rights. The foremost significance of modern democracy is that it is a way to contend for and demarcate individual rights and limit the exercise of power by the rulers. The secondary significance of modern democracy is that after demarcating individual rights, it allows fulfilling corresponding duties to those other than individuals.

Because the origin of democracy is the struggle for individual rights and because there must be clear divisions between different rights, with a definite scope, to be able to maintain order in the course of life, rule of law becomes something inseparable from democracy. Contrasting the background of democratic thought and Ruist political thought, it is not difficult to discover that there is a difference of refined and coarse, pure and motley. Therefore, I believe that in the future, democratic government can only put down stable roots and realize its highest value by further accepting Ruist thought. The reason democracy is valuable is that through contention it makes contention unnecessary, and through individuals' personal interests it achieves the public interest of the collective. But the absence of contention and public interest achieved here, as far as the practical situation, is forced by the mutual restriction of power and does not come from the self-consciousness of morality. This means it is never fully secure.

The ideas of virtue and ritual in Ruist thought are just what are needed to move from forced public interest and lack of contention based on power to moral self-consciousness. Democracy will not have a true basis until it achieves this. This point requires another essay, and I will not explain it more here. But what we cannot fail to pay special attention to here is that even if Ruism has this kind of purely political thought and even if it can establish the theoretical foundation for true democracy, nevertheless true democracy never appeared in China itself. Only democracy is the true path, the highway, for the development of human government. In Chinese history, Ruism was only able to moderate the corrosive effects of tyranny and corruption, describing a distant vision of peace and good fortune for humanity. It could not truly resolve the problems of tyranny and corruption, and still less could it find a way out of the tragic historical cycle of order followed by chaos.

Furthermore, rule by virtue is based on respect for human nature. Making the people the foundation (*minben* 民本) and democracy (*minzhu* 民主) are only separated by a small gap. The ritual in rule by ritual is the basis and standard for enacting laws. These three[35] have already entered deeply into the innermost recesses of democratic thought. The concepts of balance and the mean embedded in rule by virtue and rule by ritual are also important spiritual factors in democratic thought. Yet China itself never made the transition to democracy; in fact, since the Republic began the major and minor political schemers usually turned their backs on Chinese culture and went in an antidemocratic direction. Why was this? This is the question which we must urgently try to answer.

Kongzi, a Ruist of great achievements, said of himself that he "transmits but does not create."[36] In the *Mean* it says of him that "he handed down the way of Yao and Shun and followed the example of Kings Wen and Wu."[37] This is definitely a historical fact. The source that Kongzi handed down is surely not other than the Six Classics.[38] Ruist political thought is also put together from the Six Classics. The Classics are mainly the teachings and experiences by which the ancient emperors and kings established themselves and deigned to teach. Their value lies in the fact that they occupied the position of rulers but were able to overcome the limits of benefit and harm to the rulers' power and follow the highest reason of humanity, being truly responsible for the ruled. This is truly difficult to find in Western thought. Mr. Liang Shuming said Chinese culture was precocious regarding reason, which can also be seen here.

Ruism summed up the traditional thought of ancient China, carrying it forward and enhancing it and molding the spirit of our nation. Its contributions shine like the sun and need no further repetition. However, from the political standpoint, the thought that Ruism transmitted always took the position of the rulers to consider what to do for the ruled, trying to solve political problems from the position of the rulers. It seldom took the position of the ruled to regulate the actions of the rulers and seldom tried to resolve political problems from the position of the ruled. This makes an obvious contrast with case of modern democracy, which developed through the ruled contending with the rulers. Exactly because of this, although Ruist political thought respects human nature, makes the people the foundation, and considers the people most important, the virtue of the government is a kind of virtue that covers, like the wind blowing over the grass.[39] Ruism recommended benevolent government proceeding from a benevolent heart-mind and continuously considered various beneficial measures, including various democratic political institutions, but all of them had the characteristic of being "instituted" and "provided" ("King Wen instituted government that provided benevolence"),[40] a characteristic of "providing" and "assisting" ("providing broadly and assisting the masses").[41]

The people were always put in a passive position: even though the people were the foundation (yi min wei ben 以民為本), they could never make the leap to the stage of the people being sovereign (yi min wei zhu 以民為主). Then political matters always revolved in the hands of the rulers and ministers, meaning that true political subjectivity never evolved. All the way up to the end of the Ming, Huang Zongxi pointed out that the ruler was the guest and all under heaven is the master.[42] From there, making the leap outside the circle of rulership to think about political solutions in the people was separated merely by a thin sheet of paper, but this sheet of paper could never be broken through by those who bore responsibility in Chinese culture. When Chinese thought began to coalesce, the limitations of the historical conditions, which is to say the limitations of the unique conditions that meant political problems were only considered from the standpoint of the rulers, are worth deep thought and sighs of regret. And so in our traditional political thought, the following problems could not but happen.

First, because political thought always considered political problems from the standpoint of the rulers, all the various teachings were never able to go beyond the way of the ruler or the way of the minister, or the way of the counselor and official. Although there was refined political thought, it was always confined within these kinds of narrow topics and never was objectified to constitute true political science.[43] Therefore, this thought in itself only amounts to sprouts and buds and still has not flowered or produced fruit. (I heard this personally from Mr. Xiong [Shili] of Huanggang.)

Second, the process of rule by virtue, which proceeds from cultivating the self to governing the state and bringing peace to the world, from fulfilling one's own nature to fulfilling the nature of others, is an extension of the virtue of one person. The way of thinking in "The gentleman sets his mind on reverence and the world is thereby pacified"[44] and "All Shun did was make himself reverent and faced south"[45] is indeed possible in theory but in actuality it perhaps cannot be expected. There are massive complications in taking one person's virtue and objectifying it into society and making it into a way of implementing government. And the Chinese idea of rule by virtue left out these unavoidable complications. Actually, if political subjectivity could really be established, then the content of government could mainly be a combination of various self-administering groups, and government leaders really could reach the level of "setting their minds on reverence and the world being thereby pacified." Without political subjectivity, meaning the human nature of the people is not revealed, the practice of and response to rule by virtue will necessarily have some limitations.

Third, because there was no political subjectivity then, on the one hand, everything depended on the moral self-consciousness of the rulers, but aware of the difficulty of knowing the Way of heaven, traditional political theorists' hands were tied when it came to dealing with tyrants and corrupt officials in Chinese history. On the other hand, then even when there were sagely rulers and worthy ministers who had moral consciousness, in society there was a lack of ability to meet and respond to their virtue and bear some responsibility. Then sagely rulers and worthy ministers would feel isolated and remote, bearing too heavy a burden, and usually their strength did not follow along with their ideals. We can then understand how easy it was for the way of the gentleman to disappear and the way of the petty man to take over in the court.

Fourth, the absence of political subjectivity meant that all the mobilizing power of the government was located in the court and not in society. Intellectuals who wanted to study to make some contribution had no other outlet for their energy besides the court. If they had some dissatisfaction with the actual government, the only solution was seclusion. In these circumstances, aside from a minority who chose seclusion, intellectuals' only option was struggling for an official appointment. Those who weren't able to get an appointment felt they had not "encountered a favorable situation" and this is how society looked on them as well. These intellectuals could only vent their discontent and had simply lost any positive meaning in life.

In this way, intellectuals' energy was restricted to one goal: gaining an official position at court. They gave up on the responsibility and effort they should have directed toward all aspects of society. Then society lost the motivating energy intellectuals would have provided. Intellectuals themselves became more ignorant day by day, since their scope of activity was so limited. This turned into a fixed pattern of activity with the eight-legged essay of the civil service exam, which was also the height of their ignorance. At the same time, the power to select and dismiss intellectuals was held by those above (the emperor) rather than those below, and the emperor's moods were more important than an intellectual's scholarship or morality. For an official, keeping a watch on the emperor's moods was more important than maintaining his scholarship or morality. Then an atmosphere of competition took over and their sense of shame was lost. As a result, the descendants of the Ruists who undertook to uphold the correct transmission (*daotong* 道統) to establish the highest in humanity became for the most part the most shameless intellectuals in the world. It was like this in ancient times and even more so in the present, and intellectuals have actually turned into a burden. This is why Master Yuan said, "When there are few scholars, the world is well ordered."[46]

The Problems Ruist Political Thought Faces and Its Advancement

The four shortcomings described above are mainly historical. From a contemporary perspective, they perhaps do not cause much harm. Instead, it is another aspect of the influence of rule by virtue that obstructs political progress the most. That is the unlimited expansion of the ruling mentality, which frequently overcomes all the limits it should have, making it forever impossible to establish the fundamentals for democratic government. Rule by virtue itself does not allow this shortcoming, but in fact it is the biggest snarl in our nation's politics today.

From the point of view of rule by virtue, the affairs of the world are all internal matters of one's personality and so sagely rulers and worthy ministers have an unlimited sense of responsibility. "The Announcement of Tang" says, "Whatever crimes there are in the land, let the guilt be mine."[47] "Great Declaration" says, "Let all transgressions of the people be laid upon me, the one man,"[48] also illustrating this idea. "Yi Yin was the sage of responsibility."[49] Actually, responsibility was a common spirit all worthy ministers in China could not help having, not just Yi Yin. Hence, Ruist ethical and political thought starts with prescribing the duties one should fulfill regarding others and not with prescribing the rights one should have, as Western thought does. This is naturally a step above the spirit of Western culture. For example, "paternal care" prescribes the duty a father has to his son; "filiality" prescribes the duty of a son to his father. "Friendship of an older brother" prescribes the duty of an older brother to his younger brother; "reverence of a younger brother" prescribes the duty of a younger brother to his older brother. "Rightness of a lord" prescribes the duty of a ruler to his minister; "dedication of a minister" prescribes the duty of a minister to his lord. The others can be inferred from these examples.

Chinese culture went beyond the individual himself, beyond the concept of individual rights, and submerged the individual within the other, to the point where life and government is for the purpose of fulfilling one's duties to the other. This is precisely the reason Chinese culture can aid where Western culture is impoverished and begin a new cultural life for humanity. But as far as the whole of culture is concerned, it definitely lacks a stage of self-consciousness of the individual. As far as political thought is concerned, it lacks the stage of self-consciousness on the part of the governed. In theory, this deficiency should not be a major problem. However, in reality people have an aspect of rationality and self-control, and they also have an animal aspect of desires. Politics itself cannot be set apart from power. If a person negates his individuality based on his moral self-consciousness, then his individuality is merged within the collective. Without self-consciousness based on morality and without awareness of this individuality, his individuality becomes a passive, inactive entity, losing the ability of free, active development that is in human nature.

But in the end, those in society who have moral self-consciousness are a minority. If the majority lacks the political self-consciousness of individual rights, which brings about formation of political subjectivity, then the rulers will not be aware of the existence and restrictions of an objective political subject, and therefore without even being aware of it, will fantasize that they are the political subject (as in "I am the state," for example). Then the feeling of unlimited moral responsibility will easily change into a demand for unlimited control and power, not accepting the restrictions that a democratic government should have. The minimal demand of democracy is that a government should understand the limits of its power. The governing mentality of a modern Western democracy is like that of a limited company, while China resembles that of an unlimited company. In my view, the appearance of Yuan Shikai[50] in the Republican period and the success of Mao Zedong now can be blamed on the fact that our cultural history lacked the stage of individual self-consciousness and lacked objective restrictions on [political] power.

However, this cannot be said to be a negative influence of rule by virtue itself. Any form of government based on moral self-consciousness will necessarily have a condition of not tolerating [errors in] itself and a feeling of remorseful insufficiency. "Whatever crimes there are in the land, let the guilt be mine," is not mere modesty or a polite expression, but springs from a feeling of guilt that comes from the highest moral self-consciousness, the same as Jesus's taking the place of all humanity on the cross. For this reason, the virtuous would absolutely not feel self-satisfied that they are political leaders, still less would they use some underhanded means to contend for a position of leadership. They would naturally have a feeling of awe and reverence for the people, as it is said, "greatly in awe of the people's intent,"[51] and thus implement the concept of making the people the foundation. This is using the sense of moral responsibility to moderate political power, not using political power as a substitute for a sense of moral responsibility.

This will have the same effect as democratic government on limiting political power. Democracy starts from the need to restrict governmental interference. Because rule by virtue respects human nature, it also emphasizes simplicity and nonaction. Democracy does not have a concept of a fixed, dictatorial leader. In rule by virtue, there are the sayings, "Shun and Yu possessed all under heaven without seeking after it"[52] and "the world belongs to the public,"[53] which circulated during two thousand years of autocratic government and no one dared to deny them.

"Abdication" became the approved story in Chinese politics, so even treacherous usurpers always made a show of facing south and declining three times. This is not so different than Washington's refusal to accept lifetime presidency, which established the model for American democracy.

Furthermore, ideas like freedom of expression in democratic nations come from the concept of basic human rights. This is a firm belief that people have these rights and that the job of the government is to secure these basic rights. This of course does not constitute a problem. Ruist political thought as well always made restricting expression a great taboo. This derived from the moral self-control of the rulers and the respect for human nature in Ruist morality. This is certainly a different route than in Western freedom of expression, but the result is not different.

Only adopting the traditional Chinese political standpoint of unlimited responsibility but lacking the moral self-consciousness behind it, while also adopting the modern Western political standpoint of struggle for power but not recognizing that before it there are limits due to the basic rights of the individual (as in the present government of China): this is the most incorrigible government in the world. For example, the basic concept of law was intended to regulate relationships, restrain the rulers, and provide security to the people. But in the kind of government just mentioned, it becomes a tool to no law, much less any ritual or yielding. How did we arrive at this unprecedented disaster today? What can be done politically to save us from this disaster? Those who have a mind to care about present conditions should do some hard thinking about these questions.

From the simple discussion above, we can draw a contrast and understand that since the Republican era the government has not been a Western democratic government that is responsible for us, nor is it a Ruist government that is responsible for us. It is a political route that is a mix of Chinese and Western while being neither Chinese nor Western that is supreme. At present we can only boldly walk the road of democracy while reconsidering Ruist political thought to take the position of the ruled and bodily recognize (*tiren* 體認)[54] their situation. The first thing to do is to move political subjectivity from the rulers who have the false impression it is theirs, and return it to the people so the people have the power to defend against unvirtuous rulers. The people must go from the platitude "the people are the foundation" being mouthed by the rulers to standing on their own in democracy. Intellectuals must make a way out of the court and the pitiful mentality of sending memorials to the monarch and instead transition to finding a way for society and the public and have the fortitude to discern right and wrong for them. When it comes to judging actual political figures, we should not start from individual talent but first see their ability to establish true political subjects, meaning their ability to help realize democracy.

Our government must first have reasonable contention before it can return to reasonable absence of contention. We must first have individual independence and then a return to interdependence that goes beyond the individual. We must first have limits on government based on a concept of basic rights and then return to shaping character through ritual that surpasses rights. In sum, Ruist political thought must change from taking the rulers as the starting point and then going down to the people, to taking the ruled as the starting point and adding in the stage of self-consciousness of the individual that was neglected in our country's history. Then democracy can attain a more elevated basis through the revival of the Ruist spirit, and Ruist thought can complete its true, objective constitution through the establishment of democracy. This can not only cut through many unnecessary knotty problems, but in the struggle against authoritarianism, it can create new opportunities for good outcomes in the political future for China and for humanity.

Chapter 6

The Fundamental Character of the
Ruist Spirit, Its Limitations, and Its Rebirth

Translator's introduction: By far the longest essay in this collection, it
is one of the longest Xu ever wrote. It deals with what Xu often refers
to as the question of culture, meaning what the true spirit of Chinese
culture is and what form it should take for the modern period. As Xu
makes clear in his opening, he identifies Chinese culture with Ruism.
Furthermore, culture as he understands it is self-awareness that involves
making value judgments and choices. It is not primarily determined by
material conditions, as Marxists hold. Culture reflects thought.

In his usual fashion, Xu vociferously opposes attempts to reject
Chinese culture and overturn tradition. He points out that Western
cultures (such as the UK) have their own traditions and these did not
prevent them from becoming powerful modern states. He refuses to
accept that Chinese tradition is the reason for the lack of modernization. At the same time, he is not a fundamentalist; he recognizes that
there are problems in Chinese culture and there are strong points to
adopt from Western nations (science in particular). Yet he insists that
Chinese culture was not the reason the GMD lost the Chinese civil
war, and opposing communism does not require abandoning tradition.
The problem in his mind is rather that they were not following Chinese

Ruist Political Thought and Democracy, Freedom and Human Rights, 49–99, first published in *Democratic Review* 3, no. 10 supplement, April 1952.

culture enough, and had abandoned any sense of the value of effort to develop character.

Xu goes on to analyze the differences between Western and Chinese cultures. Western culture inherited the Greek emphasis on knowledge, making learning about the world the fundamental pursuit. This is why science developed in Europe. Chinese culture, however, always emphasized morality. Ruism has two fundamental goals: to realize the universal goodness of human nature present in everyone, and to manifest this goodness externally through correct relationships with other people. This process of building proper relationships has to start within the family, and so the family remains a crucial institution.

Although Ruism developed morality to a high degree, it was limited with regard to knowledge. Xu distinguishes two aspects of human nature: moral nature (*dexing* 德性) and cognitive nature (*zhixing* 知性).[1] Though Ruism did not neglect knowledge, it always focused on moral practice and did not pay much attention to knowledge without an immediate moral payoff. Xu contrasts this with the Western emphasis on cognitive nature which gave rise to science: it pursued knowledge regardless of whether it was useful. The spirit of empirical investigation was pushed aside in China. This is not, however, because there is anything antiscientific in Ruist thought. It simply didn't see the point of such investigation of nature.

Xu then argues that failure to develop the cognitive nature means moral practice was deficient as well. Better understanding of the world can improve moral practice, and this is how he justifies pursuing science while holding to Ruist values. As he says, scientific research can be another form of moral practice. Though Xu gives no specific examples, it is easy to see how medical research to cure diseases or economic and sociological research to alleviate poverty could be called moral practice, since the aim is to improve people's lives. Yet Xu does not address the fact that research can often be turned to destructive purposes, such as nuclear physics making it possible to build nuclear weapons. It is not clear whether he would think this should still be studied.

Xu concludes the essay by claiming that Western culture is deficient as well, in the opposite direction. It excelled at developing the cognitive nature, but could not measure up to Chinese culture in developing the moral nature. This is why the problems of Western culture (he mentions inequality) cannot be solved with scientific and technological advances. There is a crisis of value, and this is precisely where learning from Chinese culture can help. He calls for a renaissance: the way forward for

China is not to abandon its traditional culture, but to restore it and in addition adopt the best elements of Western culture.

This long essay was published as a supplement to Democratic Review 3, *no. 10, probably on April 15, 1952. It was commended by several friends after publication. Among these, one especially worthy of mention is from a letter from my old friend Mr. Wang Xinheng from May 14, in which he said, "You took what was an obscure and dull topic in Mr. Tang Junyi's writing and turned it into a call to arms with a passion like fire. It really moved me! You traced the GMD's failure to 'vulgar materialism' in thought. This point especially captured me . . ." Mr. Wang truly understood that this essay was written in a state of distress at chaotic circumstances. My purpose was not to discuss medical principles, but to provide a prescription for the patient.*

Another was from the Dean of the School of Letters at Taiwan University at that time, Mr. Shen Gangbo,[2] who in a letter from May 9 said, "Some people have been ceaselessly discussing the problem of Chinese and Western culture ever since the Sino-Japanese War [1894–95], but until now not one essay has understood both sides and written something to the point. If there are any, they must begin from your essay. Reading it, I was pleased and admiring. I was discussing it with a few colleagues today, and most of them felt that it is always the way things are, that fortune goes from one extreme to the other. Changing this convention will rely on this essay of yours . . ." This was in response to a few comparisons between Chinese and Western culture that I made. His point often made me uneasy, feeling that he spoke too lightly, and that my essay was superficial without any substance. This was the reason I didn't publish this essay in any collections before.

Recently I happened across it and read it again. I felt what I said still had the consciousness of that period, but my passion can't reach that level now. In spite of myself, I sighed with regret.
May 8, 1979
Kowloon residence, Hong Kong

Debates around This Question

What I call the fundamental character of the Ruist spirit here is in fact an attempt to give an account of the basic character of Chinese culture. Good or bad, the unifying character of the Chinese people was forged out of the Ruist spirit during the four hundred years of the Han dynasty

[206 BCE–220 CE]. Over two thousand years, consciously or unconsciously, positively or negatively, the Ruist spirit saturated every corner of actual social life. It was not until after the Opium Wars [1839–1842 and 1856–1860] that it consciously began to face arduous testing. It was not fundamentally shaken until the May Fourth movement.[3] And recently the Communist Party has been pulling it out by the roots in their "reform" movement. Ruism is not a religion, but its consistent spirit can connect to the universal and lasting in human life, which no "doctrine of one school" in the entire world can match. So there is no harm in calling it China's great irreligious religion. Some people think the reason Ruism could maintain its unique power in China for so long is because Emperor Wu of the Han listened to Dong Zhongshu and dismissed the various schools, only honoring the learning of Kongzi.[4] In addition, the rulers of later ages ceaselessly promoted it.

They fail to realize that when Emperor Wu dismissed the various schools, this merely meant that they were not officially established by the government, not that the free circulation of ideas was prohibited. Furthermore, when Western Han was founded the techniques of Huang-Lao were especially flourishing. Dong Zhongshu himself was also influenced by the Yin-Yang school. The Yin-Yang school theory of the procession of the five virtues became the common political theory among the elite at the end of the Western Han, and Wang Mang relied on it to usurp the throne.[5] As far as Ruism itself is concerned, the fourteen academicians established by the Han to promote and explain it were all of the New Text school.[6] However, the New Text commentaries were all lost until Qing dynasty scholars began searching, then finding some clues. The Ruism that was transmitted from the later Han until recent times was almost entirely Old Text. Old Text studies were not established as official in the Western Han, and like the other schools, survived as a kind of learning among the people. And so scholarship cannot rely on the government for its survival.

Chinese kings and emperors throughout history honored and promoted Kongzi: some out of personal respect and admiration formed by the social climate, some valuing Ruism as a kind of social authority. If government oversteps its role in promoting scholarship and wants to use the position of the ruling class to form a monopoly, the result will only be to strangle scholarship. In Chinese history there has always been some official learning sponsored by the government which was not greatly valued in society, and then a school would arise among the people to oppose it. The official New Text studies in the Western Han is a negative proof of this [since it lacked popularity among the people]. The reason that Ruism became the fundamental culture of China was because of society, not government. Quite the opposite; Chinese history illustrates that the Ruist spirit grew in esteem and saturated the culture through society, and was resigned to suppression and destruction under the government. The positive impact of the government on the Ruist spirit was nowhere near as great as the negative effects, and hence the diffusion of the Ruist spirit in society often met with pressure from the government and unavoidably faced resistance that cut away at it. The effect of this was that even when the Ruist spirit could have had the effect of maintaining and continuing society, it was difficult for it to have the effect of moving it forward and developing it. This is a point I want to raise again later. The only reason this essay is not titled "The Fundamental Character of Chinese Culture" is to avoid several unneeded misunderstandings, because a nation so ancient would naturally be affected by other secondary cultures in the course of its development.

Next, since I believe that the Ruist spirit is the fundamental characteristic that shaped Chinese culture, I should first give a basic explanation of the meaning of "culture." My opinion is that culture is a kind of self-awareness of human nature in regard to life, and an attitude to life (value judgments) that follows from this self-awareness. Animals are also alive, but they don't have self-awareness about life and so they don't have an attitude toward life. Hence, we cannot say that animal life has culture. After people have an attitude toward life, they begin to make choices in life. From these choices, they construct a more appropriate attitude toward life, with a more appropriate form and conditions of living. This is how culture produces civilization. There is no need to say more about how civilization can affect culture, how living conditions can affect the attitude toward life, or how these affect each other to weave together the course of history.

When one feels that the form of life and living conditions represent one's own attitude toward life, this is the harmonization of culture and civilization. When life falls into predetermined forms and conditions and one can no longer be conscious of one's attitude toward life and its significance, then civilization has separated from culture and become a dead thing. This will then cause culture to decline. When culture declines, this will inevitably result in the destruction of civilization. Economic and geographical conditions are merely incentives that human nature depends on for self-awareness and routes for self-awareness to develop. These can only be considered to be of secondary significance when it comes to the origination of culture. The self-awareness of human nature is primary. Otherwise, one cannot explain why culture, indeed identical culture, is not guaranteed to arise under identical economic and geographic conditions. I feel that bronze and iron implements, up to the electronics of the present day, are one sort of product of a period's culture. One can naturally understand a culture from these products, but one has to go a step farther. If one declares that these products are the culture of a certain period, this is not only taking a part for the whole, it is always separated by a layer, leaving one unable to explain the fact of why the same bronze and iron tools produce different sorts of cultures.

So culture is always a spiritual thing. Its origin is always found in human nature's self-awareness of life. "The Xia dynasty esteemed conscientious, the Shang dynasty esteemed respect, and the Zhou dynasty esteemed cultural refinement."[7] Whether this description of the spirit of the cultural history of the three dynasties is complete and accurate or not is another question, but it is a fact that the authors of this description were conscious of this spirit. Asking why some people in history had this self-awareness and some people did not is like asking how people happen to have souls: at present there is no way to answer this question.

Human nature contains unlimited diversity. Because the external conditions human nature relies on for consciousness and development of itself differ, human nature can never achieve full development of all its potentials at the same time. What people achieve usually inclines to one side of human nature. This gives shape to the different characteristics of world cultures. I believe that human culture can get closer to complete development through continuous contact and interaction with different cultures. However, I cannot endorse the arbitrary attitude that makes one kind of cultural characteristic the yardstick and writes off other cultures.

It should be a natural thing for Chinese people to discuss Chinese culture and the Ruist spirit that is its mainstream. But the strange thing is, it is not an easy matter to bring up this question anywhere in China. This because many people believe it represents going backward as soon as they see this sort of topic, or even that it opposes liberal democracy. Because of this, I first want to open some discussion in response to some of the popular ways of speaking on the subject.

Some people feel that as soon as one begins to talk about Chinese culture, it becomes a discussion of the "lineage of the way [*daotong* 道

統]."[8] And whoever discusses any question of "lineage" is an accomplice of totalitarianism. To me, of all the reasons for opposing talking about Chinese culture, this is one of the most absurd. Culture is a common accretion of human history. As soon as one admits there is culture, one always has to admit that there is a cultural lineage that comes from history. Lineage means transmission and inheritance. I have not discovered any culture up until now without some lineage. He who says that "lineage is wrong" actually stands in a lineage himself when he says that.[9] He believes his "lineage" is unique and so objects to others' lineage.

As far as the relation to politics, ruling groups have admittedly used their historical and cultural traditions to further their private interests. This has to be judged along with the other various conditions. And among the many conditions, using history and culture is just a kind of incidental condition of whitewashing that behavior. One cannot simply judge that all discussion of lineage is totalitarian on this basis. As far as "lineage" itself, one admittedly cannot say that there is no lineage connected with totalitarianism, but there may perhaps be lineage that is not connected with totalitarianism. To the contrary, no one won't discuss lineage now more than the Communist Party. This developed into Zhdanov's declaration on Aleksandrov's *History of Western European Philosophy* in 1937, in which he used the slogan "absolute rejection."[10] This was the height of attacks on "lineage," and also the height of totalitarianism. (The Communist Party's Cultural Revolution was also just like this. Note added on April 18, 1979.)

What Hitler boasted about was Aryan blood lineage, not the Greek or Hebrew lineage of the way. What Mussolini boasted about was the Roman "lineage of power," not the lineage of the way of Roman law, especially natural law, which originated in Rome. Which of these dictators did not nurture cultural hooligans, to use their authority to take the place of the lineage of the way of European thought? Among recent Chinese political leaders, the one who openly brought up the lineage of the way was Mr. Sun Zhongshan, yet no one can deny that he was a great leader in the democratic movement in China. In their employment of intellectuals, Chinese autocratic kings and emperors always went through the format of finding "disciples" through the civil service exam system before being able to achieve their objectives. This is in no way different from current efforts to run various [government] training programs. But identifying talent through the exam system has no relation to the lineage of the way, to the point where all true scholars in China invariably looked down on the civil service exam in any form. Using something as a pretext is in the end a pretext. Someone who will use a pretext will do that with anything. This can be understood without the need for more examples.

I cannot say that discussion of the lineage of the way is the same as democratic government. As I said above, we have to look at a number of other conditions. However, I can assert that someone who sincerely discusses the lineage of the way has an additional feeling of closeness, an additional sense of piety, and a stance of humility and respect for the history of his country and people and for the philosophical pioneers who died thousands of years before him, who went to great lengths on behalf of that culture. Compared to those utterly worthless people who ruthlessly and recklessly disparage and curse their own ancestors without stopping to think, naturally that person who respects his history can more easily approach democracy. The reason these ruthless and reckless people talk about democracy and freedom is because real power is not in their hands, and they discuss it as a shield for their personal lives and interests. If these people get power in their hands one day, then they will fulfill their ruthless and reckless ambitions. Since their thinking rejects all "lineages," they cannot but carry out a burst of censorship.[11] So I advocate not talking only about culture, but once one talks about culture, one should also talk about "lineage." Furthermore, I hope that some people come forth and resolutely make the lineage of the way their responsibility.

Next, some people mistakenly believe that the lineage of the way means tradition, and that talk of the lineage of the way means respecting tradition; that is to say, obstructing creativity. Additionally, Chinese culture lacks science, and now since we need science we should not promote Chinese culture. Does Chinese culture block modernization? Is there no culture to speak of outside of science? I will reserve these questions for the end. I would just like to point out there that there are many layers to culture. It seems that the relationship between tradition and creativity has to be addressed at a particular layer, not in an overarching fashion. Recently many people were wildly pleased to read where Arnold Toynbee in *A Study of History* pointed out the stagnating effect of tradition on culture. But they were extremely puzzled by his conclusion that Europe should return to Christian culture, when Christianity is Europe's major tradition.[12]

In fact, modern natural science, like democratic government, found its complete development in England. When historians looked into the reasons for this, for the most part they concluded that it was because England had a stable social environment for several hundred years, suited to nurturing science and democracy. The reason for this is that the British value tradition and plant their feet in tradition to advance stably. The British royal house is a kind of tradition. The Coronation Stone weighing 336 pounds, the theft of which drove the whole country into a panic, is also a tradition.[13] To people outside of Great Britain, these things have no significance at all. To the British, they serve to cement their feeling as a nation and create new vitality, because they are their traditions. The British have never felt that tradition has obstructed their creativity.

Nowadays some people do not recognize national feeling in the first place, because it is something that cannot be observed under a microscope or laid out using symbolic logic. Since the May Fourth movement, the intellectuals who have shown a little talent are like Sun Wukong, able to travel thousands of miles in one somersault:[14] with one kick they overturn Chinese culture and kick aside the farming villages where they were born and raised,[15] believing they represent ignorance due to tradition. Starting with the "Ruist shop," they have tried to overthrow every measure that the people relied on to be persons and that the nation relied on to be a nation for thousands of years. When they overthrow them and bring back the precious medicine from Lingshan,[16] the better shut their doors to live their own lives and pursue their own interests, and the worse keep down the farming communities to satisfy their Westernized urban lifestyle. They make the spiritual condition of society hang emptily, leaving it naked, and giving it a sense of inferiority like original sin. These people did the work of paving the way for the Communist Party and if even now they still don't know how to go back, they are indeed people who have forgotten their roots and don't know how to return.

There are also many people who blame the GMD's past corruption and the fall of the mainland on Chinese culture. I do not believe the Chinese culture alone can solve China's current problems. I further believe that merely endorsing Chinese culture leaves us without any way to prevent abuses of Chinese culture from having an impact. However, at the same time I might point out that blaming the corruption of the GMD and the defeat of the mainland on Chinese culture is blind absurdity. First, one should ask in universities, what percentage of courses and faculty are devoted to Chinese culture? That is, of the people who discourse on Chinese culture, how many do so with a warm and sympathetic attitude? Many people who do textual criticism followed a tradition of attacking Song-Ming pattern learning,[17] and as a result textually criticized China into a mass of blackness with nothing of value. In the GMD government, aside from the military, nine out of ten who occupy important positions are Western educated. How many of them made Chinese culture their responsibility, or used Chinese culture as the yardstick to measure the propriety of their behavior, and in so doing brought about the defeat of the GMD?

One should strictly distinguish between the abuses of a culture that happen and the poisoning that comes about from completely departing from any sort of culture and becoming an animal. Many people are sincere in their opposition to Chinese culture, but their discussion of Western culture is fake. Because of this, I don't look at these fake Westernized people and put the responsibility for the loss of China on Western culture. As far as the political aspect is concerned, the reorganization of the GMD in 1924 followed the Soviet model. After 1931, the GMD followed the Germans. When the Kong and Song families held power, they followed the merchants and compradors.[18] All the way to the escape to Taiwan, there were still people advocating turning back to imitate the Soviet Union or Germany. When these lines of thought are clarified, what do they have to do with Chinese culture? Many people feel the principles upheld by members of the GMD carry a significant flavor of Chinese culture, but they do not fully represent the spirit of Chinese culture. Because of this, it is difficult to say that this is how the spirit of Chinese culture manifests as the spirit of a contemporary political party. For example, the saying, "Obedience is the root of being responsible," naturally has a source. However, from the standpoint of Chinese culture, one should say, "Self-awareness is the root of being responsible." This is because any culture that advocates value internalism will definitely start from self-awareness in this position. And Ruism has always advocated the position that "rightness is internal"[19] and hence "being benevolent comes from oneself. How could it come from others?"[20]

The aforementioned three kinds of opposition to native culture work in concert with each other and fill the air in the schools from junior high school on up, in the government, and in the cities. The result has not been to hasten Westernization, but merely to get rid of any yardstick for a person's character. Intellectuals with any opportunity to join the ruling class slide off the cultural yardstick of character and, feeling justified and secure in the correctness of their conduct, pursue a "real" animalistic life of power, benefit, and enjoyment, instead of a false one (most intellectuals of the period believe morality, etc. are false). Most people in the upper social classes have had higher education. The impending fall of the mainland, the darkness of the government, and accompanying social chaos could seemingly be followed back for five generations. Granting that there are many conditions we are lacking, the foremost lack is the condition of character. I want to suggest the following factors explain the reason for this general atmosphere.

The first is due to the fact that a foreign nationality ruled China during the Qing dynasty and clamped down hard on intellectuals. They threatened them with prisons of words and enticed them with erudition and literary style. The cage of eight-legged essays was the low point, while the corrosion of textual criticism was the superior choice.[21] The textual criticism of the Qing dynasty was initially a tool for scholarship, but the scholars of the time imperceptibly substituted the tool for the purpose. They used words to reject thought, and took pleasure in attacking Song-Ming pattern learning, giving themselves the label "Han learning." But they completely buried the spirit of Chinese culture. This general style bears similarity to the tendencies of modern empiricism, and so the two joined together and turned into "foreign Han learning." Its special characteristic is not admitting the spiritual effect of Chinese culture, but in fact this showed that their spirit was somnolent. The same material in the eyes of cultural revivalists is alive, but to these spiritually somnolent it becomes uninteresting.

For example, the average person thinks the Renaissance started at the beginning of the fourteenth century, extending to the beginning of the sixteenth century. But when this movement began, the only old classical texts the average person could read were nothing more than a few Latin translations from the Middle Ages with which everyone was already thoroughly familiar. Not until the Council of Florence in 1438–39, when Eastern scholars of Greek took the opportunity to come seeking refuge, did research in classical Greece really begin. With the fall of Constantinople in 1453, more classical scholars moved seeking refuge, but by this time the Renaissance had been going on for more than one hundred years. The same Latin translations that people of the Middle Ages repeatedly read chapter and verse were merely commentaries. But at the start of the fourteenth century, beginning with [Giovanni]

Boccacio and [Francesco] Petrarch and other contemporaries, the same old things set off unlimited feelings of gratitude and added a new life to them, starting the trends of modernity. With no other causes, the Italian spirit revived at this period. It's like someone who has recovered from a grave illness: everything he puts in his mouth tastes fresh. Or a child from a rich family, who discovers that the simple rope chairs and paper bedcurtains of the family house, even bamboo shavings and bits of wood, all have their value and organizes them and cherishes them.

China nowadays is the exact opposite. Any culture has its deficiencies and abuses. [Chinese] intellectuals now exclusively look at their own culture in terms of its deficiencies and abuses. It's just like someone whose digestion has been dulled: when he sees some simple home cooking he is disgusted by it, and only wants to eat something spicy or sour. A profligate child considers his family's property utterly worthless, and as soon as he opens his mouth talks about wanting to make a windfall. He laughs at those who build up wealth through industry and thrift, thinking they have no prospects. Actually, the most this kind of person can do is toy with an antique or two to show off.

As long as we look into it carefully, we will find that those people who disparage their own culture can never really get into contact with the mainstream of Western culture. The most they can do is browse through a word or two [of Western languages] or a few formulas, intoxicating themselves with that attitude of toying with an antique or two or eating something spicy or sour. The shallowness of their inclinations and distortions of their spirit of course limit them and shut them off. What is even more despicable, it is not difficult to see that the more someone who seeks the limelight lacks knowledge and doesn't use his brain, the more he wants to be part of something new and stand out as different, coming out with something brand new all the time to cover up the sense of inferiority stemming from his spiritual emptiness. Because these ignoramuses fundamentally do not understand the arduous process of origin and development by which people achieved their present status, so they feel that once one talks about history and culture, one is outdated. Everywhere they listen to meaningless and ungrounded slogans, then brag to themselves how fresh and advanced they are. In fact, they are pitiful creatures who understand nothing.

Next, the May Fourth movement: one could say that it too was a spiritual awakening in modern China. It began from a sincere feeling of patriotism. In this movement, what should have happened was to take the brilliance of China and use it to criticize the abuses that had occurred, and thus welcome Western democracy and science. That would fit with the usual historical course of shifting direction to advance culturally. But the leaders of the time were impatient and couldn't wait to dig out Chinese culture entirely. Then their hatred for the black aspects of the native culture balanced against the patriotic mood of the youth, eroding it. The circumstance of this contradiction could not but make this movement come to naught and even degenerate. Just like the Heavenly Kingdom of Great Peace[22] used the slogan of the nation but only left the outer shell of the "long hairs,"[23] getting rid of the culture of the national spirit. One might say that their failure was destined.

The leaders of this [May Fourth] movement later split into two branches. One branch declared itself liberals. After they achieved their purpose of dismembering [the culture], some went into government, serving as officials without much liberty. Some closed themselves away in their homes engaging in textual criticism. In actuality, they forsook the work of constructing new thought that they should have done after dismembering the old. Gradually, they lost any influence over society and the youth. This is not saying that they intentionally shirked their work, but that they inherited the last stages of Western empiricism, absolutely rejecting idealism in the belief that it is fabricated and deceptive.[24] But, historically, any thought that has social influence includes some elements of idealism in some form. For example, the backbone of Bentham's utilitarianism is "the greatest happiness for the greatest number of people." This illustrates that utilitarianism includes elements of idealism. When these liberals rejected idealism, they unconsciously eliminated thought. After the War of Resistance (1937–1945),[25] when the country was under the oppressive atmosphere of the Communist Party, everyone anticipated someone great in thought, awaiting the return of Mr. Hu Shi from the United States.[26] And what he brought back with him was the Qixiao edition of *The Commentary on the Water Classic*.[27] Mr. Hu himself probably later realized the listless effect this produced on society, especially the youth. This is truly an example of a tragedy of that time.

Then there is the other branch, commonly referred to as the left-leaning branch, which was based in Shanghai, taking root in the universities. Starting in 1926, they propagated the gospel of Marixist-Leninist materialism from every part of the culture, embracing strength of organization and the energy of newly emerged talent. They shaped an idealistic movement without idealism, giving the youth a distant vision of a perfect future. Then the GMD governed the territory, but the CCP already governed people's minds. They divided thought into the two camps of idealism and materialism: materialism being revolutionary while idealism is reactionary. It is simple and clear; not only suitable for students above a junior high school level, but also suitable for those in the GMD who considered themselves clever. Add in the fact that for various reasons, the core anti-Communist power in the GMD mostly came from vulgar materialists. This resulted in a tension where the GMD surrendered to communism in thought while opposing it in action.

Even when many proponents of liberty and democracy did not explicitly articulate a kind of materialism, the basis of their pure empiricism, utilitarianism, and individualism is a slippery slope to an identical vulgar materialism. Additionally, Chinese production lags behind, but China does not lag in the heart-mind to pursue pleasure. Because of envy of Western pleasures as well as loathing for rural life, this is frequently shaped into thoughtless materialism, which contrasts with thoughtful materialism. Then, in all of China, whenever thought comes up, it is mostly one kind of materialism or another. The foremost characteristic of materialism is to not recognize moral, historical, or cultural values. Then naturally Chinese culture is considered to be a backward, feudal thing, which must be eliminated before one can achieve happiness.

The third cause, I fear, is that the scholars in recent years who have debated Chinese culture, regardless of whether they are for it or oppose it, all ignore the differences in the character of cultures, using the same yardstick to exaggerate and jump to conclusions. When they say Chinese culture is backward, they are using Western culture as the yardstick to measure Chinese culture. When they say Chinese culture is superior, they are using Chinese culture as the yardstick to measure Western culture. Little do they understand that measuring two cultures of different characters with the same yardstick cannot help being a kind of mistake. Adding in the fact that everyone has their prejudices and inclines toward one side, and it is even more difficult to have an evenhanded position. For example, in the *Shuowen* it says, "Ruist, comes from 'soft.' A term for practitioners of [ritual] arts,"[28] and so [opponents of Chinese culture] make Ruists out to be a school of musicians out to make an easy living and entirely dismiss the many positive examples of their vigorous spirit. The *Zuo Tradition* says, "Men's heart-minds are different even as their faces are,"[29] and based on this they judge that Chinese culture did not recognize a universal human nature even up to the Spring and Autumn period, intending to attack the Song Ruist doctrine of the identity of human nature and pattern. While they dismiss positive examples, such as, "Humans are born of the spirit of central harmony between heaven and earth,"[30] and, "The people possess this constant way, and love this perfect virtue."[31] The tendency toward this negative angle developed into people such as Cai Shangsi, degenerating to a low point.[32]

Those who take a positive stance often exaggerate a few phrases or a single word from the past. They either say that whatever the West has, we also have and there is no need to seek it outside, or they take up a few empty, grand mantras to contend with the West, believing that we are stronger than others in everything, even superior to everyone. It makes people feel Chinese culture is so blurred and dim, with no prospects.

What we require now is a kind of movement for spiritual awakening. A reaffirmation of Chinese culture is merely the natural manifestation of this awakening and its starting point. We have seen in human history cases of a nation dying out while its culture is carried on by another nation. There are absolutely no instances of a nation that has not died out eliminating the culture it created itself. As soon as someone is born, he is immersed in his own culture. No one can put himself outside it. Even those who adopt a completely negative attitude toward their own culture in reality cannot completely negate it in their own lives. It is just their lack of self-awareness that makes them unconsciously take a stand on the negative aspects of their culture. The better of those who dismiss Chinese culture in one sentence are mainly instances of the Chinese-style bad habits of the literati; the worse of them are merely Chinese-style scoundrels. It is only when someone self-consciously recognizes [the worth] of his own culture that he can take a stand on its positive aspects.

At the same time, when one has a sincerely positive attitude toward one's own culture, one will naturally have a sincerely positive attitude toward other cultures in which people have made achievements in diverse ways, and spare no effort to pursue and absorb their patterns. When we consider the cultural future of China, we should value and treasure anyone with some accomplishment in Western things. However, I resolutely oppose those who take their own narrow view, stand on a minute position with no holistic understanding of the culture, and possess a superficial and unbalanced spiritual condition in which they want to disparage everything in the world, using one [opinion] to discard a hundred other alternatives. They obstruct our rebirth and our progress.

When looking at scholarship on an individual level, most people are one-sided. If one is not one-sided, one cannot be original. But when looking at an individual's life, and especially a nation's life, they must live in a condition closer to completeness, closer to a unity in diversity. For example, England is mainly known for empiricism, but it also has its idealism, religion, ethics, and habits of democratic life, which permeate and correct each other, cooperating to become a more complete culture. When we learn from the West, every person can only learn their one-sided specialty. We should indeed learn from these one-sided studies to fill out and correct the "whole" of our lives. What is truly foolish and absurd is to want to dismiss the whole of our lives in one sentence, and hope that everyone will live in the one-sided area they study. What is more, granting that historically speaking cultural rebirth has to have some external prodding, it cannot depart from the national sentiment. National sentiment is the spiritual power that people on the brink of maturity rely on to stand up. Why did the Renaissance happen in Italy, and why did it begin by aspiring toward Rome and not Greece? These were an effect of a period of national sentiment. So another purpose of our discussing Chinese culture is without doubt to encourage this national sentiment and increase national vitality. To have creativity, a nation has to have vitality.

The Fundamental Character of the Ruist Spirit

Today I want to offer a judgment about the status of China in world cultures. In doing so, it is better to start with where it differs from Western culture rather than where they are alike. I believe that the initial motivations that led to Chinese and Western culture were different, and hence their development proceeded along two different aspects of human nature. Each formed an entirely different character. Naturally, over the long course of history a culture will never only develop along a single line. However, before humanity has become aware of their own deficiencies, their activity will also unconsciously be limited by this one fundamental character. Hence, aspects of the West that have an Asian spirit, such as pantheism or Stoicism, could never develop well. And aspects of China with a Western spirit, such as the Warring States school of names, usually came to an early end. When the fundamental spiritual characters of cultures differ, then even if they have some language and even ideas in them that are the same, this is irrelevant. In the past, Xie Xiandao[33] asked Cheng Yi [1033–1107] about the similarities between the Buddha's words and Ruism. The master said, "Although there are many similarities, they are not in the fundamentals. These all differ,"[34] which illustrates this point. In the following I will try to explain this in detail.

Although modern Western culture has its origins in both Greek and Hebrew culture, what shaped its character of studying *Scientia*[35] and thus formed the main character of modernity were the products of Greek thought. The character of this kind of study has been limited by its early focus of "natural philosophy" since it began, so that human intellect has pursued the analysis of nature. The purpose of this kind of pursuit of analyzing nature was not necessarily to understand it, but the pleasure the Greeks with leisure took in intellectual activity. Hence, the etymology of the word school, which comes from leisure.[36] The Greeks believed the greatest happiness was found in the intellectual activity of contemplation, seeking to understand truth. Intellectual activity must have an external object, and hence the Greek spirit first landed on nature [as an object], and wished to be "children of nature." Although going from a period of cosmology to a period of theories of human nature, the heart-mind of curiosity, "seeking knowledge for its own sake," could not help but be twisted by domestic troubles and foreign threats without end, they still felt the most capable, most useful, and most successful person was the "knower." So the philosophers (*Philosophieren*) are the lovers of knowledge.

This was the origin of Greek education and remained the same from beginning to end. Sophocles said, "The origin of happiness in all things is thought."[37] Aristotle said at the beginning of the *Metaphysics*, "All men naturally desire knowledge. An indication of this is our esteem for the senses; for apart from their use we esteem them for their own sake."[38] For the Greeks, knowledge was beauty and truth. The way knowledge delineated the outside world was reflected onto human life in the way they approached the question of how to live. Just as Windelband said in *A History of Philosophy*: "The philosophy of the eighteenth century, like that of the Greeks, considered it its right and duty to enlighten men with regard to the nature of things, and from this position of insight to rule the life of the individual and of society."[39]

In sum, the primary object of Greek investigation was nature— things external to human beings—and its fundamental direction of effort was toward knowledge. This is the source of the cultural inheritance of modern Europe. However, the Greeks used this kind of investigation for education, and moderns use it to pursue power. Francis Bacon said, "Knowledge is power."[40] This one sentence lays bare the spiritual core of modern Western culture. Education is something that reaches upward, while power is something that reaches forward. When Spain was active in the age of sea exploration, its coins carried the motto, "*Plus ultra* [farther beyond],"[41] which is a sign of the modern spirit. From Greek to modern culture, none of it has been about taking responsibility for people themselves, but is about getting power for humanity. The relation between humanity and nature also changed, day by day going from "children of nature" to conquerors of nature. Relations between people were exactly laid out on the basis of the tools established in the process of overcoming nature, and not on the basis of shared human nature.

It's not that modern Western culture doesn't discuss morality at all, but for the most part it erects the foundation of morality on knowledge. Pascal said, "All our dignity consists, then, in thought. . . . Let us endeavor, then, to think well; this is the principle of morality."[42] The [past] president of the American Historical Association, Carl Lotus Becker [1873–1945], opined that "knowledge" is the modern impulse in his *Freedom and Responsibility* [*in the American Way of Life*].[43] Intellect, which produces knowledge, is the principle of modern life. Naturally, one must have "integrity and good will" in addition to knowledge, but these too depend on the intellect.[44] In truth, one has to seek for the origins of modern Western morality in religion. The responsibility for morality borne by its scholarship is light, even to the point of not being responsible for it at all. And the value of a person's existence is not in his life itself for the most part, but in his persistence in the pursuit of things and in his achievements in studying things. Human value is expressed by how things are valued. The achievement of Western culture is here, and so is its problem.

The spirit of Chinese culture, which is to say Ruist culture, forms a perfect contrast with what I described above. The Greek motivation for seeking knowledge was the sense of wonder at nature made possible by leisure and the outcome of pursuing knowledge. This gave rise to cosmology in its philosophy. The practical application of the discovery of cosmological laws became science. Chinese scholarly thought originated in concern for human life. I have already said a great deal on this point, and it has almost become a conclusive judgment.[45] The "Great Appendix" to the *Changes* says, "Did not the makers of the *Changes* become concerned about calamity?"[46] It was not just those who made the *Changes*. Concern was the motivation and driving force for the pursuit of learning.

As for the content of learning, in the West it is primarily understanding nature, but in Ruism it is primarily standards for one's behavior. In the *Analects* it says:

> Duke Ai asked which disciples were fond of learning. Kongzi anwered, "There was one fond of learning, Yan Hui. He did not transfer his anger, nor make the same mistake twice."[47]
>
> Kongzi said, "The superior man does not seek to be full when eating, nor seek ease in dwelling. He is industrious in action and deliberate in speech. He goes to those who possess the way in order to be corrected. Such a person may be called fond of learning."[48]
>
> Kongzi said, "Young people should be filial at home and respectful of their older brothers when away. They should be discreet and honest and care for the masses but be particularly close with those who are benevolent. If they still have energy after accomplishing this, then they can use it to study cultural patterns."[49]
>
> Zixia said, "If someone honors worthiness and is indifferent to sexual attractiveness, is able to use all his power to serve his parents and fully exerts himself to serve his ruler, and is true to his word in his interactions with friends, then even if he says he has not studied, I would certainly say he has."[50]

What I've just quoted is the scholarly style of the Zhu and Si river valley,[51] which shaped the main content and character of Warring States Ruism that did not change significantly for two thousand years. Zhu Xi's regulations for the White Deer Grotto academy as well as Wang Yangming's tenets given to students at Longchang both adhered to this established practice without deviation. It is perfectly clear that this is very different from the spirit and target of Plato's academy as well as modern universities.

The fundamental efforts of Ruists may be summarized in the following two categories. One is to distinguish people from regular animals on the basis of the doctrine that human nature is good and morality is internal. They aim to build people up into flawless, perfect sages or benevolent people who take responsibility for the world. ("As for being

sagely or benevolent, how dare I put myself at that level?")[52] The other
is to objectify internal morality into daily use in human relations. From
practicing it in human relations, one then deepens it into "love that
bestows goodness,"[53] making relations between people and between people
and things into a kind of benevolent relationship. The internal nature
of morality due to the goodness of human nature is the benevolence of
the human heart-mind. Benevolence is put into use by practicing it in
human relations. Hence, these two aspects constitute harmonizing the
internal and external into one (the Way of harmonizing inner and outer)
and the identity of root and branch, and cannot be separated.

Although the doctrine of good human nature was clearly expressed
beginning with Mengzi, it is the orthodoxy concerning human nature
in China, not something created first by Mengzi. There was a great
controversy in Mengzi's time: whether human nature was good, bad,
both, or neither. Mengzi began from two points: that "[p]eople all have
heart-minds that are not unfeeling toward others," and that people all
have feelings of alarm and compassion, shame and dislike, deference, and
right and wrong, which shows that benevolence, rightness, ritual propriety,
and wisdom "are not welded onto me from outside, but are inherent to
me."[54] From these he reached the final conclusion that human nature
is good, and that "everyone can be a Yao or Shun [a sage]";[55] everyone
does not need to rely on outside power and can honorably stand up by
themselves. We need only have a little understanding of the arduousness
of the way the world's great religions look to outside power, the power
of gods or God, to bring people to stand up on something welded from
outside. Then we can understand the greatness of the Ruist creed, which
is rooted in oneself.

Yet Mengzi never denied the animalistic side of human beings.
He said, "That by which people differ from birds and beasts is slight,"[56]
showing that people do not differ from animals in many respects. However, if one wants to stabilize that which makes human beings human,
one can start from that slight difference and affirm human nature.
Extending Mengzi's meaning, people have a nature identical with animals
and a nature different from animals. Because it is identical to animals,
one cannot point to this part as human beings' unique characteristics,
or human nature. One has to start from where they differ from other
animals, from what human beings alone have, in order to reveal their
unique characteristics. These unique characteristics are good, and are
shared by all people, and therefore Mengzi affirmed that human nature

is good. Hence, he said, "As far as their inherent dispositions, they can become good. This is what I mean by saying [human nature] is good."[57] But in order for people to extend and fill out this slight goodness, and not let it be occluded and swallowed by their animalistic aspects—what is elsewhere called not letting the human heart-mind endanger the heart-mind of the Way—it is necessary to undergo moral cultivation and "overcome the self and return to ritual."[58]

Behind "overcoming the self and returning to ritual" there must after all be something that acts as "the master." Ruists believe that what acts as the master is the heart-mind. Each person's heart-mind serves as the master of that person. Hence, Ruist moral cultivation aims at correcting the heart-mind, nurturing the heart-mind, seeking to put the heart-mind at ease, taking hold of and preserving this heart-mind[59] (when one takes hold of it, then one preserves it), and making the heart-mind "remain in the chest cavity"[60]—making the heart-mind always the master of the person. By "taking a stand on what is greater,"[61] one makes the desires of the five senses and numerous parts that are identical to those of animals all take orders from the heart-mind. Thereupon not only is the heart-mind the heart-mind of moral pattern, the five senses and numerous parts possess moral pattern as well: this is what [Mengzi] meant by "fulfilling this body" ("Only the sage can fulfill the potential of this body").[62] Taking hold of, preserving, and nurturing the heart-mind are easier when not in contact with things, and yet the heart-mind has to be in contact with things. When it contacts things, then the feelings of happiness, anger, grief, joy, liking, disliking, and desiring inevitably arise,[63] and people's behavior gets redirected by these feelings. The feelings are influenced by matter (that is, physiological responses such as internal secretions), making it easy to err either to excess or deficiency.[64] Then when the heart-mind is directed by the feelings, its original substance becomes impossible to discern.[65]

The work of seeking to put the heart-mind at ease should be found in transforming matter.[66] Kongzi said, "Set your heart-mind on the Way, abide in virtue, rely on benevolence, and practice the arts," and "Find inspiration in the Odes, take one's stand on ritual, and complete oneself through music."[67] Practicing the arts and completing oneself through music are both ways of reconciling nature and feelings to transform the matter of one's physiology. When Kongzi talked with his disciples about how to orient one's heart-mind, he only praised Zeng Dian. This is because what Zeng Dian said illustrated good nature and feelings.[68]

Ruism does not advocate cutting off the feelings and eradicating desire, nor to let the physiological self be completely separated from the moral self, in order to avoid a sense of alienation from actual life. Rather, it advocates using learning to transform the matter [of the person], leading the feelings to follow the nature, so the physiological self completely transforms into the moral self. Then in the person's actual life, which is rational life, he lives up to the name of "rational animal." Therefore, Cheng Hao said, "Only study that reaches to the point of transforming one's embodiment is an achievement,"[69] exactly expressing this idea.

This kind of moral cultivation aimed at concentrating and molding the internal moral nature went on to develop into Song-Ming pattern learning and heart-mind learning,[70] which formed the basis of Chinese "moral humanism." Although Western humanism was on the one hand a descent from being centered on gods to being centered on humanity, on the other hand it too aimed to distinguish human beings from other animals in order to put the status of that which makes them human on firm footing. Yet this is a humanism primarily based on intellectual ability. Hence, the great masters of the Renaissance for the most part expressed themselves through their multifaceted talents. Although the Chinese side did not slight talent, its fundamental spirit was absolutely not expressed through talents. Hence, the passage from the *Analects*: "A high minister asked Zigong, 'Is your master a sage? Why does he have so many talents?' Zigong answered, 'Certainly Heaven has given to him without limit. He is nearly a sage, and in addition has many talents.' When Kongzi heard about this he said, 'The high minister knows me, doesn't he? When I was young I was lowly, so I became good at many minor matters. Does the superior man have many skills? No, he does not.'"[71] One can see a very obvious contrast here.

If internal morality is not objectified to the external, then it is not truly practiced. Hence, from the beginning Ruism has not adopted an attitude of "deep observation"[72] but takes everything back to "committed action." The five methods of study listed in the *Mean*—"learn broadly, inquire intently, reflect cautiously, distinguish clearly, and act with commitment"[73]—are not on par, but are a process of advancement. Committed action is the culmination of the first four. To act with commitment, one must objectify internal morality. Hence, Ruists especially stressed human relations and daily application. Human relations mean correct relationships between people; daily application means behavior in daily life. Each person has a certain principle they should fulfill in their relationships with others that are natural or that they inevitably enter into in the course of daily life. These principles are inherent in human nature. The realization of internal morality is in fulfilling human relations and respecting affairs (*Analects*: "respect [government] affairs and be trustworthy"; also, "in carrying out business be respectful");[74] only this can be called fulfilling the nature. Furthermore, fulfilling human relations can subsume respecting affairs, and so human relations are especially important.

Paternal and fraternal relationships are the foundation of human relations and the spontaneous visible inklings of human nature.[75] Being filial and fraternal is the foundation of human relations. "Master You said, 'The superior man focuses on the root. When the root is established, then the Way grows from it. Being filial and fraternal: are these not the root of benevolence?' "[76] Mengzi was the one to mark the term *human relations* formally, as when he said, "The three dynasties[77] also used the word *xue* for a kind of school. In all cases, its purpose was to clarify human relations," and, "Shun was wise about the myriad things and closely observed human relations."[78] Human relations as Mengzi spoke of them were also founded on being filial and fraternal. When he said, "No children in arms don't know to love their parents, and when they grow a little older, none do not know to respect their elder brothers,"[79] he was pointing to the goodness in human nature through filial and fraternal feelings.

He also said, "The substance of benevolence is serving one's parents. The substance of rightness is following one's elder brothers. The substance of wisdom is knowing these two and not abandoning them. The substance of ritual is regulating and adorning these two. The substance of music is delighting in these two."[80] We can see from these that filial and fraternal feelings are the universal character of the Ruist doctrine. Human nature with benevolence at its core is kept internally and is not apparent. What are apparent are the unanticipated feelings of loving parents and respecting older brothers. Looking closely and grasping firmly at these sorts of places, the benevolence of human nature can find its place, its basis, and one can then extend it out to humanity. Rarely does what one treats as important become unimportant, or what one treats as unimportant become important.[81] This is an iron-clad fact. The *Odes* says, "The filial son's behavior is not lacking, and he will be granted everlasting blessings,"[82] and so one can understand that "care for one's own elders and extend that to others' elders; care for one's own children and extend that to others' children"[83] is the natural extension of benevolent virtue in human nature.

Hence, filial and fraternal feelings are the starting point and fountainhead of human love. "Everyone treat their parents as parents and their elders as elders."[84] This means for everyone to make their already formed and immediate relationships into benevolent relationships. This would make a society constituted by benevolent virtue and warm feelings, and then naturally the world would be pacified.[85] In his obituary for his brother Cheng Hao, Cheng Yi wrote, "Fulfilling one's nature and perfecting one's destiny is necessarily founded on filial and fraternal feelings." Later, someone asked him, "How can one fulfill nature and perfect destiny without being cognizant of filial and fraternal feelings?" He replied,

> Later people distinguished nature and destiny from ordinary affairs. Nature, destiny, being filial, and being fraternal are just one unified thing. One can fulfill nature and perfect destiny through being filial and fraternal. Wetting down and sweeping the floor, answering and responding, and fulfilling nature and perfecting destiny are also one unified thing.[86] Among these, there is no distinction of root and branch or refined and coarse. But later people in their discussions of nature and destiny distinguished them from ordinary affairs and made them lofty and distant. That is why when I bring up being filial and fraternal, I discuss them from what is near to people. However, our time is not without filial and fraternal people who cannot fulfill nature and perfect destiny. This is because they follow them without understanding.[87]

According to another meaning of "I discuss them from what is near to people," his discussion of filial and fraternal feelings was in fact not only about them.

In the May Fourth movement, scholars on two different sides[88] only differed in degree in their opposition to being filial; they did not differ in substance. This knocked down the final Great Wall of Chinese culture and attacked the last line of defense of what makes human beings human. This joint offensive led to its natural result of struggling against parents, brothers, and elders under the Communist Party. Can we not say this represents the end of the way of human life? Facing this reality, those fake moderns who disparage being filial and fraternal as relics of feudal culture, and hence call Ruism a feudal culture, should do some self-reflection.

From the above we can see that the practice of Ruist internal morality always goes back to human relations. And when it comes to real achievement, for the most part it develops three aspects: the first is the family, the second is politics (the state), and the third is transformative education (society).

Three of the five relations[89] in Ruism fall within the scope of the family, and so "fulfilling relations" in the first place means making the family into a natural group of moral practice. Because the nucleus of Ruist thought is benevolence, and due to the character of benevolence, Ruists tend toward being dignified, at ease, and sincere, seldom changing. When Kongzi said, "The benevolent love mountains. . . . The benevolent are tranquil,"[90] this is probably what he meant. Because of this, the Ruist spirit does not put importance on change, but rather bringing out the significant implications in what is already there and giving them new value. They are gradually changed without realizing it. This form of effort has its successes and its failures, which I will not go into here.

What we should pay attention to here is that the family is humanity's natural form of association. Ruism infuses this natural association with a new life of moral practice; that is, the "rightness of filial and fraternal feeling" mentioned above. Filial and fraternal behavior in the house is, as it is put in the Great Learning, benevolence and deference: "When one household is benevolent, benevolence arises in the state. When one household is deferential, deference arises in the state."[91] When each person fulfills the duties of human life and obtains the values of human life in his family, then because he has a family, his life has space and time for [the realization of] values. Extending these vertically [through time] from the actual family, then "one's roots and branches [descendants] extend for a hundred generations,"[92] and people's lives achieve a secure place without limit in time. Expanding them horizontally [in space], "the clan is made harmonious and the nation is brought together," to the point where "all within the four seas are brothers,"[93] and people's lives achieve a secure place without limit in space. The family that the Ruist spirit connects to is itself a perfect religion without flaw, and so needs no other religion. In their realization, it is just the two words, filial and fraternal, that come from the natural revelation of the heart-mind, and their practice is where human feelings find peace. Hence, starting from the Western Han period (206 BCE–9 CE), the Ruist spirit saturated society through the family, its impact the broadest and deepest.

There is a popular folk couplet: "Enlightened instruction in the western capital; filial sons and fraternal brothers toil in the fields." These words fit very well with the guiding principle of the two centuries of Western Han, and also encompass the fundamental character of the Ruist spirit. Promoted through the Western Han dynasty, the Ruist spirit took root in the family, and thereafter the family became the firm stronghold of the union of production and culture in Chinese society. From then on, the Chinese nation had its deep power of coalescence and continuity, and completed its unique national character of dignified tenacity. Hence, it is not without reason that the Chinese nationality bears the permanent name of "Han people."[94]

Over the past two thousand years, the Chinese have met with defeat by foreigners four times and the domestic massacres are countless, but after a brief period of cultivating a different kind of life, they were able to return to their old ways. They are not like Western nations, who often die out once they face major catastrophe. This is probably because when Chinese society faces a major catastrophic threat, everyone can retreat to security in the family and circle around their ancestry, which forms a last line of defense against disaster. Once the disaster has lessened, they can extend out from their family and ancestry to restore the wholeness of production and culture in society. Furthermore, when the world is declining and the Way is weakening, and the literati and gentry have become cultural criminals, then the true Chinese spirit usually reveals itself through simple men and women, who through the integrity of their thought "hold to the virtuous Way even to death"[95] to preserve the life of the nation. This circumstance has not changed up to recent times. This too shows the depth and profundity of the diffusion of the Ruist spirit from the family on down.

Since the May Fourth movement, people have only seen the abuses within the family and have not understood the fundamental spirit of the Chinese family and the responsibility it has fulfilled to preserve and continue the nation. They felt that if only they could destroy the family, then the idea of country and a social spirit could immediately be established. It is really worth reflecting deeply once again on the present circumstances. In his 1948 work *The Reconstruction of Humanity*, the chair of the Harvard University sociology department P[itirim] A. Sorokin advocated that Western culture and society must be reconstructed. And social reconstruction in the first place needs a rational family to be the starting point for a new society. He felt deeply that the lack of a moral, secure family was a grave crisis.[96] In addition, some people believe that the reason Great Britain could progress stably was because the British make family the fortress of life. Hence, they were unlike other countries that lacked a rational family life, which led to society being rootless and adrift, with revolution happening at every turn. All of this can provide us material for reflection.

Taking responsibility for human relations, Ruists naturally have to take responsibility for government. However, due to the limitations of the historical conditions, even though Ruism had pure political theory, this theory always sought its realization by taking the standpoint of the rulers, and lacked struggle for realization from the standpoint of the ruled. Due to this, the idea of political subjectivity was never established and they were unable to go from government for the people to democracy.[97] The only effect they had was weakening the evils of the rulers; they could not entirely remove the problem of the rulers' evils. Instead, they were frequently easy to make use of for rulers who overstepped their bounds. I already showed this in "The Construction and Advancement of Ruist Political Thought,"[98] (*Democratic Review* vol. 3, no. 1) and I will not repeat the details here.

Here I should only supplement that article with this point: premodern Ruist thought on the one hand took responsibility for government, and on the other hand could not grasp the political initiative. And thus in government Ruist thought was twisted and destroyed. This frequently impacted the normal development of Ruist thought, causing the endless production of numerous thieving followers who sold out its soul. One may truly say this was a great cultural and historical misfortune. The clearest examples are the later years of the Eastern Han, Tang, and Ming dynasties, when a minority of eunuchs felt that the tastes of typical scholars who upheld integrity and honesty in government (including what is today called public opinion) were not in accord with theirs, whose word was law. Only modern totalitarians can compare with the cruelty of the way they murdered those scholars.

Due to the disaster of the Proscription,[99] the brilliant and talented fled to mysterious learning[100] and Buddhism, and the central plain of China fell into the hands of barbarians.[101] The corruption at the end of the Tang produced Feng Dao's type.[102] By the Five Dynasties the Way of the sages[103] had died out, which led to the Manchu invasion and the

Qing dynasty. Their rule of more than two hundred years caused the spirit of Chinese culture to enter into a state of slumber, transforming and turning into the unprecedented reactionary movement toward dictatorship of today. Therefore, the true Ruists of today must exert their effort toward democratization. There are those who doubt whether Ruism is compatible with democratic government, but this is a discourse that understands neither Ruism nor democracy. All doctrines that are established on the basis of internal values in thought will absolutely not accept external authority.

Modern European democracy is based on the Enlightenment of the eighteenth century, and the backbone of Enlightenment thought was natural law. Natural law philosophy originated in Rome, and this aspect of Roman thought had its source in the later Greek philosophy of Stoicism. The combination of utilitarianism, which is an inheritor of natural law thought, capitalism, and democracy is a unique product of England, but this particular combination is not necessary. The Jeffersonian democratic movement in the United States was influenced by natural law but not by utilitarianism. Hence, the idealism of American democracy is even richer. Prior to the eighteenth century, Martin Luther's Reformation and the freedom of conscience that came with it had an influence on modern democracy which no one can deny. And Luther was in reality inspired by German mysticism.[104] Also called pantheism, German mysticism is certainly a doctrine of internality of values. The internality of values in Ruist morality has already been expounded earlier. The Ruist spirit of "self-rootedness" has no need for an external God. So how could it accept an external authority with the power of coercion in politics?

Specifically in regard to this, I quote a section of Wang Yangming's *A Record of Practice*:

> [Xu] Ai asked, "In [the *Great Learning*] where it says, 'consists in having affection for the people,' Zhu Xi says that it should be read as 'renewing the people,' citing the later passage which says, 'enact renewing the people,' which seems to be evidence for this. Sir, you think it should follow the old version and keep it as 'having affection for the people.' Does this also have evidence for it?"
>
> Wang said, "The 'renew' in 'enact renewing the people' actually means the people renew themselves, different than the renew in 'consists in renewing the people': how could this be

evidence? The word 'enact' is the opposite of 'be intimate'; it does not have the meaning of having affection. The section below about governing the state and pacifying the world all sheds no light on the word 'renew.' As the text says, 'The superior man treats worthies as worthy and treats his relatives as intimate; the petty people delight in what delights them and benefit from what they find beneficial . . . as holding a baby . . . love what the people love and hate what the people hate . . . ': all these express being a parent to the people. All have the meaning of having affection.[105]

According to Wang's account, which explains "enact renewing the people" as "the people renew themselves," "renew themselves" means each of the common people stands up on his own. The "consists in" of "consists in renewing the people" means that political force does the work of renewing the people. Using modern terminology, it means political education and reform movements. None of these fit with Ruism's internalism, nor are they accepted in Ruist political thought. The way Ruism honored kings and disparaged hegemons, honored rule by virtue and disparaged rule by force, all derives from this. Ruist political thought must result in democratic government, and democratic government should take Ruist thought as its spiritual basis. All objective scholars devoted to learning and profound in thought must not take this as an overly forced interpretation.

In fact, the Ruist spirit of responsibility to humanity has, in addition to the two aspects already mentioned, another facet which is often neglected and which is truly its greatest: the facet of the spirit of transformative education. Many people say Kongzi was China's earliest educator. The word *educator* isn't exactly wrong, but it isn't exactly right either. Kongzi's spirit was actually the educative spirit of a great religious leader. Without relying on anything else, he had the thought of taking pity on humanity and took on all responsibility for them, thinking to teach and transform them. This was based on the social plane, inspiring through good faith and reasoning—entirely different than political measures. All the great world religions had to be established by making their doctrine concrete through this kind of educative spirit. Then they could call out to the human soul and meld together with it into one. Otherwise, any creed remains just talk, without much relation to people.

The reason Ruism could take the place of religion is not only because of its self-rooted moral internalism that allowed people not to need religion. It was also because of Kongzi's educative spirit, which was identical to that of the founders of the great religions, making his doctrine concrete in the Chinese nationality. This is not something with which a common philosophical doctrine can compare. Kongzi of course wanted to be employed: "If there were someone to employ me, could I not make a Zhou in the east?"[106] Politics is the shortcut for realizing ideals. However, politics depends on something else before it can be put into action, while transformative education is the work of one heart-mind and full effort can be exerted immediately.[107] Hence, Kongzi adopted an attitude of adapting to circumstances when taking or leaving employment: "When employed, put the Way into practice. When dismissed, hide it away."[108] "When the state has the Way, show yourself. When it lacks the Way, conceal yourself."[109] However, when it came to teaching others, then "instructing without tiring" often appeared along with "studying without wearying,"[110] with the same importance. The faith in and grand aspirations for humanity expressed in "With education, there are no categories"[111] can truly embrace all living beings to ascend to the sagely realm together. The *Analects* states, "I have never refused instruction to anyone who brings me as little as some dried meat."[112] Also, "It was difficult to talk with the people of Hu Village. Kongzi saw a boy from there and his disciples were confused. Kongzi said, 'I approved of admitting him without approving of what he might do when he leaves. When someone purifies himself to come to me, I accept this purification. I make no guarantees about what happens when he leaves.'"[113] Only this spirit of taking responsibility for humanity at the social level truly shows the fundamental effort and greatness involved in the concept of "human relations."

The Song-Ming study of Pattern and nature[114] was not only a resurgence of the Ruist spirit, but also a revitalization of its educative spirit. The lectures of Song-Ming Ruists represented a kind of educative spirit; to use contemporary language, they were a type of social thought movement. This spirit could cause a social object to arise, shape a social force, and establish another standard and tendency for humanity outside the court. Servants of despots, eunuchs, and the emperors' favorites and toadies all thought these lectures should be forbidden. The facts of this can all be investigated and judged by past and present. Cheng Yi once said,

A worthy person occupies the lower position, so how can he put himself forward and seek a position from the ruler? If he does seek a position, there is no way to trust him. The reason that the ancients invariably waited for the ruler to extend utmost respect and perfect ritual propriety before going to him was not that they wanted to elevate themselves as great. It was because if the ruler did not have the attitude of honoring the virtue and delighting in the Way like this, he was not worth serving.[115]

Furthermore:

When the teacher [Cheng Yi] was in the [official] seat of instruction . . . he did not seek a title for his wife. Fan Chunfu asked the reason. The teacher said, "When appointed I had no previous official position, and I still declined three times before accepting the order. Is there any reason I should now seek a title for my wife?" Fan said, "Nowadays people line up for beg for favors from the emperor. Does this conform with rightness or not? People all think they deserve it, and it does no harm." The teacher said, "It's only that officials now make a habit of begging, and easily turn into beggars."[116]

This was a common attitude toward the government on the part of Neo-Ruists. Another aspect of this attitude was using lectures for social responsibility. Zou Shouyi's "Preface to [Wang] Yangming's Literary Records" has a passage that says,

At that time there was someone who praised the old master [Wang], saying, "Of the ancients famous through the ages, some were famous for writings, someone for political service, some for moral integrity, and some for meritorious behavior. And the master [Wang] has achieved all of these. He is only missing the step of lecturing to be a complete man." The old master laughed and said, "I do wish to engage in the step of lecturing. Then even without the other four, I would not be ashamed to be called a complete man."[117]

This kind of spirit of Wang's in which lecturing is more important than meritorious government service was also common to Song-Ming Neo-Ruists.

The influence of this spirit was to give society a rational tendency outside of politics and the court, and to give form to a rational force that caused them to see despotic rulers and toadying followers of eunuchs as thorns in their sides, such that it was imperative to make use of any possible reason to prohibit and eliminate them. In incidents such as the Yuanyou proscription,[118] the banning of the false teachings in the Southern Song,[119] and the repression of the Donglin Academy at the end of the Ming,[120] those who carried out these actions naturally had their explanations for it. But from a historical perspective, they were baser and uglier than dogs or pigs. I hope this kind of episode will be forbidden for all of history.

At the same time, if China wants to survive in today's world it must have a social force that can stand up, in addition to government, that can stand on an equal footing with politics and hence be marked off from politics with a certain boundary. Then the country will be content and can grow its power. In the circumstances of being behind industrially, free academic discourse in society to arouse the human heart-mind, establish an ethos, and shape the cultural power of society to propel the other aspects is the precondition for our society to be able to stand up. This is the way forward for Chinese culture and for Chinese intellectuals, and is also the touchstone for determining whether the Chinese government will be a "big Jie" or a "little Jie."[121] So I don't feel what I've said here goes too far.

Ruist thought on human relations starts from the objectification of internal morality, ramifying to take responsibility for humanity. It starts from filial and fraternal feelings and culminates in kindness to people and animals, "becoming one body with all things between heaven and earth."[122] This process is merely the effect of putting the benevolent heart-mind into practice and connecting them together all at once. There is no separation at all here. I will only quote a section of Wang Yangming's *Questions on the Great Learning* as proof:

> The great person takes all things between heaven and earth to be one body. He looks at all under heaven as one family and all of China as one person. Anyone who distinguishes self and other on the basis of separate physical forms is a petty person. The reason the great person takes all things between heaven and earth to be one body is not because he intends to: the benevolence of his heart-mind is simply fundamentally

like this in being one body with all things. How could it only
be the great person? The heart-mind of petty persons is also
like this, but they make it petty themselves.

And so the fact that when they see a child about to
fall into a well and have a response of alarm and compassion shows that their benevolence forms one body with the
child. But a child is of the same species. When they hear
the sad cries and see the frightened appearance of birds and
beasts, they will not be able to bear it. This shows that their
benevolence forms one body with birds and beasts. But birds
and beasts are also sentient. When they see plants and trees
destroyed and broken, they will pity them. This shows that
their benevolence forms one body with plants and trees.
But plants and trees are also alive. When they see tiles and
stones smashed and broken, they will regret the loss. This
shows that their benevolence forms one body with tiles and
stones. Even the heart-mind of a petty person must have this
benevolence that forms one body with things. It is rooted in
Heaven-decreed nature, spontaneously giving off numinous
light that cannot be concealed.[123]

Furthermore, the general pattern of the five relationships is a
concrete implementation of the Ruist spirit. When a spirit is realized
in a general pattern, on the one hand it becomes more practical but on
the other hand it will gradually ossify and become unable to adapt and
change with the times. The doctrine of the five relationships took shape
more than two thousand years ago. Naturally, it cannot completely suit
the present day and has some flaws that require critique. Moreover, while
the five relationships took final shape in the Han dynasty, by this point
the original spirit had already begun to depart. In Kong-Meng thought,
dedication and filiality are kinds of virtues. In human relationships, they
are often contrasted with speech, as in, "Treat the ruler as a ruler, treat
the minister as a minister, treat the father as a father, and treat the son
as a son."[124] They are not based on distinguishing higher or lower and
leader or follower, nor based on external relationships. Han Ruists had
to adapt to requirement of the new political unity, and so in the *White
Tiger Hall Discussions* created the doctrine of the three bonds.[125] What
was a virtue of human nature intangibly became a matter of rights and
duties of external relationships. Then it lost the original significance of

human relations and at times became a tool to suppress human nature. This is the main point worth bringing up for research. However, this also has to originate in the basic spirit of five relationships thought, understanding the location of its true effort. Then critique can have the effect of expanding it and giving it new life. This is something toward which some people should exert themselves.

Limitations within Achievement

As explained above, Ruism explicates human nature from the aspect of benevolent and moral nature—these are one facet of human nature. Science cannot be achieved through this facet. Science has to rely on the development of another aspect of human nature, the cognitive nature (*zhixing* 知性), which "pursues knowledge for the sake of knowledge." Absorbed into the object, the cognitive function which pursues knowledge asks only whether its grasp of the object is true or not, and one may say that it adopts an amoral attitude. Hence, the development of the cognitive function follows the nature of the object itself, making inferences based on that. The cognitive function finds its satisfaction in the grasp of the object's law-like character. Therefore, "nature" as perceived by the cognitive function has no relation to its subjectivity; it is a purely objective nature. The mission of the cognitive function is only to plumb the object completely. In regard to the result of this contemplation, the question of the thinking subject having responsibility to put its knowledge into practice never arises. Because of this, contemplation can remove the limitations invisibly imposed by the will to act and extend its understanding step by step.

This is the backbone of Western culture and the basis for scientific achievement. The definition of philosophy that Schwegler opened with in his history of Western philosophy was, "To philosophize is to reflect; to examine things, in thought."[126] Naturally, as a definition of philosophy this requires some supplementing. However, as an explanation for what this branch of study is in Western culture, then it is a simple, clear general account.

Ruism by no means slights the cognitive function. Kongzi and Mengzi often spoke of benevolence and wisdom together. The *Mean* calls wisdom, benevolence, and courage the three universal virtues.[127] However, wisdom as Ruists call it always takes the standpoint of morality and moral practice, hence Ruist wisdom is the numinous light illuminating the internal moral subject. Extending and broadening it, it rests at making an effort on human relations. Its primary mission is not to look outside to grasp or analyze an object that has nothing to do with [moral] practice. Hence, Ruist wisdom and Western wisdom are fundamentally different in character. Kongzi said, "A benevolent person finds ease in benevolence. A wise person makes use of benevolence."[128] Mengzi said, "The substance of wisdom is knowing these two [serving one's parents and following one's older brothers] and not abandoning them."[129] The three universal virtues of courage, benevolence, and wisdom all center on benevolence; they are not on equal footing. In the *Analects*, when Kongzi said, "I once spent an entire day without eating and an entire night without sleeping to think. It was no use. It is better to study,"[130] the "no use" here means regarding morality. In Western culture, thought goes on without asking whether it's useful or not. And so Ruist wisdom only produces moral achievements; as to the achievements [brought about by] realizing morality, it does not directly lead to scientific achievement.

Cheng Yi explained investigating things[131] as follows: "Investigate and extend to things,"[132] and, "Above each thing there is a pattern, and one must exhaustively understand this pattern."[133] Zhu Xi adopted this to supplement the *Great Learning*'s definitions of investigating things and extending knowledge:

> What is meant by "the extension of knowledge consists in investigating things" [in the *Great Learning*] is that if I want to extend my knowledge, it consists in exhaustive understanding of the pattern of a certain thing. No one does not have knowledge in their heart-mind's clearest intelligence. No thing in the world does not have its pattern. It is only that there are patterns that people have not exhaustively understood and so their knowledge is incomplete. This is why the initial teaching of the *Great Learning* must be to make scholars take the existing knowledge of things in the world that everyone has, and [use it] to add to their exhaustive understanding to seek to reach the end point. When effort is applied for a long time, then one day they will suddenly achieve comprehensive knowledge that will reach into the surface and interior, the fine and the coarse, of all things. The great functions of the entire body of their heart-minds will be illuminated.[134]

According to the Cheng-Zhu account of investigating things and extending knowledge, one must distinguish subject and object, and then Pattern has already become something objective and external. Continuing this path had the possibility of developing Western-style epistemology as well as turning into science, and they made this attempt. Hence, Master Xiong Shili only adopted the Cheng-Zhu explanation of investigating things and extending knowledge in his *Essential Instructions for Reading the Classics*,[135] intending thereby to make the transition to science. His effort was painstaking. However, there is a point here that does not admit ambiguity: the "things" Cheng and Zhu referred to still mainly meant human relations and not natural objects. The purpose of investigating things and extending knowledge was still moral practice. So in his answer to Lin Qian's letter Zhu Xi wrote, "Extending one's knowledge is for the sake of realizing in practice."[136] We can see that although Cheng-Zhu came close to Western epistemology in places, the cognitive function was never liberated from morality in the end.

To the last, Zhu Xi's idea of "exhaustively investigating Pattern" never went beyond reading books. In the document he submitted to Emperor Xiaozong [1127–1194] he wrote, "In the way of study, nothing comes before exhaustively investigating Pattern, and the essence of this lies in reading books."[137] It is easy to see that his research motivation and object was very different from notable scientific examples: Isaac Newton observing an apple falling and coming up with universal gravitation, James Watt noticing boiling water forcing up the lid of a kettle and inventing the steam engine, and Francis Bacon's death. In order to test whether freezing could preserve meat, Bacon personally bought and killed a turkey, stuffing snow in its cavity, and then caught a chill and died.[138]

Wang Yangming said of Zhu Xi, "He sought for the highest good in each thing and affair, but thus put rightness outside."[139] From the standpoint of the fundamental Ruist spirit, I believe Wang was correct. The *Analects* states, "Zixia said, 'Even in minor ways there are things worth looking at. But in extending effort to what is remote, there is the concern of getting stuck, and so the superior man does not do this.' "[140] Zhu commented, "Minor ways include activities such as farming, gardening, medicine, and divination."[141] The backbone of Western learning was considered to be minor in China, while the efforts of the sages in China were considered to be nothing more than common sense in the West. The directions these cultures took from the beginning were different, and then they ended up distant and incommensurable. This is something toward which those concerned about our culture today should make an effort.

People today often say that the reason China could not achieve science is because it lacked methodology, such as logic. This claim is also ambiguous. The fundamental spirit of Ruism is as described above. The lack of logic in China certainly does not mean that Chinese thought was in a state of immaturity and could not produce logic, but rather that the method required by Ruism lay elsewhere and not in logic. The preliminary approach of study in Ruism, including things such as broad learning and interrogation of a topic, are typical.

I believe the two words "embodied recognition"[142] can represent the unique method for advancement of the Ruist spirit. Emphasizing quietude, emphasizing reverence, preserving and nurturing, and critically examining oneself all come back to embodied recognition.[143] Cheng Hao said, "Although I have learned things through study, the two words 'Heavenly Pattern' were obtained from my own embodied recognition."[144] Embodied recognition is an inward cognition that concentrates on self-illumination. It is not a process of a subject grasping an object; still less is it grasping an object's law-like character through analysis. It is the subject grasping itself. It is moral subjectivity revealing itself from among the "quasi-subjectivity" of human desires, and being affirmed and extended.

From a different aspect, embodied recognition is a process of taking emotions and thoughts that arise from contact with things and events of the world and shining the inner light of the enlightened feelings of the heart-mind on them, verifying whether they can be at peace or not before the moral subject, seeking harmony between internal and external. The process of embodied recognition simply is the process of moral practice. Therefore Song-Ming Ruists didn't refer to this as a method, but as moral cultivation (*gongfu* 工夫). Moral cultivation is a kind of real power taking effect. Nearing death, Zhu Xi specially took up a pen to write the word *arduous*. And Wang Yangming said,

> My teaching of innate moral awareness was born from a hundred deaths and a thousand hardships: it is not something easy to obtain. This is in the end the critical point for a learner [Note: meaning it is the last phase in progress along the heavenly road]. It is just unfortunate that this pattern has been sunk and buried for a long time. Learners are given trouble by the obstructions of seeing and hearing, with no

place to stick their heads out. It is inevitable that they're done in one sentence. I only fear that if learners get what is easy, what they will grasp is only a play of light and shadow, and they will be let down by their eyes and ears.[145]

I suppose it is not possible to lay out logic while engaged in concentrated moral practice.

Ruism is very close to nature. However, not in the way of the Western Romantics, who looked to nature as the place to realize their infinite yearnings. Even less in the way of scientists, who calmly and objectively analyze nature. Nature in Ruists' hearts is just the objectification of their own feelings and virtues. The names of the plants and animals in the *Odes* are just representations of the feelings and virtues of the poets, and certainly cannot constitute zoology or botany. The classifications popular among the people—such as pine, bamboo, and plum;[146] or plum, orchid, bamboo, and chrysanthemum[147]—are merely classifications that reflect people's feelings and virtues. No one can say this is a botanical classification, and nor could they say that since it is *not* a botanical classification, it lacks any meaning. Its meaning lies elsewhere. The following story best explains the attitude toward nature in Chinese culture.

> Master [Cheng] Hao said, "Zhou Dunyi wouldn't cut the grass in front of his window. When asked why, he said, 'I think of it as myself.' Was this grasping the meaning of the self-satisfaction of unending creativity? Or was it wanting to observe the flowing of the Heavenly Pattern in living things?" Zhu Xi said, "There is no need to explain. When one gets to the point, one will comprehend the pattern of itself. One must see how the significance of oneself and the significance of the grass are the same."[148]

Therefore, "Achieve the mean and harmony, and heaven and earth will find their proper places therein, and the myriad things will be nurtured therein,"[149] is just the highest plane of feelings and virtues. The value of nature is not in itself, but in how it elevates the values that are reflected in nature. In Western science, human beings also evolve in nature. According to the Ruist spirit, nature evolves in human beings.

One might say that because the cultural foundations are different, the characters of nature are also different.

As explained above, we should be forthright and admit that science is lacking in the Ruist spirit, just as it is from the Semitic spirit. However, the Ruist spirit contains absolutely nothing opposed to science. Everyone knows that modern science developed out of the Renaissance and Protestant Reformation. The Reformation influenced modern science in about three areas: first, respect for this world, and giving respect for this world a religious basis; second, spurring rational thought; and third, making professional study a divinely inspired activity, giving scholars and technologists a basis for professional thought. Of these three, the first is especially important, and it derives from German mysticism with its idea of "seeing the other shore in this world."[150] This was a major turning point in Christianity.

However, from the beginning Ruism respected this world, respected rational thought, and respected professions useful in daily life. The reason the Ruist spirit lacked science is only because its focus on moral practice limited the free development of thought: the emphasis on the moral subject imperceptibly diminished emphasis on the objectivity of things and events. However, this limitation and diminishing do not follow from the necessity of morality itself, but are only due to the initial spiritual orientation being different, with the result that the development of human nature was one-sided. Ruists were unaware that the achievement of science was achieving a different side of human nature.

Through the stimulus of modern science, China can see the whole of human nature to the greatest extent possible. It is not just a matter of the need to hasten to catch up in science. The morality of human nature can be more readily objectified to and realized in things through fulfilling the nature and completing the work of things. Then we can receive even more of the impact of morality in the daily activity of human relations and in this way continuously enrich morality. The reason Ruism differs from religion is that in Ruism, morality should not be separated from things and events but is tied to them, and from things and events it looks to complete the person. From Kongzi and Mengzi down to Cheng-Zhu and Lu-Wang, there is no difference here, and it can be rediscovered anywhere in Ruist thought.

However, Ruism connects to things and events for the sake of moral practice, and invisibly takes the measure of their value not to be in the things and events themselves, but in their relationship to moral practice. Then it becomes impossible to "investigate things and extend knowledge" to fulfill the nature of things. The problem for China is exactly that things and events are insufficient to support the demands of morality. Regarding providing broadly and assisting the masses, Kongzi sighed and said, "Why stop at benevolence? Surely one who could do that would be a sage. Even Yao and Shun would still find it difficult."[151] Developing the cognitive nature to achieve science can satisfy the requirements for providing broadly and assisting the masses, which are the requirements for morality. Furthermore, improving humanity's creative power toward things through the advancement of science and technology is not necessarily like Wang Yangming's investigation of bamboo in the courtyard, in which he investigated for three days while failing to grasp the pattern of the bamboo, and in addition falling ill. It can also reveal the secrets of the universe to our understanding, like atoms and quantum physics. It can touch off new moral problems, and structure new efforts and achievements. This is why Kongzi, Mengzi, Cheng Yi, Zhu Xi, Lu Xiangshan, and Wang Yangming were all elated by and encouraged studying without tiring and teaching without wearying.[152]

The only respect in which they differed from Western thinkers was that they encouraged everyone to use their benevolent heart-mind to guide science and make amoral science only function to perfect human morality, and not to use it as a tool of immorality. Then one can see new life and new value for science in the Ruist spirit, and increase conviction in the free development it should have. The benevolent nature and cognitive nature are merely two sides of human nature. One only needs to realize this, and then both sides can manifest more clearly. The common point of origin of effort toward these two sides is Kongzi's "no arbitrariness, no inflexibility, no rigidity, no selfishness."[153] The common ending point is as Mengzi said: "The myriad things are all complete in myself."[154] Someone who is engaged in any sort of work in a laboratory with a focused spirit, and is in a state in which their whole self is immersed in the object [of study] is just as great as someone who is engaged in moral practice and is in a state of selflessness with human desires wholly eliminated.

Stepping back a level, in his response to a letter from Sun Renfu, Zhu Xi said, "When the ancients established their doctrines, from the steps of cleaning, appropriate interaction, and proper reception, to the arts of ritual, music, archery, charioteering, calligraphy, and calculation, everyone had to restrain their minds and put their heads down to work at them without neglect. Only then could one grind down the hard and proud *qi* and enter into a state of virtue. Nowadays we don't have all these, and there is just the activity of reading, but it can still provide assistance in settling the body and mind."[155] This being the case, then if researching science and technology can settle the body and mind, wouldn't they be even better than cleaning and appropriate interaction?

Hence, scientific research can simultaneously be moral practice. Most Western scientists had religious faith. Chinese scientists can certainly have moral molding. My conclusion is that although there is no science in Ruism, it is absolutely not antiscience. The need for Ruism to have science going forward is not only that it will supplement what was lacking in the process of the development of human nature in Chinese culture. It can also assist with what our culture already developed: the benevolent nature. Benevolent nature and cognitive nature, morality and science: not only do I not see any reason why they cannot advance together, they are part of the whole of human nature. Together they are perfect, but apart, both are harmed.

Additionally, many people love to make Ruist thought into something along the lines of Western metaphysics, often forcing comparisons between it and idealism or materialism or event ontology.[156] In my view, these sorts of comparisons are mostly biased and have the danger of disregarding the true Ruist spirit.

From birth, humans are metaphysical animals, because they always want to investigate into the source of things. Naturally, Ruists want to find a source. However, the source indicated by Ruist moral doctrine is simply that people should verify it themselves through the fact that everyone has the heart-mind of compassion, approval and disapproval, yielding, and shame and dislike.[157] They simply want each individual to look for the source in his own heart-mind. This resolves question of the source of morality from each person himself, and is also the method of finding the source in what makes each person human. As far as extending upward from the heart-mind, what the source of the heart-mind is, what the origin of the universe is, Ruists of course recognized this question and Kongzi, Mengzi, Cheng Yi, Zhu Xi, Lu Xiangshan, and Wang Yangming of course thought about it, offering answers of Heaven, the decree of Heaven, and so on. But they all adopted an attitude of "draw the bow, but do not loose the arrow."[158]

From the Ruist standpoint, morality is practice. The level and domain of morality has to be realized by each person in practice. Sages and worthies teach others by showing them how to practice. If one relies only on language and writing to delineate the source of morality itself, then even if what is so delineated comes out of true and honest practice, people's acceptance of this will still only be a cognitive thing. Even when one sees something by realizing the source of morality itself through cognition, it is still, to use Zhu Xi's expression, "merely seeing a shadow from outside."[159] Furthermore, it is easy to make the basis of morality deviate. When Kongzi was asked about benevolence by his students in the *Analects*, he never described it exactly as this or that sort of thing. He rather showed them according to what they were capable of starting to put into practice. Yan Hui's level was the highest, so the level of Kongzi's answers was the highest: "Overcome oneself and return to ritual."[160]

Song dynasty Ruists, such as Zhou Dunyi, the Cheng brothers, and Zhang Zai, wanted to rescue Chinese culture from Buddhism. In order to take on Buddhism's religious statements, they spoke more about the metaphysical aspect. However, their metaphysical teaching developed from morality is absolutely not the same thing as Western metaphysics derived from the cognitive nature, even if the language is identical. Feng Youlan's thought made this kind of forced comparison between Eastern and Western thought, and took this to be the same as Chinese pattern learning and Way learning. This was way off the mark, and his flaws came out of this problem. From Zhu Xi's *Categorized Conversations*:

> The sage's words are very substantial, and further can be observed in the regular daily actions of his person . . . one doesn't need to look to the lofty. But now what people discuss is indistinct and they want to see something suspended in midair with no place to grab hold. . . . How could one obtain it . . . ? It's simply that Han Ruists were only seeking after word glosses and missed the meaning of the sages. This is why the Cheng brothers could not help but elucidate the Way and Pattern, inspiring scholars and rousing them to reach upward to seek the place where sages and worthies bent their minds. They did not anticipate that scholars now would forsake the near and seek out the distant, peering upward from below and advancing toward doctrines suspended in air, lifting up to the point that their feet no longer touch the ground.[161]

The emphasis of Lu-Wang thought was on first taking a stand on what is greater, slightly differing with Cheng-Zhu. However, this "greater" is absolutely not the sort of thing suspended in midair, as in Western metaphysics. As Wang Yangming said, "What I teach here is only teaching 'there must be work at it.' "[162] He also said, "Wanting to extend one's innate moral awareness, how could this mean faint shadows and echoes or nothingness suspended in midair? There must really be this activity."[163] Ruist thought, of course, makes examining the structure (*ti* 體) its endpoint. However, the structure Ruists speak of is for the most part the moral heart-mind.

The moral heart-mind exists in the human body and is revealed through embodied recognition and practice. One can begin to grasp the level of their heart-mind through the depth of their embodied recognition and practice. The process of embodied recognition and practice is the process of overcoming oneself and returning to ritual, and is in fact a dialectical approach. The heart-mind is in fact not in a fossilized, dead state. And so Huang Zongxi said, "The heart-mind has no original structure. Where moral cultivation reaches: that is its original structure."[164] This is not denying the existence of the structure, but rather is explaining the need to "see the structure directly and acknowledge it."[165] It is not a matter of extending cognition upward layer by layer, but a matter of approaching it layer by layer through practice. It is of course very different than the Western approaching of metaphysics formulated by extending knowledge outward. The structure of Western metaphysics is mostly outside the heart-mind. Ruists, however, absolutely do not talk of structure outside the heart-mind. It has no connection to the heart-mind of idealism, and the two cannot be compared.

Idealism and materialism have two meanings: one cosmological and one epistemological. The fundamental effort of Ruists is not directed to the question of the origin of the cosmos. Ruists only affirm the cosmos from the moral point of view.[166] Their talk of the heart-mind is simply arguing for the faculties of moral activity and receptivity. When Wang Yangming said there is no Pattern outside the heart-mind,[167] the Pattern here is also limited to the moral, and so it cannot be called a kind of metaphysical idealism. Ruism never developed the cognitive nature of knowledge for the sake of knowledge. "The function of the heart-mind is to think."[168] "Knowing is the original structure of the heart-mind."[169] For the most part they only went to this point. It would be difficult to leap to the conclusion that in terms of cognition, it is idealism or materialism. When Wang was wandering in Nanzhen and answered the question about the flowering trees,[170] this was just a moment of excitement, with a very heavy tinge of Chan Buddhism.

Ruism most emphasizes the unity of structure and function, but one cannot thereby conclude that it is a kind of metaphysical monism of idealism and materialism, or similar fabricated talk. When Li Yanping [Li Tong, 1093–1163] answered the letter of his friend Luo Bowen, he wrote, "When he started lecturing [note: he is referring to Zhu Xi], he was bound to the Way and Pattern, but now he has gradually become able to blend his explanations by blending it into places of daily use, and start moral cultivation with one intention. If he gradually matures in this way, structure and function will be unified."[171] For all Song-Ming Ruists, when they discussed the unity of structure and function they all said one should realize it in practice and moral cultivation. . . .[172]

To conclude, Ruism can have a metaphysics, but it has to be a metaphysics built out of effort based on its essential character. To use more of Mr. Ma's words, the effort should proceed from "real patterns" and cannot be only based on "abstruse talk." Even worse is to be like Feng Youlan's followers and force a framework from Western metaphysics onto Ruism, such as New Pattern Learning,[173] and so on. This destroys the lifeblood of Ruism: moral practice.

A New Life in This Time

As written above, from the perspective of the whole of human culture, the achievements of Ruism were limited by historical circumstances, and Ruism is definitely not all-encompassing or without flaw. However, if one tries to take stock of the crisis Western culture is facing as well as the dangerous situation in China at present, then the Ruist spirit, which is even now being reflected upon by those who have been through catastrophes, with the deep places of the souls of people engaged in struggle stirring, seems ready to issue forth in response. Speaking truthfully, this will be the time for new life for the Ruist spirit.

It is not merely one person at one time who has spoken of the crisis in Western culture. The locus of this crisis is precisely the opposite of that in China. The problem handed down in Chinese culture is [insufficient] material things. Because the material problem was never resolved, the recoil of this caused the human problem to fail to be resolved. The problem in front of Western culture now is in the human aspect. Because the human problem was not solved, this reflected onto material things, and made material things—which were produced by people—into fetters and threats. This resulted in the decline of Europe, which is facing the decisive test which will determine survival or destruction, just as ancient Greece and Rome did. Earlier I mentioned Sorokin's *The Reconstruction of Humanity*, in which he primarily was pointing out the problem with European sensory and emotive culture.[174] These produced a false science of people themselves, recognizing them to be only moved by desires and responsive to power, as purely physiological and material things. This led humanity to the brink of extinction, with no choice but to appeal for a reconstruction of humanity. This I already introduced. Now, as further proof, I would like to quote a section or two of the conclusions of *Man, the Unknown*, by the 1912 winner of the Nobel Prize in [Physiology or Medicine], Dr. Alexi[s] Carrel.[175]

Dr. Carrel narrates in detail the various work and achievements in modern science in regard to humanity, feeling disappointment . . .[176]

Dr. Carrel's achievements came through analysis and the use of microscopes, but he realized that there are limits to what they can do. What humanity needs to survive are more than just the fruits of analysis and microscopes. He also said, "If Newton and Lavoisier had applied their efforts to the spirit or to research on man as we do, perhaps we could achieve incomparable happiness."[177] Didn't our former sages and worthies exactly make this effort, but on a different path than Newton and others like him?

Western social science also has its brilliant achievements. However, it too is facing an unprecedented test because it is not built on the source of humanity itself. Liberalism in economics has not been able to resolve the opposition between rich and poor.[178] Yet a planned and controlled economy has the significant possibility of falling into total-itarian rule.[179] The technical efforts of economists between these two [a completely free market and a planned economy] have yet to be able to resolve this problem. As far as politics, then the views of Dr. [Carl] Becker that I cited earlier can serve as a representative. In Dr. Becker's 1940 book *Modern Democracy*, he repeatedly pointed out that the crisis in democracy comes from economic contradictions.[180] But the econ-omy doesn't become a problem due to material conditions. Technology today can resolve people's material requirements. Whether democracy can be overthrown by totalitarianism will depend on the people in the opposition of economic gain and loss. At the juncture when gain and loss affects them personally, will they be able to use democratic means to resolve the contradiction? If they are unable to use reason to resolve their problems through democratic means, the result will be to facilitate violent revolution. After discussing this back and forth, isn't the key to whether the crisis in democracy and economic contradictions can be resolved in people themselves? So the survival of European culture depends on the effort to turn around and establish "that by which people differ from birds and beasts."[181]

I look at the difficulties in European culture from a different angle: the conflict between the individual and the collective. On this point, Ruism offers a path forward, though naturally not a complete one.

In the Middle Ages in Europe, everyone lived under a unified creed of Christianity. Christianity unfolds from original sin and facing up to God. This was able to pacify the arrogant and rash Romans and the violent barbarians, arousing their spirits and orienting them upward. However, the ideas of Christianity are entirely a transcendent and external spirit. Other than having faith, an individual has no active power of self-mastery. This makes it easy to bury individual personality and in the real world spurs authoritarian rule. This is why modernity commenced with the self-awareness of personality and the individual. This is the individualism spoken of by ordinary people. However, in fact all people want to live in an orderly, unified body. No truly solitary individual can exist. Because of this, culturally individualism never overturned religion, and rationalism evolved into modern rationalism to link people into a rational unified body.[182]

However, European rationalism, built on the transcendent and external, probably shared an identical character with religion. For example, the three critical points in Hegel's philosophy of history: spirit, the state, and the individual. Spirit is the telos, the state is the material, and the individual imperceptibly becomes a means for spirit; that is, a means for the historical telos. This is why opponents of his philosophy of history called it a doctrine of puppets. Because although individuals can ascend to join with spirit with the state as the material, and hence the individual is a manifestation of the same kind as spirit, imperceptibly the individual becomes considered a second-class being. As a second-class being, it cannot but become a means for the higher-level being. Then when it comes to reality, it is impossible to say there is no possibility of this turning into totalitarian holism.

Then another group—that is, the empiricists—refused to accept rationalism in order to preserve individual freedom. They believed that as soon as one brings up rationalism, it will abet holism. Looking from the Western standpoint, this is not without reason. However, the problem lies in the fact that a thorough empiricism and individualism may coexist conceptually, but cannot coexist in real human life. Holding fast to this kind of conceptual thing in real life, the result is just to go from skepticism and nihilism to approving of nothing and achieving nothing. The other side of this coin is always to abet the power for totalitarian holism. In fact, the connection to holism is only the fault of purely external rationalism, not the fault of rationalism as such, because rationalism is not necessarily purely external.

The Ruist spirit is a transcendent and yet immanent rationalism. Its immanent aspect endorses the individual; its transcendent aspect endorses the whole. The collective manifests in the individual: there is no separate whole suspended in midair. Each individual encompasses the whole fully and completely, lacking nothing, and therefore the individual itself is the telos: the telos is not in a separate thing. When the Ruist concept of human relations manifests in reality, then although each person completely fulfills his duty toward the other, this is merely perfecting himself. He does not become a means for the other. Therefore, the measure of duty is in oneself, not in the other. "Serve the ruler with the Way, and when this is impossible, then retire."[183] How could the minister be the means for the ruler, as the petty and great dictators of the world imagine? "One flower, one world. One leaf, one *tathagata*."[184] These two sentences from Buddhism could almost be an analogy for the Ruist spirit. But Buddhism is just an empty doctrine. It still aims to leave this shore and seek the other shore, to leave this world to seek the world to come. This still divides the one and many, the individual and the collective, into two.

Ruism establishes theory on the basis of moral practice concerning human relations in daily life. It completes the collective through perfect individuals, setting up for the future with a rational present. The individual in regard to the collective, or the present in regard to the future, absolutely does not obstruct; "only the present is true."[185] This unity of individual and collective can resolve the situation in Western culture, in which individual and collective are opposed and overturn and pressure each other. Some people suspect that Ruism is a kind of Oriental collectivism. I will essay quoting the following passage for the reader to ponder from Zhao Shixia's *Postscript to the Dialogue from Yanping*:

Zhu Xi once said to me, "When I began to study, I devoted myself to vague and grandiose theories. I favored conformity and abhorred difference. I liked the grand and was ashamed of the small. When I heard Yanping's[186] teachings, I thought, why are there so many things like this? I had doubts in my mind and did not follow. In Tong'an, when I had time after my official duties, I thought over what he had said and then began to understand that he had not deceived me. What Yanping said was, the thought of our Ruist learning is different than heterodox teachings in this: Pattern is one but its allotments are many. There is no trouble with Pattern not being one. What is difficult are the many allotments."[187]

Ruist thought was understood very well in Germany in the seventeenth century. Leibniz and Wolff especially highly regarded Kongzi. Wolff also lost his post at Halle over this.[188] Leibniz felt that Western Europe was superior in theoretical philosophy, while China was superior in practical philosophy. His words were right on the mark. From the nineteenth century on, Western research on China increased daily, but its understanding of the Chinese spirit deteriorated daily. The West was ever more affected by naturalism and materialism, and so found it harder to understand Ruism. (Note added on 4/18/1979: This is directly related to the frenzied attacks on China by Western colonialism in the nineteenth century.) Furthermore, those renowned Chinese who were able to have contact with the West traded Chinese material for rice to eat while simultaneously making a name for themselves by overthrowing Ruism. Then the Ruist spirit could not contribute to Western culture and had to seek a turning point. This was China's shame, and also a misfortune for world culture.

As far as China itself is concerned, it should be discussed in three aspects: Free China and Communist rule, which mainly relate to the present political question, and the final aspect, which is the question of a way out for Chinese culture as a whole. This is the ultimate purpose for bring up this question.

For Free China, the most urgent mission at present is how to defeat communism and restore freedom to the people. I think the fact that the GMD was defeated by the CCP on the mainland cannot be assessed by the yardstick of degree of Western modernization. The CCP came out of the poor villages and backwaters. The Westernization of the GMD cadres can be vividly contrasted with the rusticity of the CCP cadres. The power of modern material that the GMD could rely on in those years was something the CCP could not match. At the same time, the CCP discussed organization, ideology, and strategy, but it's not as if the GMD did not discuss organization, ideology, and strategy. And yet, despite having an absolute advantage, the GMD suffered a crushing defeat. This is of course not because the GMD was more modernized than the CCP, but because behind their modernization, there was no soul. Hence, they lost to the CCP when it came to what is fundamental to people.

When on the mainland, the GMD could offer many good things verbally and in writing, but what each person undertook in reality was just the opposite of what was said and written. In the private and hidden aspects, GMD officers all had intelligence and ability, but in the public and open aspects, everyone was foolish and incompetent. Although the knowledge of CCP officials was limited, and what they knew was deviant and absurd, resulting in the ruin of today, they were able to fully undertake that limited knowledge, and undergo risk and hardship to realize it. They defeated the GMD in what is fundamental to people. This of course cannot be blamed only on the GMD. It is a great tragedy of the entire Chinese intellectual class.

The difficult situation of Free China now, from the GMD to ordinary society, should first be addressed by effort to take a stand on character. Only this is true self-awareness, a true change for the better. All other fake ostentation will, in my opinion, only make things worse despite the effort. All the Ruist teachings come back to wanting people to be persons of propriety. The same mission undertaken by a group of proper persons will have a completely different result than if it were undertaken by a group of shady characters. This can be said to be a self-evident principle.

Speech could be conscientious and trustworthy. Actions should be sincere and reverent.[189]

A scholar must be broad-minded and resolute.[190]

Being resolute and firm, but simple and hesitant: this is close to benevolence.[191]

Seldom are glib words and an ingratiating appearance associated with benevolence.[192]

The village worthy is the thief of virtue.[193]

That by which people differ from birds and beasts is slight.[194]

Someone without the heart of compassion is inhuman. Someone without the heart of approval and disapproval is inhuman. Someone without the heart of deferring and yield-ing is inhuman. Someone without the heart of shame and disdain is inhuman.[195]

Every responsible person in Free China, if they took stock of themselves when about to get up or when turning off the light and going to bed, then they would realize how many inhuman things they did and how many inhuman thoughts they had among the posters and slogans. They would certainly feel regretful and be at a loss, and then rise up with excitement and go attack the Communists' inhuman standpoint with the standpoint of a true person. Then there would be new life for the Ruist spirit in free China: "How could it be called a small remedy?"[196]

Then there are those who say that the way to be a person is the same, Chinese or Western, and so what need is there to bring out the Ruist spirit? In fact, one who truly puts their mind to being a [good] person will not have this question. Granting that the way of being a person is the same, Chinese people are more familiar with the Chinese way. What doubts can there be about Chinese people discussing the Chinese way? However, since many intellectuals still harbor this doubt in their breast, I have no objection to providing some explanation. In most cases, for understanding to turn into action, it requires that understanding turn into affection. It has to fit with one's life in order to become active. Humanity's greatest affections come from their own stored history. Even if I do not say that the way of being a person pointed to by Ruism is more profound and sincere than that of the West (although it is), it is the store of thousands of years of China's own history, and has imperceptibly permeated each person's life. If one has awareness of it for just a moment, then it is completely present and intimate.

This is the easiest path to arouse faith and strive for action, and is also the most universal. Japan has recently reinstated *kambun* [classical Chinese] as a required course in order to improve the upbringing of its youth. What love do the Japanese people have for *kambun*? When could they not borrow the name and make a copy of the "language of cloth and silk, the flavor of grains and pulses"[197] that *kambun* represents, the way they copy Western machines? Of course they could. But what they can't copy is the intimate affection fostered by more than a thousand years of history of *kambun* among the Japanese people.

We should take care to observe that anyone who has affection for the Western way of being a person absolutely does not object to bringing up the Ruist spirit, unless he completely doesn't understand it. Someone who disparages the spirit of Chinese culture in one breath will absolutely not accept the correct Western way of being a person. A person's feelings of admiration and reverence toward his ancestors themselves naturally and unintentionally reveal his moral character. When a person's selfishness and arrogance (there has never been a selfish person who wasn't arrogant—arrogance comes from selfishness) gets to the point where he has to curse his own ancestors to find pleasure, then in his innermost heart he surely bears enmity toward everything that is the common possession of humanity. He will especially take advantage of that which is close to his own life and easy to make into a target for releasing his enmity. So when this kind of person talks about Western culture, unless he is born to be servile he is simply borrowing it to hide his own spiteful selfishness. It is something entirely different from Western culture itself.

Next, as far as the CCP government goes, if they could abruptly have some level of realization and regret for their actions and change course, this would be to the good fortune of the world and even more a blessing for the Chinese people. However, if one truly researches this question, then [one understands that] if the CCP were to have such a realization, then what they would rely on to stand up would surely be the Ruist spirit, not Western culture. Many foreigners, Americans especially, like to say, "Chinese culture is a form of individualism. This individualism can elicit change in the Communist Party." If this individualism means rational individualism, then of course I cannot disagree. On the other hand, if it means Western utilitarian individualism,[198] then as it has nothing to do with Chinese culture that has benevolence as its core, it can have no effect on the Communist Party.

The reason communism arose, as far as its links to Western culture go, was in reaction to capitalism and individualism. As long as Western culture cannot resolve the contradictions of capitalism and individualism, the Communist Party will not seek liberation by jumping into the old circles of contradiction. Furthermore, if the CCP is to have a realization, it must include two factors. The first is a call to the benevolence within human nature in response to the endless violent struggle that is never resolved. The second is a call to [feelings for] the motherland in human nature in response to the never-ending deceit and oppression of the Soviet Union. In response to these two calls, the Ruist spirit in each person's heart will revive, they will weep bitterly over their past transgressions, and they will instantly become enlightened.[199]

As for the question of whether Free China's timing will one day ripen so they can strike back at the mainland, if some people think to take their method of controlling the people and take the people from the CCP's control, put them under their control, and do something great thereby, this is just to replace violence with violence.[200] ("Control" used to mean binding the hands and feet of the master of the house and stuffing cotton in his mouth when committing a robbery. Now people favor language control. This is why it makes people shiver without being cold.) Not only that, but a little shaman cannot overthrow a big shaman, and so in this case violence cannot replace violence. This will only increase the difficulty of striking back, something that is worth considering deeply. The people are not demanding to be released from the CCP tying their hands and feet behind their backs so some other group of people can tie their hands and feet in front. They are demanding that all things that bind the people's hands and feet—whether of iron or hemp, red or white—be thrown into the toilet forever. In my opinion, if one day we can crawl back onto the mainland and oppose the Communist Party, it should be based on Ruist love for the people. It should take people from the Communist Party's control and return them to themselves. It should allow the people to have their own households, with their own relatives and friends. It should allow them to have their own tone of life, with natural customs and human feelings, turning a forced, cold, and cruel society into a warm and natural one. Then, "the people will return like water flows down."[201] The violent organization of the Communist Party could not help falling apart.

The preceding two points [concerning the GMD and CCP] are closely founded on political need, which is absolutely necessitated by the present circumstances. In fact, culture should be responsible for politics, but not only for politics, because politics is only one part of life. It is the behavior of a totalitarian to adhere completely to politics when talking about culture. Everyone concerned about the future of humanity should make it into a profound taboo. Simplifying the Chinese political problem into a problem of CCP versus the GMD especially is a profound tragedy and deep pain of the Chinese people. Therefore, besides the above two points, I want to lay out a vision for the future of our entire culture.

Our fundamental difficulty is not only that our culture lacks the cognitive nature aspect, but even more that we could not even preserve the benevolent nature that was the achievement of Ruism. This is why I brought up the renaissance of the Ruist spirit, in order to "establish first the greater part."[202] However, this is not the conclusion of the matter. We must have a renaissance while also turning to make an effort along two lines, meaning an effort to achieve benevolence and wisdom. Western culture developed the cognitive nature and was able to preserve it, so now it needs to turn to "subsuming wisdom with a return to benevolence,"[203] evaluating and applying the achievements of wisdom in terms of benevolence. The Chinese culture of the future must restore its benevolent nature while simultaneously "turning benevolence into wisdom." That is, to put the cognitive nature in the warm embrace of the moral subject while not limiting it by the bonds of the structure of morality.[204] To have achievements in humanities and natural sciences under the auspices of the great part of humanity. Under the conditions of great awareness of the whole of human nature, creating this renaissance and turning to make an effort along two lines is not only necessary, but is absolutely possible.

The culture of benevolent nature is a culture of "Kongzi is in every person's heart-mind"[205] and in "one saying that can be practiced for one's entire life."[206] Once one has this awareness and this guidance, then the benevolent nature can move the myriad things like a spring breeze, yet without occupying the position of bearing and nurturing them. Therefore, under the conditions of the self-awareness of the whole of human nature, benevolent nature encourages the development of the cognitive nature. Otherwise, it is numb and unbenevolent.[207] Furthermore, according to the basic Ruist concepts of "one must work at it"[208] and "there is no refined or coarse, no root or branch,"[209] we should nowadays turn around and believe that fulfilling the nature of things is to fulfill one's own nature. Realizing the cognitive nature *is* realizing the benevolent nature. Concentrating one's efforts on one scientific technique *is* an individual's ultimate mission to fulfill his nature. The reason why many people now have this one technique but have not fulfilled their nature or their ultimate mission is simply that they lack this awareness and this guidance. (Refer earlier to where I quoted Cheng Yi on the fact that fulfilling one's nature and ultimate mission must be based on being filial and fraternal.)[210]

Scholars of Pattern learning developed to the point where they would "hold an inquiry based on an account of their achievements and faults"[211] to assess the good and evil of their own thoughts. This could perhaps be called a special skill that is the pinnacle of embodied recognition, but in reality it is completely locked in one level of human nature and becomes an impediment to development of the cognitive nature. There is certainly no reason to oppose this sort of effort on the part of a small group of people, but the expression of the Ruist spirit had no need to go down this road. In any case, the direction for the Ruist spirit's renaissance and new turn is to become self-aware of the whole of human nature and so make the cognitive nature and benevolent nature turn from one to the other, forget each other, and complete each other, all under the guidance of the two great essentials of human history and culture.

Then the renaissance for China will not only be of the Ruist spirit, but of the totality of human culture. It will advance toward the limitless pluralism of the whole of human nature, uphold the reality that "the myriad things nurture and do not harm each other,"[212] and constitute a new trend for China and for humanity in general. And the revolutions of the world will continue, beginning with the intellectuals of the present being able to change their thoughts from the current state of being locked in narrow-minded and despicable ways. What will make this change possible is of course still the inspiration of the Ruist spirit. Their cramped ideas which make it impossible for them to be themselves are precisely due to this. In the past, Wang Yangming once said, "When I first began to live in Longchang, I could not understand the local language. The only people I could talk to were wanderers in exile from the central lands. When I told them of the teaching of [the unity of] knowledge and action, none did not enter into it with delight. After a while, I could interact harmoniously with the barbaric locals. When I left to talk with scholars and counselors, I rather could not usually get on with them. Why? They were already full of preconceived notions."[213] Today those with whom I discuss culture are certainly also wanderers in exile from the central lands.[214] Could I also relieve them of their preconceived notions a little and set them on a broad and level road, so we could together not give up on these difficult times?

Chapter 7

The Chinese Way of Governance

After Reading *Collected Writings of Master Lu Xuan*

Translator's introduction: Although much of this substantial essay delves into the details of Tang dynasty history, it is both a deeply personal illustration of Xu's understanding of his role as a Chinese intellectual and a presentation of some of his most important political ideas. His conception of the connection between Ruism and democracy has much in common with Mou Zongsan, who was also formulating his ideas at the time that he would publish as *Philosophy of History* in 1955 and *Authority and Governance* in 1959.

The point of convergence is the idea that democracy is a way of regularizing and institutionalizing Ruist political ideals, which otherwise depended on the ruler overcoming his psychological tendencies to pursue his own interests. As Xu describes it, the goal of Ruist political thought is for the ruler to put the people first, ignoring his own preferences in order to mirror the people's preferences. This, he recognizes, is extremely difficult to do, and so there were very few sagely rulers in Chinese history. The great benefit of democracy is that it removes this from the ruler's hands and objectifies it in institutions that force those in power to follow the people's preferences, since they will be removed from office if they

Ruist Political Thought and Democracy, Freedom and Human Rights, 221–48, first published in *Democratic Review* 4, no. 9, May 1, 1953.

don't. While Xu probably overestimates the extent of this, it is a major part of his argument for why Ruism implies democracy: it better realizes the political ideals Ruists have always had.

Significant parts of the article are constituted by translations from writings by and about Lu Zhi, the Tang dynasty official. I have not translated most of these, because they are not necessary to understand Xu's interpretation of Ruist political thought and they would take up too much space. However, it is not accidental that Xu uses Lu Zhi's remonstrance with the Tang Emperor Dezong to illustrate Ruist political ideals. Lu represents the Ruist tradition of speaking truth to power, even at the risk of one's career (and at times, one's life). Although Xu politely deflects the suggestion that he is a modern-day Lu Zhi that he mentions in his author's note, there is no doubt that he felt that same responsibility to point out the transgressions of the powerful. Toward the conclusion of his essay, he mentions Lu Zhi's fate: exile until his death. Ironically, this was written not long before Xu was thrown out of the GMD, dismissed from his university position, and finally forced to leave Taiwan to spend several years in Hong Kong. All due to his criticisms of the government and agitation for more democracy in Taiwan.

Author's note: When I first became acquainted with Mr. Wang Lanseng, he shared with me a letter written to him by Mr. Zhang Minsheng. In the letter Mr. Zhang wrote that I was a modern-day Lu Xuan and Zhu Xi. No words could describe the feeling of sweating with shame I had at the time, so I wrote this essay and offered it to Mr. Zhang to express my fearful gratitude. Not long after, I met Mr. Zhang. It should not be hard to gather how I have disappointed this sincere and affable friend in recent years.

[Translator's note: Lu Zhi 陸贄, courtesy name Jingyu 敬輿 and posthumously named Xuan 宣 (754–805) was a Tang dynasty statesman and writer. For simplicity, for the remainder of the translation I refer to him as Lu Zhi irrespective of what name Xu used. At one time he was prime minister to Emperor Dezong. Xu praises him for a more acute understanding of the contradictions and tensions in Chinese political thought than most ancient thinkers. The opening section of this essay is mainly about different accounts of his life and versions of his writings in the official *Old Tang History* and *New Tang History*. As these questions are marginal to the theme of the essay, I have not translated the first section.]

II

One can say that, aside from the Legalists, all Chinese political thought is people-centered (*minben zhuyi* 民本主義); that is, the people are political subjects. Yet the actual government over thousands of years in China was despotic. The source of political power was the ruler, not the people, and so in reality the true political subject was the ruler. Because of this, when Chinese sages and worthies traced back to the root political problem, they could not help giving a rationalized place for the ruler who was the source of political power, and, at root, the way of governance discussed in the past was the way of the ruler. This is equivalent to how in democracy today, the source of power is the people and therefore nowadays the way of governance is, at root, popular will.

However, in the past in China there was a fundamental political contradiction: in the political ideal the people were subjects, but in political reality the ruler was the subject. This kind of dual subjectivity constituted an opposition that could not be reconciled. The degree to which this opposition was expressed shaped the rise and decline of order in history. So Chinese political thought always sought to dissolve the ruler's subjectivity in order to manifest the subjectivity of the world, and thus to dissolve that opposition. The tool with which the ruler displayed his subjectivity was his personal preferences and talent and wisdom. Preferences are what people have in common, and talent and wisdom are precious things in life. However, because the ruler was the ultimate locus of political power, *his* preferences, ability, and wisdom often were expressed through his ultimate political power, constituting his political subjectivity, then inhibiting [expression of] the world's preferences, ability, and wisdom, and thus inhibiting the world's political subjectivity.

Although in Chinese history the world's (which is to say, the people's) self-awareness of their political subjectivity was insufficient, yet the world is a great, objective entity. Its suppression by the ruler only added to the fundamental opposition mentioned above. At the extreme, it would burst out into chaos. Hence, Ruism and Daoism felt that what made a ruler a ruler was not increasing his ability and wisdom, but transmuting ability and wisdom into a kind of virtue. With this virtue, ability and wisdom would negate themselves (*ziwo fouding* 自我的否定);[1] preferences would also negate themselves with this virtue, so that ability, wisdom, and preferences would not fuse with political power to constitute a strong desire for domination. Furthermore, due to this self-negation [on the part of the ruler], the world's ability, wisdom, and preferences would be revealed, so that all the world could use their ability and wisdom to satisfy their preferences. This is what is called "governing the world with the world."[2] Then the ruler himself is objectified into [becoming] the world's ability, wisdom, and preferences and has none of his own. The ruler exists in a condition of nonaction (*wuwei* 無為), which is a condition of nonsubjectivity.[3] When the ruler practices nonaction, then ministers and the people have space to act. This is the true way of governance.

Laozi advocated for "doing nothing, yet leaving nothing undone."[4] Ban Gu called this "the art of the ruler facing south."[5] Zhuangzi said, "I have heard of letting the world be [being there and having it, meaning accepting whatever is present and not otherwise making anything of it], but I have not heard of governing it."[6] Although this chapter may not have come from the hand of Zhuangzi, there should be no doubt that it can represent Zhuangzi's political thought. The "Appended Phrases" of the *Changes* says, "It is through such ease and simplicity that the principles of the world obtain."[7] Kongzi said, "Yong [his student] is unaffected by the trivial" and so felt he could "face south [be the ruler]."[8] Being unaffected is close to nonaction. Kongzi went a step further and said, "How great was Yao as ruler! How lofty! It is only Heaven that is great, and only Yao modeled himself on it. How vast was his virtue! The people could not describe it."[9] (They could not discern his talent and wisdom, and so could not enumerate his meritorious virtues.) "How lofty was the way in which Shun and Yu possessed the world, as if it didn't matter to them."[10] "Was not Shun someone who ruled through nonaction? What did he ever do? All he did was make himself reverent and faced south."[11] And also, "One who rules by virtue may be compared to the Pole Star. It remains in its place while the other stars revolve around it."[12]

The "virtue" mentioned here, to put it in modern language, is a limitless motivation for good. The motivation for good—moral motivation—always involves giving up oneself to comply with others and not compelling others to accommodate oneself. The *Great Learning* as applied to government is just to put into practice "the way of the measuring line and the carpenter's square."[13] The *Mean* as applied to government is just to "govern the people with the people"[14] (meaning not to govern them according to what the ruler himself wants). In his *Assessment after Reading the "Comprehensive Mirror,"* Wang Fuzhi wanted the ruler to "be in a position where he could exist or not,"[15] making the ruler's political function to not exercise directly any political function. Huang Zongxi (1610–1695) was even clearer, saying that the world is the master and the ruler is the guest,[16] making the ruler subordinate to the people.

All these are various ways of expressing that the only way to ensure the people's political subjectivity is to overturn the ruler's. Just this is the foremost point of Chinese political thought. The various rules under this are secondary or tertiary. The ruler has to negate himself and dissolve his own political subjectivity through nonaction. He has to objectify himself and disappear into the one political subjectivity of "the world," taking the world's ability and wisdom as his ability and wisdom and taking the world's preferences as his preferences. This is the only way to resolve the contradiction between political ideal and reality. The only way to realize a kind of government of great peace wherein "The myriad things nurture each other and do not harm each other."[17]

The foundation of Ruist nonaction is benevolence, the root of the humanistic world, while that of Daoist nonaction is the spontaneity (*ziran* 自然) of the natural world. The two philosophies only separated at this point. In terms of demanding nonaction from rulers they are identical. Legalism makes ministers and the people into the ruler's tools: this is fascist thought. Yet the ruler's technique (*shu* 術) for using his tools is still to "be empty and still, waiting."[18] "An enlightened ruler remains above, doing nothing," and should "be empty, still, and engage in no activity . . . get rid of his own wisdom and cut off his own ability."[19] We can see that when a ruler displays his own existence through relying on his own wisdom, ability, and preferences, then he exists as one person in opposition to the world. When one person is opposed to the world, this not only destroys Ruist benevolence and Daoist spontaneity, it also destroys Legalist technique. One only needs to look at those rulers in history who were pleased with their own accomplishments in technique and as a result always ended up without technique[20] to understand this principle. If one's understanding doesn't reach this level, one cannot be considered to understand the basis of Chinese political thought or the causes behind the cycle of the rise and decline of order for thousands of years.

This one thread and the influence it had on history and government can be seen in every ancient thinker's doctrine and in every historical phenomenon. Although it did not constitute a complete system, it did form a strong undercurrent that could emerge at any point. And it emerged more definitely and completely in Master Lu Zhi's doctrine.

[Translator's note: Section III is again about Lu Zhi's political career and advice to Emperor Dezong. I have elided this section to focus on the general theme of proper governance rather than Lu Zhi's specific circumstances.]

IV

Lu wanted to remedy the governmental crisis of the time, which meant first resolving Emperor Dezong's isolation as well as the court's isolation. This kind of isolation stems from the opposition between the ruler and the people, which in turn derives from making the ruler's preferences, ability, and wisdom the ultimate standard. Hence, Lu wanted Dezong to get rid of his own preferences, ability, and wisdom and dissolve them into those of the people to make those manifest. This would dissolve the opposition between the ruler and the people, which is what is meant by governing through nonaction. A level up from nonaction is "assuming the blame oneself"[21] and "repenting one's mistakes."[22] The true display of blaming oneself and repenting one's mistakes is to replace suspicion with good faith, to accept criticism instead of favoring flattery, and to replace jealousy with forgiveness. Nonaction, blaming oneself, and repenting one's mistakes dissolve one's own political subjectivity; extending good faith, accepting criticism, and being forgiving display the world's political subjectivity. Then there is only one subjectivity in government, the opposition disappears, and the world achieves great peace. Lu Zhi's *Hanyuan ji*, where he speaks on behalf of Dezong and gives his responses, may be summed up in this way.

[Translator's note: The following series of quotations from Lu Zhi is omitted.]

Note: Governing the world requires an objective standard, which the ruler should follow. This is the "way" that Lu referred to when he spoke of "go against [the ruler's own] desires to follow the way."[23] However, what especially demands attention here is not just the fact that the ruler's personal desires and dislikes cannot be an objective standard for government. It is that in Chinese political thought any good abstract noun or ideology is not an objective standard that the government should follow, if it does not represent the people's preference. The objective standard for government in China is the heart-minds of the people of the world, meaning their desires and dislikes, or put another way, "popular dispositions" or "group dispositions." Mengzi talked about desire for sex and desire for beauty and said that "one who shared those desires with the people" could be king over the world.[24] Lu repeatedly emphasized "[the ruler] having the same preferences as the world,"[25] which is the way to "go against [the ruler's own] desires to follow the way." Putting this in contemporary language, what most people agree on constitutes the objective standard for government.

If an abstract noun or ideology is ossified into a rule and made the ultimate political principle that overpowers people's actual preferences, then even if it is dressed up and said to be in order to achieve the ideal future, the result is unavoidably the sacrifice of people's present preferences.[26] As a result, abstractions or ideologies themselves cannot be shown to the people, much less forcibly demanded of them. Those who present abstractions and ideologies and forcibly demand their realization are in fact a minority who occupy the position of rulers. This minority takes their own preferences and deifies them into abstractions and ideologies to overpower the world's preferences and whip the world to realize their personal preferences. But they can still sadly and shamelessly say, "I do it to realize the ideal!" Totalitarian governments led by communist parties are formed in just this way.

Chinese political thought invariably takes "the desires shared by the people" as the highest principle. The exercise of benevolence and rightness must also take its source from the best knowledge and best capability that everyone has without having to learn,[27] that which "people's heart-minds have in common."[28] Chinese political thought never establishes another principle outside of the actual preferences of the majority. It hoped that the ruler would be a sage, which seems identical to Plato's ideal of philosopher-kings. However, Plato's philosopher wielded his Idea[29] to separate the masses into classes like gold, silver, and iron[30] and execute a grand remolding of them into hatchets. The sage in Chinese political thought merely dissolves himself into the people, enabling them to realize their own preferences: a government of nonaction where everyone can "nurture life"[31] and "follow their nature."[32] They do not borrow some slogans and go carry out some reform relying on their own intelligence and ability. In other words, the sage in Chinese political thought merely transforms himself into a blank sheet of paper for the convenience of the people to draw on, rather than rigidly enforcing a picture of his own design and forcing the people to draw accordingly.[33]

Behind this idea lies an unlimited respect for and faith in human nature. This respect and faith is how the sage can display an unlimited heart-mind of benevolence. Hence, I have always felt that philosophy is a personal matter. It is something that should cover human lives broadly through using teaching (without authoritarian coercion). One cannot take philosophical concepts and ossify them into rules that become the highest political principle. The highest political principle is nothing other than the people's preferences. The government simply follows the majority and protects the minority. In view of the belief that "[the ruler's] preferences should be identical to the people's," philosophical doctrines are restricted to the category of "teachings" and teachings and politics are strictly separated.[34] This is the only way to avoid the flaw of the cunning minority using rational slogans to murder the people.

In Chinese culture, the most minimal limit in political thought is teaching those responsible for government to "like what the people like and hate what the people hate."[35] "To hate what the people like and to like what the people hate is called going against the people's nature. If one proceeds like this, one will certainly arrive at disaster."[36] As far as a political system to realize the people's preferences, Chinese political thought always advocated "both continuity and reform"[37] and modification, and in no way handed later generations a firm and unbreakable shell of a "feudal" or "patriarchal society," nor did it force people into such a system and deceive them. Chinese culture bears no fault for the current situation. The only fault of Chinese culture is that it could produce such a collection of descendants, who push all their failings back onto their ancestors and have not an ounce of shame for their own ignorance and lack of principles.

[Translator's note: Another series of quotations from Lu Zhi along with Xu's annotations has been omitted.]

In the "Great Plan" of the *Documents* it says, "Only the ruler gives favor and inspires fear,"[38] which means that the ruler holds the weighty power of reward and punishment. This idea was thoroughly revised in Ruism and Daoism (only the Legalists inherited this idea). Hence, Lu said, "Bestowing and taking away [honors] is the power of the ruler. Positions of high status are public instruments belonging to the world. One does not use public instruments to seek personal enjoyment nor use that power to vent one's wrath. . . . Creating positions with rank and salary is for sharing them with the people."[39] Someone who uses the world for selfish purposes will first act as if rank and salary are his own possessions to give. He uses rank and salary to order around those who rush after food and clothing, all to satisfy his own desire for dominance. This is what they call governing the world. Lu points out that rank and salary are public instruments, not tools for the ruler to show his pleasure or vent his anger, so that the ruler's preferences cannot be revealed through rewards and punishments. This is the first step to "making oneself reverent and practicing nonaction,"[40] and is almost the most substantive and difficult to achieve step. The above may all be said to be Lu's most fundamental understanding of the way of governance, and also what I called the primary meaning of the Chinese way of governance.

V

Nonaction is the way to prevent an opposition between the ruler and the world. However, the Fengtian incident[41] was a result of an already sharp opposition between Emperor Dezong and the world. Trying to remove that already sharp opposition through nonaction was truly an instance of a slow approach being unable to help a critical situation. Hence, Lu further urged Dezong to blame himself and repent his mistakes.[42] Non-action is like zero in mathematics, while blaming oneself and repenting one's mistakes are like negative numbers. This is why I said earlier that blaming oneself and repenting one's mistakes are one more step back from nonaction.[43] When the ruler admits his errors to the world and repents, then he is not just a zero with regard to the world, but is a negative number. Then how could the world be in opposition to him? There is no place from which to oppose. "When [Dezong] issued the pardon for Fengtian, even the warriors and hardened soldiers were moved to tears":[44] this illustrates this principle.

Someone who can truly take responsibility for his faults has already erased the division between self and others and will certainly extend good faith, accept criticism, and moreover can transmit a kind of forgiving spirit. Lu adduced many examples of this from the *Changes*, *Odes*, *Documents*, Kongzi, and Laozi, verifying it through the actions of Yao, Shun, Tang, Wen, Wu, Jie, and Zhou, as well as Emperors Taizong and Xuanzong.[45] He demonstrated that blaming oneself, repenting one's mistakes, accepting criticism, forgiveness, and so on are the one way to realize the ideal of governing the world with the world.

In Fengtian Dezong wanted Lu Zhi to investigate the causes behind the defeat [in Chang'an] and determine the most pressing tasks at that moment. Lu believed the most critical were extending good faith and accepting criticism. Dezong, however, just made excuses.

[Translator's note: Another series of quotations from Lu Zhi along with Xu's annotations has been omitted.]

Note: Extending good faith, correcting errors, and accepting criticism are the greatest virtues for a ruler, the concrete content of governing through nonaction. They are also where the central problem of the Chinese way of governance lies. In "Document on Not Putting into Effect the Prior Memorial Submitted at Fengtian" Lu cited the past to prove the present point, making repeated inferences, and in the end concluded, "Inheriting the mantle of the past comes from accepting criticism; the destruction of virtue originates in believing oneself to be already worthy."[46] Hence, accepting criticism is the specific manifestation of extending good faith and correcting mistakes. "Accepting criticism" means being willing to accept opposing views.

The ruler is the highest leader in the government. When the ruler accepts opposing views, it has the following three impacts for the ruler himself. First, it signifies admission that the government which he runs is public. Many people do not want others to express any opposing view because they consider their government theirs, and naturally bystanders should not interfere with one's private business.[47] Second, they can objectify their spirit to objective political problems.[48] Political discussion only touches on the pros and cons of objective political questions and does not touch on personal preferences or personal gain and loss. Because the pros and cons of political questions become clearer during political discussion for and against them, then in the process of objectifying their spirit, political leaders can develop [their government] toward greater perfection. When their spirit stagnates at the circle of their own flesh and blood, then purposely or not, objective political problems will always be pulled into that circle. Then they will always feel that the public affairs discussed by the people of the world are in fact discussion of their private business. The people were in fact criticizing objective problems, but he invariably feels they were criticizing him. Then how can he accept opposing viewpoints?

Finally, someone of true wisdom will certainly feel his own ability and wisdom are paltry when facing the infinite variety of truth and falsehood in the whole world. Someone with a truly benevolent mind will feel his responsibility is inexhaustible when facing the infinite varieties of joy and worry of the people. Shouldering inexhaustible responsibility with paltry ability and wisdom, naturally such a person will often feel ashamed and inadequate, only seeing his own errors and blind to his achievements. Seeing opposing views in this mood of shame and inadequacy fills a gap in his spirit. It is like getting food and drink when one is starving: How could he not accept them? People such as Stalin and Hitler just imagine the world to be a theater that performs specifically to extol and praise them, so how could they have let bystanders say anything that would throw cold water on that fantasy? From an objective political standpoint, when the people of the world express opinions about the government, including opposing views (When people in society express opinions about the government it is essentially critical. Because if they were not critical and wanting the government to do something different, why bother expressing their opinion? It seems very difficult to find people in China who understand this bit of common sense), it is the world showing itself.

The ruler encourages people to express their opinions, including opposing views, and accepts them. The ruler himself does not express his own opinions and only "[imitates the way] the suspended arm of a balance is not weighted to one side or the other, and so heavy and light show themselves and there is no room for deception. Just like water or a mirror has no idea of beauty or ugliness and beauty and ugliness display themselves, and then none can resent the result."[49] This is what is called governing the world with the world. A balance or a mirror are both examples of the nonaction of the ruler. Hence, the Chinese way of governance, which is also the Chinese way of the ruler, starts and ends with the ruler being able to listen (accept criticism). If a person can listen to what he doesn't want to hear, this is an indication of his strength and fortitude, and his vitality will be further fed by this. If a ruler only wants others to listen to him and hates it when they speak, he will be like a plant deprived of sunlight, water, and soil, his vitality stopped up. For the people, it will be as if all the oxygen has been sucked out and their breathing has been choked off. Kongzi said there is a single sentence that can come close to ruining the state: "None go against what I say."[50] How profound is his meaning! If the ruler can listen to the people, then the people will follow the commands of the court because they represent the people's [will].[51] The ruler listens and the people follow: this is a government in which there is interaction between higher and lower, a government without opposition.

[Translator's note: Section VI is another series of quotations from Lu Zhi along with Xu's annotations and has also been omitted.]

VII

Lu's political thought, as well as the entirety of Chinese political thought, may be summed as urging the ruler to

> put himself aside to follow the masses, go against his desires to follow the Way, stay away from flattery and rashness, draw near the conscientious and upright, extend utmost good faith, and eliminate rebelliousness and deception. Stop up the roads of slander and gloom and widen the gate of remonstrance and debate. . . . Record minor acts of goodness and talents to maximize the talents of the group. Forget petty flaws and petty resentments in order to discard nothing of value.[52]

In other words, he urges rulers to transform themselves morally, setting aside their own ability, wisdom, and preferences to follow those of the people. When discussing the way of governing under a despotic govern‐ ment, it is impossible to resolve the fundamental contradiction of the two political subjectivities mentioned above without getting down to this level, and [without doing so] all educational transformation would be empty. Hence, when the way of governing was discussed in the past there was no avoiding focusing on the way of the ruler. And discussion of the way of the ruler could not avoid the idea that "Yao and Shun served their lord [i.e., the people]."[53] That is, it ended up urging the ruler to be a sage practicing nonaction.

Historians often put Lu Zhi and Jia Yi[54] together and use Jia Yi's doctrine as a case in point. Ban Gu[55] said of Emperor Wen of the Han that he "cultivated himself with mysterious silence."[56] "Mysterious silence" accords very well with the conditions for being a ruler. Jia Yi's plan for securing order rarely brought up lordly virtue to Emperor Wen and merely encouraged him to put in place some measures in the spirit of grand unity.[57] This is because Jia and Lu were addressing different sovereigns and so they brought up different political ideas. However, when Jia Yi further discussed the fundamental problem of government, he said, "The fate of the world depends on the crown prince. . . . When the crown prince makes himself correct then the world is stable."[58] This is because the crown prince is the next generation's ruler. In Emperor Wen's time, there was no question of lordly virtue and so Jia Yi could not help considering the next generation. Therefore, he offered a series of ideas for the crown prince's education.

[Translator's note: A further series of quotations from Jia Yi with Xu's explanations has been omitted.]

Despite Emperor Dezong's deep recognition of Lu Zhi's worth, he still nearly had Lu Zhi executed on a pretext and ended up exiling Lu to Zhongzhou in his prime for the rest of his life.[59] Until his death, he mostly stayed shut in his house and did not dare to have visitors. This was not only a tragedy for Dezong and Lu Zhi, it was a tragedy for the whole of Chinese political history. I not only feel sympathy for Lu Zhi, I also feel sympathy for Dezong.[60] Yet if the contradiction of dual subjectivity is not resolved, this kind of tragedy can never be escaped.

Sages and worthies in Chinese history tried to eliminate this contradiction from the ruler's side, looking for a moral resolution to the contradiction. Modern democratic government resolves the contradiction through institutions. First, the source of power is moved from the ruler's hands to the people's, with "popular will" replacing "the ruler's mind." Institutionally, the government is the employee of the people. The government occupies the position of the minister in Chinese history while the people occupy the position of ruler. The people exercise the way of the ruler, expressing their agreement or disagreement with policies and then handing the responsibility for putting them into effect over to the government. Hence, the people still practice a kind of nonaction and the government then acts under this nonaction. So political leaders in a true democratic system have it much easier than the emperor did in the despotic period. The most difficult thing about being emperor, bar none, is being unable to have his own preferences. The reason he cannot have his own preferences is because he is the source of power and once his preferences merge with that power, they will batter down the people of the world's preferences and become a great evil.

But it is very difficult for a person to "rectify" and eliminate his preferences.[61] In a democracy, the leaders' preferences are separate from the source of power, so their preferences naturally have an objective restriction, which they cannot exceed to produce seeds of disorder. The flaws in their minds are not rectified, but rectify themselves. Next, in a democracy, the ruler's virtues such as emptying himself [of desires], correcting his errors, and accepting criticism are objectified into legislative government, freedom of assembly and expression, and other such objective institutions. Under these conditions, a political leader may not be a sage but he cannot help doing what a sage would do. He has to follow the results of the elections and he has to listen to the legislature's arguments. Whatever one objectively must do is subjectively easy to do. An American journalist can call [President] Truman a "horrible, despicable liar."[62] In a despotism, if the ruler could tolerate this he would be a sage. If he could not tolerate it then he would want to do something horrible and become a tyrant. But now, no matter how Truman feels about it there is nothing he can do but pay it no heed. Paying no heed does not show he is a sage, but it does show that he cannot help accepting the objective framework of a sage.

The sage ruler and way of governing that Chinese sages and worthies endured endless suffering to bring about becomes routinized in a democracy, becoming something ordinary. If Dezong had been a president or a prime minister in a democracy, I fully believe he would have surpassed Truman or Churchill because Truman didn't have his ability and wisdom, and I fear Churchill did not have his authentic demeanor. Then political theorists on the order of Lu Zhi would probably be a dime a dozen and not worth such admiration. The political contradiction in Chinese history, and the historical tragedies produced by this contradiction, can only be naturally resolved in a democratic government. For Chinese political thought to accept democracy is only to objectify the idea of political virtue already inherent in it and form it into a system everyone can follow. This is a completely logical road to follow, natural and easy, with not the slightest strained interpretation or forced conclusion.

Hence, I often say that anyone who truly understands and respects Chinese culture will certainly believe that the current efforts for democracy are a road that will make a connection to saying, "The sage at times exhausts himself." This is a development necessary for Chinese culture itself. If anyone still has doubts regarding this, I fear they are not someone who can "comprehend the changes from the past to the present."[63]

Chapter 8

Between Academia and Politics

Translator's introduction: This article was, as Xu describes, written as a response to Tang Junyi concerning the relationship between philosophical ideas and democracy and which takes priority. Tang was a close friend of Xu and also strongly influenced by Xiong Shili. Both agreed that democracy in China should be based on Ruist principles. Their disagreement was over what this means exactly. For Xu, although Ruism should be the philosophical foundation of democratic thought in China, it should not limit the operation of political democracy. A democratic government could choose laws and policies that reflect and institute Ruist values (such as filial behavior toward parents), but only if the democratic majority endorses these. Implicitly, that means the democratic majority could also choose *not* to have such policies, and this too would be a legitimate choice. Democracy constrains what doctrines can be instituted in politics, rather than doctrine constraining how democracy operates. This is what he means by democracy having primary significance and scholarship or thought having secondary significance.

The way for thought to compete is through persuasion, not coercion. Xu is very concerned about the possibility of totalitarianism, which he believes is the inevitable result of allowing doctrine to be given priority over democracy. Yet at the same time, he sees no problem with

Between Academia and Politics, 165–76, first published in *Democratic Review* 4, no. 20, October 16, 1953.

government endorsing and instituting a particular value system, as long as it is chosen democratically and minority views are protected and, hence, have the opportunity to persuade and change the majority. So although he does not specifically say so, he implies that there should be a great deal of freedom in academia and free expression in general, so minority views have a chance to be heard. His position is neither that government has to remain neutral among differing value systems (one version of contemporary liberalism), nor that any doctrine can ever come before democracy and limit democratic practice.

Mr. Tang Junyi[1] once responded to my question concerning "freedom of thought and political democracy" in a long letter, which was published in vol. 4 no. 18 of this journal. Mr. Tang gave a powerful explanation of the point "why the concepts of freedom and democracy should be of secondary significance." This has been his consistent position and it basically has no flaws. However, unless I explain myself a little, socially there might be misunderstanding of this point and even abuse. Hence, I wrote this to explain my viewpoint further.

I

Initially, Mr. Tang said my "essays on democracy over the years significantly emphasized differentiating politics and academia or thought," which is indeed the case. However, the reason I feel they should be differentiated is not that politics and academia and thought have no relation or should have no relation. Their relation may be said to be self-evident. What I wanted to say is if any doctrine or form of thought is to be implemented by the government it must, to use the old Chinese terms, pass the people's "favor and disfavor"; to use the new terminology, it must be chosen by popular will. Any "good" doctrine or form of thought and any policy that is derived from them must stop at the level of doctrine and thought if it is not favored or selected by the people. Governments certainly cannot directly compel their political realization on the grounds that they are absolutely true or good or similar reasons. When it comes to the political domain, all doctrine and thought before popular will is of secondary significance; popular will has the primary significance.

Only popular will directly determines politics. Doctrine and thought can only become political by going through the "twists and turns" of popular will. This is not to derogate academia, but to say that both academia and politics have their own sphere. The value of academia is decided within the academic sphere, not within the political sphere. If some doctrine or thought wants to realize its effectiveness politically, then it must accept the rules of the political sphere and it must go through this transition to help achieve political democracy. Otherwise, totalitarians can carry out tyrannical totalitarian rule using any doctrine or thought as a cover, and under these circumstances all can become tools for executing people. For example, the British Labour Party believes its economic policies based on socialism are the best. The Conservative Party believes the same about its economic policies based on liberalism. But whoever loses the election has to bow their head before the people's will and stand aside, waiting for the next time the people choose. This is what democracy means.

To take an extreme case, hypothetically if communism were selected by popular will, then it would take control of the government. When people reject it, then it retreats to the domain of scholarship and thought. In other words, if communists could accept that in the category of politics, it is popular will that decides ideology and not their ideology that determines popular will, and that popular will can absolutely freely change, then communists would not have to be totalitarians and communism would not have to be an ideology that kills. But the Communist Party now thinks that what they believe—from philosophy down to eating and sleeping—is the ultimate truth and ultimate good. Whenever there is disapproval of its popular will, they first exterminate the social classes that they believe are not compatible with their thought, with ultimate truth and good as their excuse or out of fanaticism. Then they go on with continuous thought pacification. And because they believe they are carrying out the Way on behalf of heaven (ideology), if this thought pacification means killing millions of people, killing for decades, they still feel no guilt. From a certain angle, rather than saying this is the fault of communism itself, it is better to say it is the fault of communism being unwilling to accept having secondary significance in politics and hence not allowing choice by popular will.

Choice by popular will and violent struggle are absolutely opposed. We should understand that the German Social Democrat Party founded by Kautsky's group[2] is also a branch of Marxism. This branch, if it obtained political power and could still have had "the majority protect the minority" and not interfere with further free choice by the people, like the British Labour Party, then we could not say that this branch is also totalitarian. Nowadays, many people think socialism means totalitarianism and only capitalism can be democratic. This way of thinking also takes ideology[3] to determine politics directly, putting ideology above popular will: in itself it is a totalistic way of thinking. Supposing popular will selects socialism freely, then if you say this is not democratic, obviously popular will is not the standard of democracy at this point and ideology is the standard. It is hard to say that in these circumstances believers in capitalism can adopt the method of a coup and reject this choice of the people, yet be called democratic.

I am not advocating for socialism here, but explaining that democratic government itself is not stuck to any specific ideology or content of thought. It builds a political form where the people can freely choose an ideology or thought. In the political sphere, this form of free choice has the primary significance and any thought or ideology is secondary. Whether a government is totalitarian or democratic is not determined by a particular thought or ideology. It is whether a form of thought or ideology—or its adherents—is willing to stand beneath this form of free choice and be bound by it that determines whether it is totalitarian or democratic. This is the reason why I advocate the differentiation of doctrine or thought and politics, and the reason why I advocate not putting any doctrine or thought within the scope of politics above democratic government, why I do not want them pressed down on top of the free choice of popular will: all of this I say from this perspective. The direct responsibility academia bears to society and the nation is done through teaching, not through ruling. Teaching is carried out in a situation of freedom, while governing always involves coercion.

II

Another reason academia and politics should be separated is the two have different standpoints on truth. I make no judgment about who may have found absolute truth at any time in history. However, the goal in scholarship is always to search for universal, proper, and absolute truth: it is the gate for humanity to pursue the truth without restrictions, demanding that people think seriously. The more seriously they think, what they grasp becomes deeper and what they are confident in becomes stronger. Then in the history of scholarship there appear many forms of thought such as idealism and materialism and other monisms. In scholarship, the successful people have some sort of monistic view; the people with real achievements invariably advocate some form of monism.

At present in China there are many people who advocate freedom of thought, but in fact they don't want to think in a free environment; they want to not think in a free environment. They have no thought of their own and so they don't understand that the end result of thinking is to endorse something (there are some who hold onto doubt until the end of their days, but they still feel they have to doubt for their entire lives, that there is something that cannot be comprehended, and this is also a kind of endorsement). Then they think that there is some absolute endorsement in thought that becomes some kind of monism, which is totalitarian, and so the only option is to eliminate scholarship and thought. On this point, I agree completely with Mr. Tang's opinion.

However, politically speaking the truth of any scholarship can only be a variable, relative truth. Government can in fact only be relatively responsible for academic truth. Individuals in government of course can have complete faith in a religion or doctrine as individuals, but they must be aware that this is a personal matter concerning them as individuals and separate their personal faith from governmental matters. Only the most confused people are unable to get clear on this point and take all their personal beliefs to be a governmental matter and everything governmental to be their personal beliefs. The purity of academia can only be secured by distinguishing the academic standpoint on truth and the political standpoint on truth. Then academia and political democracy will not impede each other and can help each other succeed.

If not, then there will be two consequences. Ever since there has been a concept of truth, there have always been two opposing sides. Many people have thought they resolved this opposition, but from history we see that they just created a new opposition. Academically speaking, uncompromising debate between opposing sides is rather a measure of how academia pushes forward. However, if the government also takes an absolute position on what is true and takes absolute responsibility for it, then it can only forcefully spread its own truth and forcefully eradicate the one that is opposed to it. This has to result in the violent work of the Communist Party called "thought reform." Some people think that without first resolving philosophical questions, we cannot resolve political questions. Then, in the space of a few days and nights, they rush out a grand philosophical system to tear down all others: this is to buy into Plato's deception about "philosopher-kings."

The second consequence is that any academic principles have to make some accommodation, large or small, when shaping political policy and being implemented. Even if it is a truth without criticism in academia, logical truths, for example. Suppose a logical positivist applied his attitude of deducing formulas to the political sphere and found that every utterance of the people had some problem: Could this still consti-tute some correct political "reference"? So in this case, logical language has to be strongly discounted. Hence, we understand that any political implementation or theoretical account of a policy cannot be considered the standard of scholarship or thought. This is a kind of modesty that those responsible for government in fact have to have. It is also a belief that those who do scholarly work have to have regarding the political domain and the independence and self-respect of academia. This is a question of the particular nature of different fields, not a matter of one being a higher level than the other.

From what has been said above, the greatest difference between politics and academia is the difference between quantity and quality. The opinions of ten thousand average people on philosophy would have a difficult time matching the opinions of one philosopher. The scientific knowledge of ten thousand average people lacks a method to match the knowledge of one scientist. Here, quality counts more than quantity, which is the essence of scholarship and thought. But in politics, the vote of a great philosopher or scientist is the same as an average person's, only counting as one vote. If he wants to exercise a greater political impact the only way to do it is to try to appeal to the sympathy of the public for his opinion. This means that quality has to have quantitative acceptance in order to make an impact in politics. In politics, quantity counts more than quality. Moving the academic emphasis on quality to politics, then we have Nietzsche and his "overman" government, which without doubt is a dictatorship.

However, this is not to say that democracy comes into conflict with humanity's qualitative advancement, but paves the road for qualitative advancement. First, in "Politics and Human Life"[4] I wrote that democ-racy is a government where the government itself limits itself. In human life, politics is limited to a position where it can exist or not in order to liberate human life outside of politics, and liberate people to live in pursuit of quality. Second, freedom in democracy is manifested in the majority safeguarding the minority, so that there is definite opportunity for them to change places [a minority opinion becoming the majority]. This allows any "quality" to fight for the chance to become the "quantity." In this way, the quality of academic doctrines still exerts its effects behind the quantitative determination of government. A dictator takes his own opinions to be qualitatively the best and hence insists on making one person's opinions into the opinions of myriads of people through coercive means, making them into robots without freedom of choice. A dictatorial world is then inevitably a materialized[5] world. In such a world it is impossible for there to be free activity of the soul or scholarship and thought. That truly becomes a quantitative world of numbers and mere things.

We should understand on a deeper level that the politics that is determined by quantity is founded on the great principle of the humanistic spirit. The humanistic spirit foremost recognizes that "life" is a value, that it is the cardinal value. Next, we may say that further demanding that "life" have some kind of meaning is the second value. This second value has to find its place in the cardinal value and cannot go around it to talk directly about the second value, especially when society is the object. Making life the cardinal value means immediate recognition of "life," an immediate recognition of quantitative value.[6] European human-ism evolved to the point of emphasizing quality in the overman, and when it made quality the cardinal value, this was a decadent mutation of humanism. Orthodox humanism always makes "life" the cardinal value.

Chinese Ruism is an obvious illustration of this direction. In the *Changes* it says, "The great virtue of heaven and earth is called life."[7] Wang Fuzhi [1619–1692][8] took "honoring life" as the primary charac-teristic of the Ruist spirit, in contrast to the naturalism of Daoism and focus on liberation in Buddhism. Hence, "caring for the living and sending off the dead without regret" is "the foundation of the kingly way,"[9] meaning that first the government must start with "quantity" and give it its appropriate place. When Kongzi said, "Give ease to the elderly . . . cherish the youth"[10] he did not ask which elderly and which youths are themselves worthy of being eased or cherished; at that time he looked only at the cardinal value. When he went to Wei, he first sighed over "how numerous [the people were]," then followed that by suggesting they should be "enriched" and "taught."[11] This is finding a place for the secondary value within the primary value. If it were Stalin, he would want first to ascertain the classes among the "numerous" people. If it were Hitler, he would want first to ascertain the "bloodlines" or "heredity" of the "numerous" people. These are examples of how dictators cannot immediately acknowledge "life" as cardinal, nor can they immediately acknowledge the primacy of "quantity."

When Kongzi saw someone bearing the population register (at that time called a *ban* 版), he stood [and bowed] from his carriage.[12] When he saw villagers playing at the game of "driving away pestilence" he put on his court dress and stood on the eastern steps,[13] displaying the utmost respect. In these instances he displayed the great humanistic spirit of immediate recognition of the value of life and people. Song-Ming Ruists for the most part emphasized attentiveness to personal morality, and so when considering the Ruist humanistic spirit from the perspective of "life" it is often concealed by the transition from the individual up to the higher moral viewpoint. When looked at this way, the Ruist humanistic spirit was deepened by Song-Ming Ruists, but it also became narrower. However, as long as they are true Ruists, they invariably cross over from the isolated, lofty place of personal morality and come to achieve an embrace of the idea, "All people are my compatriots and all things are the same kind as myself,"[14] and reveal the quantitative measure of "the streets are full of sages."[15] So an individual says to another individual that there is a distinction between the worthy and the unworthy, but an individual says to society that no one may put himself above society simply on account of his learning.

III

Considered from a different viewpoint, the account of the theory for democracy is itself a kind of thought, a kind of doctrine. Therefore, it is like the scholarship and thought of other academic fields in that it has its origin and connections to other doctrines and forms of thought. However, as far as its origins, I do not believe that it is a stage in the necessary development of absolute reason, as Hegel said. As far as its connections, they are not completely homogeneous, dependent relations. Democracy and freedom have their self-sufficient value within their own parameters. I also argue that the Ruist spirit and humanistic spirit should be the true basis of democracy, but on the one hand, this derives from the viewpoint of an individual in a culture and on the other hand, it is a way of removing obstructions and opening a clear path [to democracy] in that culture, and in this way can make both sides, democracy and Ruism, complete.

For democracy, Ruism can give it self-consciousness of its origin in human nature; for the Ruist and humanistic spirit, democracy can give them a realization in politics and a definite level of achievement. One cannot say on account of this that the Ruist and humanistic spirit encompasses democracy, nor can one say that without the Ruist spirit, the humanistic spirit, idealism, or similar views of the self-awareness of the individual that it is not fitting to talk about democratic government. China already had Ruism two thousand years ago, but up until now not only could not establish democratic government, it is still groping for an understanding of the concept. European humanism first came out of the autocratic small states of the Italian peninsula, and it was a harbinger of autocratic monarchy in European history. And in fact, the dynamism of European merchants was a strong impetus for the formation of democracy. One can thus understand that the birth of the democracy was a fortuitous combination of many different factors and it is not someone's only child.

The influence of idealism or empiricism on democracy is always a possibility, not a necessity. Plato and Nietzsche opposed democracy, and so did Machiavelli and Hobbes. (According to recent research, when Plato first arrived in Athens he wanted to be active in the democratic government, but prodded by the death of his teacher Socrates, he came to oppose democracy.) And empiricism and materialism have an even closer relationship. The average person does not recognize that there needs to be a disjunction between politics and scholarship, or that on the one hand they are connected but on the other are also self-sufficient. Then in their advocacy of democracy they are identical, but empiricists believe that they have to overthrow idealism to have democracy and idealists usually despise empiricism. This is due to the fact that they both look at the possible development of democracy from their thought as a necessity, and this necessity cannot help turning into exclusivity.

If one believes that overthrowing some school of thought in scholarship is indispensable for achieving democratic government, in scholarship I'm afraid no one can conclusively overthrow anyone else, other than with the methods of the Communist Party. Furthermore, if a dispute within academia is moved to the domain of government, this is a fundamental violation of the principle of academic freedom. This kind of exclusion itself is undemocratic, unless there is some aspect that, when applied to the issue of government, is opposed to democracy, as in Marxism-Leninism's opposition to democracy.

As for the relatedness and self-sufficiency of academia, it may be compared to Three Gorges generator project. If it is successful, this naturally originates in the power of the size of the flow in the Yangzi River above the Three Gorges. However, the water in the river cannot necessarily be turned into usable energy; in between there are a number of scientific conditions that have to be met and significant effort. Fulfilling these conditions and making the effort to complete the generator project has its own self-sufficient value, which cannot be denied. Since the age when Plato proclaimed his ideals of reason to the development of Hegel's dialectic of absolute reason, philosophical thought has always looked at the problems of various disciplines and aspects as a unified problem with a single essence. In idealism, it is a question of a higher and lower level, and it puts itself on the higher level. In empiricism, it is a question of reality and fiction: what doesn't fit with the method of one's own experience is fiction. What is real is the self.

The main purpose of Kant's three *Critiques* was probably to take the three great problems of his culture and put each into its own sphere so that they would not interfere with each other. When Kant talked about politics, he talked only about politics. For example, in *Perpetual Peace* he advocated a world confederation that would have to be formed through a group of republican states with democratic constitutions, which is to say that democracy is the foundation for peace. He did not touch on his own philosophy. This is the most equitable attitude. In the past thirty years there seem to be many scholars who have begun to admit that it is impossible to use one method to constitute a standard for all the various academic disciplines, which is really a "return to the Kantian spirit." Maybe now we can resolve many unnecessary academic disputes and launch a new direction. However, this already goes too far beyond the scope of what I can say here.

IV

In the above, I distinguished politics as an object from typical scholarship and thought. This distinction is based on taking the standpoint of scholarship to look at politics, in which politics takes on secondary significance. When taking the political standpoint to look at academia, then academia takes on secondary significance. There is no fixed, hierarchical relationship between them. But as soon as one looks at it as it is realized in the subjectivity of an individual with responsibility over government, then I completely agree with Mr. Tang's opinion. A person in himself is a "totality." In this "totality," politics is something optional, and it is a part where the bad absolutely outweighs the good. In "Politics and Human Life," I did a general analysis and concluded that the completely politicized life is the worst, the most withered and fossilized, and the most unfortunate human life. At the same time, one cannot truly understand democracy when engaging in politics on the basis of this kind of life and one will not make a real effort toward democracy. This kind of person will only discuss democracy when thwarted politically; in his mind, democracy is only the cheapest sign to hang to snatch power and profit.

Socially speaking, democracy is about limiting government to a small part of life to liberate life in other aspects of society. The purpose is not to let political activity overtake all of society so there is no other activity and the society becomes one where there are only dominators and plain slaves who are dominated. The true significance of democracy can only be realized in the lives of individuals who have a rich cultural life, whose "totality" is a totality with a rich content. Only those that have the self-awareness to realize that politics is something optional in the totality of life and a small part in which the harm outweighs the benefit can truly understand democracy. Only they can truly make the great vow[16] to make politics limited to a small part of social life, just as it is limited to only a small part of the individual's totality of life. They make the effort to realize this form of life for boundless humanity.

If this kind of person were in a state that had not yet achieved democracy, he would engage in a lifelong struggle for democracy. Otherwise, each individual could not complete his normal development, meaning he could not "follow his nature." This is exactly the same as Śakyamuni's compassionate vow to help all sentient beings enter nirvana without remainder.[17] This is the function of a purified life. This is political activity with the assistance of a rich and refined "totality" of life, and therefore it is humanized[18] politics and not politicized human life. It is a case of giving his life to jump into the muddy waters of political power[19] in order to let politics be promoted[20] and purified through its own restrictions: this is just like the great vow of the bodhisattva Dizang to dedicate himself [to saving beings] in hell.[21]

Nearly all scholars of the European Enlightenment looked at democracy as the highest [political] ideal, using everything they studied to support the struggle for democracy and freedom. In actuality, they used what they studied to support this political aspect of human life, and this is the only reason for that glorious manifestation in history. At this point, the more intelligent in our country cannot fulfill their lives in scholarship and can only turn to politics to fill out their lives. The desire for power[22] is the totality of their lives and government is precisely the location of power; hence, the entirety of their lives becomes politicized. Outside of satisfying their desire for power in government, they feel they have no other needs in life, completely unable to discover anything better than government. The average person easily uses himself as a measure to look at the objective world. When this kind of person's life is completely politicized, he naturally believes that there is only political activity in the society and that only political activity is valuable. Because of this, the only way to fit with their ideals is to make all social activity political activity and to make everything a tool for politics.[23]

Naturally, government presses down on everything under the control of this kind of person, and naturally they become the enemy of democracy. This kind of person grabs an opportunity and acquires power, believing himself to be superior. If one day their luck changes, then without knowing it they will show their worthlessness. There is no other option: there is nothing else in their lives other than being an official. So to this kind of person, it is better to die than to not be an official. Tracing this back to its source, it is because in his life he never had the education to restrain himself and guidance from scholarly culture, to the point of not enriching his "totality" of life. Then there is only politics, not human life, because the great wellspring is blocked off. Life should be enriched by scholarship, while politics spins off from life. In the past in Chinese discussions of politics, usually scholarship and the human heart-mind were first. Taking the position of an individual undertaking governmental responsibility, this is absolutely correct. I take it this this was Mr. Tang's true meaning.

Scholarship, roughly speaking, can be divided into two main categories: achieving knowledge and achieving character. Knowledge is expressed through concepts; character is expressed through dispositions. No concept can express the entire body [of knowledge], and when it comes to human life, still less could it express its totality. So conceptual study is not necessarily the sort of study that achieves character. If it could, then it would certainly have to refine itself, intentionally or not, in a period of fire in inner life, and merge with the totality of life through the dispositions. The Ruist spirit—the humanistic spirit—is not a kind of learning that is primarily conceptual. It requires knowledge—at least it does not oppose knowledge—but primarily it seeks to achieve character, not knowledge. Character is manifested as motives, a general temperament, tolerance, and integrity: these four manifest the totality of value in human life, so not only can they guide politics, they guide all activity in life, including scholarship. They give every activity its vitality and rectify their directions.

Democracy and freedom are an attitude. From a certain angle, the Ruist spirit, the humanistic spirit, is primarily about achieving the reveal of a good attitude from one's dispositions. This is being responsible to life, and so is also the origin of democracy and freedom. Democracy and freedom are precisely the objectification of the Ruist spirit, the humanistic spirit, in politics. It must do this to begin to fulfill its great purpose as an entire body of doctrine. The reason the Chinese Ruist spirit could not turn to democracy, historically and culturally speaking, was that its political development was never completed. I believe that those who grasp the true Ruist spirit today should make it their mission to realize democracy. This is the unstoppable demand the fundamental Ruist spirit makes in politics. Under the impact of the activity of this spirit, the wellspring of democratic government will increasingly flow, not stopping day or night.[24] This is completely consistent with Meng-zi's discussion of fulfilling the heart-mind and nature and, anxious and troubled, seeking the realization of the "kingly way" and "harmonizing the inner and outer ways."[25]

Government requires knowledge in order to manage the affairs of the public, so it is easy to understand the relationship between politics and learning that aims at knowledge. I will not say more here. Behind government, there is an even greater need for character, yet today the relationship between government and learning that aims at character is concealed and hard to see (in the past in China, it was held to be a self-evident principle). This is why the effort of Mr. Tang and Mr. Mou[26] in *Democratic Review* in recent years on this question is a great effort. As far as democratic freedom is concerned, this effort, as Mr. Tang has said, is an indirect discussion, a discussion of the source. I don't think the relation between these [character learning and government] can elicit controversy. If there is controversy, it is because of not enough work on persuasion and more effort needs to be applied to this. Of course, the Chinese culture talked about in the schools and the democracy and freedom street politicians talk about are incompatible and cannot be linked. This is as expected and need not be discussed more.

Chapter 9

The Culture of the Heart-Mind

Translator's introduction: This is one of Xu's most important writings on human nature and ethics, briefly summarizing his interpretation of the doctrine that he later treated at greater length in *A History of Chinese Theories of Human Nature: The Pre-Qin Period*. His central question here is the source of shared human values. His chief dissatisfaction with Western liberalism was its exclusive focus on empirical knowledge and reduction of value to something like utilitarianism: if moral virtues cannot be found scientifically, then the only source of morality is subjective feelings of pleasure and pain. For Xu, this denies the essence of humanity and reduces humans to animals.

He locates the source of value in the universal heart-mind that all people have. This obviously owes a great deal to Song-Ming Neo-Ruism, Lu Xiangshan and Wang Yangming especially, and does not appear to differ from Xu's contemporaries Mou Zongsan and Tang Junyi. Yet in this essay, Xu makes clear where he disagrees with them (though he never mentions them by name). Chinese culture is not based on metaphysical propositions, and he denies that it is a form of idealism, the interpretation Mou and Tang were developing. Xu insists that the heart-mind is not something outside the physical form; the doctrine of the heart-mind is

Collected Essays on Chinese Intellectual History, 242–49, first published in *Democratic Review* 4, no. 20, October 16, 1953.

"embodied learning," not metaphysics. It has to be realized in practice in the real world.

The way the reality of the heart-mind is known is neither through scientific investigation nor philosophical speculation. It is "embodied recognition," direct awareness of one's own moral responses to phenomena in the real world (see the introduction for more on this term). Someone who experiences these reactions cannot deny their reality. The way to understand morality is moral cultivation and action, not developing theories to justify it. If the existence of moral values cannot be confirmed scientifically, this merely shows the limits of science, not that these values are chimerical. All orthodox Chinese thought, Xu claims, starts with this heart-mind. It is Chinese culture's distinctive contribution, but at the same time it is common to all humanity and universally accessible.

Note: Xu's use of the Chinese equivalent of italics for emphasis is extraordinarily frequent in this essay. To me, italicizing all such emphasized phrases reads poorly in English, and so I have substantially reduced these.

The most fundamental special characteristic of Chinese culture is, we might say, the "culture of the heart-mind." My purpose for discussing this topic is to clarify a few misunderstandings and open a way forward for Chinese culture, because many of the present misunderstandings concerning Chinese culture are produced from misunderstanding this "heart-mind." The situation caused by these misunderstandings has led many people to feel that Chinese traditional culture accumulated over thousands of years has been forced into a situation with no way out.

The Source of Human Values

Foremost we should recognize that in the process of human cultural development, many people are searching for a solution to the problem of the source of human values. A person has to have his fundamental [value] standpoint, otherwise he will feel adrift and aimless, without direction or strength. So he must first find a standpoint before he can have confidence, a direction, and a place in which to settle. The root questions, "Where do values come from? And how can they be evaluated?" in fact are the questions of finding a fundamental standpoint in human life. Some like to think God or heaven is the source of human values. Some people take it to be something metaphysical, such as the

Forms[1] or absolute spirit.[2] Others believe it based on the benefit and
harm people do to each other[3] or reactions to environmental stimuli.
Then there is an American biologist who traces it back to protoplasm.
But where does Chinese culture believe the source of human values is?

Chinese culture spans thousands of years of history, and furthermore
the Chinese nation is a great nation. It has gone through a long process
during its actual existence and in a long process there are naturally
many twists and turns. Hence, as the culture gropes forward there are
also many twists and turns, just as the water of the Yellow River carries
along silt as it flows. In other words, there are a number of divergences
and motley things mixed in Chinese culture. There are various answers
to the question of the source of values in human life. However, when
we trace this process to its end and clear away the twists and turns and
miscellany, then we can cut to the chase and say that Chinese culture
holds that the source of values in human life is human beings' own heart-mind.
This fundamental affirmation may be said to be a special characteristic
of Chinese culture and something other nationalities do not have, with
the exception of a few twentieth-century Western thinkers who are
making an effort in the same direction but still without a breakthrough.

The heart-mind talked about in Chinese culture refers to *a part of
the physiological structure of the person*, meaning that it refers to a part of
the "five sense organs and hundred bones."[4] The function that occurs
in this part is believed to be the source of human values. It is exactly
the same as the way the eyes and ears are believed to be the source for
distinguishing colors and hearing sounds. Mengzi held the eyes and ears
to belong to the "lesser parts" because their function is lesser, and said the
heart-mind is the "greater part" because its function is greater.[5] However,
no matter whether they are greater or lesser, *they are the same in being
part of the physiological structure of the human body*. Could one say that
this part of the physiological structure is the mind of Western idealism?
Does the mind in Western idealism refer to a part of the physiological
structure of the body? So there are some hints connecting the heart-mind
of Chinese culture to an aspect of materialism, because physiology is
basically a kind of material and the function of the heart-mind is indeed
a function of a part of physiology.

There are no traces whatsoever to connect it to idealism. I must
mention in passing that there are some lines in the "Appended Phrases"
of the *Changes* that are easily misunderstood: "What is above physical
form pertains to the Way, and what is below physical form pertains

to vessels."[6] The Way mentioned here refers to the Way of Heaven. "Form" in the middle Warring States period referred to the human body, so meaning human beings. "Vessels" refers to utensils used by people. The meaning of these two sentences is that above humanity there is the Way of heaven and below humanity there are utensils. This is a *division between upper and lower based on humanity occupying the center.* And the heart-mind is in the center of the human body. If one were to finish the passage according to its original intent, then one should add a line: "What is within form is called the heart-mind." So the culture of the heart-mind, or philosophy of the heart-mind, can only be called "embodied learning" (*xing er zhong xue* 形而中學) and should not be called metaphysics.[7]

The development of contemporary science is unable to deny the Chinese culture of the heart-mind. This is because the question is not whether this function is located in the heart[8] or the brain, but rather whether the function described in Chinese culture exists in the physiology of humanity. That is, whether there are the functions described by Mengzi: the feelings of alarm and compassion, shame and dislike, approval and disapproval, declining and yielding, and so on.[9] If this kind of function does not exist in life, then there is nothing more to say. If, on the other hand, we can have embodied recognition of the feelings of alarm and compassion, shame and dislike, approval and disapproval, declining and yielding, then this proves that *there is some part of our body that possesses this function.*

It is just like how some people believe contemporary psychology cannot confirm the activity of the soul described in literature. But if the activity of the soul cannot be confirmed by doing psychology experiments, then this *is a problem with psychology itself.* The key is whether there is this activity of the soul in people's lives. If people have embodied recognition of this function in themselves, then the Chinese culture of the heart-mind is a concrete existent. This is something completely different in kind from [religious] faith or some metaphysical thing built up from speculation.

Misunderstandings of "Heart-Mind"

Many people mistakenly think that whenever the heart-mind is brought up in traditional Chinese thought it is a form of idealism, and further that idealism is inevitably politically reactionary. I have yet to see anyone find definite historical evidence or establish a solid theory to show that idealism and materialism are always politically reactionary and revolutionary, respectively. Whether this is true or not I will not discuss for now. What I want to make clear is that *the heart-mind of Chinese culture is in no way the "mind" of idealism and has no involvement with idealism.* Idealism in Chinese culture, as in "The triple world is nothing but mind and the myriad dharmas are nothing but consciousness,"[10] derives from Indian Buddhism. The controversy between idealism and materialism in Western ontology goes back very early: Is it spirit that is prior or is it matter? Does spirit create matter or does matter create spirit? Spirit is the heart-mind. Simply put, idealism is the view that mind is prior to matter and that mind creates matter. This is a question carried over from religion. However, this question certainly does not appear in every cultural system. In Chinese culture, it was never taken to be an important question that aroused controversy.

Additionally, jumping to the conclusion that the heart-mind in China is a form of idealism may be called incongruous. In his preface to *Records of Masters of Han Learning*, selected and annotated by Zhou Yutong,[11] Zhou said, "Lu Jiuyuan [Xiangshan] was an advocate of the position 'heart-mind is Pattern' . . . taking all phenomena to be produced by the heart-mind. Apart from the heart-mind all phenomena have no possibility of existence."[12] I once wrote an essay on Lu Xiangshan and read his works several times. Lu and other advocates of "heart-mind is Pattern" all believed that the ethical pattern [*lunli zhi li* 倫理之理] derived from the heart-mind, so taking it to the extreme, they said, "Heart-mind is Pattern." All phenomena (meaning the empirical world) have no relation at all with the ethical pattern that Lu was talking about. Taking the phrase "heart-mind is Pattern" and interpreting it as meaning that "all phenomena are produced by the heart-mind" is utter nonsense. Despite that, many scholars of intellectual history today are surprisingly still mired at this level of nonsense.

They make one great assumption: that any philosophy belongs to either materialism or idealism. What belongs to idealism is reactionary and what belongs to materialism is revolutionary. When the heart-mind of Chinese philosophy is categorized as idealism, as Zhou Yutong did, then Chinese culture at its most basic source is forced into a situation with no way out. On the one hand, they cannot correctly understand Western idealism, while they also have not seriously read Chinese materials. Giving a strained and forced interpretation to everything, they cannot avoid blotting out the most important aspect of Chinese culture.

The Values Manifested by the Function of the Heart-Mind

Human values are primarily manifested in the activities of morality, religion, art, cognition, and so on. In Chinese culture, they are primarily manifested in morality. However, for a very long time the Chinese, like other nationalities, attributed the source of moral values to gods or heaven.[13] Not until Kongzi did someone bodily recognize that the source of moral values is in human life. Hence, Kongzi said, "Is benevolence really so far away? If I simply desire benevolence, then it is here," and, "The key to achieving benevolence lies within yourself."[14] These sayings make it clear that the source of values is not in heaven or in gods, nor is it metaphysical. Otherwise it could not be *immediately complete*[15] *this way*. But Kongzi did not explicitly say that the source is in human life, nor did he clarify that it is the heart-mind. When Kongzi talked about the heart-mind, he still used the ordinary meaning.

The opening of the *Mean* reads, "Nature means what is mandated by heaven."[16] This may be said to be a metaphysical proposition. However, this metaphysical proposition has a unique point, which is that it is immediately realized in the person and becomes the person's essence (nature). Nature takes root within human life. Because of this, the *Mean* does not put great importance on the question of heaven, only putting importance on the question of human nature. Mengzi was the one who first definitively pointed out that the source of morality is the human heart-mind: "Benevolence, rightness, ritual propriety, and wisdom are rooted in the heart-mind."[17] This saying of Mengzi's is the conclusion of a long period of searching in Chinese culture. It is not *the conclusion of a logical inference* but is an account of an *internal experience*.[18] This one saying immediately activated the luminous function of what had been a mixed-up and chaotic life, showing that each person has a direction, a master, that can become their fundamental standpoint in life. Afterwards, Cheng Hao, Lu Xiangshan, and Wang Yangming, and others all developed from this path laid by Mengzi.

Laozi's Way has a metaphysical character. He requires people to go "embody the Way" meaning for people who are below the Way to go harmonize with the Way that is above people. One cannot say that this Way is born out of human life. Chinese culture, however, always takes the approach of proceeding from higher to lower and receiving internally what comes from outside. Zhuangzi took Laozi's metaphysical Way and realized it in people's heart-minds, believing emptiness, stillness, and clarity of the heart-mind is the Way. Hence, Zhuangzi advocated fasting of the heart-mind[19] and sitting and forgetting[20] to make the empty, still, and clear original nature of the heart-mind emerge, which is the emergence of the Way. From this, people's spirit attains great liberation.

One basic meaning of my book *The Spirit of Chinese Art*[21] was to explain that Zhuangzi's empty, still, and clear heart-mind is actually an aesthetic spirit; the source of aesthetic value is in the empty, still, and clear heart-mind. Simply put, art requires setting up the object of beauty. Purely objective things have no beauty or lack of beauty to speak of. When we consider something to be beautiful, our heart-mind exists in this empty, still, and clear state. Hence, from the Wei-Jin period on, the great painters of China pursued creativity within the empty, still, and clear heart-mind. The famous Tang dynasty artist Zhang Zao said, "Model after the maker of change [nature] outside and get inspiration from the heart-mind inside."[22] The two phrases cover the entirety of Chinese theories of painting. And to model after nature outside requires first attaining an empty, still, and clear heart-mind. The late Tang writer Zhang Yanyuan's *Records of Famous Painters throughout History* pointed out that the attainments of Wang Wei, beloved by people in the Tang, did not actually measure up to Zhang Zao,[23] which shows that the heart-mind is the source of art in China.

In the field of knowledge, one might say that the "Undoing Fixation" chapter of *Xunzi* is China's classical epistemology. Xunzi said, "How does the heart-mind know the Way? I say: it is emptiness, unity, and stillness."[24] "Emptiness" means that the heart-mind can always take in and receive [information]; "unity" means that in the act of cognition one cannot recognize two or more objects simultaneously but can only concentrate on one object, and the heart-mind will naturally concentrate on one object. In order to recognize an object clearly, one must be in a state of "stillness," and the heart-mind will naturally calm itself in the act of cognition. In other words, Xunzi understood very early that the heart-mind is the source for attaining knowledge.

When it comes to religion, primitive religion disappeared from China very early on due to the advancement of the humanistic spirit, which gradually replaced religion.[25] However, in reality there are many unsolvable problems in human life, such as life and death, a final return-ing place, and so on. For this reason, among average people demands for religion still exist, which is why Buddhism was easily accepted by Chinese people when it came east.

According to Buddhism, people can transcend the cycle of birth and death through faith in the Buddha, ascending to heaven and becoming buddhas.[26] This is a pursuit of the higher and external through faith, ful-filling people's demands for religion. But when Chan Buddhism appeared, with its beliefs of "clarify the heart-mind to see one's nature"[27] and "see one's nature and become a Buddha,"[28] then these are actually beliefs that the original heart-mind is a buddha and one should not pursue what is external and higher. In other words, when Buddhism in China developed into Chan, this meant taking religious demands and returning them to people's heart-minds, so the Chan sect is also called the "heart-mind sect." This point also existed in India but was only brought to fruition in China. Chan later developed into "scolding buddhas and cursing ancestors,"[29] only morally cultivating the heart-mind, and then there was *no religious meaning* at all. This is why many of great virtue advocated correcting the flaws of Chan with Pure Land Buddhism. The Pure Land is the same as Paradise in Western traditions, a place apart from people's actual life. However, as Pure Land developed it came to imply that the Pure Land is in the human heart-mind: a purified heart-mind is the pure land and a defiled heart-mind is a defiled land. This demonstrates that the force of taking the standpoint of the heart-mind in Chinese culture is too strong.

The Key to Understanding the Problem is the Original Heart-Mind Manifested through Moral Cultivation

What we must pay attention to is that the activity of the heart-mind described above is not at all identical to the mind as usually described or to consciousness in psychology. When it gets mixed up with other physiological functions then the heart-mind not only cannot exercise its fundamental function, it *becomes an accomplice—even the slave—of these other parts of the physiology that produce desires.* In other words, at this point the heart-mind is not the fundamental heart-mind nor does it have its original function. Naturally, it is impossible to establish the source of human values based on this. This stage falls within the scope of modern psychological research.

The heart-mind that Mengzi, Xunzi, Zhuangzi, and later Chan masters talked about goes through development and moral cultivation, liberating it from other physiological activities and acting in its original form. Only at this point is it possible to perform its functions of morality, art, and objective cognition. The other physiological activities are what Ruists called selfish desires, so Mengzi said, "For nurturing life nothing is better than reducing desires."[30] Reducing desires means to *reduce the interference of other physiological functions*, because only this way can the fundamental nature of the heart-mind be revealed. Daoists further said, "No knowledge, no desires,"[31] knowledge referring to prejudices. Escaping prejudices and selfish desires is the only way to reveal the original activity of the heart-mind so it can take control over prejudices and desires and transform them. Then and only then is the heart-mind the source of human values.

The average person does not do any moral cultivation. Does that mean that the fundamental heart-mind does not function? This is mistaken. *The fundamental heart-mind is in human life*, so that the *fundamental heart-mind of anyone at any time in any place can function*; otherwise the person is a psychological deviant. However, the average person's functioning of their fundamental heart-mind is intermittent and confused, and the life that is manifested by this is a life of mixed good and evil. If their burden of prejudices and selfish desires is light then the fundamental heart-mind will emerge more. If they have many prejudices and selfish desires, then there will be few opportunities for the fundamental heart-mind to emerge. This is the reason that the moral level of poor people and physical laborers often is higher than that of wealthy people and intellectuals.

Looking from a deeper level, how is it that the heart-mind is the source of morality, art, and cognition? This connects to many questions that still cannot be answered to this day. People in ancient times often handed these unanswerable questions over to metaphysical propositions. Mengzi said, "This [heart-mind] is what heaven gave me."[32] Cheng Yi said, "Innate ability and innate awareness have no source; they come from heaven."[33] Both statements take the question of the heart-mind and turn it into metaphysics. When a question is pursued to the end and cannot be answered, modern scholars often set up a kind of fundamental assumption, whereas the ancients often attributed it to metaphysics. Yet Cheng Hao said, "Only the heart-mind is heaven."[34] This takes what was an *unfounded metaphysical proposition* and puts it into effect *in one's own life* through an internal experience attained through moral cultivation. The proposition "Only the heart-mind is heaven" was his true experience of moral cultivation brought home, and he only dared to say it on the basis of this experience.

Chinese culture is the culture of the heart-mind. Some people think that Chinese culture is subjective, that its morality is subjective morality, opposed to anything objective. This is a great misunderstanding. The human heart-mind is the source of values; it is the moral and aesthetic subject. But "subject" does not mean "subjective." What is usually meant by subjective is one person's knowledge or desires. Revealing the fundamental heart-mind first requires "restraining oneself,"[35] having "no knowledge, no desires," and "reducing desires."[36] This means *restraining and overcoming subjectivity* through a kind of moral cultivation so that *the original nature of the heart-mind can appear.* Therefore, it is only through overcoming subjectivity that the heart-mind can be established as the source of values. At that point, the objective realm can enter into the heart-mind in its original state, not distorted by subjective prejudices and selfish desires. Then the objective realm can actually integrate with the heart-mind to be one and not two, with the heart-mind judging in a way compatible with the objective realm.

One might say that the valuing subject has to emerge before objective things can take the position they should have and attain their true value. A heart-mind that is not entangled by prejudices and selfish desires can not only distinguish good and evil, it in fact loves the good and hates evil. This can be immediately proved by the intuitive reaction when seeing a successful ethical or emotional blockbuster. In the movies, one always wants the good people to be rewarded and the evil people to get their just deserts. From this invariable tendency, which results from unspoken agreement, no matter what their conditions of life, always "people share this heart-mind, and the heart-mind shares this pattern."[37]

Conclusion: The Unique Characteristics of the Culture of the Heart-Mind

A few special characteristics of the culture of the heart-mind can be summed up as follows:

1. The function of the heart-mind is revealed *through moral cultivation*. It is *an internal experience that happens through* moral cultivation. It is an existent in itself, not something obtained through inference (like a metaphysical proposition) and so can avoid getting entangled with science.

2. The heart-mind can command other physiological functions, but it is not separate from them. Furthermore, the heart-mind's function has to go through other physiological functions to be complete. This is what Mengzi meant by "putting his physical form into action."[38] Therefore, the function of the heart-mind is certainly practical, so Mengzi emphasized "there must be constant practice"[39] and Wang Yangming emphasized "knowledge and action are one."[40] If it is just empty talk, then as Wang said, it is cut off by other selfish desires.

3. The source of human values is rooted in the heart-mind, which is to say that it is *rooted in concrete human life*. Concrete life must be lived in the various real worlds.[41] Hence, the heart-mind that is the source of culture is not separate from reality; the ideals that come from the heart-mind must blend in with life in the real world. Culture that comes out of life, is carried on in the real world, and is put into practice by the physical body is necessarily the Way of the mean. Culture that is too lofty or too extreme comes out of deep thought, passion, or inferential reasoning.

4. Any person can cast off their own selfish thoughts and prejudices in the space of a thought, meaning they can experience the function of the heart-mind. So the culture of the heart-mind is eminently immediate and complete;[42] it is popularized and socialized culture. Wang Yangming once lamented that when he was teaching in Longchang the villagers and old peasants could all understand. But when he went back to the central plains then he could not be understood by many people, because the scholars and officials of the central plains all had their own prejudices. They were not like the people of Longchang post station, who were so simple and could naturally harmonize with their own heart-minds.

5. The source of human values is in one's own heart-mind, and so Cheng Hao said, "*Each person is a naturally complete and self-sufficient being.*"[43] Only in this way is there true dignity of personality[44] and confidence in people. Moreover, each person creates an internal world in his heart-mind, finding the resting place for human life there with no need to pursue it or struggle for it outside. So this culture of the heart-mind is a culture of peace.

6. Research in Chinese culture ought to begin with *moral cultivation, personal experience, and practice*. However, this is not to dismiss the significance of analysis. Analysis needs to have these three as prerequisites. Only then can the function of analysis add reflection, thorough understanding, and expansion to personal experience and practice. Otherwise analysis can only be empty thinking.

Finally, I will close this essay with a quotation from a poem by Wang Yangming: "Each person has their own compass/The source of all transformations is always in the heart-mind/But I laugh at how I had it backwards before/Searching for it outside in leaves and branches."[45]

Chapter 10

The Creation of the Chinese Free Society

Translator's introduction: This brief essay summarizes many of the themes that occur throughout Xu's political writings: Ruists held certain political ideals (such as freedom), but were unable to realize them in their era. Democracy represents the realization of these ideals and so it is incumbent on modern Ruists to pursue democracy. This also means that Ruism is not the obstacle to democracy many people believed. Xu also displays his nationalistic bent by arguing that Kongzi had established the ideals for a free society of equals two thousand years before Europe did.

One interesting point about this essay is that Xu never draws the conclusion that some contemporary Ruists do: meritocracy is the form a modern Ruist government should take. Even as he argues that one of Kongzi's ideals is that each official should have the position that matches their ability and virtue and praises the meritocratic aims of the exam system, he never suggests giving political power based on merit. He never gives up on the goal of democracy. I can only speculate on the reasons for this difference. Probably his limited experience with democracy is one; he had very little opportunity to observe firsthand the problems with actual democratic practice.

On the other hand, he observed very clearly the problems caused by rulers who were so confident in themselves that they could accept

Between Academia and Politics, 289–94, first published in the *Central Daily News* special issue marking Kongzi's birthday, September 28, 1954.

no criticism. He was intimately familiar with the way disagreement with the government in such circumstances was politicized and critics were treated as enemies of the state. While Xu always spoke respectfully of Jiang Jieshi, he did not think Jiang's ability made him immune to error. So he has a more modest goal of making bureaucratic appointments based on ability, a practice which is hardly controversial. Everyone should have the chance to improve themselves, and earn a position commensurate with their achievements.

Kongzi established the foundation of Ruist teachings and at the same time created the Chinese free society. To me, this is the main condition for the Chinese nation's continued survival and development through countless hardships.

What I mean by the free society is that a person could improve his own position by relying on his own efforts. The difficulty and great significance of revealing this fact can be understood by comparison with other ancient societies.

Ancient Egypt, Babylon, and India were all cradles of world civilization with considerable contributions to human civilization. However, their civilizations never developed a concept or route for each person to change his own state based on his own efforts. Their ruling classes needed to meet no conditions other than class in order to be rulers. Their ruled classes—slaves and commoners—remained slaves and commoners generation after generation. They could not even imagine changing their own status under conditions they controlled themselves, other than rebellion. Rebellion in ancient times never resolved this problem, because they lacked the related concept.

As for the societies that at one time were the pinnacle of civilization, Greece and Rome, their states were made up of the class of "free persons." They maintained the freedom for an individual to improve his status through his own effort in this class. In comparison to Egypt, Babylon, and India, this was indeed a big step forward. But the class of free persons was still a minority, while the majority were slaves. Their political thought did not recognize slaves as a constituent of the state. Slaves were not included among those who could be educated and receive knowledge in the squares or academies. Their concept of "person" certainly did not have a common starting point; it was not a universal idea of persons who could enjoy basic rights. Their cultures lacked a concept of "humanity" as such. One reflection of this phenomenon is

Plato's division of people into the four grades of gold, silver, bronze, and iron.[1] The Western concept of [universal] humanity came from Jesus. Summing things up in one sentence, most people at that time were, like cattle and horses and other things, mentally and materially nailed to their original status at birth. European free society did not begin, we could say, until the Renaissance and religious Reformation.

In the above-mentioned societies entirely without freedom, everything was congealed and ossified, necessarily developing in one of two directions. The upper levels only knew how to pursue a life of material desires, slowly becoming puppets garbed in embroidery and brocade. The lower classes, without any promise of hope or opportunity, truly became animals who walked upright with neither fangs and claws nor fur or feathers. Even among animals they were the lowest. The vitality and energy of society naturally withered away, like plants in a drought. In the end, they could only dry up and die.

I have not done research on ancient Chinese history. However, according to the average circumstances of human evolution, a very long period [of Chinese history] was of course in a condition of no freedom. Certainly, a great deal of conceptual and actual work built over the time before Kongzi to move from a condition of unfreedom to freedom, However, it wasn't until Kongzi that the move toward freedom had a definite direction and systematic effort.

Kongzi's effort to move an unfree society to freedom can be simply described in the following two respects. One is the spirit and method of learning and teaching, liberating people from "nature" to establish the status of humanity firmly. He made it possible for people to stand up out of their status as a "natural entity," their status as animals, and change their rank in other people's evaluation through their own power. From lack of virtue, they could become virtuous. From lack of ability, they could become competent. Aside from the very wisest and the most foolish,[2] at every level of virtue and ability an average person can ascend or descend through their own control, no longer limited to their natural position at birth like other animals who are unable to change.

Great inspiration such as "benevolence comes from oneself"[3] was only definitively expressed by the great teachers of humanism in the Renaissance in Europe. They pointed out that freedom is the one mark that distinguishes people from animals. In China, however, this had already been established by Kongzi on the foundations of learning and teaching two thousand five hundred years ago. Chinese concepts of learning and teaching of course did not originate with Kongzi, but the foundation for making them into universal things for all humanity was definitely laid down by him. "There are no distinctions in teaching"[4] could almost not be said at all in the premodern West (Stoicism has this kind of spirit, but Westerners do not consider it the orthodoxy). Kongzi often used the phrases "learn without tiring of it" and "teach without wearying"[5] to describe himself. From the vantage point of history, it is finally possible to understand what an earth-shaking event this was, which changed people's destiny.

The second aspect is this: if a person only obtains freedom in their own virtue and ability but cannot obtain freedom in social position, then the former freedom is empty and has no real meaning. Therefore, the establishment of a free society has to break free of the classes that naturally took shape in history, and allow each person to change their class status in society through their own efforts. Kongzi never talked of a classless society (the world of the Grand Unity still has rulers and ministers);[6] people will not have a classless society. The Communist Party, which advertises themselves as having no classes, is itself the strictest pyramidal class structure.

Kongzi accepted classes (titles and divisions (*mingfen* 名分)), but what he strenuously pointed out was that classes should be based on existing conditions, so that if people can reach these conditions, they can then freely change their class position. When people have the opportunity to change their class freely, then classes change from shackles on human life to sources of encouragement. Kongzi had two positions relating to this. One was his argument that anyone occupying a certain position should have the virtue and ability appropriate for that position: this is the fundamental meaning of "rectifying names."[7] The other meaning of this position is that anyone who did not have the virtue and ability appropriate for that position should not keep it. Kongzi's respect for the titles and divisions of ruler and minister was respecting that a government should have this form of order, not a respect for a particular ruler. He adopted the attitude of a teacher instructing a student toward each ruler of his time period, guiding them on how to be a ruler and live up to that title. This can be found throughout the *Analects* and *Record of Ritual*.

He certainly did not believe a ruler could never lose his position. He wanted to answer Gongshan Furao's summons,[8] illustrating that he approved of Gongshan's rebellion. The "right to rebel" was not formally articulated in Europe until the eighteenth century,[9] but in China, in theory it was given clear form starting with Kongzi on down to Mengzi and Xunzi. Dong Zhongshu said that Kongzi composed the *Spring and Autumn Annals* "to criticize the Son of Heaven, make the lords retreat, and overthrow the counselors."[10] Dong lived under a unified dynasty respected by the world, and specially emphasized these subtle words and great meaning. Clearly, he was a true inheritor of Ruism who could explain Kongzi's true attitude toward political classes.

Everyone knows that Mengzi advocated punishing a ruler on behalf of the common man and woman.[11] Even Xunzi, who was influenced by Legalist thought in several areas (Legalism was China's totalitarian thought) twice brought up related comments: "A tradition says, 'Follow the Way, not the ruler,'" and "Maintain fidelity [to the Way] even when upper and lower trade places,"[12] indicating these were not things he made up himself, but the true Ruist inheritance. The Way is what is accepted by each person, or slightly differently, what everyone accepts from a position of equality.[13] Putting the Way above the ruler expresses that the office of the ruler cannot represent the height of class, but represents a kind of achievement of virtue and ability. The ruler is decided through the Way, which is recognized by everyone, meaning he is indirectly decided by the people.

On the other hand, corresponding to the previous point that those who have a certain position should have the appropriate virtue, Kongzi further advocated that "the virtuous must have a position."[14] "Gentleman" was a respectful term for the nobility, but in the *Analects* nine times out of ten it refers to a person of virtue. This shows that a respectful term that originally belonged to social class changed to become a term that could be attained by anyone who made effort on their character. This respectful term no longer belonged to some objective limitation, but was brought into the scope of each person's subjective control.[15] That being the case, how could there be a kind of fixed class existence such as the four classes?[16]

Politically speaking, Kongzi often dreamed of the Duke of Zhou and wanted to build "a Zhou in the east."[17] This kind of political aspiration is not something that could be realized by someone with the position of a commoner. The foundation that shaped this mentality and wish of Kongzi's was the idea that someone should have the position appropriate to their virtue. So in addition to advocating "treating relatives with affection,"[18] Kongzi even more strongly advocated "treating the worthy as worthy"[19] and "employing the worthy and promoting the capable."[20] At the same time, he opposed "filling offices based on heredity"[21] and "belittled hereditary officers,"[22] objecting to a group of men who have fixed positions as governors regardless of their virtue and ability. Kongzi believed that treating relatives with affection "reveals the tip"[23] of the virtuous nature of the inner heart-mind. It is the foundation of practicing the virtuous nature, so it has absolutely nothing to do with issues of social class. This is something anyone with a little common sense about Chinese culture can understand.

Ruism talks about ruler-minister and father-son relationships together, but these two relationships have entirely different regulations. "Fathers and sons are joined by heaven" while "rulers and ministers are joined by rightness."[24] So, "father-son relationships are based on kindness; ruler-minister relationships are based on respect"[25] (or based on rightness, respect and rightness being used interchangeably previously). This means that the ruler-minister relationship proceeds from belonging under "rightness" and should change based on rightness. "Treating the worthy as worthy" means that when a person is worthy, he should receive political recognition that he is worthy and be given the kind of position that only someone of worth and talent could fill.

This line of thought developed into China's more than two thousand years of selection by nomination and civil service exam system. I have sorrowfully pointed out the flaws with the exam system before, but from a different angle, selection by nomination and the exam system are both ways of obtaining a government position through one's own efforts. Because of this, China broke free of government by a fixed aristocracy two thousand years before Europe did.[26] This created exchange between the court and society and made it so that each man had an opportunity to advance politically through his own power.[27] This gave each man the opportunity to change his social status through his own power. So then can we not say that Kongzi created our history?

Here I can only roughly point to the outline of how Kongzi created the Chinese free society, not give a detailed account. In particular, a detailed account of Kongzi's thought concerning ritual, which is what people today fail to understand the most and is truly an issue that requires a detailed account, will have to wait for a future opportunity. However, the free society Kongzi created was never totally completed in history, because a basic political question was never resolved: the wielding of political authority. Ruists only pointed out that rulers could "be dethroned"[28] and offered abdication or punitive expeditions to remove a tyrant as the two methods of removing a ruler, while also pointing out that the power to remove a ruler ought to belong to the people. But as for how the people should go about exercising this power, they offered no answer. This had to await the realization of modern democracy.

Hence, Kongzi's doctrine continued the Chinese nation's lifeline but was unable to resolve entirely this problem faced by the nation in the political realm. As a result, from beginning to end Chinese history was in a cyclical condition of order followed by chaos. The reasons Ruism could not create the democratic form of government are many; however, if it is said that the Ruist spirit will obstruct democracy, then this either comes from a person who is an enemy of the nation with no conscience or it comes from a cultural comprador with no knowledge at all.[29] The normal development of Kongzi's political thought is necessarily to take the road toward democracy, and this democratic government would surpass (not oppose) the utilitarianism that was the basis for the establishment of European democracy.

Ruist democracy would be based on the foundation of benevolence, the highest ideal of humanity, which would make modern democracy even purer so as to resolve some political problems that cannot be resolved only through institutional measures. From the Chinese people's standpoint, someone who truly respects Kongzi should work hard for democratic government to give Kongzi's spirit a realistic political refuge. Someone who truly yearns for democracy should likewise realize Kongzi's fundamental spirit and root democracy in their own great tradition, accommodating each kind of life in society. Those superficial followers [of Kongzi] who practice favoritism cannot understand this issue, and absolutely cannot resolve this problem.

Chapter 11

The Ruist Distinction between Cultivating Oneself and Governing Others and Its Significance

Translator's introduction: The main theme of this lengthy essay is that Ruist thought applies different standards to personal morality (cultivating oneself) and politics (governing others). The aim of personal morality is to become a sage or worthy, but politics aims at a lower standard of regulating conduct. According to Xu, the most fundamental value in Ruist political thought is "life," by which he means sustaining biological life by providing for people's material needs. This is the government's primary duty. Educating the people and encouraging their moral development are secondary, and cannot justify interfering with the primary obligation.

Xu is clearly trying to distinguish Ruism from communism, which, in Leninist and Maoist forms, did rationalize causing physical harm and suffering to people in the name of moral improvement. Ruism, for Xu, never advocates this. He is probably also responding to liberal criticisms that Ruism leads to the same thing, using the coercive power of the state to enforce a specific moral view. The liberal philosopher Zhang Foquan made his influential criticism of Ruism as a kind of "pan-moralism" in his book *Freedom and Human Rights* published the same year as this article.

Ruist Political Thought and Democracy, Freedom and Human Rights, 203–20, first published in *Democratic Review* 6, no. 12, July 16, 1955.

Xu and Zhang were colleagues at Donghai University at the time, and Xu was surely aware of Zhang's views. "Pan-moralism" means to make moral value the standard for everything, so that art, science, politics, etc., are all evaluated by their contribution to individual morality. Xu rejects this, arguing Ruists apply different standards to individual morality and politics.

In the course of doing so, he again addresses the question of preferences. He has no issue with people having preferences, but insists that they cannot be the standard of moral value. Preferences are too subjective, and so morality cannot merely mean fulfilling people's preferences. There are objective standards that determine which preferences are correct and which are not. Hence, a substantial section of the essay takes issue with the historian Qian Mu, whom Xu accuses of taking Dai Zhen's thought a step forward and reducing morality to satisfying preferences. This, according to Xu, is Western utilitarianism, not Ruism.

The final section of the essay address an article by Chen Kang published in *Free China*. Chen argues that all government requires unity of thought, and unification by majority will is better than the other possibilities; hence, democracy is better than autocracy or communism. Xu objects to this. Drawing on some of his earlier work, he emphasizes that thought doesn't have to be unified. Democracy restricts certain actions by majority vote, but must protect minority opinions and give them a chance to become the majority. So he rejects Chen's premise: no government should aim at unity of thought, which will always require totalitarian means. Ruists never endorsed using coercive political power to enforce their moral values; people had to choose these on their own. There is no need to agree on moral values or the theoretical basis of democracy to agree on the value of democratic government. Xu is thus more pluralist than many other Ruists.

I

In the essay, "Explaining the *Analects* Saying 'Without the Trust of the People the State Cannot Stand'" (*Fatherland Weekly* no. 115),[1] I pointed out:

> Kongzi and Mengzi, and pre-Qin Ruists in general, obviously established different standards for cultivating oneself, meaning

for scholarship, and for governing others, meaning for politics. Cultivating oneself, the standard for scholarship, is always for natural life to elevate itself toward the moral nature. It absolutely does not establish itself on the basis of [preserving] natural life nor does it establish human values on the basis of the requirements of natural life.[2] The political standard for governing others naturally recognizes the standard of the moral nature, but this merely occupies a secondary position and the requirements of natural life for human beings occupy the primary position. Political values for governing others are primarily established upon the requirements of natural life for human beings. Other values must adhere to these [political values] and derive their value from them. (*Fatherland Weekly* no. 115, p. 8)

I have been making this point for the past four years, but this essay made it more concrete and proved more clearly what I wrote in "An Analysis of Xunzi's Political Thought."[3] There, I pointed out that the contemporary scholar Xiao Gongquan's claim in *History of Chinese Political Thought* that for Kongzi "[moral] teaching is more important than nurturing [the people's lives]"[4] is a serious mistake. I was entirely correct about this.

However, in this essay I take the approach as before of bringing out the comprehensive meaning of the entire *Analects* and *Mengzi* to reach my conclusion. Recently, I came across some material by chance that can demonstrate my point. In "Record of the Model" in *Record of Ritual*, it says, "Kongzi said, 'There is [probably] only one person in the world who loves benevolence without any [personal] desires and hates unbenevolence without any fear [of some consequences]. This is why the superior man deliberates about the Way on his own and sets laws [to govern] over the people.'"[5] And again: "Kongzi said, 'It has been difficult to perfect benevolence for a long time: only the superior man can do it. This is why the superior man doesn't burden others with or shame them for what he [alone] can do. This is why the sage does not make himself the standard for regulating their conduct. He makes it so that the people make an effort of themselves and have a sense of shame, so that they will carry out what they say.'"[6]

This chapter, "Record of the Model," mainly discusses benevolence, the central concept of Ruist thought and the highest standard for human life. However, it can only serve as the standard for cultivating oneself, and one cannot conclude that it then can be a political standard for the government to demand of the people in the course of governing others. The "Way" mentioned in "deliberates about the Way on his own" refers to the standard for being a person, which is erected on benevolence. One can only demand that this kind of standard be pursued oneself by one's own efforts. The "laws" in "sets laws [to govern] over the people" are the conventions for living for the average person in society. When these conventions are established, the Way for cultivating oneself is not used as the standard, and instead they are based on what the people can achieve. As far the standard for cultivating oneself is concerned, that [set by the governing regulations] is a kind of minimal standard. The second passage from the chapter quoted above has exactly the same meaning as the first passage, and moreover expresses it more clearly.

In addition, Dong Zhongshu promotes this kind of idea in "Standards of Humaneness and Righteousness," chapter 29 of *Luxuriant Gems of the Spring and Autumn*:

> For this reason, the superior man brought order to the internal by reverting to the proper principles to rectify the self, relying on propriety to encourage good fortune. He brought order to the external by extending his compassion to ever widening circles of activity, relying on generous regulations to embrace the multitudes. Kongzi said to Ranzi: "Those who bring order to the people first enrich them and only afterward provide them with education."[7] He spoke to Fanji and said: "Those who bring order to their persons first encounter difficulties and only afterward reap [the benefits]."[8] I understand these passages to mean that with regard to bringing order to the self and bringing order to others, the sequence followed is not the same. An *Ode* declares:

> "Give us drink. Give us food.
> Teach us. Instruct us."[9]

> To first provide them with food and drink and then educate and instruct them refers to bringing order to others. Another *Ode* exclaims:

"*Kan kan*, he that carves the wheel spokes . . .
Indeed that superior man
Does not eat the food of idleness."[10]

First the task and only afterward the repast; this refers to
bringing order to the self.

The *Spring and Autumn* censures the faults of those above and
pities the hardships of those below. . . . To search in the self
is called generosity; to search in others is called stinginess. To
censure the self for the sake of perfection is called clarity; to
censure others for the sake of perfection is called stupidity.
Therefore, to rely on the standards for ordering the self to
order others means the ruler is not lenient. To rely on the
standards for ordering others to order the self means lacking
the proper reverence in carrying out ritual propriety.[11]

When I was writing those two essays, "Explaining the *Analects*
Saying 'Without the Trust of the People the State Cannot Stand'" and
"An Analysis of Xunzi's Political Thought" I did not recall those materials. Now I will start with Ruism's fundamental spirit of respecting life,
the spirit of respecting human nature and human character, and infer
from there along with a comprehensive understanding of the entire
Analects and *Mengzi* to reach a conclusion that completely matches the
documents I quoted above. We will see from this that the fundamental
structure of a kind of thought and culture necessarily has its internal
connections. One cannot choose from peripheral areas at one's whim to
jump to incorrect conclusions or write it off entirely.

II

The reason this distinction [between cultivating oneself and governing
others] is important is twofold. On one hand, it is as I already pointed
out: if the standard for cultivating oneself is used for governing then the
principle of those like Zhu Xi, who believed that it would be better for
the people to starve than lose faith [in the government], will inevitably
turn into the Communists' wanting the people to die for their ideology.

It will turn into the tragedy of thought murdering people. On the other hand, if one regulates oneself by the standard for governing others, one will then mistakenly believe that the Ruist spirit stops at the level of natural life and thus completely obliterate the work of moral cultivation (*gongfu* 工夫) involved in cultivating oneself to "establish the highest in humanity."[12]

The Qing dynasty Ruist Dai Zhen [1724–1777] harbored a prejudice against Song-Ming Ruists and in his discussions of human nature and moral principles he primarily started from form and *qi*[13] (natural life). The activity of form and *qi* is manifested in people's preferences, and then the incorporeal was established upon these preferences [by previous Ruist philosophers]. He wrote, "Mengzi said, 'When [people with attenuated moral responses] respire day and night and take in the calm *qi* of the day, their preferences are very close to those of other people.'[14] [Correct] preferences are shown when *qi* can have some rest at ease, and hence the superior man does not treat his form and *qi* as an evil."[15] Certainly Ruism is not a religion and so does not "treat form and *qi* as an evil"; however, Ruists still want to pursue and find something that is the master over form and *qi*. What is master over form and *qi* is found in the heart-mind and nature of each person. This is one aspect of the internality of the moral subject. However, the morality which is internal to the heart-mind and nature of each person must be externally realized into what the heart-minds of people have in common, and so at the same time it goes beyond each person's subjectivity and is endowed with objective meaning. It escapes its subjective condition and becomes an objective truth.

Ruist ethics and morality ceaselessly strives toward taking shape as objective truth. Only this can "establish the highest" for humanity. Cheng [Yi] and Zhu [Xi] specially picked out the word *pattern* and believed that "nature is pattern" [*xing ji li* 性即理]. Their fundamental effort was focused here. Dai didn't understand, and that is why he criticized Cheng and Zhu:

> Cheng-Zhu [thought] made pattern into something substantial, acquired from heaven and complete in the heart-mind. They inspired later generations of the world to latch onto their own biases and call them "the pattern," which did great harm to them. They further muddled things with the doctrine of having no desires, which made the pattern more distant and made people latch onto their own biases more strongly. Then

the harm to the people was even worse. . . . If one departs
from human feelings and seeks [pattern] entirely in [one's
own] heart-mind, how could one fail to mistake one's own
opinions for pattern?[16]

Dai believed that the difference between people and animals was that
the naturalness of animals does not conform to the correct [standard] of
heaven and earth, while the naturalness of human beings can ascend to
the mean and stop there. What he meant by "the natural" is the desires
of human feelings, and what he meant by "opinions" is what is opposed
to the natural desires of human feelings, and functions to distinguish,
select, and control natural desires. Cheng-Zhu thought this was the
pattern; Dai thought it was bias.

Dai thought that the Ruist spirit started from feelings and desires;
that is, from natural life. On the one hand, he took quotes from Mengzi
such as, "Vast territory and numerous people are what the superior man
desires,"[17] and, "Fish is what I desire . . . life is what I desire"[18] to demonstrate that Mengzi founded his philosophy on desire,[19] but neglected what
Mengzi went on to say: "I will give up life and take rightness [when they
conflict]."[20] On the other hand, he cited Mengzi's saying, "One's body
and face come from Heavenly nature, but only the sage can fulfill their
potential,"[21] to serve as the evidence for his entire naturalistic philosophy, but deliberately ignored the great significance of the three words
"Only the sage . . ." In Dai's mind, there was little difference between
sages and ordinary people in terms of the achievement of their moral
nature, and so he went on to say, "The difference in material [form and
qi] between an ordinary person and a sage is nothing like the difference
between humans and [nonhuman] animals."[22] The inevitable conclusion
of naturalism is to conflate equality of human nature and personhood
with equality of knowledge and cultivation of character. Dai's idea could
stand on its own as a doctrine, much like Western utilitarianism based
on [satisfaction of] desires. There was no need to attribute it to Mengzi.
Having to attribute the ideas that he established on his own to Kongzi
and Mengzi restricted the development of his thought and also caused
damage to the Ruist spirit. This can be called combining and injuring
both.[23]

The historian Mr. Qian Mu explained Ruist benevolence entirely in
terms of "preferences" in "Kongzi's Teachings," chapter 5 of his *Explanations
of the Four Books*, finding the Ruist spirit in "preferences." To my mind,

this is an inheritance of Dai Zhen's thought, carrying it one step farther. Mr. Qian's fundamental idea is: "A benevolent person's heart-mind is upright, proceeding from the mean. He shows his true feelings to people and so he can have his own preferences. An unbenevolent person's heart-mind is selfish and self-interested, seeking to please others, and so he goes along with prevailing customs and accords with a degenerate age. He is unable have his own preferences."[24] However, benevolence cannot avoid touching on one's attitude toward others, and so Mr. Qian believes the difference between benevolence and unbenevolence is that "one who only knows his own preferences and doesn't understand that other people also have theirs is a selfish and self-interested person, and a person who lacks benevolence. Someone who infers that other people have preferences based on his having preferences is a benevolent person." And also:

> Therefore a benevolent person does not oppose preferences based on their view of self and other. An unbenevolent person does not oppose their view of self and other based on preferences. When later ages talked about benevolence they did not dare say anything about preferences, not understanding that without preferences one's heart-mind is numb and not benevolent. It is understandable why the way of benevolence was thus not made clear.[25]

As they were discussed in China, preferences referred to expressions of intent that developed from desires. One likes what conforms to one's desires and one dislikes what opposes one's desires. With preferences, there would then be actions to pursue what one liked and avoid what one disliked, actions based on intent. Animals have desires and animals have preferences. Moreover, many animals can express their preferences through their attitude, expressing their intent to pursue or avoid something. This has been demonstrated by animal psychology in recent years. Hence, preferences are not the sole possession of human beings. Furthermore, nothing can better show their true feelings of like and dislike to people than typical animals.

Next, a kind of good behavior has to be realized through preferences, and the same is true of a kind of bad behavior. Chan Buddhism expresses human morality from a negative aspect, and so does not talk about preferences. Ruism expresses human morality from a positive aspect, and so talks about preferences. Wang Yangming's emphasis on preferences was the way he personally especially emphasized the difference between Ruism and Buddhism. Ruism does not obliterate preferences, but absolutely does not establish the standard of human morality on the basis of preferences, because preferences cannot be judged good or evil in themselves. Good and evil depend on the motivation for the preference and the goal which it aims to achieve.

In other words, preferences themselves have no value; value has to be determined based on why something is liked or disliked. In the *Analects* Kongzi said, "I have never met someone who loves virtue the way they love female beauty."[26] This clearly expresses that a love for virtue is above love for beauty, and this relative placement is determined by the objects—virtue and beauty—and not by whether the true feelings of love for them are expressed. Love of beauty could always be expressed in song and someone who loves virtue could "silently set his mind on it."[27] *Analects* also records, "Zigong asked, 'Does the superior man also hate?' Kongzi answered, 'Yes. He hates those who call out the bad in others . . .'"[28] Zigong's question was motivated by a doubt about hating anything. Kongzi's response makes plain that a superior man hates what he should hate. "Disliking what he should dislike" is a restriction on disliking. On another occasion he answered Zigong's question by saying, "Better that the good among the villagers like him and the bad among the villagers dislike him,"[29] which also clearly expresses that preferences should be appropriate.

This further illustrates that the value of preferences is not in themselves but whether they are appropriate, which is an objective standard. Mr. Qian believes that "the unbenevolent seek to please others out of a selfish and self-interested mindset . . . and cannot have their own preferences."[30] In fact, someone of glib words and an ingratiating appearance[31] usually covers up his desires on the surface in order to carry out and realize his desires. When someone of glib words and an ingratiating appearance studies intensively to be able to take office, it is because an office is what he truly wants. Talk of preferences has to be connected to behavior; when someone acts to carry out his preferences, one cannot say that he "cannot have his own preferences." "When his father stole a sheep, he testified": this is to tell people the facts. "Sons and fathers cover for each other":[32] this is not to tell people the facts. People of this latter type can be said to be unable to have their own preferences. The reason a person like this cannot have his own preferences is because he has a higher moral consciousness behind him with the function of controlling or balancing his preferences.

Furthermore, a cruel and despotic person or an unrestrained and dissolute scholar can often show their true preferences. As *A New Account of Tales of the World* records,[33] the noted scholars of the Wei-Jin period [220–420 CE] were especially frank and straightforward, not dissembling. Their style is something people can long for, but it does not necessarily comport with the benevolence of which Kongzi spoke. In politics, no one surpassed the First Emperor of Qin, Stalin, and Hitler in having preferences. Those politicians who accept good advice and are checked by a legislature are foremost in being unable to have preferences. Mr. Qian also considered this point and this is why he said, "A benevolent person extends his own preferences while being aware of others' preferences. Without turning his back on others' preferences, he makes a full effort to satisfy his own preferences."[34] In this way, it seems one can give consideration to both oneself and others when it comes to preferences.

However, someone who makes a full effort to satisfy his own preferences while not turning his back on others' is certainly someone whose preferences are under control or have been corrected. Making a full effort toward one's own satisfaction is something people share with animals; there is no morality or immorality to speak of here. One cannot establish moral values here. Indulging one's own preferences while interfering with others' is called being immoral. Regulating one's own preferences and not interfering with others' can be called minimal morality. (Politics usually only demands up to this level.) Sacrificing one's own preferences in order to fulfill others' is usually called great morality.

When someone can regulate or even sacrifice his preferences, in some cases it is due to inhibition caused by external conditions, such as what was called "ritual" in traditional China or what is called "law" in the modern period. In such instances, the positive impact on behavior is due to ritual or law, not preferences themselves. In some cases, it is due to the internal moral heart-mind. The five constant aspects of human nature—benevolence, rightness, ritual propriety, wisdom, and faithfulness—well up from within and have the effect of self-regulating or transcending and transforming the preferences. In such instances, the positive impact on behavior is due to the moral heart-mind, the five constant aspects of human nature, not preferences themselves. Mr. Qian said, "Mengzi said that Gong Liu was fond of wealth and King Tai was fond of sex, but they shared them with the people, so that there were storehouses and granaries and there were no dissatisfied women or unmarried men.[35] Mengzi's teachings all came from Kongzi."[36] This response of Mengzi's was elicited by King Xuan of Qi's greed. The important part is obviously not "fondness for wealth" or "fondness for sex," but "sharing them with the people." If Gong Liu and King Tai followed their inclinations toward wealth and sex, making "their own preferences" their goal, then their intentions and desires would have only been oriented toward wealth and sex. How could they have considered the people?

The reason they could share them with the people, the reason that they could take into consideration others' preferences on top of their own, was in no way an effect of their fondness for wealth and sex in themselves. It was instead because they had a kind of distinct moral heart-mind behind or on top of their fondness for wealth and sex that guided them. From fondness for wealth and sex in themselves, there is no way to infer the conclusion to "share them with the people." Otherwise, why would the king need Mengzi to make such an effort to guide him toward it, and still be unable to share his preferences with the people? Every tyrant and corrupt official throughout history has had a love of wealth and sex. This is why the ultimate principle of government—"love what the people love and hate what the people hate"[37]—can only be realized by someone who does not have preferences of his own.

Nearly every one of the various masters of the pre-Qin period demanded that rulers govern by nonaction. "Nonaction" means to not have preferences of their own; this is how rulers must cultivate themselves. Rulers govern others by means of employing nonaction to satisfy the people's preferences and make it possible for the people to follow their preferences and safeguard their fundamental powers: this is how they govern the people. The only way to achieve the goal of governing others, which is to satisfy their preferences, is through cultivating oneself to transcend the preferences of biological life: at this juncture, cultivating oneself and governing others are necessarily connected. One could almost say that this kind of connection and distinction between cultivating oneself and governing others is the entire structure of the Ruist spirit.

Whenever preferences are brought up in Ruist documents, in nearly all cases it is to give attention to how to lead the dispositions with one's nature and not to let the dispositions obscure nature, so as to make preferences be correct. When it comes to cultivating oneself, it is rare that they establish a theory of human value directly on preferences themselves. In fact, outside of Zhuangzi, it seems that there is no such theory in any of the Daoists, Mohists, Sophists,[38] or Legalists. Wang Bi [226–249] commented on the *Changes* from a Lao-Zhuang perspective. When he explained the commentary on the words of the text of the Qian hexagram, "It manifests its fitness and constancy by making the innate tendencies of things conform to their natures," he commented. "If nature did not control their innate tendencies, how could things long behave in ways that are correct for them?"[39] This kind of cultural barrier cannot be lightly overcome. This is because once one makes preferences the basis then there are only the subjective individual impulses, and one has fundamentally denied any effort toward objective truth. This effort is something human culture has to display. Zhuangzi's chapter "Discussing the Equality of Things" is not about making them equal on the basis of an objective standard, but rather denying objective standards and denying that there are "things that all approve of,"[40] in order to return to each approving of their own preferences and equalizing things on that basis. This is finding equality in immediately recognizing the fundamental inequality of preferences. He wrote,

> If people sleep in the damp, their waists will hurt and they'll be almost paralyzed, but is this true for a loach? If they live in trees, then they'll shake in fear, but is this true of apes and monkeys? Of these three, which knows their proper place? People eat the grass- and grain-fed animals, deer eat grass, centipedes enjoy snakes, and owls and crows find mice delicious. Of these four, which knows food's proper taste? Monkeys and apes mate with each other, deer couple together, and loach swim with fish. Mao Qiang and Lady Li are considered beautiful,[41] but if fish saw them, they'd dive deep, if birds saw them they'd soar up high, and if deer saw them they'd run away in a flash. Of these four, which knows the correct standard for beauty? The way I see it, the sprouts of benevolence and righteousness, the paths of right and wrong are all mixed up and confused. How would I know the distinction between them?[42]

In the course of human life and behavior, if we just recognize pref-erences then everything stops at the subjective condition of individual lives and naturally it is not possible to recognize any common, objective standard. Without recognizing objective standards, the result is that one can only start from each individual's subjective preferences. However, according to Zhuangzi's preface in the "All Under Heaven" chapter, he recognizes that the sage-kings all "originated from one source," and furthermore, all took an affirmative attitude toward morality, benevolence, rightness, names, and laws. He also sighed and said, "The people of all under heaven did whatever they desired [their preferences], each making their own standard. How tragic! The various philosophers went in their own directions and did not come back [to the common source], and inevitably do not agree."[43] So "Discussing the Equality of Things" is likely to be some ridiculous and absurd doctrines that do not represent Zhuangzi's original idea, and therefore he was still unwilling to mix preferences with benevolence and rightness.

Wang Yangming has a passage that says, "Innate moral awareness is only an individual heart-mind of approval and disapproval. Approval and disapproval are only individual preferences. Only preferences fill out the meaning of approval and disapproval, and only approval and disapproval fill out the myriad affairs and transformations,"[44] where he seemingly slapped preferences directly on top of innate moral awareness.[45] Then he took innate moral awareness as his basis [for morality], which apparently in turn makes preferences the basis. In fact, this passage is the line that demarcates Wang from Chan Buddhism. If innate moral awareness did accept preferences and acts of approval and disapproval, then it would only be self-reflective knowledge and could not achieve positive action in human life. The key in this passage is still in innate moral awareness: only preferences that derive from direct recognition of innate moral awareness can fill out the correct meaning of approval and disapproval. Wang's "teaching of innate moral awareness was born from a hundred deaths and a thousand hardships,"[46] so one cannot say that preferences constitute innate moral awareness. In terms of moral cultivation that aims at preserving Heavenly Pattern[47] and eliminating human desires, Wang was no different than Cheng Yi and Zhu Xi. Heavenly Pattern can manifest as preferences, and so can human desires. Preferences exist in both cases, but they form in different ways. So moral cultivation does not consist in having preferences, but in whether the foundation behind the preferences is Heavenly Pattern or human desires. If one establishes [moral] theory based on preferences, then moral cultivation to preserve Heavenly Pattern and eliminate human desires is utterly useless. If one abolishes this period of moral cultivation, then the spirit of Kongzi and Mengzi, Cheng Yi and Zhu Xi, Lu Xiangshan and Wang Yangming alike will collapse.

Buddhists say, "Going straight to the mind is the Buddha Way."[48] Buddhist cultivation consists of how to "go straight to the mind," or how to "return to the fundamental mind"[49] and make "the fundamental mind the master."[50] Hence, the distinction between the human mind and the mind of the Way,[51] or between Heavenly Pattern and human desires, has to be established through a process of moral cultivation. Otherwise it is far too easy to give allegiance to a usurper. I feel Wang's account of preferences differs from Mr. Qian's, which receives further confirmation from the fact that their explanations of what it means to "control the self"[52] are completely different. Mr. Qian explains "control" as "give over," so it means to give over to the self, to follow oneself. He does not adopt the common explanation of "overcoming selfish desires," because from the standpoint where there are only preferences one cannot talk about Heavenly Pattern and human desires, and so one also cannot talk about eliminating selfish desires.

Yet Wang Yangming said,

> If people truly make an unceasing personal effort, then the deep and subtle nature of the Heavenly Pattern in this heart-mind will become apparent day by day, and the thinning of selfish desires will become apparent day by day. If one does not engage in moral cultivation to control the self, then all effort is nothing more than talk. . . . If one waits to get to the point where there are no selfish desires left to overcome before worrying about being unable to complete one's knowledge, it will not be too late.[53]

We see from this that Wang interpreted "controlling the self" as "overcoming selfish desires, and it is also very clear that he did not make preferences the basis [of morality]. Hence, I suspect Mr. Qian was influenced by Zhuangzi's "Discussing the Equality of Things" when he interpreted benevolence in terms of preferences, and boldly carried forward Dai Zhen's thought a further step. The significance of this thought can be assessed from different angles. The Renaissance return from a religious atmosphere to secular humanism seems closer to Mr. Qian's fundamental spirit. One might also say that the current spirit has seeped into his thought, of which he is perhaps unaware. However, I feel he is far from the thought of Kong-Meng, Cheng-Zhu, and Lu-Wang, which is to cultivate oneself to establish others. So Mr. Qian's essay is arranged meticulously and carefully scrutinized, and yet the sections on benevolence and related matters are unavoidably contradictory with no way of smoothing them out. I believe the initial point of divergence derives from taking the Ruist standard of governing others as the standard for cultivating oneself. This is what I sincerely wish to ask Mr. Qian to explain.

III

It is not only the case that the demand for rulers to take the people's preferences as their preferences in Ruist political thought carries with it a profound spirit of democratic thought. In addition, the distinction between the standards for cultivating oneself and governing others can resolve some theoretical difficulties where modern democracy still has no foundation, so that democracy and dictatorship will not be mixed up. This is nothing short of a miracle.

Because our country lacks real, embodied recognition[54] of democratic government, and because we have imbibed too much of the influence of communism, which reduces everything to the political, we often relate academic controversies directly to politics. Then, once advocates of freedom are not careful, they slide into the snare of totalitarianism without being aware of it. Hence, I once wrote an article called "Between Academia and Politics"[55] to draw appropriate boundaries between the spheres of politics and scholarship. On the one hand, this secures the functional apparatus of free choice in democratic government, so it does not get shaken by the truth of scholarship. On the other hand, it secures the purity and independence of scholarship from the majority rule of politics. When I wrote this article I had not yet considered that the Ruist distinction between cultivating oneself and governing others includes this kind of meaning. I was merely doing some theoretical reflections on the already accomplished fact of democratic life. Recently, when I read Professor Chen Kang[56] of National Taiwan University's article "On the Question of Unity of Thought" (*Free China* 12, no. 9), I felt that the Ruists' work here still could have a great enlightening effect in the present.

Professor Chen's article proceeds from the premise that "the thought regulating behavior within a country must be unified,"[57] bringing up four ways of unifying thought. One is the way the First Emperor of Qin [r. 221–210 BCE] did it, unifying it in himself (actually, as far as thought, Qin unified under Legalism). Another is the approach of Emperor Wu of the Han [r. 141–87 BCE], unifying it under Ruism (actually, as far as political reality goes, after Emperor Wu it was unified in the person of the emperor). Another is the approach of communism, unifying it under the party. And another is the approach of democracy, unifying it under the majority. Prof. Chen takes the standpoint that "there are a hundred kinds of errors but only one path of truth," and believes that "thought unified under the majority comes closest to absolute right and wrong and absolute benefit and harm; the possibility of it being mistaken reduced to an infinitesimal amount compared to unification under a party, a school of thought, or an individual."[58] So it goes without saying that Prof. Chen endorses unification under the majority. However, Prof. Chen believes that the first three unifying methods involve a minority oppressing the majority, which is of course not a good thing. The latter involves the majority oppressing minority views, which is admittedly better than the first three situations; "[H]owever, what did the minorities do, such that they cannot extend their rights in the same way as the majority?" Prof. Chen feels that it "cannot help but be a case of the pot calling the kettle black," and is "a problem that democracy has to explain."[59]

His own explanation is that "the minority submits to the majority . . . not that they are forced to bow to the majority." It is because the majority's view "is closer to absolute right and wrong and absolute benefit and harm. Although this view is not what the minority in fact holds, it is a better view that they could arrive at by following the same path. Hence, the majority governing the minority is in fact . . . the minority's possible (future) view governing their own actual views."[60] Since it is the minority's future selves controlling their present selves—so they are controlling themselves—there is no violation of human rights. Because Prof. Chen assumes that the foundation of democratic government lies in the truth represented by the majority, in the end he sets two conditions on the method of unifying thought in democracy: "The first is that the views of the citizens must be plural; the other is the citizens must have a scientific critical spirit and ability in logical argument."[61] I regard Prof. Chen's willingness to discuss real problems seriously as laudable. Yet he still has some misunderstandings about democracy and therefore has not resolved the problems he brings up and instead runs the risk of going in the opposite direction instead, the direction of totalitarianism.

In the first place, why is it that no one ever realized the problem of the human rights of the minority when the minority submits to the majority in democracy? Because democratic government does not actually function the way Prof. Chen thinks it does. Under a democracy, there is never a question of unifying political thought, nor does it need to be unified. Yes, at the very beginning he delimited it: "In this article, I stipulate 'thought' to refer to thought that influences behavior,"[62] distinguishing it from thought as a purely intellectual activity. But it is an extremely limited range of behavior that is decided by the majority in a democracy and requires unification. The majority of an individual's behavior, even if it has some common direction and recognizes some common standards and regulations, comes out of tradition, habit, education, and culture, among other factors. The political majority does not decide it.

The starting point of democracy is, the less governmental interference in people's lives and actions the better. If people's lives and actions are all determined by the government, then it doesn't matter how they are decided: it is still totalitarian oppression. In addition, there is, of course, a foundation in thought behind behavior, but politically speaking, the relationship between thought and behavior is not one of logical necessity. The very same form of thought can tend toward different behavior in politics, and the very same behavior can come from different forms of thought. For example, opposing communism and the Soviet Union is a common action in Free China. Liberals can endorse it, and so can those who are not liberals—even Trotskyites. Advocates of wholesale Westernization can endorse it, as can advocates of Chinese native culture. Adherents of the Three Principles of the People[63] can endorse it, and so can those who don't follow the Three Principles. [Jawaharlal] Nehru opposes communism domestically, but allies with them internationally. [Josip Broz] Tito practiced communism domestically, but internationally opposed the fatherland of communism.[64]

Democratic government is about concrete policies, not the thought behind them. This is not to deny the connection between thought and policy, but, like with the motivation behind individual behavior, to leave the theoretical basis of policy to the individual himself and for the government to let it go. Unification of policy and action does not equal unification of thought. The Communist Party especially emphasizes how thought and motives relate to behavior, based on their class theory. They believe that it is necessary to clarify everyone's motives, making theory and practice correspond, before they can be reliable. Put differently, they believe that actually to resolve political problems, it is first necessary to resolve the problem of thought, and therefore forcefully carry out brainwashing and other bloody tasks. Yet up until now, the Soviet Union has been resolving the problem of thought with political violence, not resolving political problems with thought. If one believes that the unification of a particular stage of policy in a country is a unification of thought, then government can interfere with the inner mental life of individuals and then it becomes a totalitarian government. From the standpoint of Ruism, to go from pure thought and motive to daily action, making there be not the slightest contradiction between thought and behavior, is the activity of cultivating oneself—Wang Yangming's unity of knowledge and action.[65] Ruism restricts taking what belongs to personal cultivation and making it a demand of governing from its moral standpoint. Modern democracy does not permit it from a standpoint of human rights.

What is more important is that the ultimate basis of democracy is not that the political majority can "get closer to absolute right and wrong, and absolute benefit and harm." These do not change; they are questions that belong to academia, not something that the majority can decide. I said it very clearly in "Between Academia and Politics": "The opinions of ten thousand average people on philosophy would have a difficult time matching the opinions of one philosopher. The scientific knowledge of ten thousand average people lacks a method to match the knowledge of one scientist."[66] We cannot mark philosophy and science as outside the scope of human behavior. The German philosopher Eduard Spranger [1882–1963] wrote a letter to the editorial board of *Central Review*[67] in 1950, in which he said, "If the masses are victorious (in the issue of culture) then I fear the culture of our entire world will tend toward crumbling" (see *Democratic Review* 2, no. 4). This was the pained appeal of a philosopher straddling the connecting point of two worlds, who had a deep understanding of the crisis fostered by the political majority making decisions about culture and thought.

At the same time, Prof. Chen said the Communist Party unifies thought under the party. Actually, at its base communism in theory advocates unification by the majority. This is why the symmetry of the masses and "special classes" (meaning the minority) becomes a frequently used tool in political and intellectual struggle. Its method of intellectual struggle mainly employs the "mass line," using the majority to overcome the minority. Why does it want to destroy its opponents so ruthlessly? Because it believes "the masses" are on its side, which is to say absolute right is on its side. Its opponents stand on the side of absolute wrong because of their class identity or because of a brief lack of self-consciousness.

Prof. Chen believes the decisions of the majority are "closer to absolute right and wrong, and absolute benefit and harm," and therefore, this is a direct line to the development of truth, and will become an opinion the minority cannot help accepting in the future. And so although the minority is oppressed, taking the standpoint that "there is only one path to truth" that human reason cannot help accepting, the oppression of the minority is simply their future enlightened selves oppressing their presently deluded selves. Therefore, Prof. Chen believes that "the majority and minority are equal before reason."[68] In terms of how to govern the minority, Prof. Chen naturally does not advocate the same means as the Communists, but in terms of appraising the political majority and minority by the measure of truth, they are exactly the same. Because of this, the Communist Party's purging of its opponents is merely a step in the development of these viewpoints. Using their language, it is just the complete realization of truth by means of revolution.

The submission of the minority to the majority in democracy is merely an obvious method of resolving problems by numbers. The superiority of the opinion represented by the majority is just relative and temporary, and therefore it can be changed through a specific process. The minority in a democracy is not surrendering to truth, nor is their thought being controlled by the majority. Still less is it a matter of the minority's future selves controlling their present selves. Rather, the minority exist as bold opponents. Their thought should be secured by the majority and the present minority should contend to become the future majority. Democracy is not founded on the truth represented by the majority. The minority obeying the majority is just one condition of democracy, not the only condition, and moreover, it is also a condition recognized by totalitarianism. There are also totalitarian governments in the world that are unable to become a majority. This is the lowest kind of totalitarian government. The foundations of democracy are having a peaceful process to correct governmental mistakes freely. Hence, when the minority obeys the majority, there is only meaningful democracy when the majority at the same time safeguards the minority.

Democratic government in its functioning form only more closely approaches absolute right and wrong and absolute benefit and harm when the majority and minority can freely change. This is something that cannot be captured by the content of governing by majority will. (I explained the point that democracy is a structure of government that doesn't directly relate to particular content of government in "Two Layers of the Chinese Political Problem.")[69] According to Prof. Chen, the minority side in a democracy should sooner or later disappear, leaving the side closer to absolute right and wrong and absolute benefit and harm. Prof. Chen assumes that "the minority's possible (future) view governs their own actual views." What this means is that when the minority realize their error and improve their views, they will naturally end up on the side of the majority which more closely approaches absolute right and wrong and absolute benefit and harm. This is exactly the theoretical basis of one-party government. Take a democratic nation such as England. During World War II, the Conservative Party was the majority, and then became the minority right after the war. Then it became the majority again in the last general election. This phenomenon of now being the majority, now being a minority illustrates the turning over of absolute right and wrong and absolute benefit and harm. From the standpoint of logic and reason this phenomenon of turning over shouldn't exist, but it will always exist in a democracy.

Because Prof. Chen mixes together the political and academic viewpoints, one of the conditions he gives for the approach of unifying thought in a democracy, to wit, "Citizens must have a scientific critical spirit and ability in logical argument," is not a necessary condition for the functioning of a democracy. Further, it will invisibly fall into an antidemocratic snare without realizing it. Democracy is just like Ruism, in that whatever is a unit of life is recognized to have complete and perfect value. Another implication of humanity being born free and equal is that they do not need to meet additional conditions in order to have rights. A unit of life has these rights. As long as someone is an adult who is not mentally disturbed or incompletely developed and his understanding has a basic coincidence with logic, democratic government puts complete faith in him and trusts his ability to choose, respecting his right to choose. Here, the decision is determined by a quantitative measure of which side is many and which is few, not by a qualitative measure of the value of opinions. "Ability in logical argument" is a qualitative question of scholarship. Scholarship is determined by quality; the logical ability of ten people with no training in logic is no match for one person with training in logic. From the standpoint of scholarship, ten people ought to accept the guidance of one person with training. But when casting a vote for government, one person with training in logic still counts for one vote, and should accept the common opinion of ten people with no logical training.

Assuming that a scientific critical spirit and ability in logical argument are necessary conditions for a functioning democracy, then not only are there few people in China who meet these conditions, at minimum there will not be the conditions for realizing democracy for decades. Even in England or America, the working class and farmers might not meet this requirement. Then political problems should be decided by professors of logic making some calculations or having a debate. Then we should have "philosopher-kings," whereby those with the greatest ability in logical argument should become the rulers. At minimum, for the public logic will become a mandatory course of required education, and we will have to open cram schools in logic to prepare people for elections. However, politically it is absolutely impossible to do this. In Ruism, one merely asks what the people prefer. In democracy, it is merely a choice based on the voters' own interests. The choice of the majority might be mistaken, and democracy gives people the security to correct their own mistakes freely. If one believes that the majority represents the truth, then the function of correcting mistakes in democracy will disappear, which implies that the whole function of democracy disappears.

If the political and academic viewpoints are not clarified, the damage will be as already described. However, understanding one but not the other is the way people are, so it is not at all easy to clarify them. Ruist thought is primarily "thought that regulates people's behavior." However, more than two thousand years ago it already clearly separated thought that regulates people's behavior into the two areas of cultivating oneself and governing others. The basic motive behind this distinction seems to have a deep significance still for the problem raised by Prof. Chen, and for the reality of the Communist Party. (Feng Youlan[70] once said that the Communist Party wants everyone to be a sage. Even if they really do that, there is no crime greater than to use political coercive force to make people become sages.) So we see that the goods produced by the Ruist shop apparently did not all collapse along with the May Fourth slogan.[71] I am afraid this is something Prof. Chen could not expect.

Chapter 12

Why Oppose Liberalism?

Translator's introduction: This essay was inspired by concrete political events: opposition to the education reform plan in 1956 and the resulting attacks on liberalism from Ministry of Education publications. As Xu describes, liberals were accused of being soft on communism and weakening the country's united defense against communism. There are clear parallels with the Red Scare fanned by Senator Joseph McCarthy in the United States. Xu believes these attacks were an attempt to suppress any criticism of the government.

Philosophically, the interesting aspects of the essay come from Xu's embrace of political liberalism. The contrast with many contemporary scholars of Ruism (the translator included) is clear, because they usually emphasize the differences with liberalism. As other essays discuss (notably chapter 3, "Mourning My Enemy"), Xu had strong differences with the philosophical liberals who wrote for *Free China*, yet he obviously has no issues with political liberalism. He believes individual freedom is essential to group cohesion and strength, and thus liberalism need not result in excessive individualism and lack of commitment to society. His differences with the *Free China* group were less about the result (a liberal democratic society) then the method: they wanted to eradicate Chinese tradition and Xu believes liberals also need tradition.

Ruist Political Thought and Democracy, Freedom and Human Rights, 289–99, first published in *Democratic Review* 7, no. 21, November 1956.

Xu also believes political freedom is necessary but not sufficient. Political freedom is a means; it gives individuals space to determine their own moral values and meaning in life. It is absolutely essential that they do so. Freedom from government interference in the individual's moral life is the means, not the end itself. Political freedom, as he says, must be supported by moral freedom and intellectual freedom. Liberals must stand for all three aspects of freedom, and individuals must use their freedom to make choices for their lives based on reason and conscience. In short, there is a proper way to exercise this freedom, even if Xu stops short of prescribing one kind of good life.

Recently a friend said to me, the debate between liberals and antiliberals has unfolded again, and I would like to hear your opinion on this question. In fact, I have no opinion, and the debate has only brought out a few impressions. I once formally offered some opinions on what the GMD should do going forward in Spring 1949. In those opinions there was a section analyzing why the GMD had become isolated from the intellectuals. This was primarily due to not understanding liberalism and not building good relationships with liberals. In the future the GMD must learn from this. When the GMD began to reform in 1950, they never did a serious examination of the questions of liberalism or the Three Principles of the People.[1] I was privately astonished.

Two years ago I had a serious argument with a friend, and he said I had already become a liberal. On the one hand, I was very surprised, but on the other hand, I understood through his guidance that even if someone doesn't label himself a liberal and wouldn't willingly be only a liberal, he still has to go through a phase of liberalism in the course of maturing his knowledge and character. Now that liberals are being fired upon, I intuitively felt that this is really unfortunate for the anti-Communist camp. Now that President Jiang has instructed newspapers and magazines throughout the country to express their views forthrightly to provide an occasion for selecting some to put into effect, I haphazardly wrote down some of my reflections. "Recently the edict has come down to open clear channels of communication with the government, and already I predict that the coming years will see great peace."[2] Lu You already put into words for me the feeling I had when I picked up my pen.

I

Although the word *liberalism* was not created very early, one might say that the spirit of liberalism came along with human culture. Even if one cannot find the words *liberalism* or *freedom* in it, anything that merits being called a culture has some form, some degree, of the liberal spirit moving within it. The fundamental force behind the great progress of Europe in the past three hundred years is liberalism, a fact everyone has to admit. Liberalism is the practice of people living themselves. People are not God, so anything they put into practice will have flaws, and liberalism naturally also has flaws. Hence, at the end of the nineteenth and beginning of the twentieth centuries there were constant cries about the crisis of liberalism, which led to the appearance of communism and fascism. However, as the whole world is proving, the crisis of liberalism can only be resolved through liberalism itself. Liberalism doesn't represent a certain fixed framework, but unlocks both the tangible and intangible shackles of human material and spiritual life to throw open a path to reveal human reason and conscience. It allows human reason and conscience to shine light and heat on the road in the midst of every difficulty and hardship to find a path for oneself. Leaving liberalism to resolve the crisis of liberalism is like the behavior of fascists and communists. It is just like binding one's own hands and feet and anaesthetizing one's own soul to try to get through all kinds of catastrophes. The problem we face now in the world is how to push humanity toward a greater, measureless depth.

The goal of our struggle against communism and totalitarianism is very simple: it is to liberate and revive human conscience and reason that has been bound and anaesthetized by the Communist system. It is to restore reason and conscience to each person and allow each person to rely on her own conscience to take hold of her own fate. It is to restore the freedom that makes each person a human being, and allow humanity to stand on the foundation of liberalism to struggle forward and upward. It's not that liberalism itself represents the future for humanity, because liberalism itself is just a kind of spiritual state of life. Only preserving this spiritual state can throw open the gate for humanity to go forward and upward, and provide limitless possibilities for humanity's future.

Using the term from European cultural history for the spiritual state of life in liberalism, it is "self-awareness"; using the term from Chinese cultural history, it is "being one's own master." From the moment they are born, people are thrown into an already formed tradition and society. They get buffeted around by the currents of tradition and society the way a bit of flotsam gets carried downstream by a great torrent. A few people, inspired by various sources of inspiration, stand up straight among the endless waves and currents and seek answers about the rightness and wrongness of the already formed concepts and forms of tradition and society. Their assessments of the rightness and wrongness of these relies on their own conscience and reason. They let their own conscience and reason stand above these already formed concepts and forms of tradition and society, and when they do, then tradition and society are no longer dominating an individual's life. An individual's own conscience and reason are dominating her own life. This is what "self-awareness" and "being one's own master" means. This is what liberalism means.

However, here I must explain in all seriousness that when liberals are liberated from tradition and society, this is *not* a wholesale rejection of them. Rather, it is making a new evaluation of the already formed concepts and forms, clarifying and refining them to endow them with new content. In so doing, they create a richer and more rational tradition and society. A liberal still wants to live within tradition and society. But he doesn't live passively and quiescently; he lives actively and dynamically. He continuously exercises his strength to improve and create so that tradition and society will no longer be a form of blind momentum, but illuminated by human conscience and reason, tradition and society will gradually become a product of these. This is why liberalism not only completes the individual through liberation of his spirit, but when a person completes himself as an individual, he completes the group at the same time. Even though there have been liberals who were only aware of the individual and not aware of the group, from the facts of history one can see that when there are individuals with vitality, they will form a group with vitality. So liberal nations are the most advanced, most powerful, and richest nations in history.

II

As far as our nation is concerned, the word *freedom* (*ziyou* 自由) first appeared in the annotations to the "Record of the Five Phases" in the *Han History*.[3] It appears more frequently in Buddhist books, and by the Southern Song it had become a term in common use in society. However, none of these is the direct origin of the contemporary word *freedom*. The idea that a person's success or failure should be attributed to his virtue or lack of virtue arose at the beginning of the Western Zhou, and this was the first awakening of the spirit of freedom in Chinese culture. Kongzi, who established the foundations of Chinese culture, edited down the *Odes* and *Documents*, corrected the *Rites* and *Music*, and composed the *Spring and Autumn Annals* to "to criticize the Son of Heaven, make the lords retreat, and overthrow the counselors."[4] His basis for this was naturally his own conscience and reason, not some outside authority. Otherwise, he would not dare to edit down or correct these texts, nor as a commoner would he dare to criticize and condemn powerful figures in the government. His wandering around the various states of Zhou-era China also illustrates that he relied on his own conscience and reason to find a political partner who would fit with his own ethical demands. The political authority of the lords of the time was nothing to him.

He taught that the highest goal was to pursue benevolence, but he also said, "Benevolence comes from oneself" and "do not yield even to your teacher when it comes to benevolence."[5] These are all clear instructions that people should be their own masters; he felt that only those who are their own masters can pursue benevolence. Regarding personal comportment, he said, "Clever speech and an ingratiating appearance are rarely associated with benevolence,"[6] because clever speech and an ingratiating appearance were characteristics of inferior persons who serve an authority. He pointed out that "being resolute and firm, but simple and hesitant: this is close to benevolence."[7] He sighed deeply and said, "I have never met a person of resolve," and he also said, "Even a commoner cannot have his intent taken away."[8] Zengzi, who passed on his Way "connected by one thread," said, "A scholar cannot fail to be great and firm,"[9] and, "I have heard of great valor from the master [Kongzi] . . . if I find that I am upright upon examining myself, then I will go forward even against thousands and tens of thousands."[10] Resolve, firmness, and valor are characteristics that necessarily ride along with the liberal spirit, and are also characteristics that naturally manifest when the liberal spirit becomes concrete in a person's life. A commoner not having his intent taken away and going forward against thousands are concrete expressions of opposing authority to seek freedom for individual conscience and reason.

[Ruists'] humility and adherence to ritual is an expression of their virtuous behavior and not submission. So Kongzi said, "Being reverent without ritual propriety is shameful."[11] And "excessive reverence" was something Zuo Qiuming was ashamed of, as was Kongzi.[12] When it came to Mengzi, he particularly made the point that the highest expression of the spirit of freedom is "utmost greatness and utmost strength," and so he thought that one had to "not be licentious when rich and honored, not be moved [from integrity] when poor and lowly, and unwilling to submit power and force" before one could be called a great man.[13] The "great man" is spoken of relative to those inferior, servile persons. One who does not wish to be a servile person should be a great man, and should have this elevated and honorable character possessed of the spirit of freedom.

We may therefore say that Ruism establishes a dynamic life based on the moral nature, and so the spirit of freedom becomes a dynamic expression of this aspect. Daoism seeks a mental escape from the fetters of human life, and so the spirit of freedom becomes a quiescent expression of this aspect. Ruism and Daoism are the two mainstreams of Chinese culture. If one cannot come in contact with the abundant spirit of freedom in the foundations of their thought, then one will find it impossible to come in contact with the cultural legacies they have left. All the later biased statements [about Chinese culture] came from this problem.[14] As for those who think that Chinese culture lacks the spirit of liberalism because of the (correct) belief that politically China never developed freedom and human rights, their shallowness and ignorance need no further discussion.

In the West, the spirit of freedom first became active in knowledge, while in China it first became active in morality. However, the spirit of freedom has to extend to politics; it has to have a concrete accomplishment in politics before it can become a proper system itself and provide clear, immovable guarantees for freedom in cognition and morality. Naturally, political freedom is not all of liberty. Political freedom needs to originate in intellectual and especially moral freedom, and must draw nourishment from moral freedom. This is common sense drawn from historical practice. However, what is more crucial is that humanity's greatest catastrophes and the worst suppression of human nature usually comes from politics. So the spirit of freedom in morality and in knowledge has to butt heads with politics, and must demand that politics be subordinated to each individual. Politics must be put under the control of each individual's conscience and reason, so that politics becomes a tool of each individual and no individual becomes a political tool.

The result of this effort, as everyone knows, is democratic government with human rights as its soul and a legislature as its framework. This is why the word *liberalism* did not appear until the nineteenth century when democratic government matured, even though the spirit of liberalism began at the same time as human culture. This is not without reason. The grand unification of the political framework of our nation was established based on the thought of Legalism, which opposes freedom. The continuous struggle against Legalist thought and institutions on the part of Han dynasty intellectuals was in fact a struggle to win freedom from the government. This struggle met with a tragic ending from the disaster of the Great Proscription carried out by eunuchs.[15] Thereafter, the spirit of freedom could not extend itself politically, ensuring that under the constraints of government, the life force of the whole culture, the whole nation, would turn into the tiny feet of a woman with bound feet, not getting the space to develop normally.

We should thus not find it difficult to understand the great significance of the nationalist revolution led by Sun Zhongshan for the development of our national history, which had the form of a democratic republic and which made achieving constitutional government its political goal. Sun Zhongshan made real the spirit of freedom in China in one day, which for more than two thousand years of hardship had never been realized politically. If Sun himself had lacked the spirit of freedom, he could not have had his unyielding revolutionary energy. If the goal of his revolution had not been to realize political freedom, then we cannot explain his determination to get rid of autocracy and realize democracy. However, the three principles of the people are not equivalent to liberalism, because as explained earlier, liberalism is merely a kind of spiritual attitude toward life and the three principles are a concrete idea for government. However, is it not difficult to say that the spiritual foundation that shaped the three principles was not Mr. Zhongshan's liberal spirit? Is it not difficult to say that the goal of the three principles is not to realize all kinds of freedom (including individual political freedom)?

Mr. Zhongshan said it very clearly himself: the three principles are a doctrine of the people's government, the people's ownership, and the people's enjoyment, with the people as master. The people's government, the people's ownership, and the people's enjoyment are a reversal of the traditional principles of enlightened despotism—care for the people, nurture the people, and educate the people—making the people active instead of passive. This was a watershed in distinguishing forms of government, which a common modern citizen could understand. I would like to ask, if the people have no political freedom how can they be the masters of the government? How could the government be called a democracy with the people's government, the people's ownership, and the people's enjoyment? I could say that Mr. Zhongshan's three principles of the people are liberalism's three principles of the people—a doctrine founded on liberalism. No one could interpret the three principles as a form of thought opposed to liberalism. Only Communists do this.

From the standpoint of liberalism, an individual can use his own reason to believe in the three principles, or he can use his own reason and not believe in them. But when the three principles do not hinder the free activity of each individual's reason, one need not oppose the three principles even if one does not believe in them. Minimally, the liberal three principles of the people should in theory not have this danger. An adherent of the three principles is just like a young woman advocating freedom in marriage who has already made a free choice and married someone. Marriage seems to make marital freedom disappear. How little people understand that this is precisely the result of her advocating marital freedom. Someone who only believes in liberalism and not the three principles is just like a young woman who is freely choosing her partner and does not wish to accept any constraints. This does not mean never marrying, but wanting an ideal marriage. The attitude of a liberal, as far as liberalism itself goes, is an attitude of getting rid of all constraints. However, a person's reason wants to leap out from this elimination of constraints and actively endorse something. It wants to accept active responsibility for what it endorses. An adherent of the three principles who fights against liberals is just as silly as a married woman fighting against marital freedom or cursing someone for not marrying the same husband as she.

As for my own conclusion from studying Sun's writings, his thought and ideas from before 1919 completely accord with Western democracy. Starting from 1920, he was influenced to some degree by the Soviet revolution, and the Soviet Union opposes liberalism. However, two points need additional explanation here. The first is that Sun's sympathies for the Russian revolution were exactly like the sympathies of the writer Gide and the philosopher Russell.[16] It was the natural display of a selfless great soul, searching high and low for a future for humanity. When Gide and Russell had opportunities to understand Soviet Russia's antiliberalism and its consequences, their attitudes immediately changed. This was a necessary result of the fact that their entire bodies of thought and these particular events were incompatible. From Sun's entire body of thought we can tell that if he could have lived a few more years and had an opportunity to see the true face of Soviet Russia, his attitude toward the Russian revolution would have changed completely. He would have clarified some aspects of his thought on the three principles that were influenced by communism, such as revolution to realize democracy.

Second, his "physiological" characteristic of thought after 1920 was only about correcting liberalism and not opposing it. The phrase, "Chinese people have too much freedom" appears occasionally in his lecture notes on the people's rights,[17] and this has brought about considerable misunderstanding. Someone with a little common sense can determine for himself the distance between the freedom Mr. Sun talked about here and the content of modern European liberalism. If one does not grasp the root and order the branches and uses this as an excuse to oppose liberalism, then Mr. Sun also said that the people's livelihood is communism: Are we then supposed to say the people's livelihood really is communism based on this?

The problem doesn't end here. What we are discussing now is not a question of pure thought, but is in fact a political question. The people who oppose freedom of thought are not propounding their scholarship while sitting in their studies. If they were propounding their scholarship, then there would be no harm in saying that the academic level of Free China should be a little higher than that displayed by those who now oppose freedom of thought. Most of them are standing in the imperial court and offering a defense of their own policies and behavior for propaganda purposes.[18] Because anyone who criticizes their policies and behavior is a liberal and liberalism is intolerable, naturally their criticism is not worth considering. That way they can act without scruples. They break out the sign of opposing liberalism, seemingly to defend the three principles of the people, but, in reality, do their actions represent the three principles? Was the legacy of Mr. Sun's doctrine only to teach them to consider the prestige of the government (which in reality is merely their personal benefit) and not to consider the facts? Was it to teach them that the way to maintain the government's prestige is to reject admonitions and paint over its faults, and not to reform and mend their errors?

Let us put aside those questions for now. Here, I will just give a special reminder that the basis for our current government's existence is the constitution, and its nature is constitutional government. Speaking from the point of view of legal theory and the proper system of the nation, the constitution has a direct relation to the current government and the three principles has an indirect relation. Whoever violates the constitution weakens the foundation of the government and damages its prestige. One might even say it is a form of rebellion against the nation. Rather than saying that the mission of the government now is to build Taiwan into a province modeling the three principles of the people, it would be better to say that it should be to build Taiwan into a province modeling democratic constitutional governance. If one believes that the three principles were not included in the constitution currently in effect, then the slogan of putting into practice the three principles constitutes a slogan in opposition to the constitution. How should the government resolve this contradiction?

If, on the other hand, one believes that the three principles are included in the constitution presently in effect, then this constitution represents the three principles further politically realized and codified in the legal institutions. The three principles are a belief of one party; there is room to believe in them or not. The constitution defines the polity of the nation: no one can fail to follow the constitution. Practicing constitutional government is the only way to express that the government is stable in its position and is not taking the regressive path of one-party rule. Everyone should try to consider calmly that we should not only not take this regressive path in laws and principles, but also not take it in actual power. When one understands this extremely commonplace and unchangeable principle, then one should admit that the only way to reach compromise when the different voices in politics are all muddled is through the constitution. Is the present constitution a democratic one? Or is it antidemocratic? If it is democratic, then what do the past three hundred years of history tell us: Are democracy and freedom separable or inseparable?

When realized in government, liberalism becomes the various rights of the people enumerated in the constitution. When people exercise their rights granted by the constitution but borrow the terms of some form of thought to oppose these rights, in reality they are opposing human rights. They are opposing the constitution. They are opposing the reasonable and rational foundation that the present government relied on in times of hardship. And what they want to achieve is merely their own personal interests and advantages. They want to use Mr. Sun as a shield for these personal interests and advantages. This would make him weep in his grave.

Moreover, the liberalism that is being opposed now is the doctrine most clearly separated from communism, and so is the strongest for opposing communism. What liberals demand is not their own rights or advantages. What they demand is a more stable basis for government, for the government to be more rational and effective, and for the battle lines in the fight against communism to be broader and stronger. Hence, at times they cannot help offering some criticism [of the government], that's all. Taking a general look over these past years, has there been even one instance of critical opinions against the government, whether from any body representing popular will or in the media, without offering some assistance fixing the policy?

For example, what is currently exciting direct attacks against liberalism is criticism of the education policy plan of Minister of Education Zhang Qiyun.[19] Anyone with some moral awareness and ordinary understanding who has children getting an education would try to think about it calmly and dispassionately. Even if Mr. Zhang's plan is not being put into effect in the whole province now due to some people's opposition, if one looks at the state of things where it is being given a trial in Xinzhu[20] [and extrapolates from that], what a mess the education of the whole province would be! Not a single word of Hu Qiuyuan's[21] "Additional Request for Information on the Two Policies of the Ministry of Education" brought up in the legislature on October 2 was printed in any of the major newspapers with the qualifications to fight for press freedom for the free world. Despite this, his seven questions regarding Mr. Zhang's violations of the constitution are so clear and evident, there is not the slightest room to repudiate them.

The oddest thing is that some people who themselves are not restrained by the constitution at all want to turn around and curse the liberal intellectuals who insist on respecting the constitution, who look out for the whole system of the nation, who discriminate right and wrong in opposing communism, and who don't seek the slightest personal advantage. That's right: liberals hold onto the constitution and clearly distinguish right and wrong. So they cannot avoid criticizing and correcting measures that violate the constitution and throw things in chaos. But what ism is there in the world that only permits government officials to light a fire and doesn't allow the people to light lamps? Honestly, the current circumstance is only that intellectuals don't take seriously *enough* the responsibility of their conscience and reason. They aren't *enough* of modern liberals. If one wants to leave some hope for the suffering people, then the suffering liberals must provide more hope.

Maybe some people will say that what I wrote above was theory and not reality. In extraordinary times, one cannot only talk theory and neglect reality. Theory is insubstantial and reality is solid, and so only talking theory is the view of a bookish intellectual. Correct, we are facing real problems. We should consider both theory and reality. However, the general trend of the present opposition to communism is to oppose the Communist Party for the sake of freedom. The present government of Free China is also aware of the need to increase unity. If even liberalism is put in the category of what is opposed, with whom will the government unite? If the government considers those who care about its success and so cannot help exercising a simple person's duty [to criticize] to be enemies and publicly disparages them as reactionaries, where will it look for friends? What makes me particularly sigh with regret is that before we considered ourselves inclined toward virtuous intent but in reality had to cross swords with virtuous intent, and now in reality we are in the liberty camp but in spirit often want to pick fights with liberty. The creation of this sort of comedy of errors is nothing but the result of hiding the faults and overlooking the mistakes of a small group of bureaucrats. It definitely did not come from the three principles of the people in which the GMD believes. This is worth thorough consideration by the wise President Jiang.

Note: when I wrote this essay, I was only motivated by the attacks on liberalism from some of the publications of the Ministry of Education. And also Hu Qiuyuan's additional inquiry on educational policy, which was brought to an end by the government sending Mr. Hu to fill out the delegation to the UN as a consultant.[22] *The attacks against liberalism from all sides started more than a month later.*

Chapter 13

The Fundamental Structure of Mengzi's Political Thought and the Problem of Rule of Man and Rule of Law

Translator's introduction: This article may be thought of as a companion piece to "The Origin of Kongzi's Idea of Rule by Virtue" (the following chapter), only focused on Mengzi instead of Kongzi. The structure is similar: Xu examines Mengzi's political thought, with extensive quotations to document his analysis, and uses these to argue that it does not have the implications it was commonly thought to have.

Xu's strategy here is one he frequently employs: he concedes that Mengzi did not argue for anything like modern democracy, but this was due in part to not knowing about or being able to imagine the necessary institutions and in part to facing the political reality, in which monarchy was standard. In other words, the historical situation of the time meant that Mengzi could only work within a structure in which the ruler had essentially unlimited power. However, once that is no longer the case, the ideals in Mengzi point to a different kind of political system which gives more weight to the people. As evidence, he adduces several examples in which Mengzi does suggest popular will is important for certain decisions.

Ruist Political Thought and Democracy, Freedom and Human Rights, 121–32, first published in *Fatherland Weekly* 26, no. 8, May 25, 1959.

A major focus of this article is the question of rule of law. Many Ruist scholars, including contemporary ones, argue that Ruism is a form of rule of man and opposed to rule of law. Xu argues that Mengzi recognized a need for law, and in fact that two are complementary. It is true that he believed good government needed good people in office, but it also requires objective institutions, and laws are an important part of those. When the role of law in Ruist political thought remains contested today (and currently China has no independent, neutral judicial system), Xu's arguments about the function of law are an important voice.

Author's note: This article was composed in response to an article in this journal signed by Li Qianzhe. The author supplemented it on October 26, 1959, at Donghai University.

The Attitude for Understanding History and Culture

What I want to do here is take Mengzi's political thought as representative of Ruist political thought and add a little explanation to clarify some misunderstandings. But before taking up the main question, I want to discuss a few points worthy of attention in order to be able to understand a form of historical thought.

First, the thought of people in ancient times and people in themselves is always an adaptation to some requirements of their society at the time and is always restricted by the social conditions of that time. Social environments change. We can only first try to understand a thinker and estimate the value of his thought within his social environment. A kind of thought that becomes a system of knowledge will always exercise some degree of influence over later history. But this influence is only inspirational or in principle and not a concrete blueprint; it is only a possibility, a passive influence (as the *Analects* says, "It is not the Way that makes people great").[1] Because as long as someone is a person, he should be master of himself; the ancients will certainly not dig[2] out from their tombs to lead later generations around by the nose. Taking the present social environment as the measure for evaluating the ancients' thought, despising ancient thought for being unable to be a blueprint for contemporary action, or even holding the ancients responsible for the sins of the present—all such behavior simply illustrates one's own degeneracy.

Second, Chinese culture from a very early period emphasized embodied recognition[3] and practicality, not speculation, so when the ancients expressed their thought it was often fragmentary and given in response to a specific situation, lacking the abstraction and structured form of speculative thought. But any thought that became a lineage [*jia* 家] has its internal relations containing a logical structure within its fragmented language, otherwise it could only be considered an eclectic lineage.[4] Furthermore, in what they said to address some specific facts, some of it has universal meaning behind the specifics and some of it does not. It is just as [Ernst] Cassirer said in *An Essay on Man*: thought itself is universal, unless it has not risen to the point where it can be called thought.[5] So one has to put forth a certain effort to comb through and organize the thought of the ancients to understand it. One must grasp their thought through all of their related sayings, and in addition, the meaning of one sentence can only be easily confirmed in the context of all their related sayings. One absolutely cannot pick out a phrase or two and guess the meaning as one pleases. Intellectuals of the May Fourth period frequently committed this error in their discussions of Chinese culture.

Third, some of the ancients' thoughts and intentions are right and some are wrong. Some we agree with and some we oppose, but opposing is not the same as despising or planting slander. Opposition means not accepting or further criticizing a kind of thought based on facts and reasons. Despising is an emotional response entirely inspired by practical advantages and disadvantages. If despising turns into planting slander then this is an even more illegitimate means [of opposition]. Just think: the thinkers of the past who lived lives of struggle and hardship have long since rotted in their tombs: "[I]nk from soot is silent."[6] How could they offend people today and elicit their hatred? It is like breaking furniture or scattering memorial tablets after coming home after losing at gambling or firing arrows at dead men in tombs because one is unsatisfied with reality. This might be considered the kind of bravery that can avoid direct resistance, but not the kind of bravery with promise. It seems that many people have at some point acquired a mysterious book written in invisible ink[7] and shout at and curse something they do not understand at all, just like street wanderers who think that as long as they shout loudly and adopt a weird posture then they won't have to worry about people surrounding them to watch for some excitement. The reason for this phenomenon in the realm of culture is mostly to release hatred. In fact, not only does it have nothing to do with the ancients, it has even less to do with what they said and only makes people wonder whether those who do it have the qualifications to discuss anything at all. Only those who can maintain a clear and calm mind can discuss issues.

The reason for this digression is that I have felt that Mengzi's political thought is the most difficult to misunderstand of the ancients, and yet at present there are misunderstandings of him that are difficult to imagine. I think these misunderstandings should probably not be attributed to these people's ability, but to their attitude.

The Structure of Mengzi's Political Thought

In his *History of Chinese Political Thought*, the modern scholar Xiao Gongquan said, "Mengzi's political thought became for all future time the protest directed precisely against the evils of tyranny," and also, "The theory developed subsequently in the authoritarian age that the loyal servitor would not serve another ruler [other than the one belonging to the dynasty, or surname, which he first served], was something of which Mengzi in no case could have approved."[8] These conclusions are spot on. At this point, in addition to following the structure of Mengzi's political thought and giving a general outline, I also want to supplement where Mr. Xiao's discussion is insufficient concerning the question of rule of man and rule of law in Mengzi.

In his political thought, Mengzi discussed the specific topics of benevolence and rightness and the kingly way, but this was really a way of taking a political system that started and ended with the ruler and turning it completely around into a political system for the people. After more than two thousand years to our present time, this still has not been fully achieved. Even the work of making this shift conceptually has not been achieved, but historically it represents a great matter that shook the world. Mengzi did not only subordinate the ruler's interests to the people's interests and make the people's interests the scale for assessing the success and failure of all government measures. He also took the "ritual and rightness," which Ruists had emphasized, and subordinated them to the needs of people's actual lives, making ritual and rightness exist for human life instead of making human life exist for ritual and rightness. This is why he repeatedly emphasized that "[the people] cannot have a constant heart-mind without a constant livelihood . . . in these circumstances they are only concerned with saving themselves from death, fearing their resources will not suffice. What leisure would they have to practice ritual and rightness?"⁹ Any high-sounding ism or doctrine can feign utility; only the needs of people's actual lives cannot be faked. This is the touchstone of any system of political thought. I have previously pointed out several times that classical Ruists separated the standards of personal cultivation (*xiuji* 修己) and governing others (*zhiren* 治人), by which I explained that the strict moral demands of personal cultivation in Ruism absolutely could not be turned into a tool to oppress the people.¹⁰ This is a point that was neglected by people in the past, and so is the key to many controversies in intellectual history.

Because he insists that government should take the people as the starting and end point, Mengzi clearly determines that the transfer of political power should be decided by the people. He brings up the idea of "Heaven's grant"¹¹ to deny that rulers have the right to treat political power as their personal property. In actuality, "Heaven's grant" means granted by the people. And so when King Xuan of Qi was victorious in his attack of Yan and wanted to use the traditional concept of Heaven's mandate as a basis to annex Yan ("If I do not annex it, Heaven will surely bring disaster on me"), Mengzi told him forthwith, "If the people of Yan would be pleased by your annexation, then annex it. . . . If they would not be pleased, then do not."¹² This is to say that this is something that should be decided by popular will, with no relation to the mandate of Heaven. Precisely because he believed that political power should be decided by the people, two thousand years ago he already endorsed the right to political revolution ("I have heard of the punishing of the common fellow Zhou") and the people's right to retaliate against the governors ("Now the people were able to retaliate against [the officials] at last") or replace them ("If the land within your four borders is not well governed, what is to be done?" "If [the ruler] does not listen to repeated remonstrations, he should be replaced").¹³

He was very much opposed to warfare, but he felt that Tang's attack on Ge was an instance of "avenging the common people"¹⁴ and a model of kingliness. Furthermore, he felt that the power of the people is the strongest political power, so he said, "When the people turn to [a true king], it is like water flowing downhill in a torrent: who can stop it?" "Nothing can stop a ruler who cares for the people from becoming king."¹⁵ All these illustrate that the people have the power to decide the government. These were not only considered unrealistic when heard by the rulers of the time, I fear many modern readers of Mengzi have the same feeling. But when we look over the long course of history, who can say that it is not the power of the people that completely changes the course of history?

In the past, I was like a lot of people in thinking that Mengzi's idea that the people are valuable and the ruler is not is simply the idea of the people as foundation (*minben* 民本), which is still some distance from democracy. In Xiao Gongquan's words, "Mengzi's 'importance of the people' merely commences with the idea of 'for the people' and proceeds toward that of 'of the people.' Both the principle of 'by the people,' and the institutions necessary to it, were things of which he had never heard."[16] From a current perspective, institutions for popular sovereignty are indeed something Mengzi had never heard of, but inklings of the principle of popular sovereignty can be found in Mengzi:

> The ruler of a state promotes the worthy only when necessary. . . . When your court says a man is worthy, this is not enough. When the counselors say he is worthy, this is not enough. Investigate [whether he is truly worthy] only when the people of the city say he is worthy. If you find that he is worthy, only then employ him.

> If your court says a man is unacceptable, don't listen. If the various counselors say he is unacceptable, don't listen. If the people of the city say he is unacceptable, then investigate, and if he is truly unacceptable then dismiss him. If your court says a man should be executed, don't listen. If the various counselors say he should be executed, don't listen. If the people of the city say he should be executed, then investigate, and if he truly should be executed, then execute him. So it used to be said, "The people of the city executed him."[17]

Compared to the full text, I left out two phrases: "So it used to be said, 'The people of the city employed him. . . . So it used to be said, 'The people of the city dismissed him.'" The meaning of this section is that employment, dismissals, and executions should not be decided by the ruler but should be decided by the people. The preferences of the people determine the particular content of government: "What the people desire, gather and give to them. What they hate, do not do to them."[18] And in the *Great Learning*: "Love what the people love and hate what the people hate."[19] How can reserving the political power to employ, dismiss, and execute in the people's hands not reveal the principle of popular sovereignty? However, how the people can effectively exercise this power is a question of institutions of which Mengzi indeed never thought. From this requirement of principle, which in "The Revolutions of Ritual" in the *Record of Ritual* developed into the position of "All under heaven belongs to the public. [Those in power] employ the worthy and promote the able,"[20] is a big advance in terms of institutions. In Western Han (206 BCE–9 CE) there were local elections that derived from this requirement. However, Western Han elections lacked the premise that all under heaven belongs to the public and so only had the effect of moderating the poison of despotism slightly, losing the significance of advancing toward democracy.

We should not forget, however, that Western democratic institutions centered around a legislative assembly were naturally born in city-states with populations in the tens of thousands. In some small cities of the Middle Ages they also naturally adopted this system. It was not due to the ideals of political thinkers. In Western political thought prior to the modern period, democracy was just one political system among many. It was not taken to be the best political system. Pursuing democracy as the ideal political system was something that did not happen until the latter part of the Enlightenment, after a period of despotic monarchy. Then it is understandable that ideas for healthy institutions for popular sovereignty could not arise in an agricultural society with a vast territory two thousand years ago.

Did Mengzi Not Emphasize Rule of Law?

I have only been able to describe the structure of Mengzi's political thought in an abridged fashion to this point. Later, there will be opportunities to supplement it. Now I want to turn to the issue of rule of man and rule of law in Mengzi's political thought as well as Ruist thought as a whole. The average person says Ruism only emphasizes rule of man, not rule of law, and because of this a number of accusations have been leveled against Ruists. I feel these are entirely due to misunderstandings. The importance of the people in politics cannot be denied in any age. Two thousand years ago, the world belonging to the public was just an ideal;

the source of political power was still held in one ruler's hands. When the ruler was the whole engine of government, only the ruler could become a kind of moral being. At the very least, only if the ruler controlled himself and abided by some fundamental principles of politics and human life was there any rule of law to speak of. Otherwise, with just a shake of the ruler's head all beneficial laws and grand ideas would deviate in the blink of an eye, degenerating and turning into worthless currency.

Using a constitution to control the ruler or other forms of political power is something that did not exist until the modern period. In ancient China the only option was to rely on the ruler to control himself due to his virtuous nature. Pushing it higher a level, beyond the ruler's virtuous nature there was only Heaven, but after the middle of the Western Han, rulers transferred responsibility for Heaven's changes to the high ministers. Moving down a level from the ruler's virtuous nature, ministers could only describe the actual advantages and disadvantages [of a policy], but those with power often mixed them up. So in the final analysis, no matter what, the ruler's virtuous nature was always the center. This was something unavoidable, not only before there was a concept of a constitution but even after a constitution existed, but did not yet have a true foundation or authority.

Nowadays, whenever humanity reaches a crucial juncture, behind law it is still necessary to appeal to people's conscience and reason, such as in the United Nations charter or the Universal Declaration of Human Rights.[21] Thus, if Ruists did *not* specially emphasize rule of man and the conscience and reason of those with political responsibility two thousand years ago, what else could they do? Legalists emphasized law and not people, their arguments reaching a culmination with Han Feizi. The Qin dynasty was precisely a proving ground for Legalist political thought. Yet Han Feizi died at the hands of Li Si, Li Si died at the hands of Zhao Gao, and Fusu and Huhai both met with their deaths.[22] In two reigns the dynasty fell. Is this not the most biting satire [of Legalist thought]?

As for the claim that Ruism emphasizes rule of man and not rule of law, one must first consider how law is explained. If law is understood as a modern constitution, then this concept did not exist two thousand years ago. Of course, in the past there was also the idea of eternal and unchanging laws to maintain the stability of the government. This is what Mengzi meant by "old statutes" and "the laws [*fa* 法] of the former kings."[23] This is like historical convention in England. Yet it is after all different than the contemporary concept of a constitution.

If law is understood as penal law, then Ruism in fact does not emphasize penal law, but neither does it reject penal law. Mengzi said very clearly, "When the state is at leisure, make clear its laws and punishments."[24] If law is understood as some objective political principles that should be commonly followed and institutions formed on the basis of these principles to manifest them in practice, then where did Mengzi and all Ruists *not* emphasize governing by law? Mengzi said, "The former kings had heart-minds that could not bear the suffering of others, and so they had government that could not bear the suffering of others." "The Way of Yao and Shun, without benevolent government, cannot bring peace and order to the world." "When Zichan took charge of the government of Zheng, he would take people across the Zhen and Wei rivers in his own chariot. Mengzi said, 'He was kind, but did not understand how to govern.'"[25] The instances of "govern" and "government" [zheng 政] in these quotes all mean what is typically called governing by law. "Those above have no Way on which to deliberate. Those below have no laws to hold to. When the ruler does not trust in the Way and the officials do not trust in the laws, then if the state survives it is only a matter of luck."[26] This is saying that a state will fall without rule of law. It is true that Mengzi took the traditional concept of rule by virtue and emphasized its realization in the heart-mind of the ruler, believing that the heart-mind that people could truly grasp was the basis of government. Hence, he particularly emphasized "the benevolent heart-mind" and "the heart-mind which cannot bear people's [suffering]."[27] He also emphasized "correcting what is wrong in the ruler's heart-mind."[28] Yet the heart-mind he referred to is the heart-mind in which "benevolence, rightness, ritual propriety, and wisdom are rooted."[29]

Following the fundamental nature of this heart-mind requires objectifying it into governing by law in order to resolve the actual problems of humanity. Only this can fill out the aspiration to [govern by feeling that] "if anyone in the world drowned, it was as if he had drowned them himself. If anyone in the world starved, it was as if he had starved them himself."[30] Precisely because of this, among all the political thinkers of the pre-Qin period, Mengzi put the greatest stress on economic questions and the economic system. He repeatedly emphasized, "A wise ruler regulates the livelihood of the people,"[31] meaning that they should make the people's livelihood stable through laws. At that time, all land was in the ruler's hands, so if the ruler did not regulate the people's livelihood they would have no livelihood and no way to obtain minimal means of subsistence. "Plant every household of five *mu* with mulberry trees," appears in the *Mengzi* text three times,[32] indicating that this was his economic and legislative blueprint to address the actual conditions of the time: "Never have the people been suffering more from a tyrannical government than they are now."[33] This was in order to reach his goal where "those of seventy can wear silk and eat meat and the black-haired people are neither starving nor cold."[34] In regard to artisans and merchants, he hoped to adopt methods of encouraging free development. He repeatedly advocated legal institutions: "Examine [goods] at gates and markets, but do not levy taxes on them," and, "Charge a fee for market stalls, but do not tax the goods."[35] This attitude toward artisans and merchants was shared by pre-Qin Ruists, so the *Mean* advocated "encouraging the various artisans."[36] This kind of thought continued until Xunzi was influenced by Legalism and at that point changed slightly.

Mengzi's further proposals on economic matters and rule of law are the well-field and school institutions he offered to Duke Wen of Teng. Here I will not discuss whether the well-field system actually existed in ancient times or what it was actually like, but only point out that Mengzi's proposal was an idealized version with no relation to whether it existed historically or what it was like. This was the earliest proposal for land reform in China and was influential all the way down to Sun Zhongshan's idea of equal land rights. The concept and function of education was not made explicit until Kongzi. The system of schools in the *Documents* and *Odes* appears to lack clear and reliable evidence. The transmission of political experience in the Shang dynasty probably relied on the shamans (*wu* 巫) while in the Zhou it relied on the scribes (*shi* 史). Initially, schools probably started as centers for practicing archery and caring for the elderly, with no regular educational organization.[37] Schools moved from "occasional practice" of archery and caring for the elderly to a kind of regular educational function as a result of Ruists' constant effort, and this began to take a clear shape in Mengzi's time. This was a noteworthy event in the advocacy for rule of law. It represents the [first] establishment of a separate educational system outside the government in Chinese history. In addition to the institutions of schools and the well-field, I will quote a few more specific instances of Mengzi's views on rule of law.

If you do not interfere with the proper times for farming, there will be more grain than the people can eat. If fine nets are not allowed in the ponds and pools, there will be more fish and turtles than the people can eat. If axes are only allowed in the mountain forests in the proper times, there will be more timber than the people can use.[38]

Reduce punishments and fines. Make taxes and levies lighter. Ensure the plowing is deep and easy to weed. Ensure those in their prime have time off to cultivate filiality, fraternal respect, dedication, and trustworthiness.[39]

In ancient times, King Wen governed Qi this way: he taxed one part in nine of the harvest, officials could pass their salary on to their heirs, goods were examined at the gates and markets but not taxed, and the people were not prohibited from the ponds and fish weirs. [Punishment for] criminals did not extend to their wives or children. The elderly without wives are called widowers. The elderly without husbands are called widows. The elderly without children are called the lonely. The young without parents are called orphans. When King Wen carried out governing with benevolence, he certainly made these four groups the priority.[40]

Honor the worthy and employ the able, so men of talent and distinction are in office. . . . Charge a fee for market stalls but do not tax the goods. If it complies with the [local] laws, do not charge the fee. . . . Inspect goods but do not tax them. . . . Have farmers assist [in plowing the common fields] but do not tax them. Collect the housing tax but not the idleness fee or extra cloth.[41]

To sum up Mengzi's viewpoint on virtue and law: "Goodness alone is not enough for governing. Laws alone cannot be put into practice by themselves."[42] The first sentence says that governing by people alone (goodness alone) cannot make for good government, so governing by law is also needed. The second sentence says that laws do not implement themselves, so good people are still necessary to carry them out. That is, neither laws nor people can be cast aside. However, due to the times two thousand years ago people were given slightly greater weight. Today, the greater weight should be slightly on the side of laws. However, in China which is in the midst of a period of transition, I fear it is difficult to determine which should have the greater weight.

Going back farther to Kongzi, he once said, "If you guide the people with decrees and reform them with punishments, they will evade them and have no sense of shame. If you guide them with virtue and reform them with ritual, they will have a sense of shame and correct themselves."[43] In the *Analects*, decrees generally refers to governmental commands. Governing by decrees means teaching by words; governing by virtue means teaching by example. In the *Analects*, governing by virtue means that the governors must set an example through their own lives. It did not have the broader meaning that rule by virtue later took on. Governing by virtue is to lead through one's own real life: this is rule of man. And the true spirit of ritual in governing by ritual fits exactly with contemporary rule of law. Law in Legalism carries the implication of penal law, which is not the same as contemporary rule of law. Hence, rule by virtue means advocating rule of law. The political dimension of ritual in Xunzi refers to rule of law. Mengzi also said, "When those above lack ritual propriety and those below lack education, disorderly people will arise and the state will be lost in no time."[44] *The Offices of Zhou*, also called *The Rituals of Zhou*, exclusively discussed political institutions and one could see from this alone that the political aspect of ritual Ruists talked about is rule of law. Moreover, Kongzi never neglected rule of law. And so in the Han it was often said, "Kongzi composed the *Spring and Autumn Annals* to be the laws for a dynasty."[45]

Most liable to misunderstanding is the following passage from the *Mean*: "The governments of King Wen and King Wu is described in the historical records. When the [right] men are alive, their government flourishes. When they die, their government ceases with them."[46] Based on this, many people say Ruism does not give weight to rule of law. In fact, that passage only explains the actual circumstances of the time: How could it be explained as ignoring rule of law? The *Mean* goes on to say, "Every state in the world had nine canons,"[47] and the nine canons are nine forms of settled law, each of which is then laid out in the text. If this is not rule of law then what is it? In the pre-Qin Ruist texts (such as *Mengzi*, *Xunzi*, and *Record of Ritual*) political institutions are the most detailed parts, and hence later developed in *The Offices of Zhou*. And yet people today say the same thing with different voices: Ruists only talked about rule of man, not rule of law. They carry out study without concern for the facts, they discuss without opening their minds and being frank and direct, and they take the responsibilities of people now and shift them onto their own ancestors. Thus, it is no coincidence that the intellectual class has declined.

Chapter 14

The Origin of Kongzi's Idea of Rule by Virtue

Translator's introduction: This essay stands out for Xu's sustained engagement with a foreign sinologist, the Harvard historian John King Fairbank. The genesis of this article appears to be this. Fairbank published an article in *The Atlantic Monthly* in 1966 offering his updated suggestions for U.S. government China policy.[1] Fairbank favored a realistic approach, recognizing that the CCP government was not going to be overthrown and increasing U.S. engagement with China (which Nixon would go on to do in 1971). Many intellectuals in Taiwan felt betrayed, taking Fairbank's comments as suggesting weakening U.S. support for Taiwan. More than one thousand scholars wrote an open letter criticizing Fairbank.

Later in 1966, Tao Baichuan, a GMD official, was in the United States and attempted to get a meeting with Fairbank to discuss his views on China in person. Fairbank claimed to be unable to meet with Tao, but provided him with a copy of his testimony to the Senate Foreign Relations Committee, which had been the basis for his *Atlantic Monthly* article. Tao then wrote the newspaper article Xu refers to, defending Fairbank's analysis of Chinese tradition. This deepened the controversy,

Ruist Political Thought and Democracy, Freedom and Human Rights, 99–120, first published in *Democratic Review*, September 1966.

both because Tao defended Fairbank and because of the implication that the CCP had in fact inherited Ruist tradition (which is not exactly what Fairbank wrote in his article). For Xu, this was intolerable. Complicating the situation, Tao possibly used this opportunity to misrepresent Fairbank's views. In his newspaper article, he quotes Fairbank as saying, "Communism inherited the tradition of Chinese [culture]" and, "Maoism represents 'the present of Chinese tradition.'"[2] Although Fairbank stressed the importance of understanding Chinese history for understanding the actions of the Communist government, he never said those things in either his Senate testimony or published article, though it is possible Tao drew them from another source. Regardless, Xu apparently took Tao to be reporting Fairbank's views accurately.

Xu then wrote this article, defending the Ruist concept of rule by virtue, which he thought Fairbank had argued leads to totalitarianism. (In fact, in his testimony Fairbank said no such thing but had connected the authoritarian elements of the Chinese government to Legalism.)[3] Xu offers a lengthy examination of the textual and historical basis of rule by virtue, as well as an analysis of how it works in Ruist thought. He is chiefly concerned to refute one claim by Fairbank: that rule by virtue leads to coercing the people through reward and punishment if they fail to follow the ruler's virtuous model. The core of Xu's argument is this: rule by virtue means using virtue in place of punishment, not resorting to punishment when virtue fails. It is a way of holding rulers responsible when their state is not well ordered. Kongzi's ideal was to use rituals instead of punishments, since rituals are not coercive.

Rule by virtue in its positive aspect means caring for the people and looking after their interests. It is more than refraining from using punishments. This is Xu's response to the possible objection that rule by virtue is too idealistic. He claims that if a ruler sincerely cares for the people and demonstrates this in his governing, then it is not mysterious that people will respond. Rule by virtue means using rituals to influence people, educating them, and governing in their interests. If they do this, there would be little or no need for punishments. Ruling through punishment is the Legalist method; it is what Ruists opposed. What the Communist Party followed was the Legalist tradition, not Ruism at all. So Xu argues that Fairbank has completely misunderstood Kongzi, and his views should in no way shape U.S. policy on China.

The footnotes in this essay are Xu's own, unless noted.

Chinese Culture, Beset from Both Sides

Totalitarianism and colonialism have a commonality when it comes to China: both wholly oppose traditional Chinese culture, which unfolded with Kongzi as its center. Totalitarianism does this because Chinese culture is based on the idea that human nature is good. It truly grasped the source of human dignity, equality, and peaceful interactions. This is, of course, the source of liberal democracy.[4] Hence, once totalitarians have some contact with it, they instantly realize that this voice and strength that comes from human nature is a lethal threat to them. It is very easy to understand why recently Mao Zedong's group on the mainland swore an oath to eradicate traditional Chinese culture by the roots.[5]

Colonialism does this because national self-respect comes from respect for its culture, and the awareness of the nation's independence is related to this. This is the premise and condition for the whole building of any nation. However, it is completely at odds with the colonial goal pursued by colonialism, because colonialism can only be established in a culture that feels inferior and base. Defiling and insulting one's own culture is the impetus and manifestation of this feeling of inferiority. The traditional culture centered on Kongzi, as well as the traditional culture centered on Laozi and Zhuangzi, has the character of being totally pacifistic. Anyone with a little common sense could admit this. So, during the War of Resistance when Minister of Education Chen Lifu said that advocating for Ruism was also the best way to try to achieve world peace, he was not wrong.[6]

However, in John King Fairbank's[7] memorandum sent to the American embassy in China on November 19, 1943, where he said of Chen's promotion of Ruism, "For the sake of US-China cultural relations we have to oppose it, because Ruism has an aggressive character,"[8] what is particularly worth noting is this: Fairbank was in Chongqing when he wrote this as a member of the diplomatic service sent by the United States. He sent this to the ambassador, wanting to shape official U.S. policy accordingly. It is unprecedented for a diplomatic officer abroad to want official diplomatic policy to be opposing the traditional culture of the country in which he is stationed. Some people say that he did so out of a vestigial colonial mentality. I really have no way to defend him. When he has completely opposed Kongzi, how can there still be Chinese culture? And he still mentioned "US-China cultural relations"?

Fairbank told America and China, in which anticommunists were the great majority, that the man who opposes Kongzi the most, Mao Zedong, is the true inheritor of Kongzi's tradition. This is an ingenious way of telling Americans and anticommunist Chinese, "If you want to fight against Mao, first you have to fight against Kongzi." This was an ingenious application of Fairbank's policy to tear down traditional Chinese culture.

There is a practical necessity to the colonial and totalitarian opposition to Kongzi. If we cannot convince them to give up colonialism and totalitarianism, we should not expect them to change their attitude toward Kongzi. However, according to the basic conditions for being a person, we can demand that their opposition should be founded on the true materials about Kongzi and on a normal interpretation of those materials. So here I will specifically bring up Kongzi's idea of "rule by virtue" for some examination.

The Problem with Rule by Virtue
Raised by John K. Fairbank

John Fairbank believed, "China was ruled by a great [Ruist] political fiction, the myth of rule-by-virtue. According to this, the right conduct of a superior man, acting according to the correct principles, set an example which moved others. . . . Persons too uneducated to be so moved could, of course, be dealt with through rewards and punishments. . . . This national myth of rule-by-virtue fills the Chinese historical record."[9] In the *Zhengxin Daily News* of June 6 [1966], Mr. Tao Baichuan published "A Reexamination of John King Fairbank's Public Opinions on China" in which he wrote, "I think translating it as 'rule by ritual' would better fit what Professor Fairbank said."[10] Here, I have to say something fair: according to Mr. Tao's change of translation, his understanding of this question may not match up to Fairbank's. This will naturally become clear in the later parts of the essay.

Kongzi formally brought up rule by virtue in the following *Analects* passage. "The master said, 'One who rules by virtue may be compared to the Pole Star. It remains in its place while the other stars revolve around it'" [*Analects* 2.1]. In Kongzi's mind, Yao and Shun were the highest examples of rule by virtue. We might say the following passage fully supports the previous one.

"The master said, 'Was not Shun someone who ruled through nonaction? What did he ever do? All he did was make himself reverent and faced south'" [*Analects* 15.5].[11] "Making oneself reverent" and "facing south" *are* ruling by virtue. In his *Collected Explanations of the Analects*, He Yan quotes Bao Xian: "Bao says, 'Virtue is nonaction. It means not moving like the Pole Star while the other stars revolve around it.'"[12] Bao equates rule by virtue and rule by nonaction, confirming both passages above. Bao's explanation has some basis. So in his explanation of the above passage in his *Collected Comments*, Zhu Xi also said, "Ruling by virtue means not acting and all under heaven returning to [the ruler.]"[13] A small conclusion here: rule by virtue is rule by nonaction. Nonaction, as I will later explain, means not using one's personal preferences to rule the people, and not using coercive means to rule the people. It means encouraging the people to act of themselves through one's own beneficial influence, not literally doing nothing. This has been the common opinion for over two thousand years.

What has to be investigated further is, just how should we interpret the "virtue" in rule by virtue? In *Subcommentary on Collected Explanations of the Analects*, Xing Bing said, "'Virtue' means 'to obtain.' What things obtain to live is called virtue. Pure virtue doesn't disperse. It becomes clarified by nonaction, and then the government is good."[14] This probably makes use of Laozi's thought. Xing's subcommentary was formed by editing Huang Kan's subcommentary. He was exactly like He Yan in being influenced by Laozi's thought. We will not go into the differences between Kongzi's and Laozi's thought now; let us just first point out that the meaning of his explanation here is quite vacuous and vague. In his *Collected Comments* Zhu Xi said, "The activity of virtue is obtaining. By putting the Way into practice, one obtains something in one's heart-mind."[15] This shifts from Laozi's virtue to Kongzi's virtue. It readily connects with the virtue in "Set one's intent on the Way and rely on virtue" [*Analects* 7.6].

Yet here it is still a little empty and vague. In chapter 23 of his *Categorized Sayings*, on this passage his explanation was, "If someone does good things, if it's just one or two and he's forced himself to do it, then he obtains nothing. What is meant by this sort of obtaining is becoming familiar with [good] action and feeling ease in one's heart mind."[16] Here he connects one's behavior and inner heart-mind together to explain virtue. If we are just a little flexible here, then virtue means "normative[ly correct] behavior that unites the inner and outer." Ruling by virtue means the ruler engaging in normative behavior that unites the inner and outer in governing. In the early Zhou, virtue usually indicated behavior. In the Spring and Autumn period, usually behavior that benefited others was called virtue. Among Kongzi's followers, they also connected the words to make "virtuous behavior."

Explaining the "virtue" of rule by virtue in the above manner should be close to the original meaning. We can see that Fairbank's explanation of rule by virtue as "correct behavior" is not too far off and actually Tao Baichuan's altered translation made it worse, because "virtue" can include "ritual" but it is broader than merely ritual. According to this way of explaining it, the following passages are all concerned with rule by virtue.

"The master said of Zichan, he had four aspects of the way of the gentleman. He was reverent in his own behavior, he was respectful when serving his superiors, he was kind in nurturing the people, and he was appropriate in employing the people" (*Analects* 5.16). According the *Zuo Tradition*, Duke Xiang 24, in Zichan's message to Fan Gai of Jin, he said, "Now a good name is the vehicle of virtue. Virtue is the foundation of domain and patrimony. Should one not strive to have a foundation and let it be ruined?"[17] One could say that what Zichan said also contains the idea of rule by virtue. Kongzi declared that Zichan had four aspects of the way of the gentleman, which is another way of saying that he also ruled by virtue.

"The master said, 'Yong could be put in the position facing south.' Zhonggong asked about Zisang Bozi. The master said, 'He is acceptable. He is easygoing regarding the trivial. Zhonggong said, 'Would it not be acceptable to maintain a respectful attitude and be easygoing in behavior in watching over the people? But to maintain an easygoing attitude and be easygoing in behavior is too relaxed, isn't it?' The master said, 'What Yong said is correct'" (*Analects* 6.1, 6.2). "Easygoing" is close to non-action. Maintaining a respectful attitude is virtue, and being easygoing in attitude, it is too easy to slip into a lack of virtue. So maintaining a respectful attitude and being easygoing in behavior is another way of expressing rule by virtue.

"Duke Jing of Qi asked Kongzi about governing. The master responded, 'Let the ruler be a ruler, the minister be a minister, the father be a father, and the son be a son" (*Analects* 12.11). Letting the ruler be a ruler means the ruler of the people should completely live up to the way of being the ruler of the people, or in other words, live up to the virtue of the ruler of the people. Although Kongzi here mentioned rulers, ministers, fathers, and sons, the emphasis should of course be on the ruler being a ruler, since he was responding to Duke Jing's question about governing. This also a proposal for rule by virtue.

"Ji Kangzi asked Kongzi about governing. The master responded, 'To govern means to be correct. If you lead with correctness, who would dare be incorrect?'" (*Analects* 12.17).

"Ji Kangzi was troubled by robbers and asked Kongzi what to do. The master responded, 'If you yourself had no desires, they would not steal even if you rewarded them for it'" (*Analects* 12.18).

"Ji Kangzi asked Kongzi about governing, suggesting, 'How about I execute those without the Way to help those with the Way?' Kongzi responded, 'Why do you need executions to govern? If you want goodness, the people will be good. The virtue of the gentleman is like the wind and that of the commoners like the grass. When the wind blows, the grass has to bend'" (*Analects* 12.19).

"The master said, 'If his person is correct, then the people will act without being ordered. If his person is incorrect, then even if he orders, they will not obey'" (*Analects* 13.6).

"The master said, 'If one can correct oneself, what else is there to do to govern? If one cannot correct oneself, how can one correct other people?'" (*Analects* 13.13).

"Correct" in the above mentions of "leading with correctness" and "being correct in his person" refers to correct behavior, the "virtue" in ruling by virtue. "If you could be without desires" and "if you desired goodness" are close to virtue. "Who would dare be incorrect," "they would not steal even if you rewarded them," "then the people will be good," and "they will act without being ordered" are all expressions of the effect of nonaction of rule by virtue. The three sentences beginning with "the virtue of the gentleman is like the wind" use this metaphor to explain the reason people will act without being ordered. In the passage answering Fan Chi's request to study farming, Kongzi said, "When those above are fond of ritual, the people do not dare be disrespectful. When those above are fond of rightness, the people dare not disobey. When those above are fond of honesty, the people do not dare be insincere" (*Analects* 13.4). Being fond of ritual, rightness, and honesty are the virtues of rule by virtue. The people not daring to disobey and so on express the effect of rule by virtue.

"Zilu asked about the gentleman. The master said, 'He cultivates himself to be respectful.' Zilu asked, 'Is that all?' The master said, 'He

cultivates himself to make others at ease.' Zilu asked, 'Is that all?' The
master said, 'He cultivates himself to give ease to the common people.
This is something even Yao and Shun would have been concerned
about'" (*Analects* 14.42). Cultivating oneself is being correct in one's
person: this is virtue. Cultivating oneself to give ease to the common
people is rule by virtue. The commentary on the hexagram *Fu* in the
Changes says, "'Return before going far' provides the way one should
cultivate his person."[18] Mengzi said, "Neither early death nor long life
should cause any distraction. Cultivate oneself to await them" (*Mengzi*
7A1). "Cultivating oneself" in these passages follows on the *Analects*
concept of cultivating oneself. When we get to *Xunzi*, there is the chapter "Cultivating Oneself." By the time we get to the *Great Learning*,[19]
there are not only eight steps in the process of cultivating oneself, it
also says, "From the Son of Heaven on down to the common people,
all take cultivating their person as the root."[20] This is all to say that
ordering the household, ruling the state, and bringing peace to the
world all take cultivating the person as the root. This made Kongzi's
idea of rule by virtue into a complete system. Kongzi's idea of rectifying
names inclines toward the theoretical side. What he asked was that
someone who occupied a certain position (name) in government should
live up to the reality of what this position requires. In other words, his
proposal of "let the ruler be a ruler and the minister be a minister."
For someone with the responsibilities of a political leader, this is also
rule by virtue. It is thus not difficult to understand that Kongzi's and
the entirely of Ruist political thought is all connected by the concept
of rule by virtue.

The Background of the Idea of Rule by Virtue

What I want to investigate further now is, what was the background for
Kongzi's proposing rule by virtue?

Kongzi's thought is mainly concerned with people perfecting their
personhood through self-awareness and striving upward. That is, each
person should discover and perfect their own virtue. The ruler of the
people is also a person, and further, is a person who bears a greater
responsibility. Thus, a ruler should perfect his own virtue, meaning he
first must stand up as a person. According to Kongzi's standpoint, this

is necessary. But aside from this basic standpoint, Kongzi's proposal of rule by virtue has its historical background.

Duke Ai of Lu asked Kongzi, "How can I make the people obey?" (*Analects* 2.19). Ji Kangzi asked, "What can I do to make the people respectful, dedicated, and exert themselves?" (*Analects* 2.20). We can see from these sorts of questions that conflicts between rulers and subjects had already reached a point of making the rulers uneasy. In these circum-stances, rulers usually thought that the only way these conflicts could be patched up is by increasing the demands on and control of the people, and, even further, securing these demands and control by punishment. In that case, the government would naturally become a sort of rule by punishment, making the people suffer under a tyranny.

In reality, the conflicts between rulers and subjects all stemmed from the rulers using a different standard for their own conduct than the standard that they applied to their subjects. The rulers' unreasonable demands all derived from putting their own behavior outside the stan-dard required of the people. Kongzi addressed this situation by insisting that what rulers required of the people, they must first require of and realize themselves. If they could do this, then the people would not wait for commands from the government: their behavior would naturally be consistent with the rulers'.

Just above, I brought up Ji Kangzi's question: "What can I do to make the people respectful and loyal to encourage them to be obedient?" He was asking what approach he could use to make the people "respectful, dedicated, and exert themselves." Kongzi instantly turned the question back on him and said, "If you oversee them with gravity, they will be respectful. If you are filial and kind, they will be dedicated. If you promote the good and teach the unable, they will exert themselves" (*Analects* 2.20). Those three sentences clearly indi-cate that the conflicts between rulers and ruled have to be resolved by starting with the rulers. Furthermore, looking at the *Analects*, *Mengzi*, *Great Learning*, *Mean*, and other [Ruist] classical texts, one sees that whenever they discuss government problems, especially when they discuss them with rulers, they always attribute them to the rulers and never to the people. The negative aspect of this was to reduce or even eliminate the rulers' demands on their people and give people's mental and material freedom greater security. This is the first part of the background of rule by virtue.

As I said above, the rulers' demands of the people are backed up by punishment. Since Kongzi has now turned these demands back on the ruler in the belief that this shift will bring the people to virtue and make punishments unnecessary, he has the belief that rule by virtue can replace rule by punishment. He wanted rule by virtue to replace rule by punishment.[21] This is the second part of the background of rule by virtue. In the following section, I will clearly contrast rule by virtue and rule by punishment.

"The master said, 'If you guide the people with decrees and reform them with punishments, they will evade them and have no sense of shame. If you guide them with virtue and reform them with ritual, they will have a sense of shame and correct themselves'" (*Analects* 2.3). "Decrees" means government commands; "reform" means putting in order; "punishment" means penalties. There is a point particularly worthy of attention here: the decrees and punishment Kongzi is talking about here are regular decrees and punishments, not especially irregular ones. The result of even regular decrees and punishments is that even if they can make people avoid punishment, they cannot make people feel ashamed of committing a crime in their hearts. People may still commit a crime at any time. This is to say that the effect of regular laws and punishments is still limited; they cannot fundamentally solve the problem. Laws and punishments are a kind of coercive power rulers impose on the ruled. Kongzi's dismissal of laws and punishments was due to a belief that the problems of the people could not be solved by coercive power. This carried the implication of disapproving of the essence of the governments of the time. So he hoped for "government by nonaction."

"Guide them with virtue" is the same as "leading them with correctness," another way of saying "ruling by virtue." Virtue and laws are in mutual opposition, as are ritual and punishments. Rituals and laws both prohibit people from doing wrong. The difference between them is clearly put in the "Examination of Ritual" chapter of *The Elder Dai's Record of Ritual*:

> Ritual prohibits in advance of anything happening, while laws prohibit after the wrong has occurred. . . . Ritual, ritual! It is honored for cutting off evil before it sprouts, making respect arise from the very subtle, so that the people daily move farther from evil and toward good without knowing it. Kongzi said, "I am the same as anyone when it comes to

hearing litigation. What is necessary is to make it so there is no litigation." This expresses this meaning.

When governing the people with ritual and rightness, ritual and rightness build up. When governing the people with punishments, punishments build up. When punishments build up the people's resentment multiplies. When ritual and rightness build up, the people become harmonious and close. Rulers of the world are the same in wanting the people to be good, but differ in how they try to make them good. Some guide them with virtue and teaching; others drive them with laws and decrees. Guiding them with virtue and teaching, virtue and teaching are put into practice and the people become secure and happy. Driving them with laws and decrees, laws and decrees go to extremes and the people become sad and pained. Disaster and good fortune are the responses to sadness and happiness, respectively.[22]

After development through the Spring and Autumn period, the scope of the concept of ritual had already become quite broad. In Kongzi, it lost even more of its meaning associated with the aristocracy as he endowed it with a purely moral meaning, replacing class with benevolence and rightness.[23] Furthermore, the phrase "reform them through ritual" means to realize the way of human relations in the form of reasonable behavior in daily life. Accumulating these forms of reasonable behavior, they become good customs and habits of a society. This is what is meant by "transforming the people and perfecting their customs."[24] Punishment is coercive and penal; ritual is inspiring and encouraging. Through guiding people with ritual to the point of transforming the people and perfecting their customs, on the one hand social order and freedom can reach an accommodation while on the other hand it can encourage people's spirit of actively pursuing goodness. This is what is meant by saying the people will have a sense of shame and correct themselves. According to my research, "correct" should be interpreted as being affected and moved. One Ruist political ideal is for punishments to be symbolic or put aside entirely.[25] The negative aspect of Kongzi's promotion of rule by virtue is to have there be no litigation, meaning to put punishments aside. So Kongzi even opposed Ji Kangzi's execution of those without the Way to help those with the Way. I don't understand how John Fairbank assimilates rule by virtue to rule by punishment.

The Basis of the Idea of Rule by Virtue

That being said, on what basis did Kongzi believe in the efficacy of rule by virtue? One point must be explained first. From the fact that Kongzi said, "If good men were in charge of a state for one hundred years, they could overcome viciousness and eliminate executions," and, "If a true king arose, there would be benevolence in a generation" (*Analects* 13.11, 13.12), we can see that he didn't believe the effect of rule by virtue would "respond like an echo." From many of the passages quoted above, it can appear that Kongzi said that the effect of rule by virtue was very straightforward. I think this was in order to change the direction of the governments at the time and give some encouragement. However, it is very clear that Kongzi believed that rule by virtue would necessarily have the effect of bringing about order by nonaction. One simple sentence on Kongzi's basis for this belief: it comes from faith in humanity and human nature.

Although Kongzi didn't explicitly say that human nature is good, in fact this is what he believed.[26] The ode "The Multitudes" in the "Greater Elegies" section of the *Odes* goes, "Heaven gave birth to the multitudes. When there is a thing, there is a norm for it. The people possess this constant way, and love this perfect virtue."[27] In his analysis of this ode, Kongzi said, "Did not whoever composed this ode understand the Way? When there is a thing, there has to be a norm for it. The people possess this constant way, and so love this perfect virtue" (*Mengzi* 6A6). Zheng [Xuan's] notes explain, "What the people possess is the constant Way. There are none who do not love a person of virtue."[28] Virtue is what everyone has, and is what everyone loves.

Since it is what people all love, the virtue of the ruler will naturally have an inspiring effect on the people. Kongzi said, "It was the people who made it possible for the Three Dynasties[29] to take the straight Way" (*Analects* 15.25). The straight Way is following the Way by which people are human. Its opposites are political means such as punishment and deception. The rulers of the time thought that they had to use punishment and deception to govern the people. Kongzi implied that the Three Dynasties flourished by governing the people by following the people's own Way; what the *Mean* calls "governing the people by treating them as people,"[30] with no use for punishment and deception. The people of the Three Dynasties are not essentially different from the people of today, so why cannot rulers of today take the straight Way?

In other words, why cannot they use rule by virtue? It is not difficult to infer that in the society two thousand five hundred years ago, people were especially reliant on the government and the rulers' influence on the people was especially great. If rulers themselves realized virtue, this would be realizing the latent virtue that everyone had in themselves. Kongzi's faith in government came from his faith in human nature.

This sort of idea can be found throughout Ruist classical texts. It is especially evident in the following passage from the *Great Learning*.

> What is meant by saying that bringing peace to the world depends on ordering the state is this: when those in power treat the aged properly, then filiality arises in the people. When they treat seniors properly, then fraternal respect arises in the people. When they give succor to the orphaned, then the people will not turn their backs on them. This is why the gentleman practices the Way of using himself as a measure.[31]

Those in power treating the aged properly, treating seniors properly, and giving succor to the orphaned are ways of showing that those above realize their virtue, which is the virtue everyone has. When the people are inspired this way, they immediately become filial and respectful, and will not ignore those in need. The way of using himself as a measure means the ruler uses his own virtue as the standard and spreads this to the people of the world.

The virtue possessed by everyone in the world is the same as the virtue possessed by the ruler as an individual. So another aspect of using oneself as a measure is to "love what the people love and hate what the people hate."[32] The nature of the model of rule by virtue is an inspirational nature; its character is for the ruler to limit his own power. The ultimate virtue of a ruler is to make the people's preferences into his own: this is the greatest test of rule by virtue. All totalitarian government comes from distrust of the people. The true basis of democratic government is trust in the people. The reason John Fairbank thinks Kongzi's idea of rule by virtue is a myth is because he lacks basic confidence in people themselves. He doesn't understand the background and basis of this idea, so he closes his eyes and links Kongzi to Mao Zedong. Mr. Fairbank thinks that Chinese people are ignorant but turns around and says that Kongzi is the one who thought the people of his time were ignorant. Not a single thing Mr. Fairbank said about Kongzi is anything but the exact opposite of what Kongzi thought. This is indeed peculiar.

The Positive Content of Rule by Virtue

John King Fairbank thinks Kongzi's rule by virtue is a myth, and to be realized this myth has to rely on punishments. This belief of his might come from the fact that the idea of nonaction in Daoism turned into the basis for Legalist political thought based on punishment. Given that Kongzi's political thought is also based on nonaction, Fairbank thinks it will have the same result as Daoism. What I said above, that the basis of Kongzi's idea of rule by virtue is faith in human nature, Fairbank might say is idealism or just a theory. As far as real-world government goes, it is still a myth. In response this to this, I will offer three points for examination.

The first is that Kongzi and Laozi promoted nonaction in order to do their utmost to prevent rulers from using their own preferences as the standard to govern the people, and not to say that they should not do anything at all. Laozi said, "Act without acting, and nothing will not be governed" (*Laozi* 3). Its true content is, "Assist the myriad things in being so of themselves, not daring to act" (*Laozi* 64). "Transform themselves . . . correct themselves . . . enrich themselves . . . make themselves like uncarved wood" (*Laozi* 57) are all aspects of "being so of themselves"; this means "to be this way in themselves." It is like the "self-government" we talk of now. The purpose of nonaction is precisely to let the people manage their affairs according to their own ideas. This is the basis of "Not acting, yet nothing is left undone."[33] However, although the people are that way of themselves, they still depend on the "assistance" of a sage. Assistance is still a kind of "action"; this kind of action, however, puts the people in the primary position while the ruler abides in the position of assisting them. There is no selfish interest of the ruler mixed in.

Action without selfish interest is nonaction, and therefore Laozi particularly emphasized selflessness. The substance of selflessness is that "it produces them but does not possess them, acts without relying on anything, and helps them grow without controlling them" (*Laozi* 10). The assistance that Laozi mentioned in assisting the myriad things developed into the concept of following (*yin* 因) in Shen Dao. Shen Dao said, "The

Way of heaven is such that if you follow then you will be great; if you transform then you will be insignificant. To 'follow' means to follow the dispositions of people. No person fails to act for himself. If one [tries to] transform them to make them act for oneself,[34] then one will be unable to get anyone to employ. . . . And so if one makes use of people for their own benefit and not for one's own benefit, there will be none one cannot employ. This is what is meant by following."[35] The concepts of selflessness and following are subsumed by Kongzi's thought of rule by virtue and nonaction. This is why in answering Zizhang's question, "How should one conduct oneself to work in government?" he particularly brought up, "Benefit the people with what they find beneficial" (*Analects* 20.2). We can see from this that rule by virtue is definitely not a matter of ignoring the people. In fact, it is to assist and inspire the people to carry out their own affairs.

Second, the unification of Laozi and Legalism did not derive from a necessary development of Laozi's teaching. This unification, scholastically speaking, derived from the purposeful dependence [on Laozi] of Shen Buhai and Han Feizi.[36] Politically speaking, it derived from the tendency toward Huang-Lao thought in the early Western Han dynasty, which was motivated by an emotional reaction against the Qin tyranny. In actuality, it inherited the political institutions of the Qin dynasty, which were established by Legalism. This then resulted in a situation of uniting Huang-Lao with Shen and Han. This unity had not existed in the Qin dynasty. The belief that Daoist nonaction has to lead to Shen and Han is a misunderstanding that comes from Sima Qian and others.[37] Inferring a relationship between Ruist rule by virtue and Mao Zedong thought on this basis is a forced comparison beyond all reason.

Third, I fear that Mr. Fairbank lacks a basic understanding of the positive aspect of Kongzi's rule by virtue. One cannot only blame him: it is due to past Chinese commentators not completely living up to their responsibilities. An example is Zhu Xi, in his *Categorized Conversations*: "Ruling by virtue is not wanting to go and carry out governing by means of virtue. Nor does it mean being solitary and doing nothing at all. Only that when virtue is cultivated in oneself, then the people will naturally respond to and be transformed by it. This response and transformation is not political, but in their virtue. When the rulers correct what is incorrect in the people, how could this mean doing nothing?"[38] He also said, "Ruling by virtue does not mean not using punishment or commands. Only that virtue takes precedence over them."[39] Zhu Xi's greatest mistake was to separate virtue and government action into two different things. The reason he did this was because he only thought of virtue in terms of an individual's life and did not understand that virtue is reasonable behavior that unites inner and outer.

Anything the ruler should do and can do in a reasonable way that unites inner and outer (this is sincerity) all belongs to the ruler's virtue. In other words, the ruler is a person and should first take a stand on the qualifications for being a person: this is "personal virtue." The ruler is also a ruler and at the same time must fulfill the responsibilities that entails: this is "the ruler's virtue." Personal virtue and the ruler's virtue cannot be split; personal virtue encompasses the ruler's virtue. For example, when Zilu asked about the gentleman, Kongzi said, "He cultivates himself to be respectful," and this after all means "he cultivates himself to give ease to the common people."[40] The way cultivating himself can give ease to the common people must be that starting with cultivating himself and expanding that, he can use goodness to fulfill his responsibility to give ease to the common people.

Duke Ai of Lu asked, "How can I make the people obey?" Kongzi's answer was, "Promote the upright and set aside the crooked and then the people will obey. Promote the crooked and set aside the upright, and the people will not obey" (*Analects* 2.19). A ruler's most important responsibility is appointing people. If his appointments are appropriate, then the ruler is virtuous. If his appointments are inappropriate, then the ruler is not virtuous. Whether a ruler's appointments are appropriate or not relates directly to his cultivation of himself, and so to the ruler, personal cultivation and making appointments cannot be separated. Promoting the upright and setting aside the crooked was already implied in Shun's "making himself reverent and facing south."[41] So in response to Fan Chi's question, "What did [Kongzi] mean by saying, 'Promote the upright and set aside the crooked, then you will be able to make the crooked upright,'" Zixia answered, "When Shun possessed all under heaven, he selected from among the masses and promoted Gao Yao. Then those not benevolent went far away" (*Analects* 12.22). The *Collected Explanations of the Analects* interpretation of the passage about Shun facing south is, "It means that each office had the right person and so [Shun] could govern through nonaction."[42] This is right on the mark.

In addition:

> Duke Ding asked, "Is there one saying that can make the state flourish?" Kongzi answered, "A saying cannot be expected to

do this. However, there is a saying among the people: 'It is difficult to be the ruler, and being a minister is not easy.' If the ruler understands the difficulty of being a ruler, is this not close to a saying that could make the state flourish?" The duke asked, "Is there one saying that can make the state lost?" Kongzi answered, "A saying cannot be expected to do this. However, there is a saying among the people: 'I have no joy in being a ruler, except for the fact that none go against what I say.' If what he says is good and none go against it, isn't that good? But if what he says is not good and none go against it, is this not close to a saying that could make the state lost?" (*Analects* 13.15)

Kongzi's answer to Duke Ding's question above about one saying that could make the state flourish or lost is in fact a concise and to the point answer concerning the success or failure of the ruler's way. If one understands the difficulty of being the ruler, "then one will certainly feel fear and trepidation, proceed with great caution, and not dare to neglect a single matter" (Zhu Xi's commentary). This is rule by virtue. If no one goes against his words, "then faithful words will not reach his ears, the ruler will become more arrogant day by day while the ministers become more obsequious, and in such circumstances never has the state not been lost" (Zhu's commentary quoting Fan).[43] A "saying" is a common point of discussion concerning some matter. To do things well it is necessary first to make people live up to what they say, and thus listening to what people say and taking advice and correction is one essential virtue of the ruler.

The *Mean* has: "The master said, 'How great was Shun's understanding! He was fond of asking questions and examining close words [close to matters related to the people's interests]. He concealed what was bad [concealed what was inappropriate in their language] and upheld what was good [promulgated what was appropriate in their language]."[44] In ancient times only a ruler who made himself reverent and corrected his person could do this, and further, these are entailed by making himself reverent and correcting his person. Also, "To govern a state of a thousand chariots, the ruler must respectfully attend to business and be trustworthy, moderate expenditures and care for the people, and employ them at the proper times" (*Analects* 1.5). What Kongzi said here is of course also rule by virtue, and further includes caring for and nurturing the people as part of it. To generalize in one sentence: behavior that fulfills well the responsibilities that the ruler should fulfill is all rule by virtue. Rule by virtue has certain political content; how can it be called a myth?

More importantly, rule by virtue was proposed to oppose rule by punishment. The "punishments" of "reform them with punishments"[45] are put into effect through the coercive power of the government. Reforming them with ritual does not resort to the government's coercive power. Granting that ritual brings some kind of coercion, as it developed up to Kongzi, this coercion comes from the demands of the individual's own conscience. "Master You said, 'In the application of ritual, it is harmony that is valued. This is what is pleasing in the Way of the former kings'" (Analects 1.12). "Kongzi said, 'If one can govern the state with ritual and deference, what difficulty would there be? If one cannot govern the state with ritual and deference, what use is ritual?'" (Analects 4.13). In Kongzi's view, the point of ritual in government is primarily for deference. To him, if one uses governmental pressure to realize ritual, this is no longer ritual. Hence, in order to realize government through ritual, Kongzi developed his concept of teaching, meaning education. His method was inspiration and positive influence, perfecting the virtue of each individual character according to each person's character. This can be confirmed by actual circumstances of Kongzi's own teaching.

"The master went to Wei, Ran You attending him. The master said, 'How numerous the people are!' Ran You asked, 'Since they are numerous, what should be added?' The master said, 'Enrich them.' Ran You asked, 'When there is sufficient wealth, what should be added?' The master said, 'Teach them'" (Analects 13.9). Enriching and educating the people is the general goal and content of Kongzi's rule by virtue. Enrich them first, then teach them: this imperceptibly became a great divide between Ruism and every kind of totalitarianism. Totalitarians usually control the people's bellies, often putting them in a condition of being half-starved to carry out their totalitarian education. I will not do a deeper examination of this point here. What I particularly want to bring up is how Kongzi's special proposal for providing education began to channel the function and significance of education into a government that was based on commands and punishment. This is a concept Daoism lacks and their weakness is exactly here, which was taken advantage of by Legalism.

Over more than two thousand years of despotic government, even though the educational function did not get developed completely, it still fulfilled the great function of cultivating and securing the keys for life in society. Kongzi's concept of education and rule by virtue are one and the same, and so later we have the term "virtue education." "Kongzi said, 'With education, there are no categories'" (*Analects* 15.39). The meaning of this saying is that he believed that when there is education, there are no distinctions (categories) of wise and foolish, honored and lowly, ethnicity, and so on: all people can return to goodness. This was his own experience of "instructing without tiring"[46] and also his great confidence in education. One can see from this sentence that he believed that education could solve all of humanity's problems. From Kongzi's perspective, America's current racial problems [in 1966] are the result of not doing the work of instituting equal education. Educational advancement can render government's coercive power useless. One could go as far as to say that Kongzi's idea of nonaction in government, taken to its extreme, means for education to replace government and for education to remove political thought. This is the primary content of rule by virtue.

The Development of the Idea of Rule by Virtue and Its Historical Influence

The *Analects* was recorded by Kongzi's disciples and their disciples. Passages relating to rule by virtue are scattered throughout each part of the book. It is only through meticulous discovery of the internal connections of the relevant language that we can begin to understand the idea of rule by virtue, which in fact constitutes the integrated system of Kongzi's political thought. However, it doesn't form a system in terms of the form of linguistic expression. What did form a system in terms of the form of linguistic expression is the "Duke Ai asked about government" section of the *Mean*[47]: this should be considered the initial development. This section bases goodness on personal cultivation; the five universal ways of ruler-minister, father-son, husband-wife, older brother–younger brother, and friends are the object of personal cultivation. Each person has to live in these five fundamental relationships (universal ways), and thus personal cultivation has to take these as its object. Wisdom, benevolence, and courage—the three universal virtues—are the content of personal cultivation. Making the five universal ways live up to their prescribed roles requires the spirit and ability of the three universal virtues. This is as far as the individual's personal cultivation is concerned.

If we extend it to government and rule by virtue, then it forms the system of the nine constant principles [*jiujing* 九經]:

There are nine constant principles for governing the world
and individual states: cultivate one's person, honor the worthy, have affection for relatives, respect the great ministers,
be considerate toward the whole body of officials, care for
the masses as if they were one's children, attract the various
artisans, treat the distant gently, and cherish the feudal lords.
When the ruler cultivates his person, the Way is established.
When he respects the worthy, he will avoid confusion. When
he is affectionate with relatives, his relations will have no
resentments. When he respects the great ministers, he will
not be bewildered. When he cares for the masses, they will
exhort each other to improve. When he attracts the various
artisans, then wealth and tools will be sufficient. When he
treats the distant gently, the people of the four directions will
return to him. When he cherishes the feudal lords, the world
will be in awe of him. . . .

Sending off those who depart and welcoming those who
come, praising the good and taking pity on the incapable: this
is how to treat the distant gently. Restoring broken lines of
succession, reviving states that have come to ruin, holding court
and receiving embassies at appropriate times, being generous
with those departing and accepting only minor tribute from
those who come: this is the way to cherish the feudal lords.[48]

Here, I will only explain one point: the principles of treating the
distant gently and cherishing the feudal lords in the above section are
today still perhaps the most important principles for pursuing peace
in international relations. This is a further development of the spirit
found here: "If distant people are not obedient, then develop culture
and virtue to attract them. Having attracted them, make them secure"
(*Analects* 16.1). Just where is the aggressiveness of rule by virtue that
John Fairbank pointed to?

In Mengzi, rule by virtue developed into the kingly way. Its specific
content is:

Plant every household of five *mu* with mulberry trees, and
those in their fifties can wear silk. Ensure that chickens, dogs,
and pigs do not miss their time to breed, and those in their
seventies can eat meat. Do not take time away from farming

a field of a hundred *mu*, and a family with several mouths to feed can avoid starvation. Take care with what is taught in the schools, explaining the duties of being filial and fraternal, and those whose hair is whitening will not have to bear heavy loads on the roads. For those in their seventies to be able to eat meat and wear silk while the common people are neither starving nor freezing, yet for their ruler not to become a king: this has never happened. (*Mengzi* 1A3)

Mengzi repeated the quoted material above three times, and so we can see that it is the most concrete version of the kingly way, and the most concrete content of Kongzi's rule by virtue that includes teaching and nurturing the people. What especially needs to be pointed out here is that, as far as my research shows, the Chinese concept of [formal] schooling started with Mengzi. This was a major development of Kongzi's idea of education.[49] In international politics, Mengzi brought up these principles: "Only a benevolent ruler can serve a smaller state as a larger one . . . only a wise ruler can serve a larger state as a smaller one" (*Mengzi* 2A3). These are entirely compatible with the related principles in the *Analects* and *Mean*. Is there even a hint of aggression here?

The Qin dynasty ruled by punishment. Han succeeded Qin and changed nothing. The cruelty of their punishments can be generally seen through the "Biographies of the Harsh Officials" in the *Records of the Historian* and the "Record of Punishments" in the *Han History*. The intellectuals of the Han dynasty, the Western Han especially, all wanted to change the direction of the government, which was based on punishment, and so the idea of rule by virtue was especially clear. Dong Zhongshu is a representative. His triple stratagem of heaven, earth, and humanity dresses up this great aspiration [of rule by virtue] in the clothes of yin-yang and five phases mysticism.[50] He said,

> However, when the king has something which he wants to achieve, it is fitting to seek for the beginning in heaven. The great in the Way of heaven is found in yin and yang. Yang represents virtue while yin represents punishment. Punishments are master over death while virtue is master over life. Thus, yang abides in the height of summer and looks after birth, raising, nurturing, and growing. Yin abides in the depths of winter and gathers in the places that are empty and fallow.

From this we see that heaven cherishes virtue, not punish-ment. . . . The king follows the intent of heaven when acting and so cherishes virtue, not punishment. . . . At present, eliminating the former kings' official in charge of teaching virtue and only governing the people by appointing minor officials who uphold the law is exactly the intent of cherishing punishment. (*Han History*, ch. 56)[51]

The former kings' official in charge of teaching virtue refers to the official in charge of the schools and education, responsible for replacing punishment with transformative education (*jiaohua* 教化). This in fact comes from Kongzi's idea of education, developed further by Mengzi. Dong also said,

The people's pursuit of their own benefit is like water's flowing downward. If one does not prepare carefully[52] with transfor-mative education, it cannot be stopped. . . . The ancient kings understood this clearly, so when they faced south and governed all under heaven, all made transformative education their major task. They established upper schools to teach in the capital and set up schools to transform the towns, influencing the people with benevolence, shaping them with rightness, and limiting them with ritual. Hence their punishments were extremely light and still prevented people from committing crimes. They carried out transformative education and the people's habits and customs were perfected. (Ibid.)[53]

He in no way ignored the importance of nurturing the people, so in the third stratagem he repeatedly demanded that those in power not contend with the people for benefits. He seems to have foreseen the policies that Emperor Wu would later enact for his personal benefit. He said, "When the august one seeks wealth and benefit, always concerned about lacking something, this is the idea of a commoner. When the august one seeks benevolence and rightness, always concerned about being unable to transform the people, this is the idea of a counselor."[54] However, his above proposals had to have a basic starting point: in a period of despotism, that was the reigning emperor. If the emperor does not cultivate his virtue, then there is nowhere to begin. So he also said, "The ruler of the people corrects his heart-mind to correct his court, corrects his court to correct the various officials of the government, and corrects the various officials to correct the people" (Ibid.).[55] The political demand of "returning to begin from what is honored itself" (Ibid.)[56] is exactly the beginning of rule by virtue. Putting together what Dong said, it is entirely a development of Kongzi's idea of rule by virtue. The reason he emphasized rule by virtue is precisely because of the strengthened rule by punishment from the Qin on.

In the Eastern Han, Guangwu founded the state and "governed with strictness and ferocity."[57] Among thinkers of the period, we should first put forward Huan Tan [43 BCE–28 CE]. In his *New Discourses*, chapter 2, "Kings and Hegemons," he wrote,

> In the government of the Way of the kings, they first elim-inated harms to the people and made sure their food and clothing were sufficient. Only after that did they instruct them in ritual and rightness and made them understand what was good and bad, what to discard and what to pursue. For this reason they transformed the four collectives. . . . The great accomplishment of the hegemons is to [make people] respect rulers and look down on ministers, make power unified into one person, and not to let there be two gates in government.[58] They made sure rewards and punishments were reliable, laws and decrees were widely known, the various officials were cultivated and ordered, and their awe-inspiring commands were carried out. This is the art of the hegemon. Kingship is pure; its virtue is like that [mentioned before]. Hegemony is mixed up; its accomplishments are like this. (*Collected Later Han Writings*, ch. 13)[59]

The Way of the kings Huan Tan mentions is rule by virtue. The accom-plishments of hegemony is the Legalist sort of governing, opposed to rule by virtue. It was also the spirit on which the state was founded at the time.

Du Lin's "Memorial Admonishing against Following Liang Tong's [Recommendation to] Increase Laws and Prohibitions" says,

> When human feelings are humiliated, their propensity to moderation and rightness is damaged. When laws and protec-tions increase, so does their behavior to evade them. Kongzi

said, "If you guide the people with decrees and reform them with punishments, they will evade them and have no sense of shame. If you guide them with virtue and reform them with ritual, they will have a sense of shame and correct themselves." The enlightened kings of old[60] moved and abided in generosity, rather than working to make punishments numerous. . . . When the great Han arose . . . they eliminated harsh government . . . and the people cherished broad virtue.[61] But then afterwards, regulations gradually increased, [officials] looked carefully for small faults, and slander and deception had no limits. Small gifts were collected for bribes. Minor matters that did no harm to rightness were punished with execution. Then there were no honest officials in the state and no actions completed in the homes. It got to the point where laws could not prohibit anything nor commands stop anything.[62]

Du Lin's memorial uses the facts of his time to provide proof for Kongzi's proposal of rule by virtue. Discussions like this in Chinese history cannot be counted.

I want to draw two conclusions here. First, over more than two thousand years of Chinese history, Kongzi's idea of rule by virtue had as much influence as thought could have. In a history with despotic government, it lived up to its responsibility for correcting errors. Rule by virtue connects[63] up to democracy, and can only be fully realized in democracy. If one looks at it as myth and mere decoration on the basis of the fact that it was never fully realized in history, this is because they do not understand at all the meaning of ideal thought in human life, nor do they understand the meaning ideals have for real life. Not having any realization of ideals is to have a pitch-black reality without any light.

Second, rule by virtue was proposed in response to rule by punishment. Granted that rule by virtue cannot do away with punishments in a moment, it attempts to realize the benevolent society that "must turn to benevolence in a generation" (*Analects* 13.12) through reducing the severity of rule by punishment. This is a society in which punishments have been put aside, and it definitely cannot be doubted [that this can be achieved]. I really cannot understand how John Fairbank could link rule by virtue with punishment, and still less how he could link it with Mao Zedong.

If Fairbank's mistake comes from inadequate scholarship, I could forgive it. Because so many Chinese intellectuals of reputation are wholly ignorant of their own traditional culture, how could one blame an American sinologist for this? If his mistake comes from his settled political position and so he did not hesitate to come up with an argument that goes against his own [intellectual] views, then he lacks a scholarly conscience. As a result, he not only thinks to harm China, he will actually harm his own country first. No matter how China changes, it could never change toward colonialism.[64] This is something Fairbank and those who rely on him for their living should understand. However, Fairbank's belief that the mainland, including the Communist Party, will be influenced by traditional culture no matter what is correct. But the influence of traditional culture has to oppose Mao Zedong's thought, not defend it. This is demonstrated by the current great purge.[65] I don't know what Fairbank would say in response to this iron-clad fact. (Note: This essay was originally published in *Cong-Meng Monthly*. The current version is based on the reprint in *Democratic Review* 17, no. 9.)

Chapter 15

The Question of Ruist and
Daoist Personal Cultivation in Literature

Translator's introduction: This essay is rather different than the others collected here, as it centers on literature and Xu's view on the connection between personal character and writing. It thus relates to his aesthetic theory more than his political theory. He was more conservative here. In the essay, Xu is concerned to emphasize two points. First, he agrees with the Tang scholar Han Yu's famous dictum, "Writing is to convey the Way." That is, literature should have a moral purpose. Second, despite the criticism directed at Ruism and tradition in general, it was no obstacle to the development of great literature in China. When literary creativity declined, the problem was the strictures of despotic government, not Ruism.

Going deeper, Xu claims that the resources for literary creation in China come out of Ruist and Daoist thought, especially the shared emphasis on the "empty, quiet, and still" heart-mind. He dismisses Buddhism quickly, stating that although it had some influence on the subject matter of literature, its influence on literary creativity as such was really due to where it was inspired by Daoism. Although he recognizes the major contribution of Daoist thought to Chinese literature, especially in appreciation of nature (a theme he also devel-

Sequel to Collected Essays on Chinese Literature, 1–21, not previously published.

oped in relation to visual art in his *The Spirit of Chinese Art*), he still reserves the greatest role for Ruism and its concern for society and the welfare of the people. A major source of the discussion is *The Literary Heart-Mind Carves Dragons*, a classic work on literary theory by Liu Xie from the fifth century.

What Xu here calls personal cultivation, the deep impact of Ruism and Daoism on a person's character and life—is a necessary but not sufficient condition for producing a great work of literature. Xu recognizes that wide reading is important to develop literary skill, but literary skill without personal cultivation is useless. Literature ultimately should have some moral significance, not be mere entertainment. In the best literature, subject matter and literary style harmonize and elevate each other, so even a well-written work on an insignificant (or immoral) subject can never achieve greatness.

In September 1969, I came to Hong Kong for the second time as a visiting professor in the philosophy department at New Asia College of the Chinese University of Hong Kong (the first time was the spring of 1967). I first did a routine lecture entitled "The Mission of a Philosopher." After a short time, Mr. Tang Junyi wanted me to give another talk, and then I selected the title shown above. It could be called a topic in between literature and philosophy. The response after the talk was very enthusiastic. The next day, Mr. Tang said to me, "We could all think up the content of brother Fuguan's talk yesterday, but unless it came from your mouth, it could not move the audience that way." True, looking at the content, it is quite ordinary. Add to that the fact that I was in a new environment preparing materials for class and extremely busy, I therefore didn't polish it into a paper. Now there is overgrown grass on Mr. Tang's grave[1] and I myself have developed this chronic disease (stomach cancer) in my declining years. Whenever I think of the past, my sorrow is without end. Now I cleaned up the remaining draft of that talk and fixed it up a little, and after ten days made it into a chapter of this book. Although the argument is a little more detailed than it was when I gave the talk, that spirit and energy that moved the audience then has gone with time, not to return. Each time I think of this, my melancholy feeling redoubles.

Afterthought under the lamp on November 29, 1980

I

What I should first explain is that the literary creativity of a people will necessarily be influenced by the traditions and popular currents of thought of that people, whether that influence is positive, negative, deep, or shallow. From Western Han on, nearly all Chinese literature was influenced directly and indirectly by Ruist and Daoist thought. Beginning with the Six Dynasties, Buddhism was added. Proceeding a step farther from thought is personal cultivation. What I mean by "personal cultivation" is transforming and elevating a person's life through thought, making abstract thought take shape as a concrete personality. At this point, the influence of personal cultivation on creative work is total, proceeding up from the root. What is commonly meant by thought influence is fragmentary, proceeding out of external conditions and chances. The two move along a single thread, but differ in depth and thus also differ in purity.

The next thing to explain is that personal cultivation is usually realized in life and does not necessarily develop into writings; in fact, it cannot develop into writings. This is because personal cultivation can form the motivation for creative work, but cannot directly form the effort for it. The effort of creative work requires focused effort (*gongfu* 工夫) outside of personal cultivation. At the same time, literary creativity does not necessarily depend on personal cultivation. The original literature came out of the spontaneous affective inspiration[2] of the emotions, with the addition of innate talent in expression. At this point, there is no influence of thought to speak of: How could it depend on personal cultivation? Therefore, the original literature of each people, folk songs, usually appeared before the creation of writing, and even if it were after the creation of writing, even illiterate people could create folk songs.

As for the appearance of literary authors, they naturally must have some fundamental learning, and even more must have creative experience obtained from past literary works in order to acquire creative affective inspiration and technique. The greater the author, the more profound this focused effort must be. Du Fu wrote, "If one has read over ten thousand scrolls, putting one's pen to paper will be spirit-like." He further urged his son, "Study thoroughly the patterns of *Selections of Refined Literature*."[3] Both remarks speak to this point. This can also be called a kind of cultivation, but it is literary cultivation. When literary cultivation is profound and inclining toward maturity, then it advances into personal cultivation, but this is not to say that personal cultivation is the premise or fundamental condition of creation. The individual character (nature and emotions) of an author that literature reflects is usually the individual character of his original life, not necessarily the character arrived at through cultivation.

However, literature and art are founded on the mutual involvement of the creator's subjectivity (soul or spirit) and the subject matter's objectivity (events or things). It is not only the case that without the object that the subject thinks of or is affected by, the material would not enter into the scope of artistic creation. It is also the case that the creator's subjectivity can mold and elevate or diminish it, shaping it into multiple different layers. Although she gives expression to the objective events or things that enter into the scope of artistic creation in an imagistic way, the image of a successful work is necessarily the value or meaning of some objective events or things. The value or meaning of objective events and things, considered in themselves, is usually concealed rather than manifest, depending on the creator's discovery. This is the first meaning of creation.

The greatest difference between the value or meaning of objective events and things discovered by artists and writers and the "laws" of objective events and things discovered by scientists is that laws have only one stratum and thus a fixed definition. Once discovered, it is fixed in one place and does not change. Values and meaning have limitless strata—high, low, deep, shallow, and so on—and could be said to fluctuate with no fixed place. This is the reason the same objective events and things as subject matter can admit infinite creativity. The discovery of the strata of the values and meaning of objective events and things is not related to the objective events and things themselves; objective events and things are colorless and neutral.[4] It is determined by the stratum of the creator's subjective spirit. If the stratum of the creator's subjective spirit is high, the stratum he discovers in objective events and things will likewise be high; if it is low, the stratum he discovers in objective events and things will likewise be low.

The fundamental measure that determines the value of a work is the creator's power of discovery. For a creator to possess unique power of discovery, she must have outstanding spirit. To have outstanding spirit, she must have outstanding personal cultivation. China grasped the inseparable relation of "work and person" about 1,600 years earlier than the West. (See my "On the Literary Style of *The Literary Heart-mind Carves*

Dragons.") Hence, it is a natural development to go from demanding raising the level of works to demanding raising the level of persons, and then to bringing up the great significance of personal cultivation in literary and artistic creation.

II

In China, only the two philosophies Ruism and Daoism arose out of reflection on real life and approached mastery over the heart-mind or nature of concrete life. They transform the miscellany of life through revealing the latent virtue of the heart-mind and nature, elevating and purifying life. In this way they manifest in real life, correcting its direction and establishing the foundations of value in human life. Therefore, only Ruism and Daoism bear the meaning of personal cultivation. This is because this kind of personal cultivation flowers and bears fruit in real human life. Its effect is not limited to being the basis of literature and art, but it can also become the basis of these.

After Indian Buddhism began to flourish in China, its influence on literature was usually in the areas of good and bad, karma and retribution. This is just influence in the layer of thought, not influence that comes out of personal cultivation. What had influence on literature from personal cultivation is generally considered to be Chan Buddhism. However, speaking factually, the influence that Chan had on literature was established on the stage in the process of personal cultivation where Chan fit with Daoism—Zhuangzi especially. If Chan had gone up one level higher, it would have removed the conditions for literary achievement. Therefore, the great influence that Chan had in culture, literature, and the arts that Japanese scholars extol was actually reviving the influence of Zhuangzi's thought in a new body. An attempt to compare the *Zhuangzi* of Daoism and *The Platform Sutra* of Chan follows:

1. Motivation
   Daoism: release the shackles of the spirit
   Chan: put the mind to the question of life and death

2. Cultivation
   Daoism: no knowledge, no desires
   Chan: eliminate the three poisons of greed, hatred, and ignorance

3. Advanced stage

    Daoism: "The heart-mind of the ultimate person is like a mirror"[5]

    Chan: "The heart-mind is like a clear mirror"[6]

4. Final result

    Daoism: "Brings things to completion with no harm"[7]

    Chan: "There is originally not one single thing"[8]

From the above comparison, Daoism and Chan are only compatible in points 2 and 3. But if this were all that there is to Chan, it would not be Chan. What makes it Chan is that it necessarily goes back to "There is originally not one single thing."

Daoism, with the mirror-like heart-mind, can go back to employing things, letting them come without welcome and letting them go without being attached ("not sending off or welcoming"),[9] joining in the spontaneity of things and completing their great beauty. This is what "bringing things to completion with no harm" means. This can be turned into literature and art. Chan goes back to "there is originally not one single thing." Outside of achieving emptiness, there is nothing else it aims to achieve. The literati Chan monks who thought they derived benefit from Chan in their poetry in reality derived benefit from being berated by the Fifth Patriarch, and took their stand on the "heart-mind is like a clear mirror" that is identical to Daoism. With this as their basis, they were in essence following Daoism, not Chan. Therefore, here I only bring up Daoism and not Buddhism, and one could also say that Daoism includes Buddhism.

III

Beginning in Western Han, Ruist scholars began to pursue the two philosophies of Ruism and Daoism in response to various demands. As far as life, society, and government manifested in their writings, beginning with Jia Yi[10] the active aspect of a work usually derived from Ruism. When things could not be helped and they shifted from active to passive, then they shifted from Ruism to Daoism. Among Ruist scholars of the time, probably Ban Gu[11] is the lone exception. This illustrates that the greater writers of the Han period were simultaneously influenced by both

Ruism and Daoism to a greater or lesser extent. However, Han scholars usually explored Ruism and Daoism from outer to inner, unearthing the heart-mind or nature in life. They skipped over the process of cultivation of letting the heart-mind or nature flourish outwardly and were instead inclined to the outward construction of a great fictitious system, not necessarily grasping the issue of heart-mind or nature. This is especially evident in Daoism. This is why they accepted the passive attitude and approach to life of Daoism, but did not necessarily grasp the "empty, still, and clear" heart-mind.[12] This made it difficult to have philosophical influence that shaped the external to then become internalized personal cultivation. With regard to Ruism, they also emphasized active efficacy, which is still some distance from the effort of personal cultivation.

Following the three violent attacks on intellectuals of the Proscription of the Eastern Han, the conflict between Cao [Shuang] and Sima [Yi], and the Disturbances of the Eight Princes,[13] the active spirit of Ruists naturally went into hiding. What took its place was the new metaphysics of "nothingness as structure," what was then called mysterious learning.[14] This speculation covered over its passive and escapist attitude toward life. This was the first period of mysterious learning, which took Laozi as its basis. This kind of mysterious learning influenced literary creativity, and then appeared, "In the Zhengshi period, poetry was for elucidating the Way (extolling and elucidating Daoist thought)[15] and poems were intermixed with the spirit of transcendence (going beyond the heart-mind of the real world). The followers of He Yan[16] led the multitudes into shallowness," and, "East of the Yangzi River, poetics drowned in the fad for mystery. . . . Although [the writers there] all had literary style, none could compete [with earlier writers]."[17] Putting it in contemporary language, this is poetry of abstract philosophy. This kind of poetry comes out of the external shaping influence of Daoism, not out of internal personal cultivation.

However, the mysterious atmosphere of Eastern Jin was mainly based on Zhuangzi. Under the long influence of *Zhuangzi* studies, they unknowingly collided with Zhuangzi's "empty, still, and clear" heart-mind. In chapters 2 through 4 of my *The Spirit of Chinese Art*, I already repeatedly pointed out that the "empty, still, and clear" heart-mind is the heart-mind of direct interaction of humanity and nature and realizes the beauty of nature. I then said that this is the principal aspect of the artistic spirit. Therefore, the conscious discovery of the beauty of nature and the positing and development of literary and artistic theory all appeared in this period. Advancing a step from this is the personal cultivation posited by Daoist thought of the "Spiritual Thought" chapter of Liu Xie's *The Literary Heart-mind Carves Dragons*. He said, "Therefore in writing think as a potter's wheel (like a potter uses the wheel to make vessels, meaning molding and raising). Value is in being empty (empty because without prejudices) and still (still because of not being roiled by desires). Dredge and cleanse the five organs. Wash and purify the spirit."[18]

According to Zhuangzi, the original aspect of the heart-mind is "empty, still, and clear." Liu didn't mention "clear" in that sentence; with "empty" and "still," "clear" is self-evident. To value being able to be empty and still to preserve the original aspect of the heart-mind, with the heart-mind as master of the body in order to think as a potter's wheel in writing, which is to mold and raise the level and efficacy of the activity of one's own literary soul—this is to consciously cultivate the person according to Daoist thought and make it the foundation of raising one's creative ability. The two sentences below appear in the "Knowledge Roamed North" chapter of the *Zhuangzi* and express realizing the effort of cultivating emptiness and stillness.[19] This is the highest peak that the influence of mysterious learning on art and literature reached after two hundred-some years of influence, put in writing through the pen of Liu Xie. Hence, the attitude toward writing that he promoted was, "Control the heart-mind to nurture one's technique, let no tasks burden your thoughts, and one's writing will be beautiful and its meaning evident. There is no need to labor one's emotions."[20] This forms a very clear contrast with Lu Ji's *On Literature*,[21] in which he promoted an assiduous and active spirit.

Furthermore, the nurturing of *qi* that he discussed in the "Nurturing Qi" chapter is different than that of Mengzi, which came before, and that of Han Yu, which came after. It is, in fact, the advice of Daoism's view on nurturing life for literary authors. He believed, "Follow one's intent and gather harmony, then patterns will meld together and the emotions will be free. If one bores in and sharpens excessively, then the spirit will be exhausted and the *qi* will decline."[22] Even more from the Three Dynasties to the Spring and Autumn period, "even though the tendency to greater embellishment grew with the passing of time, it still accorded with what was in their breast, not dragging their work beyond the bounds of their talent." Then, "From the Han to the present day . . . they strained themselves with thought."[23] He advocated following one's feelings in an easy manner, bringing them together gently. . . . In literary writing, the essential thing is to be temperate and appropriate. Cleanse and harmonize the heart-mind and modulate the *qi*. If irritated, immediately put it aside so as not to become obstructed. When ideas come, open one's mind and make the pen follow, but when ideas hide away, cast the pen aside and roll up the mind. Easy wandering dispels weariness and chat and laughter cures exhaustion. . . . Although this is not a wondrous technique like embryonic breathing,[24] it is one method of protecting the *qi*.[25]

Summing up, his meaning is, "Pacify and treasure the primary[26] spirit. Store and nurture the pure *qi*. When water is still, it mirrors. When fire is calm, it is bright."[27] One could say these are a development of the previous four lines from "Spiritual Thought" quoted above. We can see from this that he had a unified understanding of the question of cultivation, and the basis of his thought came from Daoism. Going beyond this, the only option is to leave home and become a monk, and so Liu Xie, author of *The Literary Heart-mind Carves Dragons*, became the Buddhist monk Huidi.

I already stated previously that Daoism, as material for literary cultivation, took a passive attitude toward life, society, and government. What formed the motivation for creativity and served as the object for creativity was usually interest in nature. Because of this, Liu Xie wrote the especially notable chapter "The Natural World," He said, "This is why the four seasons cycle around, but to bring them into metaphors requires emphasizing repose. The movements of the natural world are manifold, but the words to analyze them must honor simplicity."[28] "Honoring simplicity" is a question of skill. "Emphasizing repose" is the state of an empty and still soul. How does one bring them into metaphors while emphasizing repose? As he already stated, "When water is still, it mirrors. When fire is calm, it is bright." Natural scenery, which has no connection to the benefits and harms of the human world, can only manifest its beauty by entering into an empty and still heart-mind. Su Shi's "Sending Off Master Can Liao" in which he wrote: "If you want the language of your poems to be wondrous, have no distaste of emptiness and stillness. Still, you then understand the various motions. Empty, you then accept the myriad horizons,"[29] also expresses this kind of meaning. A further step following the circulation of mysterious learning was Emperor Wen (Xiao Gang) of Liang's "writing must be unrestrained,"[30] and from here, Li E's "They accumulated volumes which didn't go beyond images of the moon or dew. Their gathered records filled trunks, but they were just descriptions of wind and clouds."[31] This is exactly a continuation and development of that line of thought.

IV

Given what I have said above, how is it that many people believe that the Way of "The Source of the Way" chapter [of *The Literary Heart-mind Carves Dragons*] is the Way of spontaneity, and I insist it refers to the Way of heaven, and that this Way of heaven is directly realized in the Way of the Duke of Zhou and Kongzi? This is quite simple. The "patterning" of the first paragraph refers to art. When this paragraph begins with "the sun and moon are repeated jade disks," this is the artistic form of the Way of heaven.[32] Going on, he talked about human beings, the soul of the myriad things born from the artistic Way of heaven, who are born with artistry. He believed that this is a natural principle. This does not touch on the "spontaneity" of Daoism.

Why, then, did Liu Xie write chapters such as "Confirming the Sages" and "Honoring the Classics"? Moreover, from reading the entire book, he strongly reveres the Ruist sages and classics, far more than Daoism. Here, I have four points to mention and explain.

First, Ruism and Daoism have something in common: both start from the real world, breathing together with the people of the real world, and put their effort on solving problems in the real world. We may say that that Daoism's "empty and still heart-mind" and Ruism's "heart-mind of benevolence and rightness" are two aspects of the same heart-mind, both things that people have from birth. In the course of real life, each person freely switches between them without being aware of it. Ruism developed the "benevolent and right" aspect, and need not, as the Song Ruists did, reject the "empty and still" aspect. Kongzi himself brought up the idea that "the benevolent are still."[33] Daoism developed the "empty and still" aspect, and need not, as the "Robber Zhi" chapter of the *Zhuangzi* did, reject the "benevolent and right" aspect. Therefore,

Laozi and Zhuangzi mentioned "great benevolence" and "great rightness," and looking into them fully, they never ceased being concerned about the people of all under heaven. It was Daoism after Lao-Zhuang, especially Wei-Jin mysterious learning, that separated from society. The free switching between Ruist and Daoist spirit in life and in literary creation is, we might say, the common thread from the Han on. Therefore, Liu Xie did not feel any contradiction in adding Ruism's practical managing of worldly affairs to Daoism's personal cultivation.

Second, one can achieve a thorough appreciation of the beauty of nature merely relying on the empty and still heart-mind, but it is impossible to ensure that this appreciation can be put down in writing. To be able to put it in writing further requires accumulation of learning and development of expressive skill. Therefore, after the four lines quoted above he added, "Accumulate learning in order to store up treasures, deliberate on pattern to enrich one's talents (this refers to expressive ability), read deeply to fathom the source of enlightenment (study and read the works of various authors in order to thoroughly understand the changes of each literary style), and learn to the utmost to make one's expression pleasing (through unceasing practice, achieve facile use of words and language in expression)."[34] The first two phrases deal with accumulating learning, the last two with developing expressive skill. Only by filling out the empty and still heart-mind with these two conditions can one create something lasting.

However, here he has already broken free of the bonds of Daoism and entered into the territory of Ruism. This is because the transmission of Ruism developed history and culture, becoming the unifying thread of learning. In the "Honoring the Classics" chapter, he said, "The roots coil deep; the branches and leaves are tall and thick. This is how even though the events are long past, the remaining meaning is renewed daily. . . . Scholars of later ages took them up and did not feel they were outdated. The cultivated of the past used them long and did not feel they were ahead of their time. They can be compared to Mt. Tai, which gives rain all around it, or the Yellow River, which waters a thousand *li*."[35] He further said, "If one accepts the classics in order to set out one's principles and ponders the elegies to enrich one's language, it is like taking to the mountains to get copper for casting or boiling sea water to get salt."[36] This is no empty talk. Furthermore, pursuing learning with an empty and still heart-mind will only make it more effective, with absolutely no interference. Xunzi believed the heart-mind being "empty, still, and unified" was the fundamental condition to understanding the Way, demonstrating this.[37]

Third, Liu did literary criticism through literary development. He therefore endorsed, "Follow the root to search out the leaves, and the movements of one's thought will be perfect of themselves."[38] One can only seek the root of writing becoming literature in China in the Ruist Classics. In "Honoring the Classics," he wrote,

> The *Changes* is the starting point of the discussion, persuasion, rhyming narrative, and preface genres. The *Documents* is the source of the royal command, policy, encomium, and memorial genres. The *Odes* established the basis of the rhapsody, elegy, song, and judgment genres. The *Rites* is the origin of the inscription, eulogy, admonishment, and prayer genres. The *Annals* is the root of the chronicle, biography, oath, and proclamation genres.[39] They reached new heights in establishing models and opened up expanses at vast distances. This made it possible for the hundred masters to leap up, but in the end they returned within the circle of the Classics.[40]

What this is about is exactly the fact of literary development. When one seeks the root in literary development, one naturally connects back to the Zhou period and Kongzi.

Fourth, Liu's fundamental intent in writing *The Literary Heart-Mind Carves Dragons* was to rescue, in form and content, the literature of the time, which was in decline. And form and content, Liu believed, could not be separated. He said, "Early Song writing was errant and novel."[41] In regard to literature of his own Song dynasty, his attitude was that "they were written recently and are easy to understand, and so I will not make an effort to grade or rank them";[42] however, the one word *errant* can summarize them. This kind of criticism can be found throughout the book. In conclusion, in regard to form, it "lost substance and became peculiar"[43] because of a tendency to error, and in regard to content, it became shallow and useless because of the atmosphere of mysterious learning. Liu wanted to "correct errors and overturn shallowness," could find no way to do so in "free conversation with an excess of *qi*," and had to "go back to honoring the Classics."[44]

In facing challenging circumstances, he never failed to trouble himself to save the world, and therefore wanted to pull literary form and content back to the Ruist great unifying thread of the practical achievement of ordering the world. However, he still wanted to preserve the achievements since Han-Wei times in expressing emotions and stylistic elegance. After seeing Kongzi in a dream, he wrote *The Literary Heart-Mind Carves Dragons* with "Confirming the Sages" and "Honoring the Classics" as the center. This does not contradict at all his promotion of Daoist emptiness and stillness for literary cultivation. We need only pay attention to those in the present who are strongest in their opposition to Kongzi and Ruism, and usually have the deepest prejudices with the most vulgar and despicable minds. This can shed light on the significance of the empty and still heart-mind.

V

From the literary standpoint, the first to self-consciously and clearly pursue the effort of personal cultivation from Ruism was probably Han Yu (768–824).[45] Although the preface to "Biographies of Writers" in the [*New*] *Tang History* says, "Writing went through about three changes over the three hundred years that Tang ruled the world,"[46] the main current inside and outside the court was the parallel prose style of the east of the Yangzi River. This kind of writing with an ossified form was inevitably weak in energy and structure and vague in content, and so the ancient prose movement had already begun with Xiao Yingshi, Li Hua, Du Guji, and Quan Deyu,[47] demanding to rescue faulty writing with simplicity. However, it only attained success with Han Yu, who set down the foundation for later development. In thought, although the Tang dynasty had begun by advancing Ruism, Buddhism, and Daoism together, after Xuanzong [r. 713–756] Buddhism became dominant. Before Han Yu, the ancient prose movement had not explicitly brought up a movement in thought that would resonate with the form of ancient prose. Han Yu not only put forth the principle that "writing is to convey the Way," demanding that the content of a piece of writing determine its form, he went farther and made Ruist benevolence and rightness the material for personal cultivation. The natural fusion of literary form and content would evolve out of the natural fusion of the Way with the author's life, and thus achieves the highest state in writing. Looking at it this way, Su Shi's comment that "Han's writing arose from the decline through the eight dynasties,[48] and his Way was to save the drowning of the world" is not without foundation.[49] I will expand on this a little with Han's "Letter in Reply to Li Yi."

> If you seek to attain the level of the ancients in establishing words (ancient prose), don't look for achievement to be swift and don't be seduced by the prospect of power. Nurture the root and await the fruits. Add the grease [to the lamp] and expect the light. When the root is luxuriant, the fruits will grow. When the grease is rich, the light is bright. The harmony of the words of a benevolent and right person is just like this.[50]

The "ancient" in that letter is directed to the "contemporary" situation. "The establishment of language in ancient times" means ancient prose, and is directed against the contemporary form of parallel prose. This contemporary writing was a long-lasting trend, and writing in this way was easy because it was formulaic. Ancient prose was writing that opposed this trend. It was difficult because it was creative, and so he wrote, "Don't look for achievement to be swift." Contemporary parallel prose was suited to pursuing a reputation and meeting official demands, while ancient prose was no use for these. One could say that ancient prose was independent creation for the purpose of satisfying the requirements inherent to writing itself, so he said, "Don't be seduced by the prospect of power." This new form of contemporary writing, which united opposition [to parallel prose] with the prospect of power was a new creation from engagement with ancient prose. It required a deeper and more expansive mind to form a lasting, unchanging creative motivation. This then required personal cultivation . . .[51]

Making Ruism the basis of regular personal cultivation, shifting and elevating one's entire life to make it a life of Ruist moral reason and then responding to objective things and events, one will inevitably and naturally feel an unlimited sense of responsibility toward life, society, and government. As far as (but not merely limited to) literary creation, it will open a limitless spring of creativity, from which to look down at contemporary writing that consists of the wriggling and squirming pursuit of the private interests of personal fame and wealth. In his "Memorial to Yueyang Tower," Fan Zhongyan wrote,

Alas! I have looked for the benevolent heart-mind of the ancients. They were perhaps different than those two kinds (becoming happy or sad in response to the scene). Why is this? They did not become happy because of things; they did not become sad because of meeting with misfortune. When in a high position at court, they worried about the people. When far away among the rivers and lakes,[52] they worried about their ruler. When employed they worried; when retired they worried: when did they have time to be joyful? They would surely say, "I worry before the rest of the world worries, and I feel joy after the rest of the world feels joy!"[53]

These lines can probably describe one or two results of personal cultivation with Ruist thought.

VI

I have some opinions I need to bring up and expand on here.

First, the fundamental conditions for literary creativity—and what determines whether it is deep or shallow, great or minor—come from deep feeling in the author's concrete life; whether that feeling is deep, shallow, great, or minor; as well as expressive ability. As long as an author has lofty, pure sentiments and deep sympathy, he can then have lofty, pure, and deep affective inspiration. This shapes the motive for creation and makes writing a great work possible. At this point, Ruism, Daoism, and all other forms of thought are merely external influences which may be present or not. One absolutely may not hold up Ruism, Daoism, or any form of thought and put it in command over all literary works, ancient and modern, nor put it in command over the oeuvre of one author. This is especially clear in the case of poetry. However, another point that cannot be ignored is: Even if an author or artist has never made Ruism and Daoism the material for their cultivation[54]—even if they're a foreigner who hasn't even heard of Ruism and Daoism—in the activity of their creative soul they will usually have a place that unknowingly accords with the benevolent, right, empty, and still heart-mind grasped by Ruism and Daoism.

This is because the heart-mind grasped by Ruism and Daoism, unlike the philosophy of [ancient] Greece, does not follow logical inference and push forward and up (actually outward), but is a deep, submerged reflection carried on in the midst of life, and what it verifies are two kinds of foundational, original spiritual conditions. Proceeding only from embodied recognition of this spiritual condition in itself, and not beginning from the form or structure of expressing this spiritual condition, one should then recognize the truth of the judgment, "People share this heart-mind, and the heart-mind shares this pattern."[55] Anyone can on their own discover and reach the place of the source of life that Ruism and Daoism discovered and reached, without going through the structure that they expressed. What makes great writers and artists the world over great is precisely the fact that they realize this to a more profound level than the average person. I have therefore felt in recent years that facilitating connection between China and the West through art and literature would be much easier and more natural than through philosophy.

At the same time, I should point out that not only was Ruist thought's great contribution to literature primarily in deepening, elevating, and broadening authors' affective inspiration; we should likewise try hear the sound of deep sighs in the unconventional nature of the language in the classics of Daoist thought, of which *Laozi* and *Zhuangzi* are the foremost. Yes, they seek liberation from these deep sighs, letting the spirit find a place of repose. From this they went on to develop nature and pastoral poetry in which appreciation was foremost. But without *deep sighing, there is no true feeling of liberation.* And there is *ceaseless gliding* between "affective inspiration" and "appreciation," not a boundary that cannot be passed over. Not only was affective inspiration greater than appreciation in the "Song of Feelings" by Ruan Ji and "Dark Rage" by Ji Kang, who were both strongly influenced by Daoism, isn't it also hard to say that there was only appreciation and no affective inspiration in Tao Yuanming's pastoral poetry? A single author can have works that incline toward *affective inspiration* and others that incline toward *appreciation*. A clear example of this is Wang Wei's works primarily of appreciation such as "Azure Field" and "Wang River," which are completely different from his works that came from affective inspiration, such as "Song of Yi Gate" and "The Old General," and yet came from the same hand. The reason Wei-Jin period poems of mysterious learning have no value is because they not only had no affective inspiration, they had no genuine appreciation either, and merely made being mysterious into a dogma.

Second, there is the question of whether following the principle of "writing is to convey the Way" promoted by Han Yu, which progressed into carrying out personal literary cultivation on the basis of Ruist thought, ended up restraining the development of literature. Put another way: the question of whether emphasizing morality ended up fettering literature. This question was first raised with the opposition to the Song Ruists of the Qian-Jia school[56] and following from that, their opposition to the ancient prose of the Tongcheng school.[57] It then progressed through the May Fourth period and down to contemporary literary and artistic schools who imitate Western irrationalism, and especially in the "praise-singing"[58] school, which was particularly developed under [Communist] despotism, one could say the issue grew more and more heated. It got to the point where once someone said a certain work followed the principle of "writing is to convey the Way," it was knocked down. I should take this opportunity to clarify this issue.

The first point is this: if a writer's soul and moral norms are in fact two separate things, the motivation to write does not come out of the affective inspiration of the moral soul at all, but only from words, with moral norms added on top, or even used as a mask. At this point, morality becomes a rigid doctrine, and any such doctrine will have the effect of fettering and constraining. Naturally it will restrain the development that literature rightly demands.

Next, if, as described earlier, morality becomes internalized through a process of cultivation, and internalized as the author's heart-mind, then heart-mind and morality are one. In that case, the courageous and benevolent heart-mind derived from morality deepens and broadens the motivation and objects of affective inspiration. An author can see what others cannot, feel others cannot, and say what others cannot. This can only elevate and expand the quality and domain of literary works: What constraint could there be? The true classics, great works of all times and places, don't hang out a sign proclaiming their morality, but invariably have in them a kind of deep moral implication that arouses their vitality. The form of realizing morality can change, but the fundamental spirit of morality must be that which is innate in human nature. It must be that which the individual and the group need. There is a well-known saying in the West: "Land barren of morality is land barren of literature." This is something worth pondering for the wise of today who follow along with the trends while lacking principles of their own.

Moreover, all human culture in the end comes out of the survival and development of humanity itself, and literature is no exception. If morality truly fettered literature, and therefore it was necessary to oppose morality by means of literature, then in the circumstances in which humanity had to choose one of them, for their own lasting benefit they would have to choose morality and give up literature. I believe pornographic and black comedy authors who go against morality for their own personal gain are no different than drug dealers.

In fact, the true greatest obstacle that constrains the development of literature is long-term despotic government. If one were to assess the works of the various masters[59] as literary works, then the pre-Qin writings, including the *Odes* and *Songs of Chu*, would be the peak of Chinese literary development. Why is this? Because despotic government had not yet appeared. The reason Eastern Han literature doesn't measure up to Western Han is because the circumstances of the dynasty's founding and its measure of language were broader in the Western Han. The reason Song literature is inferior to Tang, Ming is inferior to Song, and Qing is inferior to Ming (other than literature of the Ming-Qing boundary and the period following the Xianfeng and Guangxu emperors)[60] is because despotism became worse generation after generation. The reason works of quality often appeared during the period of dynastic transition is this was a time when the old and new despotisms were still disjointed. Why did the Chinese authors of the thirties lose their luster under Communist rule? Why did praise-singing, opposition to morality, human nature, and all cultural products reach an unprecedented height? Because Mao Zedong's despotism reached unprecedented heights.

Literary life is inspired by the irrational in the world and humanity. Under despotism, there are knives and saws in front and boiling cauldrons behind,[61] and exile, starvation, and freezing fill the space between them to establish a forbidden zone that human conscience cannot touch. Everything was the darkest, cruelest, and most opposed to human nature, and the stricter the forbidden zone prohibited and the longer this went on, the more people became numb. Some became reptiles going over to the opposite side. The greatest authors could not but consciously or unconsciously limit their affective inspiration to seek the existence of the most basic conditions for life, or would compromise their skill when expressing their affective inspiration to go back to what is called "gentle and sincere."

I will attempt to use the great writer Su Shi as an example. In March 1079 (when he was forty-four), He Zhengchen and others picked out some words from Su's poems, accused him of disrespecting the emperor, and had him jailed at the censorate. They hoped to use fourteen of his ordinary poems to get him sentenced to death. This was the famous Crow Terrace poetry trial.[62] From a contemporary perspective, his poetry occasionally reveals a sense of indignance that came out of his affective inspiration. Without even some indignance, why write poetry at all? And yet it was due to this that the great genius was trapped: "My spirit is startled by boiling water and fire—my fate is like a chicken's."[63] Although he was spared due to the intervention of Emperor Shenzong's mother, at the time near death, he was instead allowed to settle in Huangzhou,[64] then exiled to Huizhou[65] and eventually to Qiongzhou.[66] These were all questionable punishments involving words. Although Su usually relied on Daoist thought as a way to divert himself from his predicaments (the former and later "Ode to Red Cliff" being especially clear examples), when he got to Qiongzhou, he had to give vent to his anger and grief at ending his life under a despotism in language neither Ruist nor Daoist.[67] Countless geniuses throughout Chinese history were oppressed by this kind of despotism until they died. Many now do not understand Chinese literature and the whole of Chinese learning from this fundamental place, nor understand why it continuously took the path of decline, and instead push the responsibility for this onto Ruism's moral teachings. It has got to the point where modern intellectuals with a modicum of innate moral awareness and consciousness have no place to preserve themselves and no home to return to—angrier and more sorrowing than Su Shi. And then they have a lofty discussion on literary creativity. It all makes it impossible for me not to feel wan and perplexed.

Notes

Introduction

The account of Xu's life is based primarily on his own autographical writings, information provided by his son Hsu Woochun (Xu Wujun), his brief chronological biography that is appended to Xu, *Wars of Words and Translations*, and Liu and Xie, *Chronological Table*.

1. Different sources have different dates of his birth. This is due to the fact that Xu uses the Chinese lunar calendar when mentioning when he was born, raising questions about the equivalent date in the Western calendar. I follow the date given in Huang, *A Question of Morality in Politics*, 6; Liu and Xie, *Chronological Table*, 1.

2. Xu, *Reflections*, 65.

3. Hence, Thomas H. C. Lee's statement that the New Ruists refused GMD support is not strictly accurate. Xu in fact sought it out. Nor was Xu's later move to Hong Kong voluntary, as Lee implies. Lee, "Chinese Education and Intellectuals."

4. This began before the move to Taiwan, but Xu does not address this period much.

5, Xu, *Chinese Theories of Human Nature*, preface, 6.

6. Xu, "Mourning Xiong Shili," 341.

7. *Analects* 12.12.

8. Here and throughout the book, I use "New Ruist" in a narrow sense, meaning specifically the contemporary Ruists who took the Mengzi–Wang Yangming side concerning human nature and knowledge of morality, influenced by Xiong Shili.

9. Xu, *Between Academia and Politics*, 450–52.

10. *Mengzi* 2A6.

11. Liu, *Confucianism in the Eyes of a Confucian Liberal*, 68.

12. Xu, *Chinese Theories of Human Nature*, 125.

13. Ibid., 195.

279

14. Ibid., 460.

15. While it would go too far afield to consider the research here in any depth, some modern experimental philosophy confirms that studying philosophy as an academic endeavor has little impact on behavior. See Schwitzgebel, "Do Ethicists Steal More Books?" and Schwitzgebel and Rust, "The Moral Behavior of Ethicists."

16. Xu, *Chinese Theories of Human Nature*, 258. He also develops this point in chapter 5, "The Construction and Advancement of Ruist Political Thought."

17. It is similar to Hobbes and Xunzi, though of course neither reach the conclusion of democratic government.

18. Xu, "Literary Records of Xu Fuguan," 144. Originally written in 1963. For unknown reasons, Xu used his old style name.

Chapter 1

1. Xu was an officer in the Chinese army during the War of Resistance against Japan, retiring in 1946.

2. A collection of model exam papers for use in preparing for the civil service exams (which no longer existed at the time).

3. *Jinshi* (admitted scholar) was the title given to those who passed the final and most difficult national exam.

4. 譚延闓, 1880–1930. Tan was a GMD official. His final office was premier of the Republic of China government.

5. The Four Books are the *Analects*, *Mengzi*, *Great Learning*, and *Mean*, recommended by Zhu Xi for beginning a Ruist education. The Five Classics are the *Odes*, *Documents*, *Changes*, *Record of Ritual*, and *Spring and Autumn Annals*.

6. These are various collections of classical writings. *Broad Debates of Donglai* (東萊博議) was written in the Southern Song by Lü Zuqian (1137–1181) for exam preparation. *Ancient Writing Styles in One Hundred Chapters* (古文筆法百篇) was compiled by Li Jiufu and Huang Fulin in the Qing dynasty. *Zenith of Ancient Writings* (古文觀止) also dates to the Qing dynasty, compiled by Wu Chucai and Wu Tiaohou. *Annals Easy to Understand* (綱鑑易知錄) was a Qing compilation of historical writings edited by Wu Chucai, Zhou Zhijiong, and Zhou Zhican. *Imperial Comments on the Comprehensive Mirror [of the Past], Edited for Perusing* (御批[歷代]通鑑輯覽) was a collection of historical writings compiled for and commented on by the Qianlong emperor in 1768.

7. In 1905.

8. 聊齋志異. A well-known collection of fantasy tales compiled by Pu Songling and published in 1766.

9. The educational system at the time divided primary schooling into common elementary and high elementary school. The high elementary program

began at age thirteen and took three years, after which students could enter middle school.

10. A city in Hubei.

11. The Tongcheng school was a group of writers associated with Tongcheng in Anhui. It was noted for fidelity to traditional Ruist principles and opposition to excessively flowery writing.

12. Another city in Hubei.

13. *Xunzi*, "Encouraging Study," 1. https://ctext.org/xunzi/quan-xue#n12247.

14. Liang Qichao 梁啟超 (1873–1929) was a writer and political reformer. After fleeing to Japan after a failed effort at political reform, he became an influential writer and publisher, helping to introduce Western ideas to China. Liang Shuming 梁漱溟 (1893–1988) was a scholar of Buddhism and Ruism, and around the time Xu is writing about had become professor of philosophy at Beijing University. Wang Xinggong 王星拱 (1887–1949) was an educator and chemist, at the time professor of chemistry at Beijing University. Hu Shi 胡適 (1891–1962) was also a professor of philosophy at Beijing University, where he was one of the foremost advocates for Western methods in scholarship. In some other works, including later in this essay, Xu is extremely critical of Hu's approach to humanistic study.

15. Traditional Chinese books were bound together with threads.

16. In Wuhan city.

17. Xu had joined the army that year.

18. Sun's main political idea, the three principles are democracy, nationalism, and welfare. See chapter 13 for more.

19. Xu initially went to Japan to study at Meiji University in 1928. He returned to China a year later, then went back to Japan in 1930 and enrolled in the Japanese army officers' school.

20. Soviet Marxist theoretician Abram Deborin (1881–1963). In 1931 he was criticized in a Central Committee resolution.

21. Yan'an was the headquarters of the CCP at the time.

22. Carl von Clausewitz (1780–1831) wrote a book *On War*, still unfinished at the time of his death.

23. Yang Jie 楊杰 (1889–1949) was an officer the in the GMD army and government, and author of several books on warfare.

24. The temporary capital during the war with Japan, in Sichuan.

25. Reading 叩 instead of 扣.

26. 熊十力, 1885–1968. Lecturer in philosophy first at Beijing University, then Nanjing University and author of *New Treatise on the Uniqueness of Consciousness* 新唯識論 (1932). Xiong is considered one of the first New Ruist philosophers. During the war he fled to Sichuan, where the meeting Xu describes took place.

27. Wang Fuzhi 王夫之 (1619–1692) was a noted scholar of the Ming-Qing period. *Assessment after Reading the* Comprehensive Mirror (讀通鑑論) is his

assessment of an earlier work of history, *The Comprehensive Mirror in Aid of Governance* (資治通鑑), the *Comprehensive Mirror* of Wang's title.

28. 文心雕龍, a classical work on literary theory from the fifth century CE written by Liu Xie.

29. 史記, the pioneering work of history by Sima Qian completed in the first century CE.

30. The German historian Leopold von Ranke, 1795–1886; the Italian philosopher and politician Benedetto Croce, 1866–1952; the German historian Friedrich Meinecke, 1862–1954 (this identification is uncertain); and the German neo-Kantian philosopher Ernst Cassirer, 1874–1945.

31. Zhu Xi (1130–1200) and Lu Xiangshan (1139–1192) were both major Neo-Ruist philosophers of the Song dynasty.

32. At this time, Hu Shi (1891–1962), one of the leading proponents of Westernization in China and Taiwan, was president of Academia Sinica. New Ruists such as Xu were highly critical of his philological and document-based approach to humanistic research.

33. The point is difficult to capture in English. What he means is that he would only read the best books, though this is his personal standard of quality.

34. Lu Xun (1881–1936) was one of the pioneers of modern Chinese fiction and an influential figure in the New Culture movement. Kawakami Hajime (1879–1966) was a Japanese Marxist economist.

35. The British political theorist and economist Harold Laski (1893–1950).

36. Lai Zhide 來知德 (1525–1604) was a noted scholar of the *Classic of Changes*. Xu names the various relations that Lai used to explain the sequence of hexagrams, but it is virtually impossible to give satisfactory English equivalents.

Chapter 2

1. Jiang's birthplace in Zhejiang province.

2. A village within the Fenghua district.

3. Reading 處 instead of 置. That is, the Nationalists had a military and political organization, but were about to lose China. The liberals had no effective political organization and little influence.

4. This was probably 1946–48.

5. Both were also students of Xiong Shili and would go on to become major New Ruist philosophers.

6. About fifteen thousand U.S. dollars.

7. Zheng Yanfen 鄭彥棻 (1902–1990) and Tao Xisheng 陶希聖 (1890–1988) were both GMD government officials.

8. 張丕介 (1905–1970) had been an official in the Ministry of Education. Later he was one of the founders of New Asia College with Qian Mu and Tang Junyi.

9. More literally, "practicalism and contradictionism."

10. Qian Mu was already a noted historian.

11. See "Why Oppose Liberalism" chapter 13 for more on Hu.

12. This may be the same 鄭竹園 (1927–) who later went to the United States and became a professor of economics at Ball State University.

13. A CIA-supported organization founded in 1951 to promote U.S. interests in Asia. It was the precursor to The Asia Foundation.

14. Xu wrote this in the early stages of the Cultural Revolution.

15. A newspaper published in Hong Kong from 1925 to 1995.

16. 謝幼偉 (1905–1976), a former GMD army officer and government official, who went on to be a professor at several universities in Taiwan.

17. See the introduction for more on this concept.

Chapter 3

1. Xu does not specify the currency, but presumably he meant new Taiwan dollars, which would have been a little less than one hundred U.S. dollars. If he meant Hong Kong dollars, then it would have been more than five hundred.

2. This would have been in 1964.

3. Possibly he means *The Future of Chinese Culture* 中國文化的展望 (1965), probably Yin's best-known work.

4. 陳鼓應 (1935–), a student of Yin's and later a well-known scholar of Daoist philosophy.

5. 張灝, professor emeritus of history at Ohio State University.

6. Yin had been professor of philosophy. In 1966 he was not offered continued employment.

7. 1883–1969. Jaspers was a German psychiatrist and philosopher.

8. A genre of unsystematic brief aphorisms and dialogues, common in Chan Buddhism and Neo-Ruism.

9. Some of these are appended to Xu's essay. I have not translated them here.

10. Xu's commonly used name had been Foguan, which he later changed to Fuguan at the suggestion of Xiong Shili.

11. Reading 辯證 for 辯正

12. A slightly altered version of a couplet from Lu You's (1125–1210) poem "Roaming the Mountains to West Village."

13. An allusion to the opening chapter of the *Zhuangzi*.

14. These are all Xu's parenthetical insertions.

15. The other philosophers Yin mentioned to Xu, Tang Junyi and Mou Zongsan, were known for their deep interest in Hegel and Kant, respectively.

16. That is, they had no backbone. On the two handles, see *Han Feizi*, chapter 7. https://ctext.org/hanfeizi/er-bing.

17. "Superstition" is literally "god who subdues mountain [spirits]" (*zhen-shanshen* 鎮山神). The point is uncertain but Xu seems to mean the complete faith in science as the solution to all problems that some subscribed to.

18. He was sixty-six at the time.

Chapter 4

1. The distinction between structure (*ti* 體), which does not change, and function (*yong* 用), which does change, is important in much of Chinese philosophy.

2. 慧業, literally "wisdom karma." In Buddhism, karma is often extended to mean the latent seeds that have not yet been activated.

3. In other words, there is no such thing as a form that has no content.

4. A common saying in historical writings.

5. Xu had worked in government himself.

6. Reading 楨 instead of 貞.

7. See "Why Oppose Liberalism?" chapter 12 for details.

8. Xu probably means the initial 1911 revolution to establish a republic, and the 1913 second revolution aimed at ousting Yuan Shikai.

9. Yuan Shikai (1859–1916) was a general in the Qing army and chosen as president shortly after the Republic was established. In 1915 he declared himself emperor. Widespread revolts forced him to abandon this attempt and he died not long after.

10. After Yuan's death the central government of China collapsed and the country was divided among several warlord factions.

11. The *baojia* system was a sort of local government and militia in which a certain number of households (called a *bao*) had a head official responsible for security, tax collecting, and other government functions.

12. Wang, *The Classic of Changes*, 130.

13. A term from *Laozi*, ch. 5; https://ctext.org/dao-de-jing#n11596. It means something that can be destroyed once its purpose has been served.

14. This appears to be the original title of what was published as *Philosophy of History* in 1955.

15. Xu's word is rational (*heli* 合理), but Hegel and Mou both used substantial.

16. Hegel, *Lectures on the History of Philosophy, 1825–6*, 1:88–90.

17. Mou, *Philosophy of History*, 62–73.

18. Ibid., 189–93.

19. Ibid., 167–70. For an English examination of Mou's terminology, see Elstein, *Democracy in Contemporary Confucian Philosophy*.

20. 智性 would ordinarily mean "wisdom," but as Xu makes clear, what he has in mind is the knowledge of the external world, in which he believes Western culture excelled.

21. Approximately US$500–750. Per capita GDP in Taiwan in 1951 was US$158 by comparison.

22. "Distinguished talent," an unofficial title used for those who passed the initial exam of the civil service system. He is suggesting that this relied on connections more than an objective measure of ability.

23. Presumably, Xu is referring to the Political Consultative Assembly in 1946, which included representatives of the GMD and CCP as well as other parties.

24. Reading "power" (*quanli* 權力) rather than "right" (*quanli* 權利) here.

25. One of the three principles.

26. Reading 遂性養生 instead of 遂生養性 in keeping with Xu's frequent usage elsewhere.

27. John 10:1–2, King James version.

28. An allusion to *Zhuangzi*, "The Human World," 5; https://ctext.org/zhuangzi/man-in-the-world-associated-with#n2743.

29. This must be related to Japan's surrender at the end of World War II, but it is not exactly clear what Xu means.

Chapter 5

1. As Xu makes clear farther down, he has in mind the leaders of the May Fourth movement who rejected tradition.

2. See the introduction for Xu's understanding of Ruist humanism.

3. For more on this idea, see chapter 15.

4. *Odes* #260. https://ctext.org/book-of-poetry/zheng-min.

5. This sentence borrows several terms from the *Zhuangzi*.

6. *Analects* 12.17.

7. *Analects* 2.1.

8. *Mean* 33. https://ctext.org/liji/zhong-yong#n10293.

9. *Great Learning* 1–2. https://ctext.org/liji/da-xue#n10382.

10. *Documents*, "Canon of Yao," 1. https://ctext.org/shang-shu/canon-of-yao#n21033.

11. *Documents*, "Counsels of Gao Yao," 1–2. https://ctext.org/shang-shu/counsels-of-gao-yao#n21086.

12. The two sovereigns were the legendary sage-rulers Yao and Shun. The three kings were the founders of the ancient dynasties of Xia, Shang, and Zhou: Yu, Tang, and Wu (sometimes including King Wu's father Wen as a founder of the Zhou).

13. *Documents*, "The Great Plan," 1. https://ctext.org/shang-shu/great-plan#n21271.

14. A common saying that derives from Zhu Xi's comment on *Analects* 15.24. See *Collected Commentary on the Four Books*, https://ctext.org/si-shu-zhang-ju-ji-zhu/wei-ling-gong-di-shi-wu.

15. *Mengzi* 6B2.

16. *Analects* 12.19.

17. *Mengzi* 2A2.

18. *Documents*, "Songs of the Five Sons," 2. https://ctext.org/shang-shu/songs-of-the-five-sons#n21145.

19. Durrant, Li, and Schaberg, *Zuo Tradition*, 1025. The bracketed text is Xu's addition which does not match the original.

20. Xu argued this at length in *A History of Chinese Theories of Human Nature: The Pre-Qin Period*.

21. *Documents*, "Counsels of Gao Yao," 2; https://ctext.org/shang-shu/counsels-of-gao-yao#n21092; "Great Declaration," 2. https://ctext.org/shang-shu/great-declaration-ii.

22. Durrant, Li, and Schaberg, *Zuo Tradition*, 97, 343.

23. *Speeches of the States*, "Speeches of Lu I," 1; https://ctext.org/guo-yu/lu-yu-shang#n24554; "Speeches of Zhou II," 24. https://ctext.org/guo-yu/zhou-yu-zhong#n24506.

24. *Mengzi* 7B14.

25. A paraphrase from a letter of exhortation by Zhang Yungu (?–631). Liu, *Old Tang History*, 190a.4992.

26. Zhu Xi's comment on *Analects* 1.12. See *Collected Commentary on the Four Books*, https://ctext.org/si-shu-zhang-ju-ji-zhu/xue-er-di-yi.

27. Xiong, *Essential Instructions*, 1:62.

28. *Analects* 2.3.

29. Liu et al., *The Huainanzi*, 503.

30. *Mengzi*, 4B29, 4B20.

31. *Great Learning*, 11. https://ctext.org/liji/da-xue#n10392.

32. *Record of Ritual*, "The Minor Rituals," 1. https://ctext.org/liji/qu-li-i#n9481.

33. *Analects* 4.13. The word "can" is missing from Xu's quotation.

34. *Great Learning*, 1. https://ctext.org/liji/da-xue#n10382. Xu adopts Zhu Xi's emendation that replaces *qin min* (being intimate with the people) with *xin min* (renewing the people).

35. Rule by virtue, the people as foundation, and rule by ritual.

36. *Analects* 7.1.

37. *Mean* 31. https://ctext.org/liji/zhong-yong#n10291.

38. *The Odes, Documents, Changes, Rituals, Spring and Autumn Annals,* and the lost *Music* classic.

39. *Analects* 12.19.

40. *Mengzi* 1B5.

41. *Analects* 6.30.

42. Huang, *Waiting for the Dawn: A Plan for the Prince*, 92.

43. There was little examination of the objective institutions and policies that would make for better government, only exhortations to those in power to rule well.

44. *Mean* 31. https://ctext.org/liji/zhong-yong#n10291.

45. *Analects* 15.34.

46. Yuan Mei 袁枚 (1716–1797), a Qing dynasty poet and essayist. The quote is from "On Scholars," in *Collected Writings from the House on Xiaocang Hill*, chapter 1, 31. https://ctext.org/wiki.pl?if=en&chapter=866326.

47. A paraphrase rather than a quote. *Documents*, "The Announcement of Tang," 1. https://ctext.org/shang-shu/announcement-of-tang#n21168.

48. *Documents*, "Great Declaration II," 2. https://ctext.org/shang-shu/great-declaration-ii.

49. *Mengzi* 5B1. In some interpretations, *ren* 任 means to seek employment rather than responsibility, which is clearly what Xu intends.

50. Yuan Shikai 袁世凱 (1859–1916) was a general in the Qing army and chosen as president shortly after the Republic was established. In 1915 he declared himself emperor. Widespread revolts forced him to abandon this attempt and he died not long after.

51. *Great Learning*, 8. https://ctext.org/liji/da-xue#n10389.

52. *Analects* 8.18.

53. *Record of Ritual*, "Revolutions of Ritual," 1. https://ctext.org/liji/li-yun#n9872.

54. See the introduction for more on this idea.

Chapter 6

1. He developed this in greater detail in *A History of Chinese Theories of Human Nature*.

2. 沈剛伯 (1896–1977) was the person who would go on to recommend Xu for a position at Donghai University.

3. May 4, 1919, saw widespread protests against the Treaty of Versailles in which the German concessions in China were given to Japan. This broadened into criticism of Chinese tradition and movement for modernization.

4. In most historical accounts, Emperor Wu established Ruism as the official philosophy on the advice of Dong Zhongshu starting in 140. Many recent scholars have challenged this.

5. In this schema, a dynasty was identified with one of the Five Phases (wood, fire, earth, metal, water), each corresponding with a particular virtue.

6. The New Text school referred to certain traditions of classics and commentaries that were written in the newer script in the Han dynasty, as

opposed to the Old Text works which allegedly used the script before it was standardized.

7. Ban, *Han History*, "Biography of Dong Zhongshu," 56.2518. Xu's original quote has a mistake. I've translated according to the original source.

8. As used in Ruist thought, the term refers to a kind of doxography, used to define who truly inherited and carried on the Ruist tradition. Various scholars have debated who was and was not in the lineage of the way.

9. Although the language suggests Xu is talking about someone specific, he does not say who it is.

10. Andrei Zhdanov (1896–1948) was an important Soviet politician and potential successor to Stalin. Georgy Aleksandrov (1908–1961) was also a Soviet official. He succeeded Zhdanov as head of the Propaganda and Agitation Department of the Central Committee until his removal in 1947 when his book was denounced. Presumably Xu meant 1947 rather than 1937.

11. Literally, "burning and burying," an allusion to the First Emperor of Qin, who was said to have burned the books and buried the scholars alive.

12. E.g., Toynbee, *A Study of History*, 9:618–37.

13. Xu is referring to the Stone of Scone, used in the coronation ceremonies first of Scottish kings, then later by English monarchs after the stone was taken by King Edward I. In 1950, four Scottish students stole the Stone from Westminster Abbey and brought it back to Scotland to draw attention to Scottish nationalism.

14. Sun Wukong, also known as the Monkey King, is one of the main characters in the classic Chinese novel *Journey to the West*. In the novel, Sun used his considerable magical powers to help the monk Xuanzang bring back Buddhist scriptures from India.

15. Xu often described himself as the son of farmers.

16. Lingshan is a mountain often mentioned in Chinese mythology. Here, Xu uses this as a metaphor for importing ideas from the West.

17. *Lixue* 理學, the branch of Neo-Ruism associated with Cheng Yi and Zhu Xi.

18. Xu probably means Kong Xiangxi 孔祥熙 (H. H. Kung. 1881–1967) and Song Ziwen 宋子文 (Soong Tse-ven, 1894–1971). Both held several significant positions in the GMD government. Kong was married to Song Ailing, whose younger sisters were married to Sun Zhongshan and Jiang Jieshi. Song Ziwen was also part of that family, and thus Kong's brother-in-law.

19. *Mengzi* 6A5.

20. *Analects* 12.1.

21. Eight-legged essays (*bagu wen*) were a formulaic way of writing required for the examinations.

22. The Taiping rebellion (1850–1864) was a religious and nationalistic uprising against the Qing dynasty, led by Hong Xiuquan who believed himself to be Jesus's younger brother. Xu here uses the name of the Taiping state.

23. A nickname for Taiping followers, because they did not shave their foreheads and braid their hair in the Manchu style, letting it grow long.

24. When Xu and other New Ruists use the term *idealism*, this is not at all subjective idealism, like Berkeley's, in which all is mind. The meaning is closer to the Marxist understanding of idealism. It could also be called "rationalism," in that they uphold a priori knowledge beyond tautologies, specifically that moral knowledge is a priori and universal.

25. Also called the Second Sino-Japanese War, this is the Chinese term for the part of World War II fought in China to resist the Japanese invasion.

26. Hu Shi, one of the prominent May Fourth leaders as a professor at Beijing University, was also a strong advocate of liberalism. He was the ambassador to the United States from the Republic of China from 1938 to 1942.

27. An ancient work of geography, on which Hu did textual research.

28. *Shuowen jiezi*, 9.4935. https://ctext.org/shuo-wen-jie-zi/ren-bu1#n31384. The *Shuowen jiezi* is the earliest extant Chinese dictionary, which gave speculative etymologies of words often based on similarity of pronunciation, as in this example.

29. Durrant, Li, and Schaberg, *Zuo Tradition*, 1289; slightly modified.

30. Ibid., 803.

31. *Odes* #260. https://ctext.org/book-of-poetry/zheng-min.

32. 蔡尚思, 1905–2008. Cai was an influential scholar of Chinese thought on the mainland, spending most of his career at Fudan University in Shanghai. He published extensively on Ruism and the history of Chinese thought.

33. Xie Liangzuo 謝良佐 (1050–1103), a disciple of Cheng Yi.

34. *Reflections on Things at Hand*, "On Heterodoxy," 12. https://ctext.org/wiki.pl?if=gb&chapter=69918.

35. Italics indicate that Xu used this word in the original text.

36. In Greek, *skholē*.

37. Xu was mixed up. The meaning of the actual line is rather the opposite. In one translation, it reads, "Life is sweetest when one lacks sense." Sophocles, *Ajax*, l. 555. http://www.perseus.tufts.edu/hopper/text?doc=Perseus%3Atext%3A1999.01.0184%3Acard%3D545.

38. Aristotle, *Metaphysics*, 3. A more literal rendering of Xu's Chinese version would be, "All people from birth hope to have knowledge. A proof of this is the delight they take in sense perception. Sensory perception has no relation to practicality; it is loved purely for itself."

39. Wilhelm Windelband (1848–1915) was a German philosopher. Windelband, *A History of Philosophy*, 4.

40. In *Meditations Sacrae*, "Of Heresies," Bacon wrote, "Knowledge itself is power," though he was referring specifically to God's knowledge. Bacon, *The Works of Francis Bacon*, 14:95.

41. Xu's translation would more literally read, "Still at the other side."

42. Pascal, *Pensées*, 116, no. 347.

43. Becker, *Freedom and Responsibility*, 49–50.

44. Ibid., 50.

45. See chapter 11, "The Ruist Distinction between Cultivating Oneself and Governing Others and Its Significance."

46. Wang, *The Classic of Changes*, 87. This is the source of Xu's well-known concept of "concern consciousness" (*youhuan yishi* 憂患意識). See the introduction for more.

47. *Analects* 6.3.

48. Ibid. 1.14.

49. Ibid. 1.6.

50. Ibid. 1.7.

51. Two rivers in the ancient state of Lu, Kongzi's homeland.

52. *Analects* 7.34.

53. Although not an exact quote, the term "bestow goodness" comes from the *Odes* #247. https://ctext.org/book-of-poetry/ji-jui.

54. *Mengzi* 2A6, 6A6.

55. Ibid. 6B2.

56. Ibid. 4B19.

57. Ibid. 6A6.

58. *Analects* 12.1.

59. *Categorized Conversations of Master Zhu*, "Holding and Guarding," 55. https://ctext.org/zhuzi-yulei/12#n587343.

60. A slight modification of a saying attributed to Cheng Yi, *Reflection on Things at Hand*, "Preserving and Nurturing," 36. https://ctext.org/wiki.pl?if=en&chapter=395496#p37.

61. *Mengzi* 6A15, referring to the heart-mind.

62. Ibid. 7A38.

63. These are known as the seven feelings, and were an important topic in Neo-Ruist thought.

64. An allusion to *Analects* 11.16.

65. Xu is following conventional Neo-Ruist thought, which distinguished the fundamental nature prior to embodiment from the actual embodied nature. The former is perfectly good, while the latter can go wrong due to the influence of bodily responses, as Xu describes here.

66. I.e., one's physiological responses.

67. *Analects* 7.6, 8.8.

68. See ibid. 11.26.

69. *Reflections on Things at Hand*, "Overcoming the Self," 26. https://ctext.org/wiki.pl?if=gb&chapter=245164.

70. *Lixue* 理學 and *xinxue* 心學, two branches of Neo-Ruism.

71. *Analects* 9.6.

72. 觀照, a term associated with Buddhism.

73. *Mean* 22. https://ctext.org/liji/zhong-yong#n10282.

74. *Analects* 1.5, 13.19.

75. It is probably not accidental that Xu only specifies male relationships here.

76. *Analects* 1.2. Xu also repeats the quote in note 45 above.

77. Xia, Shang, and Zhou.

78. *Mengzi* 3A3, 4B19.

79. Ibid. 7A15.

80. Ibid. 4A27.

81. A paraphrase of the *Great Learning* 2. https://ctext.org/liji/da-xue#n10383.

82. *Odes* #247, "Having Drunk," 5. https://ctext.org/book-of-poetry/ji-jui#n16397.

83. *Mengzi* 1A7.

84. Ibid. 4A11.

85. *Great Learning* 1. https://ctext.org/liji/da-xue#n10382.

86. Qv. *Analects* 19.12.

87. *Reflections on Things at Hand*, "Way of the Family," 11. https://ctext.org/wiki.pl?if=gb&chapter=722654.

88. Xu presumably means communists and liberals.

89. Ruler-subject, husband-wife, father-son, older brother-younger brother, and friend-friend.

90. *Analects* 6.23.

91. *Great Learning* 11. https://ctext.org/liji/da-xue#n10392.

92. *Odes* 235, "King Wen," 2. https://ctext.org/book-of-poetry/wen-wang#n16211.

93. *Analects* 12.5

94. "Han people" is the Chinese term for the majority ethnicity in China.

95. *Analects* 8.13.

96. Sorokin, *The Reconstruction of Humanity*, 144–49.

97. "Government for the people" is my loose translation of 民本 *minben*, more literally "the people as foundation"; that is to say, the purpose of government is to take care of the people. In Chinese, the semantic relation between this and democracy (*minzhu* 民主) is more obvious.

98. Chapter 5 in this volume.

99. The Great Proscription erupted out of a conflict between eunuchs and regularly appointed bureaucrats. The eunuchs had the support of the emperor and succeeded in having many of their rival officials killed and many more banned from office for life. See Twitchett and Loewe, *Cambridge History of China, Vol. 1*, 328–30.

100. *Xuanxue* 玄學, a philosophical school that focused more on abstract metaphysics than practical politics.

101. Xu is referring to the fact that after the fall of the Eastern Han dynasty (220 CE), what had been the political and cultural heartland of China was ruled by a succession of non-Chinese invaders for several centuries.

102. Feng Dao 馮道 (882–954) was an official famous for his willingness to serve a succession of short-lived dynasties rather than staying loyal to one ruler.

103. Reading 聖 instead of 生.

104. It is not clear to whom Xu is referring, but he may have had in mind pre-Reformation German theologians such as Meister Eckhart.

105. *Complete Works of Wang Yangming*, "Knowledge and Action 1," 1. https://ctext.org/wiki.pl?if=en&chapter=915813.

106. *Analects* 17.5.

107. Xu appears to mean that political achievement depends on having office, which Kongzi never did for long, while his achievements in education only relied on his own effort.

108. *Analects* 7.11

109. Paraphrasing ibid. 8.13.

110. Ibid., 7.2.

111. Ibid. 15.39.

112. Ibid. 7.7.

113. Ibid. 7.29.

114. The term Xu uses here is *lixing* 理性, which is elsewhere translated as "reason"; however, context argues for interpreting it as two separate but related concepts in this case.

115. *Reflections on Things at Hand*, "Taking and Leaving Office," 1. https://ctext.org/wiki.pl?if=gb&chapter=506911.

116. Ibid., 31–32. https://ctext.org/wiki.pl?if=gb&chapter=506911.

117. *Complete Works of Wang Yangming*, "Quieting the Heart-mind 10: Prefaces," 14. https://ctext.org/wiki.pl?if=en&chapter=308795.

118. In the early twelfth century, grand councilor Cai Jing acted to exile and blacklist remaining officials who opposed the New Policies of Wang Anshi during the reign of Song Zhezhong (the Yuanyou period), and forever bar their descendants from taking office. See Levine, *Divided by a Common Language*, ch. 6.

119. The teachings of Zhu Xi and many other prominent Neo-Ruists were banned by order of grand councilor Han Tuozhou from 1196 to 1202. See Levine, 167–68.

120. From 1625 to 1627, the eunuch Wei Zhongxian persuaded the Tianqi emperor to have the leaders of the Donglin movement arrested and killed, and the Donglin faction eliminated. See Dardess, *Blood and History in China*.

121. Jie, the last king of the Xia dynasty, is a byword for a tyrant in Chinese. Xu thus uses this allusion to ask how tyrannical the Chinese government will be.

122. The quote is from Cheng Hao. *Reflection on Things at Hand*, "Substance of the Way," 20. https://ctext.org/wiki.pl?if=gb&chapter=145840#p21.

123. *Complete Works of Wang Yangming*, "Awakening to the Genuine 7," 4. https://ctext.org/wiki.pl?if=en&chapter=480845#p740.

124. *Analects* 12.11.

125. The three bonds are ruler-minister, father-son, and husband-wife. *White Tiger Hall Discussions*, "Three Bonds and Six Regulations," 1. https://ctext.org/bai-hu-tong/san-gang-liu-ji#n53154.

126. Schwegler, *A History of Philosophy*, 11. https://www.gutenberg.org/files/41412/41412-h/41412-h.htm.

127. *Mean* 20. https://ctext.org/liji/zhong-yong#n10280

128. *Analects* 4.2.

129. *Mengzi* 4A27. See note 76 for the full quotation.

130. *Analects* 15.31.

131. A key Neo-Ruist term.

132. Zhu, *Collection of Zhu Xi*, "Answering Jiang Degong," 2114.

133. *Reflections on Things at Hand*, "Extending Knowledge," 9. https://ctext.org/wiki.pl?if=en&chapter=910491#p10.

134. *Collected Commentaries on the Four Books*, "Great Learning, 6. https://ctext.org/si-shu-zhang-ju-ji-zhu/da-xue-zhang-ju#n89503.

135. Xiong, *Essential Instructions*, 1:187–92.

136. Zhu, *Collection of Zhu Xi*, "Answering Lin Qian," 1725.

137. Zhu, "Memorial Sent to the Secondary Palace," 564. https://ctext.org/wiki.pl?if=en&chapter=675594#p380.

138. The story of Bacon dying of a chill brought on during an experiment with freezing is recorded by John Aubrey in his *Brief Lives*, although in Aubrey's account it was a chicken rather than a turkey and Bacon did not kill or clean the bird himself. Aubrey, *Brief Lives*, 16.

139. *Complete Works of Wang Yangming*, "Knowledge and Action 1," 3. https://ctext.org/wiki.pl?if=en&chapter=915813#p5.

140. *Analects* 19.4.

141. *Collected Commentaries on the Four Books*, *Analects* 19.4 https://ctext.org/si-shu-zhang-ju-ji-zhu/zi-zhang-di-shi-jiu#n90117.

142. See the introduction for more.

143. These are terms for various practices of self-cultivation advocated by Neo-Ruist thinkers. "Emphasize quietude" is from Zhou Dunyi, "emphasize reverence" and "preserve and nurture" were used by Cheng Yi and Zhu Xi, and "critically examine oneself" appears frequently in Zhu Xi's writings.

144. Zhen, *Collected Writings of Xishan*, 350. The word in the original is *tiyan* 體驗, personal or embodied experience, rather than *tiren* 體認 as Xu has quoted.

145. *Complete Works of Wang Yangming*, "Awakening to the Genuine 10," 23. https://ctext.org/wiki.pl?if=en&chapter=480845#p991.

146. These are symbols of steadfastness, since they do not wither in the winter.

147. These are symbols for each of the four seasons, common in painting.

148. *Categorized Conversations of Master Zhu*, "Writings of the Masters Cheng 2," 83. https://ctext.org/zhuzi-yulei/96#n598180. Xu's quote deviates slightly.

149. *Mean* 1. https://ctext.org/liji/zhong-yong#n10263.

150. "Other shore" is a common Buddhist term for salvation, in the Buddhist case nirvana. Here Xu applies it to the Christian idea of heaven.

151. *Analects* 6.30.

152. Ibid. 7.2.

153. Ibid. 9.4.

154. *Mengzi* 7A1.

155. Zhu, *Collection of Zhu Xi*, "Answering Sun Renfu," 3312.

156. The Chinese term comes from the Chinese translation of Bertrand Russell's *History of Western Philosophy*, where in the last chapter he describes the ontology of the philosophy of analysis as consisting of event elements rather than material elements. Russell, *A History of Western Philosophy*, 2:1058.

157. *Mengzi* 2A6, where these are said to be the sprouts or sources of benevolence, wisdom, ritual propriety, and rightness, respectively.

158. Ibid. 7A41. It is used as a metaphor for not making the Way too obvious.

159. Zhu, *Collection of Zhu Xi*, 3052–53.

160. *Analects* 12.1

161. *Categorized Conversations of Master Zhu*, "Master Zhu 10: Instructing the Disciples 1," 30. https://ctext.org/zhuzi-yulei/115#n599405. Another extended quote from Zhu Xi is excised for space.

162. *Complete Works of Wang Yangming*, "Knowledge and Action 2," 116. https://ctext.org/wiki.pl?if=en&chapter=915813#p234.

163. *Complete Works of Wang Yangming*, "Awakening to the Genuine 7," 14. https://ctext.org/wiki.pl?if=en&chapter=480845#p750.

164. *Scholastic Records of Ming Ruists*, "Huang Lizhou's Preface," 1. https://ctext.org/wiki.pl?if=en&chapter=632135#p2.

165. A saying common in Chan Buddhism.

166. The construction here is odd, but probably Xu means that Ruists regard the moral order as immanent in the cosmos.

167. *Complete Works of Wang Yangming*, "Knowledge and Action 1," 10. https://ctext.org/wiki.pl?if=en&chapter=915813#p12.

168. *Mengzi* 6A15.

169. *Complete Works of Wang Yangming*, "Knowledge and Action 1," 12. https://ctext.org/wiki.pl?if=en&chapter=915813#p14.

170. In response to a student asking whether the flowering trees that they saw on their walk were not separate from his heart-mind, Wang responded, "These flowers are not outside of your heart-mind." *Complete Works of Wang Yangming*, "Knowledge and Action 3," 63. https://ctext.org/wiki.pl?if=en&chapter=915813#p311.

171. Li, *Collection of Li Yanping*, 4.

172. An extended quotation from Ma Yifu is excised for space.

173. *Xin lixue* 新理學, Feng's name for his philosophy.
174. Sorokin, *The Reconstruction of Humanity*, 101–107.
175. Xu's original text calls him "Alexin," and says he won the Nobel Prize in science.
176. Extensive quotations from Carrel are omitted for space. The sections Xu quotes can be found in Carrel, *Man, the Unknown*, 278–79, 280.
177. Xu cites the Japanese translation. The original reads, "If Galileo, Newton, or Lavoisier had applied their efforts to the study of body and consciousness, our world probably would be different today." Carrel, 23.
178. Xu may have in mind the economic liberalism of someone such as F. A. Hayek, whose ideas were influential around this time—something closer to what today would be called libertarianism.
179. This in in fact the central argument of Hayek, *The Road to Serfdom*.
180. Becker, *Modern Democracy*, ch. 2.
181. *Mengzi* 4B19.
182. There is a distinction here that is impossible to reflect accurately in English, and the meaning of which is uncertain. The first term for rationalism Xu uses is *helizhuyi* 合理主義; the second is *lixingzhuyi* 理性主義. The latter is the common Chinese term for rationalism, while the former is an alternative translation used sometimes in Japanese, but rarely in Chinese. "Modern rationalism" would ordinarily mean the Enlightenment philosophy of Descartes, Leibniz, and others, but it is not clear what the other "rationalism" would mean. Possibly Xu is thinking of early religious philosophers such as Augustine and Aquinas.
183. *Analects* 11.24
184. *Recorded Sayings of Yushan*, ch. 7. *Jiaxing Tripitika* 40.B494.
185. *Categorized Commentary on Sutra of the Original Vow of the Bodhisattva Dizang*, X21.384, 752b.
186. "Yanping" is another way of referring to Li Tong (1093–1163), Zhu Xi's teacher.
187. Zhao, "Postscript to Dialogues with Yanping."
188. In 1721, Wolff gave a lecture, "Discourse on the Practical Philosophy of the Chinese," in which he compared Kongzi favorably to Jesus and praised the Chinese for having morality without religion. He was attacked for his views and in 1723 dismissed from his position and exiled from Prussia by King Frederick William I. Louden, "What Does Heaven Say?," 73–74.
189. *Analects* 15.6.
190. Ibid. 8.7.
191. Ibid. 13.27.
192. Ibid. 1.3.
193. Ibid. 17.13
194. *Mengzi* 4B19.
195. Ibid. 2A6.

196. Ibid. 7A13.

197. Xu paraphrases the idiom *bubo shusu* 布帛菽粟, meaning something very ordinary but necessary to life.

198. Rather than the utilitarianism of John Stuart Mill, Xu seems to mean individuals selfishly pursuing their own interests.

199. Literally "become buddhas" (*chengfo* 成佛), though here it seems intended metaphorically.

200. Xu is hinting at the GMD plans to take back the mainland, President Jiang's goal.

201. A paraphrase of *Mengzi* 4A9.

202. A paraphrase of ibid. 6A15.

203. This appears frequently in modern Ruist writings, but no source is given.

204. Xu is hinting at the criticism of Ruism as "pan-moralism" by Taiwanese liberals, which they held responsible for the failure of China to modernize.

205. *Complete Works of Wang Yangming*, "Quieting the Heart-mind 8," 495. https://ctext.org/wiki.pl?if=en&chapter=308795#p1788.

206. *Analects* 15.24.

207. This can also mean "unfeeling."

208. *Mengzi* 2A2.

209. Paraphrase of Cheng Yi in *Reflections on Things at Hand*, "Way of the Family," 11. https://ctext.org/wiki.pl?if=gb&chapter=722654.

210. See note 83.

211. The source is unknown.

212. *Mean* 31. https://ctext.org/liji/zhong-yong#n10291.

213. *Complete Works of Wang Yangming*, "Quieting the Heart-mind 10: Prefaces," 31. https://ctext.org/wiki.pl?if=en&chapter=308795#p2052.

214. A reference to self-chosen exile outside of China.

Chapter 7

1. A rare instance of Xu using Hegelian terminology. Mou Zongsan had already begun talking about the self-negation of the moral subject in 1951 (Chan, *The Thought of Mou Zongsan*, 114), but it is not clear if Xu was inspired by this or whether he picked up the idea from Tang Junyi.

2. *Guanyinzi* (also known as *Wenshi zhenjing*), "Polarity," 1. https://ctext.org/wenshi-zhenjing/san-ji#n279943.

3. I take Xu's point to be not that the ruler literally has no ability, wisdom, or preferences, but that for the purpose of governing he ignores these and instead acts according to what the people want and what they think should be done. For more on his concept of nonaction, see chapter 14.

4. *Laozi* 37, 48.

5. Ban, *Han History*, 30.1732.

6. *Zhuangzi*, "Letting Things Be," 1. https://ctext.org/zhuangzi/letting-be-and-exercising-forbearance#n2777. The bracketed comment is Xu's.

7. Wang, *The Classic of Changes*, 48–49.

8. *Analects* 6.1, 6.2. The bracketed comment is Xu's. The ruler traditionally occupied the north position in the hall, facing south. Hence, "facing south" is a metonym for occupying the ruler's position

9. *Analects* 8.19.

10. Ibid. 8.18.

11. Ibid. 15.34.

12. Ibid. 2.1.

13. *Great Learning* 12. https://ctext.org/liji/da-xue#n10393.

14. *Mean* 13. https://ctext.org/liji/zhong-yong#n10273.

15. Wang Fuzhi (1619–1692) was a noted scholar of the Ming-Qing period. *Assessment after Reading the "Comprehensive Mirror"* (讀通鑑論) is his assessment of an earlier work of history, *The Comprehensive Mirror in Aid of Governance* (資治通鑑), the *Comprehensive Mirror* of Wang's title. No such quote appears in this text.

16. Huang, *Waiting for the Dawn: A Plan for the Prince*, 92.

17. *Mean* 31. https://ctext.org/liji/zhong-yong#n10291.

18. *Han Feizi*, "Way of the Master," 1. https://ctext.org/hanfeizi/zhu-dao#n1902.

19. Ibid., 1, 2. https://ctext.org/hanfeizi/zhu-dao.

20. That is, they lost their thrones.

21. Durrant, Li, and Schaberg, *Zuo Tradition*, 167.

22. Found in many classical texts, e.g., *Mengzi* 5A6.

23. Ouyang and Song, *New Tang History*, "Biography of Lu Zhi," 157.4916. Xu's quotation deviates slightly.

24. *Mengzi* 1B5.

25. Lu, *Collected Works of Lu Zhi*, "Document Offered at Fengtian on the Most Pressing Current Affairs," 367.

26. There can be little doubt that Xu has in mind the sacrifices demanded to achieve the communist utopia.

27. Best knowledge (*liangzhi* 良知) and best capability (*liangneng* 良能) come from *Mengzi* 7A15. *Liangzhi* became the central concept in Wang Yangming's thought, where it means a kind of innate moral awareness.

28. *Mengzi* 6A7.

29. Xu adds the capitalized English word in his text.

30. A reference to *Republic*, Book III. https://www.gutenberg.org/files/1497/1497-h/1497-h.htm.

31. *Zhuangzi*, "Essentials for Nurturing Life," https://ctext.org/zhuangzi/nourishing-the-lord-of-life.

32. Xu uses this phrase often. It appears in many traditional sources and there is no indication from where Xu may have drawn it.

33. This is a puzzling aspect of Xu's thought to me. He appears to oppose *any* attempt for those with political power to provide leadership on any question, or to try to persuade the people at all. He gives little consideration to whether the majority at times *ought* to change their preferences. See Elstein, *Democracy in Contemporary Confucian Philosophy*, 83–84.

34. See chapter 8 for more on this.

35. *Great Learning* 12. https://ctext.org/liji/da-xue#n10393.

36. Ibid.14. https://ctext.org/liji/da-xue#n47493. Xu's quotation deviates slightly.

37. A phrase drawn from Yang Xiong's *The Classic of Supreme Mystery*, "Glitter of Supreme Mystery," 4. https://ctext.org/taixuanjing/tai-xuan-ying#n284 786.

38. *Documents*, "Great Plan," 8. https://ctext.org/shang-shu/great-plan#n 21279. Not an exact quotation.

39. Lu, *Collected Works of Lu Zhi*, 699, 703.

40. Paraphrasing *Analects* 15.5.

41. In 783, soldiers in the capital of Chang'an rebelled when they were not given the rewards they felt they deserved. Emperor Dezong was forced to flee to the city of Fengtian, where he was besieged by rebel armies. It was not until the following summer that the rebels were defeated and Dezong was able to return to Chang'an.

42. On New Year's Day 784, Dezong issued a pardon to the soldiers and commanders involved in the rebellion, excepting only the ringleader, and blamed himself for the events at Lu Zhi's urging.

43. A step back in this case meaning a step away from the opposition between the ruler and the world.

44. Ouyang and Song, *New Tang History*, "Biography of Lu Zhi," 157. 4932.

45. Yao, Shun, Tang, Wen, and Wu were all legendary sage rulers frequently praised by Ruist authors, while Jie and Zhou were the last kings of the Xia and Shang dynasties, respectively, classical examples of how tyranny led to downfall. Taizong and Xuanzong were earlier Tang emperors.

46. Lu, *Collected Works of Lu Zhi*, 385.

47. It is worth keeping in mind that when Xu wrote this, Taiwan was a one-party state under martial law, and any political party other than the GMD was strictly forbidden.

48. Xu's use of "objectify" (*keguanhua* 客觀化) is quite idiosyncratic. As should become clear, what he means is the ruler broadening his concern to the public as a whole when considering governmental policies, rather than focusing mainly on his family.

49. Lu, *Collected Works of Lu Zhi*, "Document Requesting Allowing the Various Ministers to Discuss [Government] Affairs with Respect," 402.

50. Paraphrasing *Analects* 13.15.

51. Although Xu never mentions Rousseau here or in any other writings that I am familiar with, the parallels are striking.

52. Lu, *Collected Works of Lu Zhi*, "Document on Describing the Source to Move Good Fortune," 362–63.

53. If this is a quote, I have not been able to identify the source.

54. 賈誼 (c. 200 BCE–168 BCE), a Western Han scholar and official.

55. 32–92 CE, author of the *Han History*.

56. Ban, *Han History*, "Record of Laws and Punishments," 23.1097.

57. Ban, "Biography of Jia Yi," 48.2230–56.

58. Ibid., 48.2251.

59. Zhongzhou was a town in Sichuan, which would have been far from the political center at the time.

60. It is difficult not to conclude that Xu saw himself as a modern-day Lu Zhi, and probably thought of his relationship with President Jiang as mirroring Lu Zhi's relationship with Emperor Dezong.

61. For reasons that are not fully clear, Xu uses the word from the *Great Learning* (*ge* 格) that Wang Yangming explained as meaning "to rectify."

62. It is unclear whether Xu is referring to someone actually saying this of Truman.

63. *Han History*, "Biography of Sima Qian," 62.2735.

Chapter 8

1. 唐君毅 (1909–1978), another major New Ruist philosopher, friend of Xu, and frequent contributor to *Democratic Review*. He is often mentioned in Xu's writings.

2. Xu is apparently referring to Karl Kautsky (1854–1938) and the Social Democratic Party. Kautsky was not one of the founders of the SDP, but he was an influential member until splitting from the party in 1917.

3. *Zhuyi* 主義, literally "ism."

4. *Between Academia and Politics* 95–100, not translated here.

5. 物化, which would be more literally rendered "thingified"; that is, a world in which people are made into things.

6. That is, each instance of (human) life has the same value and value is not determined by the quality of that life

7. Wang, *The Classic of Changes*, 77; slightly modified.

8. A noted scholar of the late Ming-early Qing period.

9. A paraphrase of *Mengzi* 1A3.

10. *Analects* 5.2.

11. Ibid. 13.9.

12. Ibid. 10.16.

13. Ibid. 10.10. I presume Xu refers to this rite as a kind of trick or game to indicate he doesn't believe it actually works.

14. Zhang Zai, "Western Inscription," 2. https://ctext.org/wiki.pl?if=en&chapter=847353.

15. *Complete Works of Wang Yangming*, "Knowledge and Action 3," 100–101. https://ctext.org/wiki.pl?if=en&chapter=915813#p348. Xu's quotation deviates slightly.

16. In Buddhism, this refers to the vow a bodhisattva makes to liberate all sentient beings.

17. Also called final nirvana, the ultimate stage of Buddhist awakening when a living being has exhausted his or her remaining karma.

18. Xu makes a verb out of "human life" (*renshenghua* 人生化) in a way that is impossible to translate into grammatical English.

19. The text has *quanli*權利 (rights) rather than *quanli* 權力 (power), but the latter fits the context better.

20. 超升 *chaosheng* in Buddhism also means the ascension of a person to the Pure Land, and given the Buddhist language throughout this paragraph, Xu is probably playing on that meaning as well.

21. Dizang (Skt. Kṣitigarbha) is one of the most important bodhisattvas in East Asian Buddhism. According to the *Sutra of the Original Vow of the Bodhisattva Dizang* (T13.412) he vowed to save all beings from hell before becoming a Buddha.

22. As above, the text has *quanli*權利 (rights) rather than *quanli* 權力 (power), but Xu appears to mean the latter.

23. Xu seems to be hinting obliquely at the president of the Republic of China, Jiang Jieshi.

24. An allusion to *Analects* 9.17 and *Mengzi* 4B18.

25. The "kingly way" is a common phrase in the *Mengzi*; the latter phrase does not appear.

26. 牟宗三 (1909–1995), another major New Ruist philosopher, friend of Xu, and frequent contributor to *Democratic Review*. He is often mentioned in Xu's writings.

Chapter 9

1. The Platonic Forms.

2. A reference to Hegelian philosophy.

3. A hint at utilitarianism.

4. A traditional way of referring to the entire body.

5. *Mengzi* 6A15.

6. Wang, *The Classic of Changes*, 67; slightly modified.

7. Xu is playing on the Chinese word for "metaphysics," *xing er shang xue* 形而上學, literally the study of what is above or beyond form. In opposition to those who treat the heart-mind as something metaphysical beyond the physiological body (this is probably directed to Mou Zongsan and Tang Junyi, among others), Xu insists it is part of the physical person.

8. The word here is also *xin* 心 but he clearly means the physical organ specifically.

9. *Mengzi* 2A6.

10. A common saying in Chinese Buddhist texts, which Xu could have drawn from any number of sources.

11. Zhou Yutong 周予同 (1898–1981) was professor of classics at Fudan University in Shanghai. His edition of Jiang Fan's *Records of Masters of Han Learning* was first published in 1934.

12. Jiang, *Records of Masters of Han Learning*, 1:10. Xu's quote elides the part where Zhou says Lu's philosophy is a form of idealism.

13. See the introduction for Xu's views on religion.

14. *Analects* 7.30, 12.1.

15. A technical term in Chan Buddhism meaning fully manifest and present already, usually with the additional connotation of manifesting in everyday phenomena.

16. *Mean* 1. https://ctext.org/liji/zhong-yong#n10263.

17. *Mengzi* 7A21.

18. See the introduction on internal experience.

19. Zhuangzi, "The Human World," 2. https://ctext.org/zhuangzi/man-in-the-world-associated-with#n41958.

20. *Zhuangzi*, "The Great Ancestral Master," 9. https://ctext.org/zhuangzi/great-and-most-honoured-master#n2760.

21. Xu published this book in 1966, so this section must be a later addition to the essay when it was revised for publication in book form.

22. Zhang Yanyuan, *Record of Famous Painters through the Ages*, "Later Tang," 31. https://ctext.org/wiki.pl?if=gb&chapter=722335#p33.

23. Ibid., "On Painting Landscapes, Trees, and Rocks," 1. https://ctext.org/wiki.pl?if=gb&chapter=129615#p28.

24. *Xunzi*, "Undoing Fixation." https://ctext.org/xunzi/jie-bi#n12613.

25. See the introduction for Xu's views on religion.

26. To say the least, not a very accurate characterization of much of Buddhism.

27. A phrase that appears in many Buddhist texts, such as *Exposition of the Diamond Sutra*, X25.508, 868c.

28. A phrase that appears in many Buddhist texts, such as *New Commentary on the Flower Garland Sutra*, T36.1739, 740a.

29. A phrase that appears in many Buddhist texts, such as *Urging Entry to the Gate of Chan*, T48.2024, 1098a.

30. *Mengzi* 7B35. https://ctext.org/mengzi/jin-xin-ii#n1875. The original text has "nurturing the heart-mind."

31. *Laozi* 3.

32. *Mengzi* 6A15.

33. His comment on *Mengzi* 6A15 in Zhu Xi's *Collected Commentaries on the Four Books*. https://ctext.org/si-shu-zhang-ju-ji-zhu/jin-xin-zhang-ju-shang#n90374.

34. Cheng and Cheng, *Collected Works of the Cheng Brothers*, 15. The saying is not attributed to Cheng Hao.

35. *Analects* 12.1.

36. See notes 30 and 31.

37. Wen, *The Child Heroes*, 124.

38. *Mengzi* 7A38.

39. Ibid. 2A2.

40. One of Wang Yangming's key doctrines. One important discussion of it is in *Complete Works of Wang Yangming*, "Record of Knowledge and Action 1," 8. https://ctext.org/wiki.pl?if=en&chapter=915813#p10.

41. "Real world" is something of a technical term for Xu. It means the world of action and interpersonal relations, as opposed to thought and speculation.

42. See note 15.

43. A paraphrase of Cheng and Cheng, *Collected Works of the Cheng Brothers*, 1.

44. See the introduction to chapter 4 for more on this term.

45. *Complete Works of Wang Yangming*, "Record of Quieting the Heart-mind 1," 495. https://ctext.org/wiki.pl?if=gb&chapter=308795#p1788.

Chapter 10

1. This is found in Book III of the *Republic*, but there Socrates says that it is a useful lie, which Xu ignores. https://www.gutenberg.org/files/1497/1497-h/1497-h.htm.

2. "Only the very wisest and the most foolish do not change" (*Analects* 17.3).

3. *Analects* 12.1.

4. Ibid. 15.39.

5. Ibid. 7.2, 7.34.

6. The Grand Unity is a classical political and social ideal, described in *Record of Ritual*, "The Revolutions of Ritual," 1. https://ctext.org/liji/li-yun#n9872.

7. *Analects* 13.3.

8. *Analects* 17.5.

9. Xu is off by a few years. It was defended by John Locke in his *Second Treatise on Government* published in 1689.

10. Recorded in *Records of the Historian*, "Grand Historian's Preface," 16. https://ctext.org/shiji/tai-shi-gong-zi-xu#n9286.

11. *Mengzi* 3B10.

12. *Xunzi*. "The Way of the Minister," 2, https://ctext.org/xunzi/chen-dao#n12452; "The Way of the Minister," 9, https://ctext.org/xunzi/chen-dao#n12459.

13. Xu wrote this seventeen years before John Rawls published *A Theory of Justice*. The similarity is startling.

14. There is no such quote in the *Analects*, though rulers are generally urged to employ the virtuous.

15. "Subjective" here does not mean relative or arbitrary at all, but only that the term was based on an individual's moral achievement, not the class into which they were born.

16. Xu uses the Chinese translation for the four *varnas*, the foundational divisions of traditional Indian society.

17. *Analects* 7.5, 17.5.

18. This phrase appears in many Ruist texts. It is attributed to Kongzi in the *Mean* 20. https://ctext.org/liji/zhong-yong#n10280.

19. *Analects* 1.7.

20. *Elder Dai's Record of Ritual*, "Ruler's Words," 7. https://ctext.org/da-dai-li-ji/zhu-yan#n44439.

21. *Documents*, "Great Declaration," 1. https://ctext.org/shang-shu/great-declaration-i#n21247.

22. *Gongyang Tradition*, Duke Yin 3rd year, 3. https://ctext.org/gongyang-zhuan/yin-gong-san-nian#n56466.

23. I have not found any attribution of this phrase to Kongzi.

24. The latter phrase is attributed to Yin Chun in Zhu Xi's *Collected Commentaries on the Four Books*, *Analects* 3.19. https://ctext.org/si-shu-zhang-ju-ji-zhu/ba-yi-di-san#n89666. I have not found any instance of the former phrase.

25. *Mengzi* 2B2.

26. As a historical claim, this is dubious.

27. Xu's text has "each person," but the civil service exam system was always restricted to men.

28. *Mengzi* 5B9.

29. The term *comprador* is of Portuguese origin and referred to local brokers or managers who worked with European firms in East Asia, selling their products in China. Xu's metaphor thus suggests someone who makes money or derives other benefit from importing a foreign culture.

Chapter 11

1. Reprinted in *Ruist Political Thought and Democracy, Freedom and Human Rights*, 193–202.

2. "Natural" here means something like "biological"; that is, the demands of life as a physical being. It is not "natural" as opposed to "cultural."

3. Reprinted in *Ruist Political Thought and Democracy, Freedom and Human Rights*, 133–55.

4. Not a direct quote, but the idea is expressed in Xiao, *History of Chinese Political Thought, Volume One*, 110–11.

5. *Record of Ritual*, "Record of the Model," 13. https://ctext.org/liji/biao-ji#n10308.

6. Ibid., 21. https://ctext.org/liji/biao-ji#n10317.

7. *Analects* 13.9.

8. Ibid. 6.22.

9. *Odes* #230. https://ctext.org/book-of-poetry/mian-man.

10. *Odes* #112. https://ctext.org/book-of-poetry/fa-tan

11. Dong, *Luxuriant Gems of the Spring and Autumn*, 316–18; slightly modified.

12. Zhou Dunyi, *Explanation of the Depiction of the Great Ultimate*, 13. https://ctext.org/wiki.pl?if=gb&chapter=870107.

13. In Song-Ming and later Ruism, *qi* means roughly physical stuff, matter-energy.

14. *Mengzi* 6A8. Here, *qi* is used in its older sense of breath or air.

15. Dai, "On the Good," *Complete Works*, 6:19.

16. Dai, "Letter in Response to Admitted Scholar Peng Chongchu," *Complete Works* 6:362.

17. *Mengzi* 7A21. Xu's text has ± instead of ±.

18. Ibid. 6A10.

19. Dai, "Letter in Response to Admitted Scholar Peng Chongchu," *Complete Works* 6:358.

20. *Mengzi* 6A10.

21. Ibid. 7A38.

22. Dai, "On Reading the Discussion of Human Nature in the 'Appended Phrases' of the *Changes*," *Complete Works* 6:351.

23. A twist on a traditional saying: "When Ruism and Buddhism are combined, both are perfected; when they are separated, both are injured."

24. Qian, *Explanations of the Four Books*, 1:65.

25. Ibid., 1:66.

26. *Analects* 9.18, 15.13.

27. Paraphrased from ibid. 7.2.

28. Ibid. 17.24.

29. Ibid. 13.24.

30. See note 25.

31. *Analects* 1.3.

32. Ibid. 13.18.

33. A fifth-century CE collection of anecdotes and conversations compiled by Liu Yiqing 劉義慶.

34. Qian, *Explanations of the Four Books*, 1:66.

35. Paraphrasing *Mengzi* 1B5.

36. Qian, *Explanations of the Four Books*, 1:69.

37. *Great Learning* 12. https://ctext.org/liji/da-xue#n10393.

38. *Mingjia* 名家, also known as the school of names.

39. Wang, *The Classic of Changes*, 130.

40. Zhuangzi, "Discussing the Equality of Things," 11. https://ctext.org/zhuangzi/adjustment-of-controversies#n2729.

41. Both were noted for their beauty.

42. Zhuangzi, "Discussing the Equality of Things," 11. https://ctext.org/zhuangzi/adjustment-of-controversies#n2729.

43. Zhuangzi, "All Under Heaven," 1. https://ctext.org/zhuangzi/tian-xia#n3014. Most scholars doubt this chapter was composed by Zhuangzi.

44. *Complete Works of Wang Yangming*, "Knowledge and Action 3," 77. https://ctext.org/wiki.pl?if=en&chapter=915813#p325.

45. Innate moral awareness (*liangzhi* 良知) is Wang's term for the faculty that recognizes good and evil and hence constitutes the basis for moral judgments.

46. *Complete Works of Wang Yangming*, "Quieting the Heart-mind 10," 32. https://ctext.org/wiki.pl?if=en&chapter=308795#p2053.

47. A Neo-Ruist term meaning the way the world should function.

48. A phrase found in many Buddhist texts.

49. *Sutra Collecting the Buddha's Past Actions*, T3.190, 733a.

50. I have not found this specific phrase in any Buddhist text.

51. These are important terms in Neo-Ruism. They come from *Documents*, "Counsels of Yu the Great," 13. https://ctext.org/shang-shu/counsels-of-the-great-yu#n21076.

52. *Analects* 12.1.

53. *Complete Works of Wang Yangming*, "Knowledge and Action 1," 59. https://ctext.org/wiki.pl?if=en&chapter=915813#p61.

54. See the introduction for more on embodied recognition.

55. See chapter 8.

56. Presumably 陳康 (1902–1992), professor of philosophy at National Taiwan University. His primary field was ancient Greek philosophy.

57. Chen, "On the Question of Unity of Thought," 5.

58. Ibid., 7.

59. Ibid.

60. Ibid.

61. Ibid.

62. Ibid., 5.

63. See "Why Oppose Liberalism?" chapter 12 for more.

64. Xu presumably is referring to Tito's split with the Soviet Union.

65. Wang famously claimed that no one who truly knows the good fails to act on it. See "The Culture of the Heart-Mind," chapter 9, for more.

66. See chapter 8.

67. *Chūōkōron* 中央公論, a Japanese literary magazine.

68. Chen, "On the Question of Unity of Thought," 7.

69. See chapter 4.

70. Feng Youlan 馮友蘭 (1895–1990) was another contemporary Ruist philosopher, best known for his *History of Chinese Philosophy*. He remained in mainland China after the revolution. The source of this comment is unknown.

71. Allusion to a slogan popularized by Hu Shi, "overthrow the Ruist shop." Chen mentions it in his article.

Chapter 12

1. Sun's main political idea, the three principles are literally people's power, the nation, and people's livelihood, or democracy, nationalism, and livelihood or welfare. See Sun, *Three Principles*.

2. A quote from the poem "Thoughts on the Newly Arrived Summer" by Lu You (1125–1210).

3. The canonical history of the Western Han dynasty written by Ban Gu and Ban Zhao, completed in 111 CE. It is not clear which annotations Xu means, but it does not appear in the *Han History* text itself. It does appear in some other works from the Eastern Han.

4. *Records of the Historian*, "Grand Historian's Preface," 16. https://ctext.org/shiji/tai-shi-gong-zi-xu#n9286. There it is attributed to Dong Zhongshu.

5. *Analects* 12.1, 15.36.

6. Ibid. 1.3.

7. Ibid. 13.27.

8. Ibid. 5.11, 9.26.

9. Ibid. 8.7.

10. *Mengzi* 2A2.

11. *Analects* 8.2. The quote deviates slightly.

12. Ibid. 5.25.

13. *Mengzi* 2A2, 4B2.

14. Xu appears to have in mind the rejection of tradition, particularly around the May Fourth period.

15. The Great Proscription erupted out of a conflict between eunuchs and regularly appointed bureaucrats. The eunuchs had the support of the emperor and succeeded in having many of their rival officials killed and many more banned from office for life. See Twitchett and Loewe, *Cambridge History of China, Vol. 1*, 328–30.

16. French author Andre Gide (1869–1951), winner of the 1947 Nobel Prize in literature, and British philosopher Bertrand Russell (1872–1970), one of the founders of analytic philosophy and winner of the 1950 Nobel Prize in literature.

17. Sun expressed related ideas throughout his second lecture on the people's rights. In particular, see Sun, *The Three Principles of the People*, 122.

18. "Imperial court" is used as a metaphor for the government.

19. 張其昀 (1901–1985) was minister of education of the Republic of China from 1954–58. He attempted to institute educational policies to promote loyalty to the GMD. I thank Huang Chun-chieh for this information. For more on the general efforts by the GMD to encourage nationalism and anticommunism, see Lee, "Chinese Education and Intellectuals," 140–42.

20. A city on the west coast of Taiwan about eighty miles southwest of Taibei.

21. 胡秋原 (1910–2004), an author and politician in Taiwan.

22. Huang Chun-chieh suggested to me that this was offered to him as a quid pro quo: he would get a trip to New York at government expense in exchange for dropping his criticisms.

Chapter 13

1. *Analects* 15.29.

2. Reading 鑽 instead of 攢.

3. See the introduction for more on this idea.

4. Xu refers to the traditional classification of thought into distinct lineages or schools, as they have been called: Ruism (*Rujia*), Daoism (*Daojia*), Legalism (*Fajia*), and so on.

5. Something close to this idea can be found in Cassirer, *An Essay on Man*, 70–71.

6. If this is indeed a quote, the source is unknown.

7. A trope common in martial arts stories, in which a book with some unique fighting technique is written in invisible ink that can only be revealed and read through a secret process.

8. Xiao, *History of Chinese Political Thought, Volume One*, 160, 163. Bracketed text in the original. Slightly modified to use Mengzi instead of Mencius. Other quotations from Xiao in this chapter are also so modified.

9. *Mengzi* 1A7.

10. See chapter 11.

11. *Mengzi* 5A5.

12. Ibid. 2B10.

13. Ibid. 1B8, 1B12, 1B6, 5B9.

14. Ibid. 3B5.

15. Ibid. 1A6, 1A7.

16. Xiao, *History of Chinese Political Thought, Volume One*, 161.

17. *Mengzi* 1B7.

18. Ibid. 4A9.

19. *Great Learning*, 12. https://ctext.org/liji/da-xue#n10393.

20. *Record of Ritual*, "The Revolutions of Ritual," 1. https://ctext.org/liji/li-yun#n9872.

21. The Universal Declaration of Human Rights was adopted by the General Assembly in 1948.

22. Han Feizi was a major Legalist philosopher. Li Si and Zhao Gao were officials in the Qin government. Fusu and Huhai were two heirs of the first emperor of Qin.

23. *Mengzi* 4A1.

24. Ibid. 1A4.

25. Ibid. 2A6, 4A1, 4B2.

26. Ibid. 4A1.

27. Ibid. 4A1, 2A6.

28. Ibid. 4A20.

29. Ibid. 7A21.

30. Ibid. 4B29.

31. Ibid. 1A7. The precise quote only appears once, but Xu probably means Mengzi frequently expressed this sentiment.

32. Ibid. 1A3, 1A7, and 7A22. Mulberry leaves were used to feed silkworms, so this meant providing each household with the means to produce silk.

33. Ibid. 2A1.

34. Ibid. 1A3, 1A7.

35. Ibid. 1B5, 2A7.

36. *Mean* 21. https://ctext.org/liji/zhong-yong#n10281.

37. I omit citations of earlier glosses on "archery" and "caring" which Xu argues were mistaken.

38. *Mengzi* 1A3.

39. Ibid. 1A5.

40. Ibid. 2B5.

41. Ibid. 1A5.

42. Ibid. 4A1.

43. *Analects* 2.3.

44. *Mengzi* 4A1.

45. Paraphrase of *Records of the Historian*, "The Grand Historian's Preface," 17. https://ctext.org/shiji/tai-shi-gong-zi-xu#n9287.

46. *Mean* 20. https://ctext.org/liji/zhong-yong#n10280.

47. Ibid. 21. https://ctext.org/liji/zhong-yong#n10281.

Chapter 14

1. Reprinted in Fairbank, "New Thinking about China."—Tr.

2. Tao, "A Reexamination of John King Fairbank."—Tr.

3. John K. Fairbank, *U.S. Policy with Respect to Mainland China*, 164–65.—Tr.

4. A few of us have been doing considerable research and exposition on the significance of this aspect of Chinese culture over the years.

5. The Cultural Revolution had begun earlier in the year—Tr.

6. 陳立夫 (1900–2001) was minister of education from 1938 to 1944—Tr.

7. John King Fairbank (1907–1991) was an influential professor of Chinese history at Harvard. During World War II he worked for U.S. government offices in China—Tr.

8. From State Affairs Council 1943 on international relations, 38, cited in Liang Hejun, "Did Fairbank Change Mao? Did Mao Change Washington?" *Zhengxin Daily News*, June 28 [1966, 2].

9. Cited in Cao Min, "An Examination of Mr. Tao Baichuan's 'Reexamination of John King Fairbank,'" *China Magazine* 4, no. 6 (June 1966): 33. [Cao took these quotes from Tao Baichuan's original article: see next note. Instead of translating Xu's quotation, I have quoted from Fairbank's original testimony, Fairbank, *U.S. Policy with Respect to Mainland China*, 99–100.—Tr.]

10. Tao Baichuan 陶百川 (1903–2002) was a GMD politician who occupied several government posts. In his newspaper article, Tao relates how he attempted to set up a meeting with Fairbank to discuss the U.S. government's China policy, but he was unable to. He says that Fairbank sent him a copy of Fairbank's testimony to the Senate Foreign Relations Committee on China. This appears to have been the source of the quotes in Tao's article attributed to Fairbank, but Tao does not specify. Tao Baichuan, "A Reexamination of John King Fairbank's Public Opinions on China 費正清對華言論的再檢討," *Zhengxin Daily News*, June 6, 1966, 1—Tr.

11. The ruler traditionally occupied the north position in the hall, facing south. Hence, "facing south" is a metonym for occupying the ruler's position—Tr.

12. Xing Bing, *Commentary and Subcommentary on the* Analects, 2.1. https://ctext.org/lunyu-zhushu/wei-zheng#n92265—Tr.

13. *Collected Comments on the Four Books*, Analects 2.1. https://ctext.org/si-shu-zhang-ju-ji-zhu/wei-zheng-di-er#n89622—Tr.

14. Xing Bing, *Commentary and Subcommentary on the* Analects, 2.1. https://ctext.org/lunyu-zhushu/wei-zheng#n92265—Tr.

15. The first sentence is indeed from *Collected Comments on the Four Books, Analects* 2.1. https://ctext.org/si-shu-zhang-ju-ji-zhu/wei-zheng-di-er#n89622. The second is instead found in *Categorized Conversations of Master Zhu,* "Analects 5," 13. https://ctext.org/zhuzi-yulei/23#n588981—Tr.

16. *Categorized Conversations of Master Zhu,* "Analects 5," 13. https://ctext.org/zhuzi-yulei/23#n588981—Tr.

17. Durrant, Li, and Schaberg, *Zuo Tradition,* 1127—Tr.

18. The line statements were probably complete by the early or middle Warring States period. See my *A History of Chinese Theories of Human Nature* ch. 7. [The quote is from Wang, *The Classic of Changes,* 287—Tr.]

19. The *Great Learning* was probably complete around the time of the Qin unification.

20. *Great Learning* 2. https://ctext.org/liji/da-xue#n10383—Tr.

21. This might represent coercive measures generally—Tr.

22. *The Elder Dai's Record of Ritual,* "Examination of Ritual," 2–4. https://ctext.org/da-dai-li-ji/li-cha#n44478. The quote is *Analects* 12.13—Tr.

23. In the *Analects,* we find, "If a person is not benevolent, what has he to do with ritual? If a person is not benevolent, what has he to do with music?" and "[The gentleman] makes rightness his substance and puts it into practice by means of ritual" [3.3, 15.18]. These passages regulate ritual with benevolence and rightness.

24. *Record of Ritual,* "Record of Education," 1. https://ctext.org/liji/xue-ji#n10099—Tr.

25. These phrases occur in a number of Ruist texts—Tr.

26. See *A History of Chinese Theories of Human Nature,* ch. 4.

27. *Odes* #260. https://ctext.org/book-of-poetry/zheng-min—Tr.

28. Zheng, *Zheng's Notes on the Mao Odes,* 144—Tr.

29. The Three Dynasties are the Xia, Shang, and Zhou—Tr.

30. *Mean* 13. https://ctext.org/liji/zhong-yong#n10273—Tr.

31. *Great Learning* 12. https://ctext.org/liji/da-xue#n10393—Tr.

32. *Great Learning* 12. https://ctext.org/liji/da-xue#n10393. Xu's move here is clever: if the ruler can use himself as a standard for the people, due to their common humanity, then the people can also be the standard for the ruler—Tr.

33. *Laozi* 37, 48—Tr.

34. Meaning the ruler—Tr.

35. Translation from Harris and Shen, *The Shenzi Fragments,* 112., slightly modified to accord better with Xu's interpretation—Tr.

36. Two other Legalist thinkers—Tr.

37. In *Records of the Historian,* Laozi and Han Feizi's biographies are in the same chapter. [Sima Qian is the author of *Records of the Historian,* the first great historical work in China—Tr.]

38. *Categorized Conversations of Master Zhu,* "Analects 5," 5. https://ctext.org/zhuzi-yulei/23#n588973—Tr.

39. Ibid. 6. https://ctext.org/zhuzi-yulei/23#n588974—Tr.

40. See section II—Tr.

41. See section II—Tr.

42. Xing Bing, *Commentary and Subcommentary on the* Analects, 15.5. https://ctext.org/lunyu-zhushu/wei-ling-gong#n93033—Tr.

43. *Collected Comments on the Four Books,* "Analects," 13.15. https://ctext.org/si-shu-zhang-ju-ji-zhu/zi-lu-di-shi-san#n89944—Tr.

44. *Mean* 6. https://ctext.org/liji/zhong-yong#n47447. The bracketed additions are Xu's—Tr.

45. See section III—Tr.

46. *Analects* 7.34—Tr.

47. The *Mean* is divided into upper and lower chapters. The upper was composed by Zisi; the lower by his disciples. What I quoted here is from the upper chapter. For a detailed examination, see *A History of Chinese Theories of Human Nature,* ch. 5.

48. *Mean* 21. https://ctext.org/liji/zhong-yong#n10281—Tr.

49. See *A History of Chinese Theories of Human Nature,* ch. 9.

50. The five phases are wood, metal, fire, water, and earth. See Dong, *Luxuriant Gems,* 450–55 for their role in his thought—Tr.

51. Ban, *Han History,* 56.2502.—Tr.

52. Literally, make dikes and embankments—Tr.

53. Ban, *Han History,* 56.2503–04—Tr. There are a couple of errors in Xu's quote; translation follows the original.

54. Ban, *Han History,* 56.2521—Tr.

55. Ibid. 56.2502–2503—Tr.

56. Ibid. 56.2502—Tr.

57. Fan, *Later Han History,* 41.1400—Tr.

58. I.e., to have one political authority—Tr.

59. *New Discourses,* 6. https://ctext.org/wiki.pl?if=gb&chapter=458238#p7—Tr.

60. A following phrase, "had deep knowledge and far-reaching thought," is missing from Xu's text—Tr.

61. This is referring to the Western Han. He is taking liberties for the sake of making a point, not giving the facts.

62. Fan, *Later Han History,* 27.937–38—Tr.

63. Reading 貫 for 實—Tr.

64. Xu's remark looks ironic in light of recent developments in China's relations with its neighbors—Tr.

65. Xu probably means the demotions of officials who opposed the Cultural Revolution, notably Liu Shaoqi and Deng Xiaoping—Tr.

Chapter 15

1. Tang had died in 1978.

2. I have used this to translate *ganfa* 感發, which might be more verbosely rendered "a feeling which must be expressed." It is an important ingredient in writing, as Xu makes clear, but I wanted to illustrate that it is a specific kind of inspiration, which comes from the author's deep feelings being aroused by something.

3. 文選, a famous anthology of Chinese literature from about the third century BCE to the fifth century CE compiled by Xiao Tong 蕭統, son of Emperor Wu of the Liang dynasty.

4. Xu here uses the Buddhist term *wuji* 無記 which refers to a dharma that is neither good nor evil.

5. Paraphrasing *Zhuangzi*, "Responses of Emperors and Kings, 6. https://ctext.org/zhuangzi/normal-course-for-rulers-and-kings#n2768.

6. *Platform Sutra of the Sixth Patriarch*, T48.2008, 348b.

7. *Zhuangzi*, "Responses of Emperors and Kings, 6. https://ctext.org/zhuangzi/normal-course-for-rulers-and-kings#n2768.

8. *Platform Sutra of the Sixth Patriarch*, T48.2008, 349a. As Philip Yampolsky discusses, this phrase does not appear in the Dunhuang manuscript of *The Platform Sutra* and must have been a later addition. Yampolsky, *The Platform Sutra*, 94.

9. *Zhuangzi*, "Responses of Emperors and Kings, 6. https://ctext.org/zhuangzi/normal-course-for-rulers-and-kings#n2768.

10. 賈誼, c. 200–169 BCE, a famous Han dynasty author.

11. 班固 32–92 CE, author of the *Han History*.

12. Paraphrashing *Zhuangzi*, "Gengsang Chu," 16. https://ctext.org/zhuangzi/geng-sang-chu#n2901.

13. The Great Proscription erupted out of a conflict between eunuchs and regularly appointed bureaucrats. The eunuchs had the support of the emperor and succeeded in having many of their rival officials killed and many more banned from office for life. See Twitchett and Loewe, *Cambridge History of China, Vol. 1*, 328–30. On the conflict between Cao Shuang and Sima Yi, which eventually resulted in Cao Shuang's execution, see Dien and Knapp, *Cambridge History of China, Vol. 2*, 82–83. The Disturbances of the Eight Princes was a series of political struggles from 290 to 311 involving eight princes of the Sima family. For details see Dien and Knapp, 92–94.

14. *Xuanxue* 玄學, a philosophical school that focused more on abstract metaphysics than practical politics.

15. Parenthetical comments in quotations are Xu's own insertions.

16. 何晏 c. 195–249 CE. A major mysterious learning thinker and author of an important commentary on the *Analects*.

17. *The Literary Heart-mind Carves Dragons*, "Elucidating Poetry," 3–4. https://ctext.org/wenxin-diaolong/ming-shi.

18. Ibid., "Spiritual Thought," 2. https://ctext.org/wenxin-diaolong/juan-liu#n108353.

19. I can only speculate that a quotation was left out in typesetting. No quote from *Zhuangzi* follows.

20. *The Literary Heart-mind Carves Dragons*, "Spiritual Thought," 3. https://ctext.org/wenxin-diaolong/shen-si#n108354.

21. 陸機, 261–303. *On Literature* is his best-known piece, a rhapsody on the principles of composition.

22. *The Literary Heart-mind Carves Dragons*, "Nurturing *Qi*," 1. https://ctext.org/wenxin-diaolong/yang-qi#n108459.

23. Ibid., 2. https://ctext.org/wenxin-diaolong/yang-qi#n108460.

24. A Daoist technique of breath control that purported to achieve breathing without the mouth or nose, like an embryo in the womb.

25. *The Literary Heart-mind Carves Dragons*, "Nurturing *Qi*," 5–6. https://ctext.org/wenxin-diaolong/yang-qi#n108464.

26. Xu has 元 here, while most texts have 玄.

27. *The Literary Heart-mind Carves Dragons*, "Nurturing *Qi*," 7. https://ctext.org/wenxin-diaolong/yang-qi#n108465.

28. Ibid., "The Natural World," 4. https://ctext.org/wenxin-diaolong/wu-se#n108495.

29. Su Shi, "Sending Off Master Can Liao." https://fanti.dugushici.com/ancient_proses/71322.

30. Xiao Gang, "A Warning to [My Son] Daxin, Duke of Dangyang," *Complete Writings of Liang*, 11.3. https://ctext.org/wiki.pl?if=gb&chapter=557314.

31. From a letter Li E submitted to Emperor Wen of Sui. Wei, "Biography of Li E," *Sui History*, 66.1544.

32. Liu, *The Literary Heart-mind Carves Dragons*, "The Source of the Way," 1. https://ctext.org/wenxin-diaolong/yuan-dao#n108162.

33. *Analects* 6.23.

34. Liu, *The Literary Heart-mind Carves Dragons*, "Spiritual Thought," 2. https://ctext.org/wenxin-diaolong/juan-liu#n108353.

35. Ibid., "Honoring the Classics," 3. https://ctext.org/wenxin-diaolong/zong-jing#n108176.

36. Ibid., 5. https://ctext.org/wenxin-diaolong/zong-jing#n108178.

37. *Xunzi*, "Undoing Fixation." https://ctext.org/xunzi/jie-bi.

38. Liu, *The Literary Heart-mind Carves Dragons*, "Form and Nature," 3. https://ctext.org/wenxin-diaolong/ti-xing#n108358.

39. Many of these terms for writing genres have no close English equivalent, and translations should be considered approximate.

40. Liu, *The Literary Heart-mind Carves Dragons*, "Honoring the Classics," 4. https://ctext.org/wenxin-diaolong/zong-jing#n108177.

41. Ibid., "Understanding Change," 2. https://ctext.org/wenxin-diaolong/tong-bian#n108367. I skip several additional quotes in which Liu criticizes contemporary writing.

42. Ibid., "Ordering of Talent," 9. https://ctext.org/wenxin-diaolong/cai-lve#n108506.

43. Ibid., "Fixing the Propensities," 7. https://ctext.org/wenxin-diaolong/ding-shi.

44. I've skipped another long quotation here.

45. 韓愈 Han Yu was a noted Tang dynasty writer and one of the pioneers of the return to Ruism.

46. Ouyang and Song, "Biographies of Writers," *New Tang History*, 201.5725.

47. 蕭穎士 707–758; 李華, 714–774; 獨孤及, 726–777; 權德輿, 759–818; all Tang dynasty writers and officials.

48. The dynasties from Qin through Sui.

49. Su, "Stele at the Temple of Han, Lord of Literature." https://fanti.dugushici.com/ancient_proses/71722.

50. Han, "Letter in Reply to Li Yi." https://fanti.dugushici.com/ancient_proses/72260.

51. Skipping another long quote

52. "Rivers and lakes" is a colloquial term for being on the margins of society

53. Fan, "Memorial to Yueyang Tower." https://fanti.dugushici.com/ancient_proses/47517. Fan Zhongyan 范仲淹 (989–1052) was a prominent Song official and scholar.

54. Reading 修 for 休.

55. Wen, *The Child Heroes*, 124.

56. Another name for Qing dynasty evidential studies, which developed during the Qianlong and Jiaqing periods.

57. The Tongcheng school was a group of writers associated with Tongcheng in Anhui. It was noted for fidelity to traditional Ruist principles and opposition to excessively flowery writing.

58. A pejorative term for art and literature that focused on extolling the achievements of socialism in China.

59. 諸子, the Chinese bibliographical category that includes philosophical works.

60. Xianfeng reigned 1850–1861, Guangxu 1875–1908. Xu seems to mean roughly the second half of the nineteenth century.

61. A play on the expression "to be cut up and boiled in a cauldron," meaning as a punishment.

62. Crow Terrace was a nickname for the imperial censorate, which prosecuted the case. Su Shi was the most prominent of many accused of lèse majesté. For more details see Hartman, "The Inquisition against Su Shih."

63. "Sent to [My Brother] Ziyou from Prison." Translation from Fuller, *The Road to East Slope*, 247.

64. A district in Hubei.

65. A city in Guangdong.

66. A district on Hainan Island.

67. I omit another quote from a poem of Su's.

Bibliography

Works by Xu Fuguan

Xu, Fuguan. *A History of Chinese Theories of Human Nature: The Pre-Qin Period* 中國人性論史: 先秦篇. Taibei: Commercial Press, 1990.

———. *Between Academia and Politics* 學術與政治之間. Taibei: Student Books, 1985.

———. *Miscellaneous Writings of Xu Fuguan: Reflections* 徐復觀雜文: 記所思. Taibei: Times Publishing, 1980.

———. "Old Dreams—Tomorrow 舊夢.明天." In *Literary Records of Xu Fuguan: Literature and Art* 徐復觀文錄: 文學與藝術, Vol. 3. Taibei: Huanyu, 1971.

———. *Ruist Political Thought and Democracy, Freedom and Human Rights* 儒家政治思想與民主自由人權. Edited by Xiao Xinyi蕭欣義. Revised edition. Taibei: Student Books, 1988.

———. *Sequel to Collected Essays on Chinese Literature* 中國文論文集續篇. Taibei: Student Books, 1982.

———. "The Culture of the Heart-Mind 心的文化." In *Collected Essays on Chinese Intellectual History* 中國思想史論集. Taibei: Student Books, 1988.

———. *The Finest Selected Writings of Xu Fuguan* 徐復觀文錄選粹. Edited by Xiao Xinyi 蕭欣義. Taibei: Student Books, 1980.

———. *Wars of Words and Translations* 論戰與譯述. Taibei: Zhiwen, 1982.

Traditional Chinese Sources

Analects 論語. Chinese Text Project. https://ctext.org/analects. 2019.

Ban, Gu 班固. *Han History* 漢書. 12 vols. Beijing: Zhonghua shuju, 1975.

Categorized Conversations of Master Zhu 朱子語類. Edited by Li Jingde 黎靖德. Chinese Text Project. https://ctext.org/zhuzi-yulei. 2019.

Cheng, Hao 程顥, and Cheng Yi 程頤. *Collected Works of the Cheng Brothers* 二程集. Edited by Wang Xiaoyu 王孝魚. Second edition. 2 vols. 理学丛书. Beijing: Zhonghua shuju, 2004.

Collected Commentaries on the Four Books 四書章句集注. Edited by Zhu Xi 朱熹. Chinese Text Project. https://ctext.org/si-shu-zhang-ju-ji-zhu. 2019.

Dai, Zhen 戴震. *Complete Works of Dai Zhen* 戴震全書. Edited by Zhang Dainian 張岱年. Vol. 6. 7 vols. 安徽古籍丛书. Hefei, China: Huangshan shushe, 1995.

Documents 尚書. Chinese Text Project. https://ctext.org/shang-shu. 2019.

Dong, Zhongshu 董仲舒. *Luxuriant Gems of the Spring and Autumn*. Translated by Sarah A. Queen and John S. Major. Translations from the Asian Classics. New York: Columbia University Press, 2016.

Durrant, Stephen W., Wai-yee Li, and David Schaberg, eds. *Zuo Tradition | Zuozhuan: Commentary on the "Spring and Autumn Annals."* 3 vols. Classics of Chinese Thought. Seattle: University of Washington Press, 2016.

Elder Dai's Record of Ritual 大戴禮記. Chinese Text Project. https://ctext.org/da-dai-li-ji. 2019.

Fan, Ye 范曄. *Later Han History* 後漢書. Beijing: Zhonghua shuju, 1975.

Fan, Zhongyan 范仲淹. "Memorial to Yueyang Tower 岳陽樓記." Chinese Ancient Poetry. https://fanti.dugushici.com/ancient_proses/47517. 2021.

Gongyang Tradition 公羊傳. Chinese Text Project. https://ctext.org/gongyang-zhuan. 2019.

Great Learning 大學. Chinese Text Project. https://ctext.org/liji/da-xue. 2019.

Guanyinzi 關尹子. Chinese Text Project. https://ctext.org/wenshi-zhenjing. 2019.

Han Feizi. *Han Feizi* 韓非子. Chinese Text Project. https://ctext.org/hanfeizi. 2019.

Han, Yu 韓愈. "Letter in Reply to Li Yi 答李翊書." Chinese Ancient Poetry. https://fanti.dugushici.com/ancient_proses/72260. 2021.

Harris, Eirik Lang, and Shen Dao 慎到. *The Shenzi Fragments: A Philosophical Analysis and Translation*. Translations from the Asian Classics. New York: Columbia University Press, 2016.

Huan, Tan 桓譚. *New Discourses* 新論. Chinese Text Project. https://ctext.org/wiki.pl?if=gb&res=367423. 2019.

Huang, Zongxi 黃宗羲. *Scholastic Records of Ming Ruists* 明儒學案. Chinese Text Project. https://ctext.org/wiki.pl?if=en&res=450463. 2019.

———. *Waiting for the Dawn: A Plan for the Prince*. Translated by Wm. Theodore De Bary. Translation from the Asian Classics. New York: Columbia University Press, 1993.

Jiang, Fan 江藩. *Records of Masters of Han Learning* 漢學師承記. Edited by Zhou Yutong 周予同. Electronic reprint. Vol. 1. 2 vols. Taibei: Academy of Chinese Libraries Higher Education Committee, 2009.

Jiaxing Tripitika 嘉興大藏經. Cbeta.org. 2019.

Laozi 老子. Chinese Text Project. https://ctext.org/dao-de-jing. 2019.

Li, Tong 李侗. *Collection of Li Yanping* 李延平集. Congshu jicheng 2047. Beijing: Zhonghua shuju, 1985.

Liu, An 劉安, John S. Major, Sarah A. Queen, Andrew Seth Meyer, and Harold D. Roth, eds. *The Huainanzi: A Guide to the Theory and Practice of Gov-*

ernment in Early Han China. Translations from the Asian Classics. New York: Columbia University Press, 2010.

Liu, Xie 劉勰. *The Literary Heart-Mind Carves Dragons* 文心雕龍. Chinese Text Project. https://ctext.org/wenxin-diaolong. 2021.

Liu, Xu 劉昫. *Old Tang History* 舊唐書. Beijing: Zhonghua shuju, 1975.

Lu, Zhi 陸贄. *Collected Works of Lu Zhi* 陸贄集. Edited by Wang Su 王素. 2 vols. 中国历史文集丛刊. Beijing: Zhonghua shuju, 2006.

Mean 中庸. Chinese Text Project. https://ctext.org/liji/zhong-yong. 2019.

Mengzi 孟子. Chinese Text Project. https://ctext.org/mengzi. 2019.

Odes 詩經. Chinese Text Project. https://ctext.org/book-of-poetry. 2019.

Ouyang, Xiu 歐陽修, and Song Qi 宋祁. *New Tang History* 新唐書. Beijing: Zhonghua shuju, 1975.

Record of Ritual 禮記. Chinese Text Project. https://ctext.org/liji. 2019.

Reflections on Things at Hand 近思錄. Edited by Zhu Xi 朱熹 and Lü Zuqian 呂祖謙. Chinese Text Project. https://ctext.org/wiki.pl?if=gb&res=675972. 2019.

Sima, Qian 司馬遷. *Records of the Historian* 史記. Chinese Text Project. https://ctext.org/shiji. 2019.

Speeches of the States 國語. Chinese Text Project. https://ctext.org/guo-yu. 2019.

Su, Shi 蘇軾. "Sending Off Master Can Liao 送參寥施." Chinese Ancient Poetry. https://fanti.dugushici.com/ancient_proses/71322. 2021.

———. "Stele at the Temple of Han, Lord of Literature 潮州韓文公廟碑." Chinese Ancient Poetry. https://fanti.dugushici.com/ancient_proses/71722. 2021.

Taisho Tripitika 大正新脩大藏經. Cbeta.org. 2019.

Wang, Bi 王弼, ed. *The Classic of Changes: A New Translation of the I Ching as Interpreted by Wang Bi*. Translated by Richard John Lynn. Translations from the Asian Classics. New York: Columbia University Press, 1994.

Wang, Yangming 王陽明. *Complete Works of Wang Yangming* 王陽明全集. Chinese Text Project. https://ctext.org/wiki.pl?if=en&res=684746. 2019.

Wei, Zheng 魏徵. *Sui History* 隋書. 6 vols. Beijing: Zhonghua shuju, 1973.

Wen, Kang 文康. *The Child Heroes* 兒女英雄傳. Edited by Miao Tianhua 繆天華. Taibei: Sanmin shuju, 2017.

White Tiger Hall Comprehensive Discussions 白虎通. Compiled by Ban Gu 班固. Chinese Text Project. https://ctext.org/bai-hu-tong. 2019.

Xing, Bing 邢炳. *Commentary and Subcommentary on the* Analects 論語注疏. Chinese Text Project. https://ctext.org/lunyu-zhushu. 2019.

Xu, Shen 許慎. *Shuowen jiezi* 說文解字. Chinese Text Project. https://ctext.org/shuo-wen-jie-zi. 2019.

Xuzangjing 續藏經. Cbeta.org. 2019

Xunzi. *Xunzi* 荀子. Chinese Text Project. https://ctext.org/xunzi. 2019.

Yang, Xiong 揚雄. *The Classic of Supreme Mystery* 太玄經. Chinese Text Project. https://ctext.org/taixuanjing. 2019.

Yuan, Mei 袁枚. *Collected Writings from the House on Xiaocang Hill* 小蒼山房文集. Chinese Text Project. https://ctext.org/wiki.pl?if=en&res=900026. 2019.

Zhang, Yanyuan 張彥遠. *Records of Famous Painters through the Ages* 歷代名畫記. Chinese Text Project. https://ctext.org/wiki.pl?if=gb&res=214894. 2019.

Zhang, Zai 張載, "Western Inscription 西銘," *Collected Writings of Zhang Zai* 張載文集. Chinese Text Project. https://ctext.org/wiki.pl?if=en&chapter=847353. 2019.

Zhao, Shixia 趙師夏. "Postscript to Dialogues with Yanping 延平答問跋." In *Dialogues with Yanping* 延平答問, 683. Siku quanshu 712. Hangzhou: Hangzhou Publishing, 2015.

Zhen, Dexiu 真德秀. *Collected Writings of Xishan* 西山文集. Siku quanshu 1208. Hangzhou: Hangzhou Publishing, 2015.

Zheng, Xuan 鄭玄. *Zheng's Notes on the Mao Odes* 毛詩鄭箋. Taibei: Xuehai Publishing, 2001.

Zhou, Dunyi 周敦頤. *Explanation of the Depiction of the Great Ultimate* 太極圖說. Chinese Text Project. https://ctext.org/wiki.pl?if=gb&res=602558. 2019.

Zhu, Xi. *Collection of Zhu Xi* 朱熹集. Edited by Guo Qi and Yin Bo. 10 vols. Chengdu: Sichuan Educational Press, 1996.

Zhuangzi 莊子. Chinese Text Project. https://ctext.org/zhuangzi. 2019.

Other Works

Aristotle. *Metaphysics*. Translated by G. Cyril Armstrong and Hugh Tredennick. Reprint. The Loeb Classical Library 271. Cambridge: Harvard University Press, 2003.

Aubrey, John. *Brief Lives*. Edited by Oliver Lawson Dick. London: Secker and Warburg, 1950.

Bacon, Francis. *The Works of Francis Bacon*. Edited by James Spedding, Robert Leslie Ellis, and Douglas Denon Heath. Vol. 14. Boston: Taggard and Thompson, 1864.

Becker, Carl L. *Freedom and Responsibility in the American Way of Life*. New York: Alfred A. Knopf, 1945.

———. *Modern Democracy*. New Haven: Yale University Press, 1941.

Cao, Min 曹敏. "An Examination of Mr. Tao Baichuan's 'Reexamination of John King Fairbank,' 陶百川先生費正清再檢討的檢討." *China Magazine* 中華雜誌 4, no. 6 (June 1966): 3.

Carrel, Alexis. *Man, the Unknown*. New York and London: Harper and Brothers, 1935.

Cassirer, Ernst. *An Essay on Man: An Introduction to a Philosophy of Human Culture*. New Haven: Yale University Press, 1944.

Chan, N. Serina. *The Thought of Mou Zongsan*. Modern Chinese Philosophy 4. Leiden: Brill, 2011.

Chen, Kang 陳康. "On the Question of Unity of Thought 論思想統一問題." *Free China* 自由中國 12, no. 9 (May 1955): 5–7.

Dardess, John W. *Blood and History in China: The Donglin Faction and Its Repression, 1620–1627*. Honolulu: University of Hawai'i Press, 2002.

Dien, Albert D., and Keith N. Knapp, eds. *The Cambridge History of China, Volume 2: The Six Dynasties*. Cambridge; New York: Cambridge University Press, 2019.

Elstein, David. *Democracy in Contemporary Confucian Philosophy*. Routledge Studies in Contemporary Philosophy. New York: Routledge, 2014.

Fairbank, John K. "New Thinking about China." In *China: The People's Middle Kingdom and the U.S.A.*, 91–102. Cambridge: Belknap Press of Harvard University Press, 1967.

———. U.S. Policy with Respect to Mainland China, § Committee on Foreign Relations (1966).

Fuller, Michael A. *The Road to East Slope: The Development of Su Shi's Poetic Voice*. Stanford: Stanford University Press, 1990.

Hartman, Charles. "The Inquisition against Su Shih: His Sentence as an Example of Sung Legal Practice." *Journal of the American Oriental Society* 113, no. 2 (1993): 228–43.

Hayek, Friedrich A. von. *The Road to Serfdom*. Chicago: University of Chicago Press, 1980.

Hegel, Georg Wilhelm Friedrich. *Lectures on the History of Philosophy, 1825–6*. Translated by Robert F. Brown. Rev. ed. Vol. 1. 3 vols. The Hegel Lectures Series. Oxford; New York: Clarendon Press; Oxford University Press, 2009.

Huang, Zhaoqiang 黃兆強. *There Is of Course a Question of Morality in Politics: A Look at Xu Fuguan's Political Thought* 政治中當然有道德問題: 徐復觀政治思想管窺. Taibei: Student Books, 2016.

Lee, Thomas H. C. "Chinese Education and Intellectuals in Postwar Taiwan." In *Postwar Taiwan in Historical Perspective*, edited by Chun-chieh Huang and Feng-fu Tsao, 135–57. Studies in Chinese Global Affairs 1. Bethesda: University Press of Maryland, 1998.

Levine, Ari Daniel. *Divided by a Common Language: Factional Conflict in Late Northern Song China*. Honolulu: University of Hawai'i Press, 2008.

Liang Hejun 梁和鈞. "Did Fairbank Change Mao? Did Mao Change Washington? 費正清改造了毛澤東? 毛澤東改造了華盛頓?" *Zhengxin Daily News* 徵信新聞報. June 28, 1966, 2.

Liu, Honghe. *Confucianism in the Eyes of a Ruist Liberal: Hsu Fu-Kuan's Critical Examination of the Confucian Political Tradition*. New York: Peter Lang, 2001.

Liu, Tongzu 流通組, and Xie Yingxing 謝鶯興, eds. *Chronological Table of Professor Xu Fuguan* 徐復觀教授年表初編. Taizhong: Donghai University Press, 2017.

Louden, Robert B. "'What Does Heaven Say?' Christian Wolff and Western Interpretations of Confucian Ethics." In *Confucius and the Analects: New Essays*, edited by Bryan W. Van Norden, 73–93. Oxford; New York: Oxford University Press, 2002.

Mou, Zongsan 牟宗三. *Philosophy of History* 歷史哲學. Revised edition. Taibei: Student Books, 1988.

Qian, Mu 錢穆. *Explanations of the Four Books* 四書釋義. Vol. 1. 2 vols. Taibei: Zhonghua wenhua, 1953.

Pascal, Blaise. *Pensées*. Translated by W. F. Trotter. The Modern Library. New York: Random House, 1941.

Plato. *The Republic*. Translated by Benjamin Jowett. Project Gutenberg. https://www.gutenberg.org/files/1497/1497-h/1497-h.htm. 2019.

Russell, Bertrand. *A History of Western Philosophy* 西方哲學史. Third edition. Vol. 2. 2 vols. Taibei: Wu'nan Books, 1991.

Schwegler, Albert. *A History of Philosophy in Epitome*. Translated by Julian H. Seelye. Third edition. New York and London: D. Appleton, 1864.

Schwitzgebel, Eric. "Do Ethicists Steal More Books?" *Philosophical Psychology* 22, no. 6 (December 2009): 711–25.

———, and Joshua Rust. "The Moral Behavior of Ethicists." In *A Companion to Experimental Philosophy*, edited by Justin Sytsma and Wesley Buckwalter, 225–33. Malden, MA: Wiley-Blackwell, 2016.

Sophocles. *Ajax*. Translated by Richard Jebb. Cambridge: Cambridge University Press, 1893. http://www.perseus.tufts.edu/hopper/text?doc=Perseus%3Atext%3A1999.01.0184.

Sorokin, Pitrim A. *The Reconstruction of Humanity*. Boston: The Beacon Press, 1948.

Sun, Wen 孫文 (Zhongshan). *The Three Principles of the People* 三民主義. Taibei: Zhongyang wenwu gongying she, 1985.

Sun, Zhongshan 孫中山. *Three Principles English Reader*. Edited by Baen Lee. Shanghai: Commercial Press, 1937.

Tao Baichuan 陶百川. "A Reexamination of John King Fairbank's Public Opinions on China 費正清對華言論的再檢討." *Zhengxin Daily News* 徵信新聞報. June 6, 1966, 1.

Toynbee, Arnold J. *A Study of History*. Vol. 9. 12 vols. London; New York; Toronto: Oxford University Press, 1954.

Twitchett, Denis, and Michael Loewe, eds. *The Cambridge History of China, Volume 1: The Ch'in and Han Empires, 221 B.C.–A.D. 220*. The Cambridge History of China. Cambridge: Cambridge University Press, 1986.

Windelband, Wilhelm. *A History of Philosophy, with Especial Reference to the Formation and Development of Its Problems and Conceptions*. Translated by James H. Tufts. Second Edition. New York: Macmillan, 1901.

Xiao, Gongquan [Hsiao Kung-ch'üan]. *History of Chinese Political Thought, Volume One*. Translated by F. W Mote. Princeton: Princeton University Press, 1979. http://site.ebrary.com/id/11017666.

Xiong, Shili 熊十力. *Essential Instructions for Reading the Classics* 讀經示要. Vol. 1. 2 vols. Taibei: Mingwen shuju, 1999.

Yampolsky, Philip B., trans. *The Platform Sutra of the Sixth Patriarch: The Text of the Tun-Huang Manuscript*. New York: Columbia University Press, 1967.

Index

rights and duties, 78
science and, 58, 84, 91, 99–100, 116
wisdom and, 117
Western Han, 108, 225–26, 247, 253, 261, 264, 276
Windelband, Wilhelm, 99
Wolff, Christian, 130, 295n188
Wu, Emperor, 86, 200, 254, 287n4
Wu, King, 74, 230
wuwei, 140. *See also* nonaction

Xia dynasty, 88
Xiao Gongquan, 187, 222, 224
Xiong Shili
    embodied recognition and, 11
    heart-mind and, 72
    New Ruists and, 279n8
    political thought and, 76
    science and, 118
    Tang Junyi and, 151
    Xu's meetings with, 4, 21, 26
Xu Fuguan
    overview of, xiii–xv, 1–18
    cancer and, 260
    death of, 5
    education of, 3–4, 21–30
    influence of, 18
    military service of, 3–5, 21, 25, 280n1
    teaching career of, 4, 27
    See also specific topics
Xunzi
    heart-mind and, 171, 173, 270
    Legalism and, 228
    morality and, 8
    rebellion and, 180–81
    ritual and, 230

Yan'an, xiii, 3, 25
Yang Jie, 25, 281n23

Yan Hui, 124
Yao, 68–69, 74, 102, 122, 140, 148, 227, 236
Yin Haiguang, 5, 9, 18, 37–44
Yin-Yang school, 86
Yu, 79, 140
Yuan Shikai, 57, 79, 284n9

Zhang Foquan, 5, 185–86
Zhang Qiyun, 217
Zhang Yanyuan, 171
Zhang Zai, 124
Zhdanov, Andrei, 89, 288n10
Zhou Dunyi, 120, 124
Zhou dynasty, 7, 88
Zhou Enlai, xiii, 4
Zhou Yutong, 169, 301n11
Zhuangzi
    benevolence and, 269
    heart-mind and, 171, 265–66
    literature and, 263, 265–66
    pacifism and, 235
    preferences and, 195–98
    south-facing ruler, 140
    Xu's study of, 23
Zhu Xi
    education and, 101, 122, 130
    knowledge and, 117–18
    morality and, 119, 124
    pattern and, 72, 118, 120, 190–91, 197
    renewing the people, 110
    self-cultivation and, 189, 247
    virtue and, 237, 247–49
    Xu's study of, 27
Zichan, 227, 238
Zigong, 104, 193
Zilu, 239–40, 248
Zixia, 101, 248
Zuo Qiuming, 211
Zuo Tradition, 96, 238

CPSIA information can be obtained
at www.ICGtesting.com
Printed in the USA
LVHW111725220922
728951LV00004B/38

9 781438 487168